BEYOND BENEFIT COST ANALYSIS

Beyond Benefit Cost Analysis

Accounting for Non-Market Values in Planning Evaluation

Edited by

DONALD MILLER
University of Washington, USA

DOMENICO PATASSINI
IUAV University of Venice, Italy

Routledge
Taylor & Francis Group
LONDON AND NEW YORK

First published 2005 by Ashgate Publishing

Reissued 2018 by Routledge
2 Park Square, Milton Park, Abingdon, Oxon OX14 4RN
605 Third Avenue, New York, NY 10017

First issued in paperback 2021

Routledge is an imprint of the Taylor & Francis Group, an informa business

A Library of Congress record exists under LC control number: 2004117606

ISBN 13: 978-0-815-38773-2 (hbk)
ISBN 13: 978-1-351-16268-5 (ebk)
ISBN 13: 978-1-138-35659-7 (pbk)

DOI: 10.4324/9781351162685

Contents

List of Figures

List of Tables

List of Contributors

Ernest Alexander. Emeritus professor of urban planning at the University of Wisconsin-Milwaukee, USA; Principal in APD–Alexander planning & design, Tel-Aviv, Israel. E-mail: eralex@inter.net.il.

Angela Barbanente. Professor in urban and regional planning at the II Facoltà di Ingegneria (2nd Faculty of Engineering) of the Politecnico di Bari (Polytechnic of Bari), Italy. E-mail: abarba@poliba.it.

Tüzin Baycan Levent. Professor of urban and regional planning at the Şehir ve Bölge Planlaması Bölümü (Department of Urban and Regional Planning) of the İstanbul Teknik Üniversitesi (İstanbul Technical University), Turkey; Researcher at the Afdeling Ruimtelijke Economie (Department of Spatial Economics) of the Vrije Universiteit Amsterdam (Free University of Amsterdam), The Netherlands. E-mail: baycan@arch.itu.edu.tr.

Dino Borri. Professor of Urban Planning of the DAU (Dipartimento di Architettura e Urbanistica (Department of Architecture and Planning) at the Politecnico di Bari (Polytechnic of Bari), Italy. E-mail: borri@poliba.it.

Maria Cerreta. Contract researcher at the Dipartimento di conservazione dei beni architettonici ed ambientali (Department of Conservation of Architectural and Environmental Assets) at the Università degli Studi di Napoli Federico II (University of Naples 'Federico II'), Italy. E-mail: cerreta@unina.it.

Grazia Concilio. Researcher of the DAU (Dipartimento di Architettura e Urbanistica (Department of Architecture and Planning) of the Politecnico di Bari (Polytechnic of Bari), Italy. E-mail: concilio@poliba.it.

Paola Cossettini. Environmental engineer at VESTA – Venezia Servizi Territoriali e Ambientali (Venice Territorial and Environmental Services), Italy. E-mail: p.cossettini@vestaspa.net.

Steve Curwell. Professor at the SCPM (School of Construction and Property Management) of the University of Salford, UK. E-mail: s.r.curwell@salford.ac.uk.

Simin Davoudi. Professor of planning and environment, Director of CUDEM (Centre for Urban Development and Environmental Management) at Leeds Metropolitan University, UK and President of AESOP (Association of European Schools of Planing). E-mail: s.davoudi@leedsmet.ac.uk.

Enrico De Polignol. Town planner at the Servizio Pianificazione Ambientale (Environmental Planning Service) of the Comune di Venezia (Venice City Council), Italy. E-mail: e.depolignol.sia@comune.venezia.it.

Pasquale De Toro. Contract researcher at the Dipartimento di conservazione dei beni architettonici ed ambientali (Department of Conservation of Architectural and Environmental Assets) at the Università degli Studi di Napoli Federico II (University of Naples 'Federico II'), Italy. E-mail: detoro@unina.it.

Luigi Fusco Girard. Professor in economics and environmental evaluation and director of the Dipartimento di conservazione dei beni architettonici ed ambientali (Department of Conservation of Architectural and Environmental Assets) at the Università degli Studi di Napoli Federico II (University of Naples 'Federico II'), Italy. E-mail: girard@unina.it.

Markus Hedorfer. Town planner and GIS specialist, professional (HeSc, GISURB) at Venice-Mestre, Italy. E-mail: hedorfer@gisurb.it.

Abdul Khakee. Emeritus professor in policy analysis and urban management at the Avdelning för Samhällsbyggnad (Division of Urban Studies) of the Kungliga Tekniska Högskola (Royal Institute of Technology), Stockholm, Sweden. E-mail: abdul.khakee@pol.umu.se.

Nathaniel Lichfield. Town planner and economist, professional (Lichfield Planning) at London and Lincoln, UK; Emeritus professor in economics of environmental planning at University College London. E-mail: n.lichfield@lichfield planning.co.uk.

Patrizia Lombardi. Researcher at the DICAS (Dipartimento Casa-Città, Department of Housing and City) of the Politecnico di Torino (Polytechnic of Turin), Italy. E-mail: patrizia.lombardi@polito.it.

Donald Miller. Professor in urban design and planning at the Department of UDP (Urban Design and Planning) of the University of Washington at Seattle, USA. E-mail: millerd@u.washington.edu.

Peter Nijkamp. Professor in regional and urban economics and in economic geography at the Faculteit der Economische Wetenschappen en Bedrijfskunde (Faculty of Economics and Business Administration) of the Vrije Universiteit Amsterdam (Free University of Amsterdam), The Netherlands. E-mail: pnijkamp@feweb.vu.nl.

Chiara Paneghetti. Chemist at the CORILA – Consorzio Ricerche Laguna (Lagoon Research Consortium), Venice, Italy, until 2003; now at Technital SpA, Venice. E-mail: c.paneghetti@technital.inet.it.

Maria do Rosário Partidário. Professor in environmental planning, strategic and environmental impact assessment at the UNL (Universidade Nova de Lisboa, New University of Lisbon), Portugal; Researcher at the CESUR (Centro de Sistemas Urbanos e Regionais, Centre for Urban and Regional Systems) of the UTL (Universidade Técnica de Lisboa, Technical University of Lisbon). E-mail: mp@fct.unl.pt.

Domenico Patassini. Professor in planning evaluation techniques at the DP (Dipartimento di Pianificazione, Planning Department) of the Università IUAV di Venezia (IUAV University at Venice), Italy. E-mail: domenico@iuav.it.

Barry Pearce. Dean, Director of Studies and Senior Lecturer in Land Economy, Magdalene College, University of Cambridge, UK; Coordinator of the Cambridge–MIT Joint Urban Design Studio. E-mail: bjp2@cam.ac.uk.

Enrico Rinaldi. Architect at the CORILA – Consorzio Ricerche Laguna (Lagoon Research Consortium), Venice, Italy. E-mail: rinaldi@corila.it.

Jonathan Rosenhead. Professor of Operational Research at the London School of

Economics, UK. E-mail: j.rosenhead@lse.ac.uk.

Franco Selicato. Professor of Urban Planning of the DAU (Dipartimento di Architettura e Urbanistica (Department of Architecture and Planning) of the Politecnico di Bari (Polytechnic of Bari), Italy. E-mail: selicato@poliba.it.

Carmelo Torre. Researcher of the DAU (Dipartimento di Architettura e Urbanistica (Department of Architecture and Planning) of the Politecnico di Bari (Polytechnic of Bari), Italy. E-mail: torre@poliba.it.

Henk Voogd. Professor of planning at the URSI (Urban and Regional Studies Institute) of the University of Groningen, The Netherlands. E-mail: h.voogd@frw.rug.nl.

Christopher Yewlett. Lecturer in Planning and Transport and Course Director of the MSc Planning and Transport at the Cardiff School of City and Regional Planning of the University of Cardiff, Wales, UK. E-mail: yewlett@cardiff.ac.uk.

Preface

Evaluation of planning options has become a principal means of informing and supporting decision making. It is often required by law, and just as frequently important in judicial proceedings to demonstrate that decisions are not arbitrary. Early planning evaluation focused on comparing alternatives on the basis of their relative efficiency. Consequently the emphasis was on measuring the inputs and outcomes in economic or monetary terms.

More recently, decisions have become both more complex, and more recognized as being complex. This has led to development and use of a number of methods and strategies for dealing with the effects of planning alternatives in other than money equivalents. This book introduces and critically assesses a number of ways to deal with values that do not lend themselves to using money as their measurement, and demonstrates the application of these approaches in practice cases.

Earlier versions of several of the chapters that follow were presented at a two-day workshop on evaluation in planning, held at Ca' Tron, the home of the Planning Department, IUAV University, Venice, Italy in February, 2003. Main research activities of the Department are focused on management of urban changes seen from an interdisciplinary perspective. What paves the ground to this approach is the presence among affiliated teachers and researchers of a number of experts in economics, sociology, law, urban design and planning. Besides, the Department delivers advanced training courses: two PhD programmes, the first on Analysis of public policies and the second on Analysis and governance for a sustainable development; four second degree masters on Evaluation of urban, regional and environmental policies, Urban and regional planning for developing countries, Remote sensing and geographical information systems, RIDEF (on energy policy), two first degree masters on Mediterranean mediation: investment and integration and Logistics and multi-modal transport. As for the present book, the Department provides technical and financial support to publications and diffusion of the research results in the mentioned domains.

We wish to thank Professor M. Reho, Director of this Planning Department for the accommodation and financial support for this workshop, and to Professors D. Borri and L. Fusco Girard and their institutions in providing financial and scientific support for this initiative. This was the fifth workshop in a series on planning evaluation to bring together practicing planners and researchers from a number of countris. The earlier workshops took place in Umea, Sweden in 1992, Valenzano, Italy in 1993, London, UK in 1996, and Groningen, The Netherlands in 1998.

Major thanks in preparation of this book goes to M. Hedorfer, who formatted the text, revised figures and tables, and was responsible for the final copy. Our thanks also to the staff at Ashgate for helping to make this project enjoyable. Finally, to all of the contributors, our thanks for their helpfulness and understanding throughout the process of preparing this book.

Donald Miller and Domenico Patassini
Seattle, Washington (USA) and Venice (Italy)

List of Abbreviations

AAAI	American Association for Artificial Intelligence.
ACI	Average Consistency Index in the *AHP*.
ADA	Americans with Disabilities Act of 1990.
AESOP	Association of European Schools of Planning.
AHP	Analytical Hierarchy Process. *MCA* method.
AI	Artificial Intelligence.
AIS	Artificial Intelligent System.
AISRe	Associazione Italiana di Studi Regionali (Italian Regional Science Association). Italian Section of the *RSAI*.
AuReS	Automa Rendita Specializzato (Specialized Rent-of-Land Automaton). Cellular automata software developed by E. Rinaldi of the *ELGIRA* work group.
BASICS	Battelle Scenario Inputs to Corporate Strategies. Scenario-creating future research software developed by S. Millett from Battelle Memorial Institute at Columbus, OH (USA). During further development BASICS has been renamed to *SFI*.
BCA	Benefits Cost Analysis.
BGA	Ben Gurion Airport (נמל התעופה בן גוריון), Tel-Aviv, Israel.
BSc	Bachelor of Science. See also *MSc*.
CA	Computational Agent.
CAF	Common Appraisal Framework (UK).
CAUPR	Center for Architecture & Urban Planning Research at the at the University of Wisconsin-Milwaukee (USA).
CBA	Cost Benefit Analysis. See also *COBA* and *CoBA*.
CBR	Case-Based Reasoning.
CD	Controlled Dispersion. A spatial development scheme. See also *CU* and *MU*.
CEBE	Centre for Education in the Built Environment.
Centro	Corporate name of the West Midlands Passenger Transport Executive (UK).
CEQ	Council of Environmental Quality (USA).
CFA	Cash Flow Analysis.
CI	Consistency Index in the *AHP*.
CIA	Community Impact Analysis.
CIA/E	Community Impact Analysis/Evaluation.
CIE	Community Impact Evaluation.
CMD	Cognitive Moral Development. A moral reasoning theory developed by L. Kohlberg (1927-1987).

CMP	City Master Plan. Often used as synonym of *PRG* when referred to Italian contexts.
CNR	Consiglio Nazionale delle Ricerche (Italian National Research Council).
COBA	Cost Benefit Analysis. A computer program originally developed by the *DoT*, and actually supported by the *DfT*. See also *CBA* and *CoBA*.
CoBA	Cost Benefit Analysis. See also *CBA* and *COBA*.
CORILA	Consorzio Ricerche Laguna (Lagoon Research Consortium). Research consortium at Venice, Italy.
CR	Consistency Ratio in the *AHP*.
CSERGE	Centre for Social and Economic Research on the Global Environment (UK).
CSH	Critical Systems Heuristics.
CSTB	Centre Scientifique et Technique du Bâtiment (Scientific and Technical Building Centre). A French State-owned industrial and commercial corporative.
CU	Concentrated Urbanization. A spatial development scheme. See also *CD* and *MU*.
CVM	Contingent Valuation Method. A direct valuation study method.
DCA	Department of Constitutional Affairs (UK). Ceated on 12 June 2003 within the British consitutional reform as the successor of the 'Lord Chancellor's Department'.
DDA	Disability Discrimination Act. Australian DDA of 1992, British DDA of 1995.
DEFRA	Department for Environment, Food and Rural Affairs (UK). Created in June 2001 by the merger of the environmental responsibilities of the former *DETR* and the functions of the former *MAFF*.
Delphi	The Greek town. Here always used to refer to the homonymous group decision process developed by the *RAND* Corporation in 1969.
DETR	Department of the Environment, Transport and the Regions (UK). 1997–2001. The DETR has been created in June 1997 by bringing together the former *DoE* and the former *DoT*. Re-organization of the departmental structure in June 2001 lead to the new *DTLR*, which took over responsibilities from the Home Office and ceded the responsibily for the environment to the new *DEFRA* and other issues to the *DTI*.
DICAS	Dipartimento Casa-Città del Politecnico di Torino (Department of Housing and City of the Polytechnic of Turin, Italy).
DfT	Department for Transport (UK). Created in May 2002 by detaching the transport functions from the former *DTLR*.
DG	Directorate-General. The European Commission is administrated through 36 DGs and Services (similar to ministries).
DL	Decreto-Legge (Italian Decree-Law).
DM	Decreto Ministeriale (Italian Ministerial Decree).

DoE	Department of Environment (UK). 1970–1997. The DoE was created in 1970 by the merger of the Ministry of Transport, Housing and Local Government and the Ministry of Public Buildings and Works. The responsibility for transport has been transferred to the new *DoT* in 1976. In June 1997 the DoE has been merged again with the DoT to form the new *DETR*.
DOI	See *USDOI*.
DOT	See *USDOT*.
DoT	Department of Transport (UK). 1976–1997. Until 1976 the responsibility for transport was covered by the *DoE*. In June 1997 it has been merged again with the *DoE* to form the new *DETR*.
DP	Dipartimento di Pianificazione dell'*IUAV* (Planning Department at the *IUAV*).
DPCM	Decreto del Presidente del Consiglio dei Ministri (Decree by the President of the Council of Ministers). In Italy, the official denomination of the Prime Minister is 'President of the Council of Ministers'.
DPW	Department of Public Works.
DSS	Decision Support System.
DTI	Department for Trade and Industry (UK).
DTLR	Department for Transport, Local Government and the Regions (UK). 2001–2002. Created in June 2001 as the successor of the former *DETR*, the DTLR has been dismantled in May 2002. Its responsibilities for transport have been moved over to the new *DfT*, while most of the other functions have been brought to the new *ODPM*. The responsibilities for the Electoral Commission and related functions have been transferred to the Lord Chancellor's Department, which has subsequently been absorbed by the new *DCA*.
DU	Dipartimento di Urbanistica dell'*IUAV* (Department of Urbanistics at the *IUAV*).
e-	Electronic. In compound words, such as e-democracy, e-governance, e-voting, and alike.
EA	Environmental Assessment.
EAR	Ethical Artificial Reasoner.
EC	European Commission. See also Note 12 at p. 308.
EIA	Environmental Impact Assessment.
EIS	Environmental Impact Statement.
Électre	Elimination et Choix Traduisant la Réalité (Elimination and Choice by Translating Reality). Familiy of outranking methods.
ElGiRA	Électre – Giuditta – REC – AuReS. The acronym refers to these four modules by which the overall evaluation model was initially composed. Subsequently it has however been enriched with additional modules, while single modules were partially dropped. Nevertheless, the ELGIRA work group decided to retain the initial acronym in order to avoid confusion.

EO	Executive Order of the President of the United States.
EP	European Parliament. See also Note 13 at p. 308.
EPA	Environmental Protection Agency (USA).
ESDP	European Spatial Development Perspective (EU).
ESI	Economisch en Sociaal Instituut van de *VU* (Economic and Social Institute of the *VU*).
ESPON	European Spatial Planning Observation Network. A *EC* programme.
FZK	Forschungszentrum Karlsruhe (Research Centre Karlsruhe, Germany).
GAIA	Geometrical Analysis for Intercative Assistance. Outranking method.
GAM	Goal Achievement Matrix.
GDP	Gross Domestic Product.
GEC	Global Environmental Change.
GIS	Geographical (or Geospatial) Information System.
Giuditta	Gestione Informatizzata di Tollerabilità Ambientale (IT-Driven Environmental Tolerability Management). Human risk modelling software developed by the Province of Milano (Milan, Italy) in collaboration with URS Dames & Moore, Milano.
GPG	Good Practice Guide. Guides published by the *ODPM*.
HMSO	Her Majesty's Stationery Office (UK).
HPM	Hedonic Price Method. An indirect valuation study method.
HUD	United States Department of Housing and Urban Development.
HW	Highway.
IA	Impact Assessment.
IAIA	International Association for Impact Assessment.
ICC	Interdisciplinary Catalogue of Criteria.
ICT	Information and Communication Technology.
IDF	Israel Defense Forces. Official English acronym and name respectively of צה"ל and צבא ההגנה לישראל.
IFS	Interactive Future Simulations. Scenario-creating future research software developed by S. Millett from Battelle Memorial Institute at Columbus, OH (USA); formerly *BASICS*.
IIED	Internationl Institute for Environment and Development.
IOER	See *IÖR*.
IÖR	Leibniz-Institut für Ökologische Raumentwicklung e.V., Dresden (Leibniz Institute of Ecological and Regional Development, registered association, Dresden, Germany).
INTELCITY	Towards Intelligent Sustainable Cities. Project IST-2001-37373 (see also *IST*) of the European Union.
IPiGeT	Istituto di Pianificazione e Gestione del Territorio del *CNR* di Napoli (*CNR*-Istitute for Planning and Management of the Territory at Naples). The IPiGeT, founded in 1980, has been definitively closed in 2003.
IRR	Internal Rate of Return.

IST	Information Society Technologies. European Union programme family name.
IT	Information Technology.
ITAS	Institut für Technikfolgenabschätzung und Systemanalyse des *FZK* (Institute for Technology Assessment and Systems Analysis of the *FZK*).
IUAV	Università IUAV di Venezia (IUAV University at Venice, Italy). Originally 'IUAV' meant 'Istituto Universitario di Architettura di Venezia' (Venice University of Architecture).
IVM	Instituut voor Milieuvraagstukken van de *VU* (Institute for Environmental Studies of the *VU*).
JRC	Joint Research Centre. A Directorate General of the *EC*.
KS	Knowledge Society.
LPA	Local Planning Authority (UK).
LRT	London Regional Transport (UK).
LSE	London School of Economics (UK).
LTP	Local Transport Plan (UK).
LTT	Local Transport Today. A journal.
MAFF	Ministry of Agriculture, Fisheries and Food (UK). Its functions have been transferred in June 2001 to the new *DEFRA*.
MAGUS	Modelling Access with GIS in Urban Systems. A project undertaken by the University College Northampton (UK).
MCA	Multicriteria Analysis.
MCDA	Multi-Criteria Decision Analysis.
MIT	Massachusetts Institute of Technology (USA).
MoDe	Montagne di Degrado (Mountains of Deprivation). Cellular-automata software developed by E. Rinaldi of the *ELGIRA* work group.
MMS	Multi-modal Study.
MP	Master Plan.
MPB	Master Plan delle Bonifiche (Reclamation Master Plan). Referring to the Porto Marghera 'National Interest Site' near Venice, Italy.
MSc	Master of Science. See also *BSc*.
Mt	Megatonne. One million tonnes, or one billion ($1 \cdot 10^9$) kg.
MU	Multipolar Urbanization. A spatial development scheme. See also *CD* and *CU*.
NAIADE	Novel Approach to Imprecise Assessment and Decision Environments. A multicriteria method (and software). Developed at the Ispra (Italy) site of the *JRC*.
NAW	National Assembly for Wales.
NCPB	National Council for Planning and Building (הארצית לתכנון ובניה המועצה, Israel).
NEJAC	National Environmental Justice Advisory Council (USA).
NEPA	National Environmental Policy Act (USA).

NGO	Non-governmental organization.
NHS	National Health Service (UK).
NPV	Net Present Value.
OCDE	Organisation de coopération et de développement économiques. Official french name of *OECD*.
ODPM	Office of the Deputy Prime Minister (UK). Created in May 2002, it received responsibilities for policy on housing, planning, devolution, regional and local government and the fire service, among which also those of the former *DTLR*.
OECD	Organisation for Economic Co-operation and Development. See also *OCDE*.
OPRAF	Office of Passenger Rail Franchising (UK).
OR	Operational Research.
PAH	Polycyclic aromatic hydrocarbons.
PBS	Planning Balance Sheet.
PPG	Planning Policy Guidance Note (UK).
PPP	Policies, plans and programmes. In the context of *EIA*: 'EIA of PPP'.
PREVA	Preferences, values and aspirations.
PRG	Piano Regolatore Generale (Italian Land-Use Plan). In English often referred to as the City Master Plan (*CMP*). Local plan at the township (municipality) level.
Prométhée	Preference Ranking Organisation Method For Enrichment Evaluations.
PRUSST	Programma di Riqualificazione Urbana e di Sviluppo Sostenibile del Territorio (Italian Urban Redevelopment and Sustainable Development Programme).
PRU	Piano di Recupero Urbano (Italian Urban Renewal Plan).
PSM	Problem Structuring Method.
PUR	Polycentric Urban Region.
RAND	Research and Development. The name of a non-profit research organization: RAND Corporation at Santa Monica, CA (USA).
RBCA	Risk-Based Corrective Action. Human risk modelling methodology (and software) developed by the United States Environmental Protection Agency. The developers of RBCA indicate that the acronym should be pronounced like 'Rebecca'.
REC	Risk – Environment – Costs. A methodology (and software) to carry out evaluation of soil clean-up options. Developed by the 'REC Consortium' in the Netherlands.
RMK	Risico – Milieu – Kosten. The original Dutch name of *REC*.
ROME	Reasonable Maximum Exposure. Human risk modelling software developed by the Italian National Environmental Protection Agency in collaboration with URS Dames & Moore.
ROW	Right Of Way.
RPG	Regional Planning Guidance Note (UK).

RSAI	Regional Science Association International, Urbana, IL (USA).
RTD	Research, Technological Development & Demonstration.
SAST	Strategic Assumption Surfacing and Testing.
SCA	Strategic Choice Approach. A *PSM*.
SCBA	Social Cost-Benefit Analysis.
SCPM	School of Construction and Property Management at the University of Salford (UK).
SEA	Strategic Environmental Assessment.
SEAn	Strategic Environmental Assessment Analysis.
SEM	Societé à Economie Mixte (French Mixed Economy Company).
SIA	Strategic Impact Assessment.
SIROCCO	System for Intelligent Retrieval of Operationalized Cases and Codes. A *CBR* retrieval and analysis system developed by B. M. McLaren at the University of Pittsburgh, PA (USA).
SIS	Sistema Informativo dei Suoli (Soil Information System). The reclamation-oriented land information system at the Venice Municipality, Italy.
SITA	Società Italiana Trasporti Automobilistici SpA (Italian Motor Transport Company, Ltd). An important Italian private transport company.
SMART	Specific, measurable, achievable, realistic, and timed.
SODA	Strategic Options Development and Analysis. A *PSM*.
SpA	Società per azioni (Italian Private Limited Company).
SRA	Strategic Rail Authority (UK).
SRI	SRI International. Research institute with its headquarter at Menlo Park, CA (USA). Originally 'SRI' meant 'Stanford Research Institute'.
SSM	Soft Systems Methodology. A *PSM*.
SSSI	Site of Special Scientific Interest (UK).
STU	Società di Trasformazione Urbana (Italian Urban Transformation Company).
SUD	Sustainable Urban Development.
SWATS	South Wales Area Traffic Study.
TaeD	Dipartimento di Tecnologie dell'Architettura e Design 'Pierluigi Spadolini' dell'Università di Firenze (Pierluigi Spadolini Department of Technology of Architecture and Design of the University of Florence, Italy).
TCM	Travel Cost Method. An indirect valuation study method.
TEN	Trans-European Networks. A *EU* concept. See also *T-TEN*.
TSO	The Stationery Office. A subsidiary of The Stationery Office Holdings Ltd., the official publishing service privatized from *HMSO* in 1996.
T-TEN	Transport Trans-European Networks. See *TEN*.
UCO	Use Classes Order (UK). Complete name: 'The Town and Country Planning (Use Classes) Order 1987'. Often also employed as syn-

	onym of the classes (A1-A3, B1-B8, C1-C3, D1, D2) themselves defined by the 1987 Order.
UDP	1. Unitary Development Plan (UK). Development plan at the District or Unitary Authority level. 2. Urban Design and Planning. A Department at the *UW*.
UN	United Nations.
UNDP	United Nations Development Programme.
URGE	Urban Green Environment. EU project 'Development of Urban Green Spaces to Improve the Quality of Life in Cities and Regions'.
USDOI	United States Department of Interior.
USDOT	United States Department of Transportation.
USEPA	See *EPA*.
UW	The University of Washington at Bothell, Seattle, and Tacoma (USA).
VROM	Volkshuisvesting, Ruimtelijke Ordening en Milieubeheer (People's Housing, Spatial Planning, and Environmental Management). Name of a Dutch ministry: Ministerie van VROM (Ministry of VROM). VROM is often also translated as 'Spatial Planning, Housing, and the Environment'.
VTT	Valtion teknillinen tutkimuskeskus (Finnish State Technical Research Centre).
VU	Vrije Universiteit Amsterdam (Free University at Amsterdam, The Netherlands).
WAG	Wales Assembly Government (UK).
WB	World Bank.
WO	Wales Office (Swyddfa Cymru, UK). The successor of the former Welsh Office, established in 1964, and whose powers have been devolved in 1999 mainly to the *NAW*. The actual *WO* 'is the key Government figure liasing with the devolved administration in Wales and represents Wales' interests in the [UK] Cabinet and in Parliament'. See the *WO* web site at http://www.walesoffice.gov.uk for details.
WTA	Willingness To Accept.
WTO	World Trade Organization.
WTP	Willingness To Pay.

The List of Abbreviations does not contain common English language expressions like e.g. (exempli gratia, for instance), i.e. (id est, that is), viz. (videlicet, namely), vs. (versus), etc. (et cetera), country acronyms, such as EU (European Union), UK (United Kingdom) or USA (United States of America), nor official US state abbreviations.

Chapter 1

Introduction — Accounting for Non-Market Values in Planning Evaluation

Donald Miller and Domenico Patassini

1.1 Introduction

This book deals with strategies and techniques for identifying, measuring and incorporating non-market values in planning evaluation methodologies. It is in response to the shortcomings of benefit cost analysis that, while it has been the conventional means of evaluating planning options, has long been criticized because it requires all effects of these options to be expressed in monetary terms.

This book presents a range of approaches for accomplishing the major purposes of evaluation used in urban and regional planning. These purposes include providing an explicit, replicable basis for public assessment of alternatives, and for debate on the merits of these alternatives, as a contribution to deliberate and informed decision making (Rietveld, 1980; McAllister, 1979). Growing demand for public involvement and for accountability in decision making requires better means for accommodating a broad range of concerns in planning evaluation (Miller, 1999; Woltjer, 2001; Parkin, 1993).

Although considerable effort has been directed by economists to the task of finding market values for the effects of planning options (Nas, 1996; Pearce, 1971), for many of the most important issues in the decision-making process these measurements have been invalid, unreliable, or both (Glasser, 1998; Barrow, 1997). Methodologies examined in several of the following chapters include effectiveness-cost and multi-criteria analysis, and the book explores how these have been applied in practice in developing special-issue plans, complex regional development strategies, and efforts to analyze the environmental justice and other ethical implications of major infrastructure projects. Use of scenarios and problem structuring methods by stakeholder groups also are explored as means of narrowing the range of options when uncertainty makes estimating future levels of performance especially difficult.

Several techniques for measuring and for estimating non-market values, for use by these various methodological approaches, are critically assessed. These include land use and development indicators employed by a national planning system, the incidence and degree of environmental impacts on various social groups, and survey opinion data concerning the nuisance and desirability effects of alternative designs for public facilities. Organizational impediments and requirements for using assessment evidence in responsible decision making are explored. Throughout, the problems of complexity and resulting uncertainty are explicitly addressed. A common theme among the contributions that follow is a strong tendency for the process of decision making to focus on those aspects that are measured, and thus the pressure to develop valid metrics for all of the objectives and concerns that the decision making should address.

The contributions to this book come from people engaged in research and practice from ten countries: in Europe, North America, the U.K., and the Middle East. Most of these contributions are based on actual cases, and so provide demonstrations of ways that the ideas presented can usefully inform planning practice elsewhere. This practical information will be of interest both to those engaged in developing planning evaluation and those who are the users of this evaluation in decision making. Additional audiences include people in academic programs preparing for professional planning practice, and researchers concerned with improving both quantitative and qualitative approaches to evaluating decision options.

1.2 Measuring the effects of planning alternatives

The important role of evaluation in developing planning recommendations is to compare alternatives under consideration with each other and with the purposes that the final choice is intended to serve (Nijkamp, 1974; Beuthe, Eeckhouldt and Scannella, 2000). In this way, a large list of alternatives may be reduced to a smaller number so that the decision-making process is manageable and efficient (Lai and Hopkins, 1995; Bauer, 1997). Similarly, evaluation helps in ranking the alternatives in that final list, and often in measuring how much better some alternatives are that others in meeting the purposes that the decision should address (Hill and Tzamir, 1972; Janssen, 1992).

To accomplish this, the evaluation methodology or procedure that is used needs to employ evidence concerning the performance of each alternative. Since most decisions concerning plans, policies, program or projects involve meeting several objectives, the task of designing or choosing what kind of evaluation to employ requires that it be able to deal with multiple objectives, and requires devising valid measures or metrics for estimating likely performance of alternatives in accomplishing each of these objectives. And if the evaluation is intended to facilitate comparing alternatives based on their expected performance over several objectives, the measurements used need to be converted into a common scale or index that summarizes the appraisal of each alternative.

Benefit cost analysis is the traditional means of accomplishing this. Dating from the 1920s, this application of allocational economics was first used to compare alternative designs for major public works projects such as dams for flood control and navigation where the questions to be answered were the best location, number, and sizes of these dams. In this analysis, costs are usually the capital and operating expenses of implementing a design. Benefits are the outputs or outcomes of the project, usually first estimated in physical terms such as flood damage prevented or reduced time for shipping by water, and these estimates are then converted into monetary terms. To develop a summary performance figure for each alternative that is evaluated, the estimated costs are subtracted from the benefits for each year of the project, and these net benefits are discounted to account for the effect of time in delayed consumption. The discounted net benefit for each alternative can be used to identify which of these options is most efficient (Andrieu, 1977; Lichfield, 1964).

The design of benefit cost analysis is intended to address specific concerns. That is, it is designed to assess several alternatives, each of which is intended to accomplish one specific objective. And it is designed to assess these alternatives only on a single basis: in terms of which promises to result in the greatest return to society for the investment. As an exercise in economics, benefit cost analysis is not intended to address other public policy concerns such as distributional fairness or the use of non-renewable resources, unless these can be expressed in monetary terms (Prest and Turvey, 1965; Sugden and Williams, 1983).

While most costs of inputs are usually fairly easy to measure in market terms, it is often difficult to do the same with benefits. For example, to place a price on a beautiful view, efforts are made to find out what people might be willing to pay either to obtain it or not to lose it, and survey results on these two situations tend to differ (McPherson, 1992; Lindsey, Paterson and Luger, 1995; Biermann, 1999). Or for instance, what is the value of a life saved or a disability avoided by investing in a safety feature for a highway or an environmental regulation? At times, this has been measured in terms of the projected earning power of an individual less their living costs, which suggests that retired people may have a negative value and children a reduced value since their earning years are ahead of them (Portney and Harrington, 1995; Cropper and Portney, 1992).

These examples illustrate a major shortcoming with benefit cost analysis, with its requirement that all of the effects that are included in the evaluation must be translated into market terms. This is a problem because many of the effects that are produced by planning options that are under review are not market goods: they are not consumables that are exchanged between willing buyers and sellers, where the price paid represents the full cost of production and the full value to the consumer (Mishan, 1974; Lichfield, Kettle and Whitbread, 1975; Self, 1975).

Largely in response to this shortcoming, a number of alternative evaluation methodologies have been developed, that seek to incorporate and account for important non-market values of features of planning alternatives. For example, one of these is the planning balance sheet or score card (Lichfield, 1968; Lichfield, 2001), which estimates the market good effects of alternatives, but also uses natural measures such as acres, housing units, and minutes saved for those effects for which there are no clear prices. This evidence is not converted into a common metric and a single summary figure for each alternative such as is provided by discounted net benefit numbers, but instead is left as a display for those involved in the decision process to consider and use in comparing alternatives.

Another methodology is multi-criteria evaluation. First called the goals achievement matrix method (Hill, 1968; Hill, 1973; Miller, 1980; Hill, 1985), this approach assesses planning options in terms of how well each performs with respect to a number of criteria (Voogd, 1983). These criteria are measurable statements of the several objectives or purposes that the final decision is intended to serve (Nijkamp, 1979). These criteria commonly use a number of metrics that are standardized, usually in terms of the rate of accomplishing each objective. These effectiveness scores are then weighted on the basis of the relative value attached by the stakeholders to each criterion (Voogd, 1997; Brill et al., 1990; Miller, 1985). When this is done, a weighted sum of the effectiveness scores for each alternative can provide a summary score for comparison with the comparable figures for each of the other options. While this approach can incorporate prices of goods where this is appropriate, it also facilitates including non-market goods in an accountable and useful manner (Munda, 1995; MacDonald and Faber, 1999).

1.3 Methods and approaches for dealing with non-market values

The planning balance sheet and multi-criteria methodologies are but two approaches used in planning practice to provide a fuller analysis of options than that afforded by benefit cost analysis (Hopkins, 1984; Fishburn, 1978). The following chapters include a number of additional procedures that deal in a creditable way with effects for which markets are limited or do not exist. Some of these additional approaches also prove to be more useful in dealing with decisions that are complex. This complexity may result from confusion over goals and objectives. Or it may stem from limited cause and effect understanding of some of the features of the options, that limit technical estimation of their performance. When decisions are complex for these and other reasons, methodologies such as developing and inspecting scenarios, or deliberative processes aimed at improving how problems are defined and structured, are proving to be effective means of incorporating concerns that are important to sound decision making, but for which there are no market prices.

The organization of this book consists of four parts. The first of these is the most detailed and provides accounts of technical methods for evaluating non-market effects of alternatives. The five chapters of the second Part present separate methodologies for considering non-market goods, each of which deal with progressively more complex planning situations. The third Part reports on the use of scenarios as an approach to comparing alternatives. The fourth Part focuses on how organizational design affects decision making, and thus the requirements for information.

Methods and applications

The five chapters in Part I deal with operational approaches for incorporating non-market values in solving problems. Each of these contributions is based on a case study that demonstrates how the method works and the problems with it. The first contribution, by Voogd, examines several schemes for rating the design of routes and urban spaces for their accessibility by someone in a wheelchair, and finds flaws of oversimplification with most of them.

The subject matter of this contribution is important because demand for public policy and programs that respond to physical limitations is increasing as older cohorts in the population grow larger. Voogd's inquiry is a practical illustration of the need to incorporate non-market values into evaluation methods, especially in recognizing and accommodating the needs of people with various disabilities.

The second contribution dealing with methods, by Miller, addresses ways to go about dealing with the environmental justice implications of alternative plans or projects. This kind of social fairness analysis seeks to answer the questions: whether and to what extent are low income and minority populations disproportionately adversely impacted by each of several planning options, and when this occurs how can these impacts be mitigated or compensated?

This topic complements the one addressed by Voogd in focusing on the social equity issues that are beyond efficiency analysis. After outlining the procedure to estimate and deal with the environmental justice aspects of a proposal, Miller presents and critically assesses a case in which this was undertaken, and identifies problems in defining a base-line population, inadequacies of secondary-source date, and difficulties in defining and evaluating types and levels of impacts on populations in different areas.

In the third chapter of this Part, Yewlett provides a detailed overview of the use of planning evaluation in assessing transport projects in the United Kingdom since the 1960s. In doing so, he points out how basic benefit cost analysis of roads projects evolved into a new, broader appraisal framework in the 1990s. This now commonly used approach includes wider treatment of externalities and distributional effects, as well as fiscal and economic issues.

This new approach was first applied to the Newport Multi-Modal Study in South Wales, and employed a number of non-market criteria including reducing reliance on the private car, reducing greenhouse gas emissions, and avoiding adverse landscape impacts. Since these effects are estimated and presented in a range of metrics, the intent of this evaluation is to provide a 'consequence display' facilitating public review and dialogue.

The chapter by Baycan Levent and Nijkamp explores alternative ways to evaluate urban green spaces. This includes their differentiating between social, ecological, economic and planning values of these green spaces and mapping these to illustrate instances in which the values are shared and those in which they are not. This leads to a discussion of both the economic and non-economic approaches to estimating the value of likely effects of plans and projects, especially as these treat environmental concerns. They look specifically at types and values of urban green space, differentiating those aspects that lend themselves to monetary and to non-monetary valuation.

This is then applied in developing an extensive listing of criteria and sub-criteria, and indicators for each of these, which are of utility for assessing the relative desirability of alternative schemes for providing urban green. This listing grows out of the EU project: Development of Urban Green Spaces to Improve the Quality of Life in Cities and Regions (URGE).

The final chapter in this Part — by Patassini, Cossettini, De Polignol, Hedorfer, Paneghetti, and Rinaldi — presents and assesses an application of an analytical process for evaluating alternative plans for reclaiming and redeveloping a major brown-field site. The case is the Porto Marghera area of mainland Venice: a large, contaminated, industrial area.

This analytical process, called ELGIRA, consists of four models, that assess each of several options in terms of cost, risk, and environmental merit in a manner that facilitates dialogue among several contributing disciplines, and among several groups of stakeholders with differing interests. Initial tests of the ELGIRA process indicate that it produces useful and reliable input to deliberations, and helps to reach the compromise decision required in a project of this size and involving many agencies and private parties.

Methodological approaches — new strategies

The five contributions in this second Part of the book speak in broader terms than do the chapters in Part I, since they deal more with methodologies than with discrete methods. Each of these methodologies is a complete evaluation framework or process, and each represents an effort to deal with a high level of complexity that the methods presented in the earlier Part are not wholly effective in treating. The first chapter of Part II addresses Community Impact Evaluation (CIE) that is the most conventional of these methodologies and deals with relatively simple problems. The next two chapters explore uses of indicators and Strategic Impact Assessment (SIA) that endeavor to deal with greater complexity. The fourth chapter of Part II deals with ways of structuring problems that respond to complexity that is so great that model-based approaches fail, where the intention is to assist in fully defining the situation and the options rather than providing numerical scores concerning the most desirable choice. The fifth chapter provides a synthesis in that it combines several methods and approaches.

In his contribution, Lichfield argues that the impacts that should be measured and valued in evaluation should be the consequences that positive and negative externalities or spill-over effects have on various population groups. He encourages including the costs that the people who are impacted would have to incur to avoid undesirable intrusions.

Lichfield makes the case that Community Impact Evaluation (CIE) facilitates this by including all impacts whether or not these are transformed into market values, and that it includes the social distribution of these impacts as well. He then offers advice on how to structure and use CIE to meet these objectives.

After defining land use and environmental planning indicators and reviewing their application, especially in ex post evaluation of policy and plans, Pearce analyzes both the political and technical problems in designing and using these indicators. He focuses on five 'technical problems' that are shared by efforts to estimate market-equivalent measures of the effects of planning options. Many if not most of these problems stem from how indicators are frequently designed and used in practice, rather than being intrinsic to indicators as a means of accounting for effects that defy measurement in monetary terms. These conclusions are important cautions to observe in responsible practice.

In the third contribution to Part II, Partidário discusses the development and use of Strategic Environmental Assessment (SEA) in several EU nations, and reviews the application of this methodology in a range of planning and policy undertakings. Because SEA commonly deals with strategic objectives and vision statements, and so operates at a more general level than do project-based Environmental Impact Statements, it is often less technical and more political in nature. Based on experiences with SEA, Partidário argues for a more advanced version that she calls Strategic Impact Assessment, which would be more responsive to decision making by, for example, providing just-in-time information and engaging more participants in the process.

In the fourth chapter of this Part, Rosenhead provides a brief but complete overview of Problem Structuring Methods (PSM): a set of decision-support approaches that foster systematic exploration of a range of alternatives, and supplement model-based analysis with deliberation that makes use of the informed judgments of participants. He identifies five specific approaches that have been developed separately, but each has been designed to cope with the uncertainties raised by very complex problems, and with criteria that are difficult to measure, not least in market terms. Several applications illustrate the range of kinds of decision situations that these PSMs are especially suited to address. Rosenhead points out that we now have some experience with applying PSMs to urban planning, and that these cases illustrate how this methodology can provide significant support for communicative action approaches in planning.

As the title of the fifth chapter suggests, Fusco Girard, Cerreta and De Toro present both a general discussion of the need to include non-market concerns in planning evaluation, and present a case study which illustrates an approach that accounts for ecological and social/cultural values, in addition to efficiency concerns. The case involves design of a sustainable transport system for the Sorrento Coast in Italy, that balances environmental and development needs.

The methodological approach that was used integrates several of the methods and strategies presented earlier in this book, including Problem Structuring Methods and multi-criteria and multi-group evaluation methods, and also employs elements of scenario building and analysis that are discussed in the next Part. Consequently, this application of a cyclical evaluation process provides a synthesis of a number of the other contributions to this book, and a demonstration of how several methods and approaches may be combined in practice.

Scenarios as an exploratory approach

Part III extends the discussions in Part II, in that the three chapters of this Part address scenario building, with an emphasis on posing and comparing possible desirable and undesirable outcomes, rather than designing specific planning or policy options and trying to estimate the performance of each of these. The first two chapters in Part III both deal with scenario building and its use in general terms, and provide demonstrations of using this approach. The third contribution looks at a major feature of this approach: how ethical issues can be treated and the trade-offs of these with other concerns such as economic efficiency.

The chapter by Lombardi and Curwell reports on their work exploring how information and communication technologies can be used for the sustainable development of cities. This initiative brought together experts in these developing technologies, and in sustainable urban development, to design five alternative city scenarios that accomplish this goal.

After describing each of these scenarios, the authors apply an analytical hierarchy process as a means of comparing them on the basis of six sets of concerns. Pilot tests of this approach, involving a small number of respondents, illustrate how this procedure operates and suggests its promise for broader application.

In the second contribution to Part III, Barbanente and Khakee provide a critical review of using scenarios of desirable futures in evaluating policy and planning options. As they note, scenarios are especially useful in stimulating reflection about possible futures and to suggest if-then arguments, and they make the case that exploratory evaluation is different than conventional evaluation in terms of function, knowledge, and organization or responsibility. They then demonstrate an interactive scenario construction process using two southern Mediterranean cases, in which alternatives were assessed on the basis of preferences, values, and aspirations. They conclude that desirable scenario development embraces uncertainty and non-market values with greater success than does trend-based forecasting.

The final chapter in this Part — by Borri, Concilio, Selicato, and Torre — addresses the ways of defining or prescribing the ethical concerns that should provide the framework for specifying the ends or criteria used in planning evaluation. Their discussion includes the possible ethical conflicts between, for example, economic and social ends such as choosing less profitable options that provide more collective consumption goods or desirable redistribution results. They illustrate this with two case studies, and suggest a methodological approach employing artificial intelligence.

Organizational and institutional context of evaluation and decision

Part IV of this book consists of two chapters in which features of organizational design, especially of governmental units, are assessed in terms of how they foster or impede the use of information in making creditable decisions. In doing so, these contributions step away from considering methods or methodologies, and focus instead on preconditions for evaluation in any form having effect and incorporating non-market values.

The first of these two chapters, by Davoudi, examines the quality of governance relations in polycentric urban regions. This provides the basis for developing a framework for evaluating governance capacities that support collective action. The proposed framework includes a number of criteria that can be used both in designing more effective institutions and in evaluating their likely effectiveness. These criteria recognize the importance of intellectual, social and political capital. This analysis focuses primarily on the five major metropolises in Europe.

In the final contribution, Alexander argues that institutional design is likely to be more important to the quality of decision making than are consciousness of values or norms, or improving the technology of methods used in evaluation. He reasons that if planning is a political process, then evaluation is the institutional framework or arena for resolving conflicting claims. Important questions are who participates, and what are their prescribed roles and status as these affect the outcome?

To illustrate and test this argument, Alexander presents and analyzes six case histories of complex decision making to assess the influence of the formal planning evaluation that was done. He then proposes a framework for institutional design at various scales, including rules, procedures and organizational structure that will be effective in incorporating diverse values and preferences and achieve desired market and non-market objectives.

1.4 Conclusion

Albert Einstein once observed: 'Not everything that can be counted counts, and not everything that counts can be counted.' To this statement might be added that what is not counted is likely not to count, or at least to count for less, in public decision making. This is an incentive to find ways to circumvent the limitations of requiring that all concerns be measured in monetary terms as required by benefit cost analysis.

This book describes and illustrates a number of ways to incorporate non-market values in explicit planning evaluation. It also presents some additional approaches that seek to deal with concerns that defy measurement in a reliable and valid manner: to make count what cannot be counted. It is to be hoped that this book will encourage and inform efforts to improve planning evaluation in ways that result in its providing better and more useful evidence for public decision making.

References

Andrieu, M. (1977), 'Benefit cost evaluation', in L. Rutman (ed.), *Evaluation Research Methods: A Basic Guide*, Sage, Beverly Hills, CA (USA), pp. 219-232.

Bauer, W. (1997), 'General plan evaluation criteria — an approach to making better plans', *Journal of the American Planning Association*, Vol. 63, No. 3, pp. 329-344.

Barrow, C. (1997), *Environmental and Social Impact Assessment*, John Wiley & Sons, New York, NY (USA).

Beuthe, M., Eeckhouldt, L. and Scannella, G. (2000), 'A practical multicriteria methodology for assessing risky public investment', *Socio-Economic Planning Sciences*, Vol. 34, No. 2, pp. 121-139.

Biermann, S. (1999), 'The strategic identification of suitable land for low income housing: A case study from South Africa', in J. Thill (ed.), *Spatial Multicriteria Decision Making and Analysis*, Ashgate, Aldershot (UK).

Brill, E., Flach, J., Hopkins, L. and Renjithan, S. (1990), 'MGA: a decision support system for complex, incompletely defined problems', *IEEE Transactions on Systems, Man and Cybernetics*, Vol. 20, No. 4, pp. 745-757.

Cropper, M. and Portney, P. (1992), 'Discounting human lives', *Resources*, No. 108, pp. 1-4, Resources for the Future, Washington, DC (USA).

Fishburn, P. (1978), 'A survey of multiattribute/multicriterion evaluation theories', in S. Zionts (ed.), *Multiple Criteria Problem Solving*, Springer, Berlin (Germany), pp. 181-224.

Glasser, J. (1998), 'On the evaluation of "sicked problems"', in N. Lichfield (ed.), *Evaluation in Planning — Facing the Challenge of Complexity*, Kluwer, Dordrecht (The Netherlands), pp. 229-249.

Hill, M. (1968), 'A goals-achievement matrix for evaluating alternative plans', *Journal of the American Planning Association*, Vol. 34, No. 1, pp. 19-29.

Hill, M. (1973), Monograph Series No. 5, *Planning for Multiple Objectives*, Regional Science Research Institute, Philadelphia, PA (USA).

Hill, M. (1985), 'Can multiple-objective evaluation methods enhance rationality in planning?', in M. Breheny and A. Hooper (eds.), *Rationality in Planning: Critical Essays in the Role of Rationality in Urban and Regional Planning*, Pion, London (UK).

Hill, M. and Tzamir, Y. (1972), 'Multidimensional evaluation of regional plans serving multiple objectives', *Papers of the Regional Science Association*, No. 29, pp. 139-165.

Hopkins, L. (1984), 'Evaluation of methods for exploring ill-defined problems', *Environment and Planning B: Planning and Design*, No. 11, pp. 339-348.

Janssen, R. (1992), *Multiobjective Decision Supports for Environmental Management*, Kluwer, Dordrecht (The Netherlands).

Lai, S.-K. and Hopkins, L. (1995), 'Can decision makers express multiattribute preferences using AHP and MVT? An experiment', *Environment and Planning B: Planning and Design*, Vol. 22, No. 1, pp. 21-34.

Lichfield, N. (1964), 'Cost benefit analysis in plan evaluation', *Town Planning Review*, Vol. 35, No. 2, pp. 159-169.

Lichfield, N. (1968), 'Economics in Town Planning: A basis for decision making', *Town Planning Review*, Vol. 39, No. 1, pp. 5-20.

Lichfield, N. (2001), 'The philosophy and role of community impact evaluation in the planning system', in H. Voogd (ed.), *Recent Developments in Evaluation — In Spatial, Infrastructure and Environmental Planning*, Geo Press, Groningen (The Netherlands), pp. 153-

173.

Lichfield, N., Kettle, P. and Whitbread, M. (1975), *Evaluation in the Planning Process*, Pergamon, Oxford (UK).

Lindsey, G., Paterson, R. and Luger, M. (1995), 'Using contingent valuation in environmental planning', *Journal of the American Planning Association*, Vol. 61, No. 2, pp. 252-262.

McAllister, D. (1979), *Evaluation in Environmental Planning*, MIT Press, Cambridge, MA (USA).

McPherson, E. (1992), 'Accounting for benefits and costs of urban greenspace', *Landscape and Urban Planning*, Vol. 22, pp. 41-51.

MacDonald, M. and Faber, B. (1999), 'Exploring the potential of multi-criteria special decision support systems: A system for sustainable land-use planning and design', in J. Thill (ed.), *Spatial Multicriterion Decision Making and Analysis*, Ashgate, Aldershot (UK), pp. 353-377.

Miller, D. (1980), 'Project location analysis using the goals achievement method of evaluation', *Journal of the American Planning Association*, Vol. 46, No. 2, pp. 195-208.

Miller, D. (1985), 'Equity and efficiency effects of investment decisions: multi-criteria methods for assessing distribution implications', in A. Faludi and H. Voogd (ed.), *Evaluation of Complex Policy Problems*, Delftsche Uitgevers Maatschappij BV, Delft (The Netherlands), pp. 35-50.

Miller, D. (1999), 'Design and use of urban sustainability indicators in physical planning — a view from Cascadia', in D. Miller and G. de Roo (eds.), *Integrating City Planning and Environmental Improvement*, Ashgate, Aldershot (UK), pp. 283-305.

Mishan, E. (1974), *Cost-Benefit Analysis, An Informal Introduction*, Allen and Unwin, London (UK).

Munda, G. (1995), *Multicriteria Evaluation in a Fuzzy Environment: Theory and Applications in Ecological Economics*, Physica-Verlag, Heidelberg (Germany).

Nas, T. F. (1996), *Cost-Benefit Analysis — Theory and Application*, SAGE Publications, Thousand Oaks, CA (USA).

Nijkamp, P. (1974), 'A multicriteria analysis for project evaluation', *Papers of the Regional Science Association*, No. 35, pp. 88-111.

Nijkamp, P. (1979), *Multidimensional Spatial Data and Decision Analysis*, Wiley, New York, NY (USA).

Parkin, J. (1993), *Judging Plans and Projects — Analysis and Public Participation in the Evaluation Process*, Ashgate, Brookfield, VT (USA).

Pearce, D. (1971), *Cost-Benefit Analysis*, Macmillan, London (UK).

Portney, P. and Harrington, W. (1995), 'Health-based environmental standards: balancing costs with benefits', *Resources*, No. 120, pp. 7-10, Resources for the Future, Washington, DC (USA).

Prest, A. and Turvey, R. (1965), 'Cost-benefit analysis: a survey', *The Economic Journal*, Vol. 75, No. 3, pp. 683-712.

Rietveld, P. (1980), *Multiple Objective Decision Methods and Regional Planning*, North-Holland Publishing Company, Amsterdam (The Netherlands).

Self, P. (1975), *Econocrats and the Policy Process: The Politics and Philosophy of Cost-Benefit Analysis*, Macmillan, London (UK).

Sugden, R. and Williams, A. (1983), *The Principles of Practical Cost-Benefit Analysis*, Oxford University Press, Oxford (UK).

Voogd, H. (1983), *Multicriteria Evaluation for Urban and Regional Planning*, Pion, London (UK).

Voogd, H. (1997), 'On the role of will-shaping in planning evaluation', in D. Borri et al. (eds.), *Evaluating Theory-Practice and Urban-Rural Interplay in Planning*, Kluwer, Dordrecht (The Netherlands), pp. 23-24.

Woltjer, J. (2001), 'Evaluating complex decision-making processes: an assessment of Dutch communicative planning initiatives', in H. Voogd (ed.), *Recent Developments in Evaluation*, Geo Press, Groningen (The Netherlands), pp. 85-109.

PART I
METHODS AND APPLICATION

Chapter 2

Evaluation of Visitability of Public Urban Places

Henk Voogd

2.1 Introduction

People are different with different abilities and with different perceptions of difference. It is increasingly recognised in geography and planning that this must have consequences for the way urban spaces are considered (Butler and Parr, 1999; Imrie and Hall, 2001). Accessibility is for many disabled persons, who otherwise fear social exclusion, a human rights issue (Young, 1990). When a built environment is accessible and hence visitable by all people, it benefits everyone — not only disabled persons but also people with buggies, children, and elderly with or without luggage, shopping trolleys, and walkers. By visitability is meant here the availability of a continuous accessible path of travel for all people between public areas. Individual access to the built environment without the assistance of someone else is a basic civil right of all individuals. Evidently, urban planners and all others who help in shaping the built environment should have people of all abilities in mind.

Basic elements of a visitable site, i.e. a place accessible for all people, include the following (Wijk, Drenth and van Ditmarsch, 2001):

- Accessible parking spaces (including some that are van accessible), with spaces of appropriate aisle widths to enable a person with a wheelchair or scooter to move into and out of a van or car;
- Accessible parking spaces provided closest to the entrance of a building or buildings;
- Appropriately sized kerb cuts and ramps;
- Appropriately marked crosswalks and signage;
- Exterior routes, with appropriate surfaces, which must provide unobstructed circulation to all relevant areas;
- Connections between all relevant areas, including connections to adjacent sites.

How can the 'visitability' principle be implemented? The basic elements mentioned above suggest that it is a simple matter of applying the right technical norms and standards, of evaluating the city areas by means of such a checklist and then by correcting the undesirable situations. However, practice in many cities teaches us

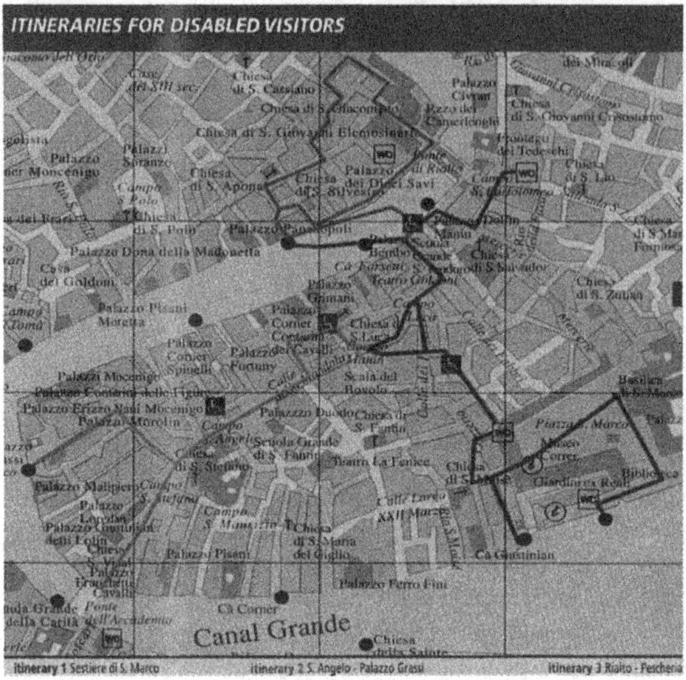

Figure 2.1 Map of Venice illustrating the limited visitability of parts of the city for wheelchair visitors, denoted by shaded streets
Source: Venice City Council (2004), *Itineraries for Disabled Visitors*

that this is not yet, or seldom, happening because of conflicting interests.

Cities can be seen as a conglomerate of public and private spaces with different access to different people. Some people have access to all public spaces; others have only limited access, due to the fact that they cannot overcome the barriers that surround these spaces. An example is given in Figure 2.1.

This chapter analyses some approaches for evaluating visitability. Although many more people may benefit from a good accessibility of places, e.g. people with buggies or heavy luggage, disability activists and their supporters have set the tone of this discussion. In the next section their argument will be briefly outlined. In addition, attention is paid to the criteria by which visitability can be evaluated if a checklist approach is followed. Currently available technologies, like GIS, make it possible to arrive at 'tailor-made' spatial evaluations whereby different impairments can be taken into account. However, such an approach also has some drawbacks.

There is general agreement nowadays that a proper evaluation of the visitability of a site can only be done in an 'inclusive' way, i.e. by using the expertise of those who have one or more impairments. However, little is known about the most effective way of using this expertise. In this contribution a proposal is made for increasing our professional knowledge about this problem by applying a 'cluster evaluation' (Barley and Jenness, 1993) of experiences in many different cities.

2.2 Visitability by legal arrangements

If we define a 'disabled' person as somebody who needs auxiliary equipment in order to compensate for bodily shortcomings, it would fit to a majority of the population. Many people need glasses, contact lenses or false teeth to 'survive' in this modern society! Although they would be very handicapped without their equipment, we generally do not call them 'disabled'. However, there is no fundamental difference between spectacles and wheelchairs, provided that the environment allows the use of this equipment. Both wheelchair and spectacles attempt to reduce the consequences of impairment. This illustrates that the term 'disability' can have many different interpretations and is therefore hard to define in an unambiguous way (Oliver, 1996).

In practice very often a medical definition is given, i.e. referring to a defective limb, organism or mechanism of the body. The message generated from this definition is, according to sensitive disability activists, that the 'disabled' person is inferior to the 'abled' person, thereby neglecting that 'abled' persons also have many different capacities. Many authors therefore recognise that the term 'disability' is a social construct (Gleeson, 1998; Gleeson, 1999; Fincher and Jacobs, 1998; Butler and Parr, 1999). For instance, dyslectic people would never have been judged as disabled in the 'paperless' Middle Ages, while in the same period smart people with 'two left hands' probably would have been considered as very handicapped. A disability is therefore often defined as the disadvantage or restriction of activity caused by a contemporary social organisation which takes no or little account of people who have physical impairments and thus exclude them from the mainstream of social activities (Butler and Bowlby, 1997; p. 411). This is called the social definition of disability, which has stimulated the thinking about visitable environments.

Disability activists in the United States have been very successful in the past in creating legislation that makes public spaces in cities accessible to disabled people. The ADA (Americans with Disabilities Act) of 1990 is seen by many as an example for the rest of the world. The same is true for the Australian DDA (Disability Discrimination Act) of 1992. However, so far there have hardly been proper follow-ups in other 'civilized' countries. The British DDA (Disability Discrimination Act) of 1995, for instance, has been criticized for its lack of 'teeth' (Gooding, 1996; Imrie and Hall, 2001). In the Netherlands state concern is still largely focused on providing support for elderly and dependent citizens. The focus of the Dutch *Wet Voorzieningen Gehandicapten* (Disability Facilities Act) of 1994 is on providing free auxiliary equipment and mobility facilities such as cheap use of door-to-door taxis. However, no special legal regulations exist yet with respect to the visitability of the built environment. It only takes the form of a handbook with recommendations and advice to developers and architects (Wijk, Drenth and van Ditmarsch, 2001). The implementation of access is left at their discretion.

The legal model of rights like ADA and DDA serves as a necessary framework for implementing some essential goals with respect to improving the lives of disabled persons. But it also has its limitations as Clear and Gleeson (2002) outline. They argue that rights-based legal frameworks have not significantly challenged the systems and practices that oppress disabled people and create exclusionary social spaces of work, community and home life. Without fundamental change in the material conditions of people's lives, oppressive systems are left largely untouched. Mental changes of the 'abled' population should be aimed at, which obviously needs time. Oppression of disabled is more the result of 'ignorance' of differences than 'unwillingness' to cope with differences. Communicative planning approaches may therefore be essential for an inclusive treatment of disability issues (Aslaksen et al., 1997).

2.3 Visitability by checklist evaluation

The legal model is especially applicable to national policy-making. At the local level the visitability of sites can be improved by adopting a planning approach based on checklist evaluation. Matthews and Vujaković (1995) have studied the barriers of site access and mapped the experiences of wheelchair users. This resulted in a list of barriers ranked by importance (see Table 2.1).

The list of barriers in Table 2.1 can be used as criteria for evaluating the quality of a site or route for wheelchair users and for developing an urban visitability improvement programme. A very interesting example of such an approach is the MAGUS project of the University College Northampton (Beale et al., 2000; Beale et al., 2001). Here the abbreviation MAGUS stands for 'Modelling Access with GIS in Urban Systems'. Also in this project wheelchair users were asked to mention the most important barriers: see Table 2.2.

In the MAGUS project the barriers of Table 2.2 are used as mapping criteria in a Geographical Information System (GIS). This results in so-called access surfaces. By means of an opinion poll among 400 wheelchair users, the researchers of MAGUS used the average rankings of the importance of barriers as weights. In addition, six types of surfaces were tested and also given an impedance score: concrete (1), paving (1.2), tarmac (1.3), brick (1.6), grass (6), gravel (8). The quality of a kerb has been determined by regression analysis of the appreciation of wheelchair users and nine variables of a kerb, i.e. height, surface, slope, camber, orientation, width, bull nose, brick runner and curvature. By using network analysis tools from the Arc/Info GIS program, 'least impedance' routes are calculated based on minimizing barrier weightings associated with a route. The following formulae have been used (Beale et al., 2001; modified)[1]:

$$\begin{aligned} \text{Impedance} &= l \cdot [35W(10-b)+R] \\ \text{Uphill} &= l \cdot (W \tan\theta + R) \\ \text{Downhill} &= l \cdot (W \tan\theta - R) \end{aligned} \tag{2.1}$$

Table 2.1 Visitability barriers in urban areas, in rank order according to Matthews and Vujaković (1995)

Rank	Barrier
1	High kerbs and/or lack of dropped kerbs
2	Steep gradients or ramps
3	Uneven paving slabs
4	Rough or cobbled surfaces
5	Slippery surfaces
6	Narrow pavements
7	Street furniture poorly placed, restricting access
8	Congested pavements
9	Steps without adjacent ramp
10	Dropped kerbs on roads not adjacent to each other
11	Difficult camber on pavement
12	Deep gutters along roadside, impeding crossing
13	Busy roads
14	Lack of resting places on slopes and ramps
15	Handrails not provided on ramps
16	Insufficient designated road-crossing places
17	Drains near to dropped kerbs
18	Cars parked adjacent to dropped kerbs
19	Raised manhole covers at road-crossing points
20	Poor pathway maintenance leading to problems of fouling by dogs and litter

Source: Adapted from Matthews and Vujaković (1995), 'Private worlds and public places — mapping the environmental values of wheelchair users'

Table 2.2 Barriers and the impedance scores by type of wheelchair user in MAGUS model, low scores represent high levels of impedance

Rank	Barrier	Manually Assisted	Self Propelled	Motorised
1	Steps	1	1.17	1
2	High kerbs	2	2.25	2
3	Deep gutters	3.42	3.83	6
4	Gravel surfaces	5.71	3.75	4
5	Lack of dropped kerbs	5.14	5	4
6	Narrow pavements (< 1 m)	7.28	6.83	8
7	Steep gradients	6.57	6	7.5
8	Adverse cambers	6.57	8.08	7.5
9	Poor pathway maintenance	8.14	8.41	7
10	Cobbled surfaces	9.14	9.67	8

Source: Adapted from Beale et al. (2001), *Modelling Access with GIS in Urban Systems (MAGUS)*

where:

- W is the wheelchair user's weight (on average 75 kp, where 1 kp = 9.807 N, i.e. the gravitational force of a mass of 1 kg),
- l is arc length (in m),
- $\tan\theta$ is slope in decimal degrees,
- R is rolling resistance (in kp),
- b is barrier impedance score (in a range of 1 – 10, where low numbers indicate high impedance).

In this way GIS enabled access surfaces to be transposed into routes that both advised about levels of impedance and which offered the capability for informed decision-making by wheelchair users and urban planners.

By comparing Table 2.1 and Table 2.2 the conclusion can be drawn that a number of aspects are dominant in the evaluation of visitability of sites for wheelchair users. All barriers mentioned in Table 2.2 also appear in Table 2.1. However, the rankings differ. For instance, a comparison shows that in the MAGUS survey 'steps' were seen as the most important barrier, whereas the earlier investigation of Matthews and Vujaković (1995) ranked this at the 9th position. This is remarkable and it illustrates once again that rankings based on opinion polls are strongly time and place dependent, and thus difficult to generalize. From a theoretical point of view, this is a critical element in the MAGUS model, that is calibrated by means of average rankings of opinions.

Another assumption behind MAGUS, however, seems more important. The quality of routes is defined as the aggregate of the impedance scores. This means that a so-called compensatory evaluation model is used, i.e. a low score in a route — implying high impedance — can be compensated by a few high scores further on the route. Thus a route with scores of $9+8+1=18$ can be recommended as better that a route with scores of $5+5+5=15$, while the first route, because of steps, is inaccessible while the second route is accessible but with great difficulties. It is unclear how MAGUS is solving this theoretical problem.

A similar problem exists with respect to the length of a route. Because the quality of a route is determined by an additive relationship between impedance scores, long routes are 'by definition' less attractive than short routes. As an illustration: $9+8+1=18$ is more attractive than a route consisting of $4+4+4+4=16$, whereas a wheelchair user may consider the second route as the *only possibility* to visit a site if he or she is unable to climb steps (denoted by impedance score 1).

No doubt, the great strength of a GIS approach like MAGUS is that is forces people to think about urban barriers and the subject of visitability. It is an excellent tool for illustrating those aspects of the built environment that need improvement. However, apart from providing that kind of substantive information, it is also of crucial importance that factors are revealed that hinder or stimulate visitability. In other words, identifying design feature that facilitate access for those who must use wheelchairs can encourage actors with power in planning processes to arrive at more visitable cities.

2.4 Visitability by cluster evaluation

A GIS approach attempts to make a copy of the built environment. However, in order to improve the environment for planners it is more important to know how to cope with the processes that determine a built environment. As Imrie and Hall (2001) illustrate, there are many (often implicit) reasons why developers and others responsible for the built environment do not want to assist in making places visit-able for everyone. The cost is one of the most important arguments. Social opposition for other reasons is not unlikely. For example, Dear et al. (1997) conclude that:

> One of our saddest professional experiences ... is to encounter community opposition of such virulence that it prevents much-needed services from being provided to disabled people. ... we understand that the establishment of a facility for people with disabilities is at base a form of boundary transgression, threatening to break down the symbolic and spatial barriers between normal and abnormal and eroding the social distance which supports the diametric opposition between self and Other. (Dear et al., 1997; p. 474)

However, in many civilized countries we see a growing attention among public decision-makers to include the disabled in their policymaking. For instance, each municipality in the Netherlands is obliged by law to have an advisory council on disability affairs. This council must give invited and uninvited advice to local authorities about all policies that may affect disabled persons. It would be very interesting to evaluate the results of these councils in terms of making cities more visit-able.

One way to approach this is to perform a so-called cluster evaluation (Barley and Jenness, 1993). This approach has been developed by the Kellogg Foundation (2001) for assessing its projects. The information collected through cluster evaluation is originally to enhance the effectiveness of grant making, clarify the strategies of major programming initiatives, and inform public policy debates. Cluster evaluation deals with the evaluation of groups of projects. It is a means of determining how well the collection of projects fulfils the objective of systemic change. Stakeholder participation is seen as essential, which implies for disabled people that an inclusive approach is followed. The focus of cluster evaluation is on ascertaining lessons learned, not on judging individual projects. It is therefore different from ex post project evaluation.

The basic question to be answered by cluster evaluation could be 'how do disability councils affect public policy-making?' or 'how is the organisation of these councils — e.g. its position in local networks — affecting its effectiveness?' or 'which sectors of public policy have been influenced and how and why?' The advantage of cluster evaluation is that participants do not need to fear its results, which is a drawback of many other forms of evaluation (Worthen and Matsumoto, 1994).

A cluster evaluation of local visitability policy could also be usefully performed in an international setting, since its prime objective is to learn lessons about systemic change. It would be very interesting to start an international comparison of municipalities with respect to their disability policies, notably the visitability of their cities.

2.5 Some concluding comments

The population does not consist of 'the average person' but of different people with different functional abilities (Fincher and Jacobs, 1998). This should lead to a different way of developing and presenting planning proposals as well as consequential evaluations.

Generally the needs of people are changing when they grow older, leading to different consumption patterns with different implications for urban planning and land use. As our life expectancy increases, needs to be met by the built environment change. We are more likely to experience disability as a result of aging and live with it for many years to come. Our environment, however, may not be so easily or inexpensively modified to suit our changing needs.

Evaluation of visitability not only implies gaining insight into substantive urban barriers, but also into organisational barriers. It is therefore crucial to obtain a better understanding in processes and instruments that improve the quality of life of disabled persons. This contribution has discussed three fundamentally different approaches to improve access of urban spaces, viz. the legal approach focussing on prescribing standards and norms for the built environment, the checklist approach focussing on mapping and physically avoiding urban barriers, and the cluster evaluation approach focussing on organisational learning and systemic change.

The examples in this contribution, however, were mainly limited to one type of disability, viz. the wheelchair user. Obviously, there are other kinds of impairments that should influence the built environment. People with visual impairments, for instance, may also benefit from the removal of the barriers mentioned in the previous section, but they additionally need other considerations such as a signage system that is adapted to their handicap (Golledge, Klatzky and Loomis, 1996; Imrie, 1996). It is therefore essential that not only wheelchair users are the subject of study, as has been the focus in this contribution, but also that other minority groups with special environmental requirements are taken into consideration.

Note

1 Editors' note: the formulae for uphill and downhill impedances could also be simplified by setting first

$$\text{Uphill} = \quad f(\theta) = l \cdot (W|\tan\theta| + R) \tag{2.2}$$

and then

$$\text{Downhill} = -f(\theta) \tag{2.3}$$

which means that both, uphill and downhill impedance values are computed by multiplying the absolute value of angle θ (which is negative in the downhill case) with the wheelchair user's weight W, by then summing the result with the rolling resistance R, and by finally multiplying the two addenda with the line length l. The difference between uphill and downhill is therefore given only by the preceding sign (positive in the uphill and negative in the downhill case), exactly as in the formulae presented by H. Voogd at p. 18.

References

Aslaksen, F., Bergh, S., Bringa, O. R. and Heggem, E. K. (1997), *Universell utforming. Planlegging og design for alle* (Universal Design. Planning and Design for All), Statens råd for funksjonshemmede (Norwegian State Council on Disability), Oslo (Norway). English version available at http://www.independentliving.org/docs1/nscd1997.html.

Barley, Z. A. and Jenness, M. (1993), 'Cluster evaluation: A method to strengthen evaluation in smaller programs with similar purposes', *Evaluation Practice*, Vol. 14, No. 2, pp. 141-147.

Beale, L., H. Matthews, Picton, P. and Briggs, D. (2000), 'MAGUS: Modelling Access with GIS in Urban Systems: An Application for Wheelchair Users in Northamptonshire', in CNR-IROE (ed.), *Proceedings 6th ERCIM Workshop 'User Interfaces for All', 25-26 October 2000*, CNR-IROE, Firenze (Italy).

Beale, L., H. Matthews, Picton, P. and Briggs, D. (2001), *Modelling Access with GIS in Urban Systems (MAGUS)*, University College Northampton, Northampton (UK), http://www.magusonline.org.uk/docs/MAGUS%20Review%20Report.pdf.

Butler, R. and Parr, H. (eds., 1999), *Mind and Body Spaces*, Routledge, London (UK).

Butler, R. and Bowlby, S. (1997), 'Bodies and Spaces: an exploration of disabled people's experiences of public space', *Environment and Planning D: Society and Space*, Vol. 15, No. 4, pp. 411-433.

Clear, M. and Gleeson, B. (2002), 'Disability and Materialist Embodiment', *Journal of Australian Political Economy*, Vol. 49, pp. 34-55.

Dear, M., Wilton, R., Gaber, S.L. and Takahashi, L. (1997), 'Seeing people differently: the sociospatial construction of disability', *Environment and Planning D: Society and Space*, Vol. 15, No. 4, pp. 455-480.

Douglass, M. and Friedmann, J. (eds., 1998), *Cities for Citizens*, Wiley, London (UK).

Fincher, R. and Jacobs, J. (eds., 1998), *Cities of Difference*, Guildford Press, New York, NY (USA).

Gleeson, B. (1998), 'Justice and the disabling city', in R. Fincher and J. Jacobs (eds.), *Cities of Difference*, Guildford Press, New York, NY (USA), pp. 89-119.

Gleeson, B. (1999), *Geographies of Disability*, Routledge, London (UK).

Golledge, R.G., Klatzky, R.L. and Loomis, J.M. (1996), 'Cognitive mapping and wayfinding by adults without vision', in J. Portugali (ed.), *The Construction of Cognitive Maps*, Kluwer Academic Publishers, Dordrecht (The Netherlands), pp. 123-141.

Gooding, C. (1996), *Blackstone's Guide to the Disability Discrimination Act 1995*, Blackstone Press, London (UK).

Imrie, R. (1996), *Disability and the City*, Paul Chapman Publishing, London (UK).

Imrie, R. and Hall, P. (eds., 2001), *Inclusive Design, Designing and Developing Accessible Environments*, Spon Press, London and New York.

Kellogg Foundation, W.K. (2001), *Evaluation Handbook*, Kellogg Foundation, Battle Creek, MI (USA), http://www.wkkf.org/Pubs/Tools/Evaluation/Pub770.pdf.

Matthews, M.H. and Vujaković, P. (1995), 'Private worlds and public places — mapping the environmental values of wheelchair users', *Environment and Planning A*, Vol. 27, No. 7, pp. 1069-1083.

Oliver, M. (1996), *Understanding Disability: from theory to practice*, Macmillan, London (UK).

Venice City Council (2004), *Itineraries for Disabled Visitors*, Venice City Council Official Web Site, Italy, http://www.comune.venezia.it/mappe/disabili/piantina_eng.asp.

Wijk, M., Drenth, J. and van Ditmarsch, M. (eds., 2001), 4th revised edition, *Handboek voor Toegankelijkheid* (Accessibility Handbook), Elsevier, Doetinchem (The Netherlands).

Worthen, B.A. and Matsumoto, A. (eds., 1994), 'Conceptual Challenges Confronting Cluster Evaluation', in American Evaluation Association (ed.), *Annual Meeting of the American Evaluation Association*, AEA, Boston, MA (USA), http://www.aglec.unl.edu/rockwell/worthen.txt.

Young, I.M. (1990), *Justice and the Politics of Difference*, Princeton University Press, Princeton, NJ (USA).

Chapter 3

Methods for Evaluating Environmental Justice — Approaches to Implementing U.S. Executive Order 12898

Donald Miller

3.1 Introduction

Urban planners have long been concerned about social fairness in the programs and projects undertaken by the units of government that they serve. Both they and elected officials are aware that every development decision has redistributional effects: a reshaping of who gets and who pays. Elected officials are alert to these effects since they need the votes of at least half of their constituents, although they may not want distributional information to become public knowledge. The codes of professional conduct of planners usually call for these implications to be made public, especially if those who are less well-off disproportionately bear the costs.

A principal reason why social distributional impacts are not more widely a feature of the professional practice of planners is that methodologies for accomplishing this are not highly developed (Miller, 1985). In the U.S., this situation is changing as the result of Executive Order 12898, which requires federal agencies to develop and employ ways for assessing whether actions that they are contemplating disproportionately adversely affect low-income or minority populations. While this order now applies only to federal agencies, even local projects using federal funds must include this sort of assessment in the environmental impact statements for them. This contribution explores these policy initiatives, develops an evaluation method to implement it, and discusses how this method can be integrated with a participatory strategy of planning. This contribution also critically reviews an application of this federal requirement: the environmental justice evaluation for a light rail transit project in Seattle, Washington that is supposed to get modest federal financial support. This case is useful both for illustrating how environmental justice assessment can be applied in practice, and for investigating some of the difficulties that can arise when this kind of planning evaluation is undertaken.

3.2 The nature of environmental justice

Environmental justice refers to fairness in the social distribution of various physical factors that affect quality of life and healthful conditions. It can be applied in assessing differences in the environmental features that various groups of people, defined by income or other social characteristics, currently live with. Evaluation of this kind can be used to prioritize public interventions to improve environmental qualities so that the results are fairer. Alternatively, predicting both positive and negative environmental impacts of alternative plans or project designs is useful in estimating the redistributional effects of these actions on various population groups, this can be the basis for selecting from among alternatives in a manner that reduces or avoids increasing inequities, and even be a basis for redesigning options so that they avoid becoming a greater burden on especially sensitive groups of people.

Evaluating social justice as a routine part of urban planning has proved to be difficult for several reasons. First, the distribution of costs and benefits over segments of a population is at the center of political economy, and the basis of controversy (Mier, 1993). Second, there are no widely creditable ways of defining what constitutes fairness (Miller, 1985). Instead there are a variety of definitions, ranging from equality of outcomes, to equality of inputs, to distributing net benefits on the basis of what each group contributes, for example through taxes. In addition, there are several approaches to subdividing the population for purposes of addressing social equity. The principal approach is by current access to resources, and so by income and wealth. Most definitions focusing on this dimension consider options that deliver more benefits to the less well-off to be progressive in their redistributional effects (Bryant, 1995). However, other approaches to defining fairness classify groups by location such as neighborhood or country, and by gender or other social characteristics. Definitions of sustainability focus on generations in prescribing that resources be used today in a manner that does not limit the options of future generations.

Since there is no fundamental definition of what distribution constitutes social fairness, but rather that any definition is based on judgment, choosing among these approaches is a political rather than a technical function (Seley, 1983). In the U.S., a general definition has emerged through a political process reflected in court decisions, legislation, and executive decisions. At the national level, environmental justice has come to mean fairness in treating and involving all people in the process of designing, deciding, and implementing environmental regulations in a manner that is nondiscriminatory on the basis of race, income, or national origin. Further it requires that minority or low-income people not be disproportionately affected by the negative environmental impacts of governmental actions. The political process by which this definition was arrived at involved a number of investigations of who lived nearby toxic waste dumps and other environmental affronts, and years of advocacy by church and ethnic groups (Miller, 2001).

A third difficulty in incorporating environmental justice into conventional urban planning practice is methodological. This has to do both with how to measure the environmental effects of alternatives on people, and how best to account for affected groups. In measuring environmental effects, what sorts of impacts should be included and should they be measured in terms of inputs, for example amount of pollution present, or in terms of outputs such as the health and other consequences of exposure? Similarly, determining who is being impacted at varying intensities is difficult, as is defining the characteristics of these people as a basis for determining whether the result is socially unfair.

These three sets of problems largely explain why little evaluation of environmental justice has taken place, even though statements concerning the need to address this are often seen in the planning and environmental management literature as well as in social criticism. Attention to resolving these issues has only recently become a part of the public agenda, most promisingly as part of the new federal mandate.

3.3 The Federal Governmental mandate in the United States

American presidents can approve executive orders that direct the actions of administrative agencies. With Executive Order 12898, Federal Actions to Address Environmental Justice in Minority Populations and Low-Income Populations, President Clinton directed each federal agency to adopt, as part of its mission, responsibility for evaluating and mitigating '...disproportionately high adverse human health or environmental effects of its programs, policies, and activities on minority and low-income populations in the United States' (Federal Register, 1994).

Note that both low-income and minority populations are identified for attention, that effects on health and other environmental effects such as nuisances are to be assessed, and that these assessments are to be made for federal agency programs, policies, and activities. The institutional arrangements for accomplishing this are spelled out in an accompanying Presidential Memorandum, which charges the Environmental Protection Agency (EPA) to take lead responsibility for implementing these requirements and the Office of Environmental Justice within EPA was set up to manage this function. Each federal agency must include environmental justice analysis in their National Environmental Policy Act (NEPA) practices and procedures whenever a contemplated action requires an environmental impact assessment. Furthermore, in each such instance, the lead agency must assist affected communities to participate in the NEPA process, including arranging meetings at convenient times and locations, providing effective notice for these, and supplying critical documents including information concerning human health effects. The EPA must review the environmental impact assessment documents and procedures to determine that the originating agencies have adequately addressed environmental justice concerns.

Complementing the responsibilities of the EPA, the Council on Environmental Quality (CEQ) is directed to assist in developing general principles for integrating environmental justice assessments with other environmental assessment issues, and exercising oversight in implementing EO 12898 (CEQ, 1996). CEQ guidelines include assuring effective representation and participation of affected groups as environmental justice is addressed, and requiring that assessment of impacts include possible cumulative effects of exposure to environmental hazards, as well as socioeconomic factors that may increase vulnerability to these exposures. These guidelines also call for collaboration between the lead agency and affected disadvantaged groups in developing alternatives to reduce these effects, and in developing ways to mitigate remaining effects. Even so, these guidelines stop short of specifying the methodology to be used in evaluating environmental justice. Instead of prescribing practices that should be followed, agencies have been encouraged to exercise initiative and to develop prototypes that can lead to improvements: a process of learning from experience. For example, one agency has enlisted churches and other associations in which members of ethnic communities are active as means of communicating effectively with these populations (USDOI, 1995). Another agency is breaking down the life cycle of hazardous waste sites and industrial facilities to trace the environmental effects of designs and decisions made at different phases in building and operating these.

Executive Order 12898 makes evaluating the environmental justice effects of planning and programs undertaken by federal agencies a central feature of their decision-making processes. This appears to be a unique requirement among national governments, and may well encourage similar initiatives elsewhere. While this order does not stipulate the methodology to be used in evaluating environmental justice, the principles included in the order suggest a procedure that will be explored in the next section of this contribution.

3.4 A fundamental approach for evaluating environmental justice of decision options

While no methodology was specified in the EO 12898 or the accompanying memorandum, and agencies were delegated the responsibility of designing methods that respond to the particular kinds of programs and permits under consideration, the definition of intent does suggest a general procedure to employ (NEJAC, 2004). This involves comparing the proportions of low-income and minority populations that would be adversely impacted by a proposed project, with the composition of a larger population, in order to determine if less advantaged people were disproportionately affected. Following this reasoning, environmental injustice occurs in situations in which the percentages of less advantaged residents of areas receiving negative environmental impacts are greater than those same percentages for a larger population. The difference in these rates provides a measure of this injustice, and can guide efforts to mitigate these environmental effects.

This evaluation methodology consists of six steps or activities that represent a logical sequence, since several of these tasks depend on earlier ones. Using this process iteratively and being alert to ways in which feedback from several of the latter tasks can avoid it becoming linear and thus overly limiting. The six tasks include:

1. Mapping the environmental effects generated by a proposal,
2. Enumerating the impacted populations,
3. Establishing a base-line group,
4. Comparing the rates of impacted minority and low-income populations with counterpart rates for the base-line population,
5. Public outreach and participation in reviewing and understanding the environmental effects, and
6. Designing mitigation responses, through this participation.

The first four of these tasks are analytical, largely technical activities, while the last two depend on public consultation aimed at engaging the judgments of affected parties (Sager, 1994).

Mapping the estimated spatial extent of the environmental spillovers from the proposed action is the first step in this process. Plume models are a common device for predicting levels of pollution impact on surrounding resident or working populations. For example, five classes of degree of impact were mapped for each of several kinds of pollution in Dutch integrated environmental zoning (Miller and de Roo, 1996). Since the purpose of estimating the spatial extent of these adverse effects is to relate these to the populations who are impacted, employing analysis zones that are also used for reporting demographic data facilitates this task. For this reason, spatial units such as census tracts, block groups and blocks used by the U.S. Census are especially appropriate (Miller, 1980).

The second task is to analyze the characteristics of the populations within the affected analysis zones. Of specific interest are the proportions of these populations that are low-income or minority. Absolute numbers need to be used as well, since using only rates of less advantaged populations can obscure differences in the population size of various zones or study areas. For example, using rates alone could result in an impacted area with a small population but a largely minority population being regarded as of greater consequence than an area with a larger minority and total population, but with a lower proportion of the total population being minority.

The proportion of less advantaged populations in affected areas is compared with comparable proportions for a larger or base-line population for purposes of assessing whether members of these groups are unfairly adversely impacted. This base-line population can be defined in several ways. For example, the base-line population may be that of the local jurisdiction, the state, or even the nation. Each of these choices will in most cases provide different results. For example, minority populations may be more concentrated in cities than distributed throughout an entire metropolitan region. In this case, the differences in percentages of impacted minority populations would be smaller if the city population were taken as the base-line than it would if the metropolitan population were taken as the base-line.

The fourth step in this generalized evaluation procedure is to compare the rate or percent of the less advantaged populations with the counterpart rates for the larger population to determine if low-income or minority populations are disproportionately disadvantaged by the proposals being assessed. Thus, for example, if 30 per cent of the impacted population in an area were minority, and 12 per cent of the larger population were minority, then the difference of 18 per cent of impacted minority population would be a measure of the extent to which this group is disproportionately adversely affected.

This calculation is similar to the minimum requirements approach in differentiating local-serving from export economic activity, and tends to share the assumption that deviation from common distributions are noteworthy. On the other hand, this is the measure of significance that is referenced in the wording of Executive Order 12898, and is consistent with subsequent guidelines from the EPA and the Council on Environmental Quality (Williams et al., 1995). Again, it is worth noting that comparing rates of contribution by particular groups to the total population, both in impacted analysis zones and in base-line populations, will tend to mask the total effects of pollution in terms of how many people are impacted. Furthermore, using the differences in population percentages in impacted areas and in larger areas assumes that the residual between these is an appropriate criterion. Doing this tends to minimize the significance of impacts on those less advantaged people who are not part of the residual; that is the proportion of the affected population that matches the larger or base-line population.

Following these four analytical tasks are two activities that depend on and use the results. The executive order specifies that there be public participation in the process of determining the fairness of the distribution of negative effects, and gaining an understanding of the severity and implications of these effects (Krimsky and Plough, 1988), and in seeking acceptable ways to mitigate these effects (Hillier, 1998). While the affected populations are the major target of this requirement, it may be that including members of the larger or bench-mark population will build a political constituency that will aid in implementing the resulting decisions (Dryzek, 1990). As noted earlier, securing participation from the less advantaged people who are impacted by the environmental spillovers of proposed options requires special effort. These people are not usually skilled or comfortable with participating in public dialogue of this sort, nor do they tend to have discretionary time to allocate to this (Sager, 1994). Enlisting community leaders and using media that are trusted by these populations are among the techniques that can be employed (Ozawa, 1991).

The sixth and final task is designing responses to the negative environmental spillovers of a contemplated action, with the aim of eliminating any environmental injustice. There are essentially three ways of accomplishing this: reduction, mitigation and compensation. Reduction commonly involves changing locations or changing technology of the sources of pollution, for example, so that undesirable impacts become less of a problem. Mitigation involves actions that shield people from the effects of remaining environmental impacts, such as erecting noise barriers or moving people out of harm's way. Compensation seeks to find ways of providing goods to offset negative effects that can not be reduced or mitigated, such as through providing direct payments or providing desirable facilities and services that counter the remaining nuisance (Kunreuther and Easterling, 1996).

Engaging affected parties in designing and negotiating these responses serves several purposes (White and Ratick, 1989). It helps affected parties gain an understanding of the impacts that will be generated and their consequences (Krimsky and Plough, 1988). Since valuation of these impacts depends on the judgments of those being affected, involving these parties is essential to these values being expressed accurately (Williams and Matheny, 1995; Miller, 1997). Finally, participation helps to assure that solutions to environmental problems adequately improve the conditions of those being impacted (Forester, 1993; Miller and de Roo, 1999).

This sequence of six tasks is an effort to identify a fundamental framework for evaluating environmental justice that responds to the purposes and intent of Executive Order 12898. It is a generalized approach that identifies much of the analysis that is required, and in this form raises some questions concerning the adequacy of this analysis — such as using rates when absolute numbers are needed as well. While clearly this framework needs to be adapted to various situations, it does begin to make operational the broad policy guidelines of this initiative to address issues of fairness. The following case will demonstrate how this approach has been applied in a major transit project, and analysis of this application will help to identify possibilities and difficulties in doing this.

3.5 An assessment of the environmental justice analysis for the Central Link Light Rail Project in Seattle

The urbanized portions of three counties in the central Puget Sound region form Sound Transit, a taxing district to provide heavy rail commuter service, regional express bus service, and light rail transit service. The first phase of the light rail element was to have run for 26 miles from Northgate Shopping Center at the northern boundary of Seattle, south and through downtown Seattle, and continuing to SeaTac Airport just beyond the southern boundary of Seattle.

Bids for 21 miles of this project, stopping at the University of Washington campus on the north, came it at about twice the budget estimates. In the immediate future, Sound Transit plans to build 14 miles of this light rail facility, south from downtown Seattle and short of reaching SeaTac Airport, through predominately low income and minority neighborhoods. This fourteen-mile portion, of what in time is supposed to be a light rail facility linking Tacoma on the south and Everett to the north, was estimated in the plans as having the lowest rider-ship of any portion of the larger system, and is often referred as connecting downtown Seattle with nowhere.

The Central Link project provides an interesting urban case for applying environmental justice analysis for critically evaluating the effectiveness of the methodology used. In this contribution, data for the planned 21 mile route are included to provide a basis for comparing estimated effects on people living in areas adjacent to the route north of downtown Seattle, and the route on which construction will begin shortly that is south of this business district.

The Central Link Draft EIS (USDOT, 1997) responds to Executive Order 12898 and the 1997 U.S. Department of Transportation Order on Environmental Justice (USDOT, 1998), and does so by documenting the impacts and population characteristics along alternative routes. This report also addresses efforts to inform and involve low-income and minority populations in the development of plans.

An early issue to resolve in undertaking this analysis was securing data on the spatial distribution of low-income and minority populations. Effort was made to find recent or current sources that could be used to update 1990 Census data to 1997. Unfortunately, current school enrollment and public health department data are collected at census tract or larger spatial units and thus are not as detailed as needed. Although commercial data bases which updated 1990 counts include racial information at the block group level, it was concluded that the 1990 Census data were the most complete and comprehensive and thus were used for the environmental justice assessment.

A second set of operational questions are the population percentages to be used in defining low-income and minority areas, and choice of the reference or base-line population for determining this. Neither EO 12898 or the DOT Order specify criteria for these definitions, but the CEQ (1998) NEPA guidance suggests either the criterion of areas exceeding 50 per cent or areas with 'meaningful greater' percentages than in the reference area. For this project, meaningfully greater was defined as the affected population that is one standard deviation above the mean for the reference population. Reasons for this are that it is low enough to compensate for under-representation of minority and low-income people because of undercounting, and that the 1990 Census was out of date, but high enough to avoid misrepresenting areas with concentrations of disadvantaged people.

Specifying the reference population requires choice among alternatives as well. The mean of the population in the Sound Transit service and taxing district was chosen since this region includes the urbanized portions of these counties and is the basis for compliance reporting. The mean composition of this population was 16 per cent minority and 9 per cent low-income. Respective figures for the three municipalities through which the light rail line will run were 24 per cent and 12 per cent, and for the areas adjacent to the whole Central Link route and around the stations were 36 per cent minority and 16 per cent low-income. The lower threshold provided by using the population of the service district as the base-line assures that impacts on people in these groups will not be minimized, and best matches the local concept of a minority/low-income community.

Determining and mapping low-income populations is complicated by definitions and data sources. While the DOT Order on environmental equity specifies the poverty guidelines of U.S. Department of Health and Human Services as the basis for low-income, these poverty levels are based on family size and data for this combination of characteristics is suppressed in the Census for small areas. Instead, as CEQ and EPA recommends, the Census statistical poverty threshold was used. The smallest spatial unit for which this evidence was available is the Block Group, which is used. Recalling that the low-income population of the service district was 9 per cent, one standard deviation is 21 per cent, and thus Census Block Groups in which more than 21 per cent of the population were below the poverty level were identified as low-income.

Identifying and locating minority populations is a little less difficult. Racial information is available at the Census Block level, although this leads to undercounting Hispanic persons. The smallest enumeration unit was chosen, as with low-income population, to minimize overlooking pockets of minority people. Since minority contribution to the population of the service district was 16 per cent, one standard deviation is 34 per cent. Thus Census Blocks with 34 per cent or more non-white residents were classified as minority populations for this analysis.

To summarize, the mean and standard deviation for percentage minority and percentage below poverty, using 1990 Census data, were calculated for the population of the Sound Transit service district. Those Census Blocks with high minority populations along route alternatives for the initially planned 21 mile light rail project tend to concentrate just south of downtown Seattle, and continue south for about 4.3 miles along Martin Luther King Jr. Way to near the southern boundary of the city, as illustrated by Figure 3.1 Block Groups with more than 21 per cent of the people having incomes below the poverty level were mapped as low-income areas, and are similarly located: mainly south of downtown, as presented in Figure 3.2.

For purposes of mapping the impacts of the Central Link project, the NEPA definitions of significant adverse effects were used. Types of effects include those affecting health, community cohesion and economy, displacement, and pollution. Several kinds of impacts of concern were identified through consultation with members of neighborhoods in the vicinity of the alternative light rail routes. Most of the environmental impacts were evaluated in other portions of work on the Draft EIS, and their spatial extent was compared to the mapped locations of low-income and minority populations.

Uncertainty affected mapping and measuring these environmental effects since route and station decisions were yet to be made. An approximation was provided by combining possible alternatives into three prototypes for the complete Central Link project. One prototype includes elements which would most affect mapped low-income and minority populations, a second was designed to have moderate disproportionality, and a third would most avoid concentrations of these populations. These three prototypes provide a general indication of the impacts resulting from ways in which the whole project might be designed, which can help to inform public discussion and in determining the preferred alternative.

Residential displacements and property encroachments were an important category because up to 500 dwelling units might be acquired. The impact on target populations was estimated on the basis of their percent representation in the blocks and block groups where property would be acquired for each alternative segment of the project (Table 3.1). When these segments were combined to form the three prototypes, each of these complete system schemes had disproportionate impacts as presented in Table 3.2, especially along possible routes south and east of downtown Seattle.

Neighborhood impacts, in terms of disruptions of movement patterns and quality of life, emerged as a major source of concern in discussions with community groups. Some of these qualities were treated under displacements, traffic, and other specific

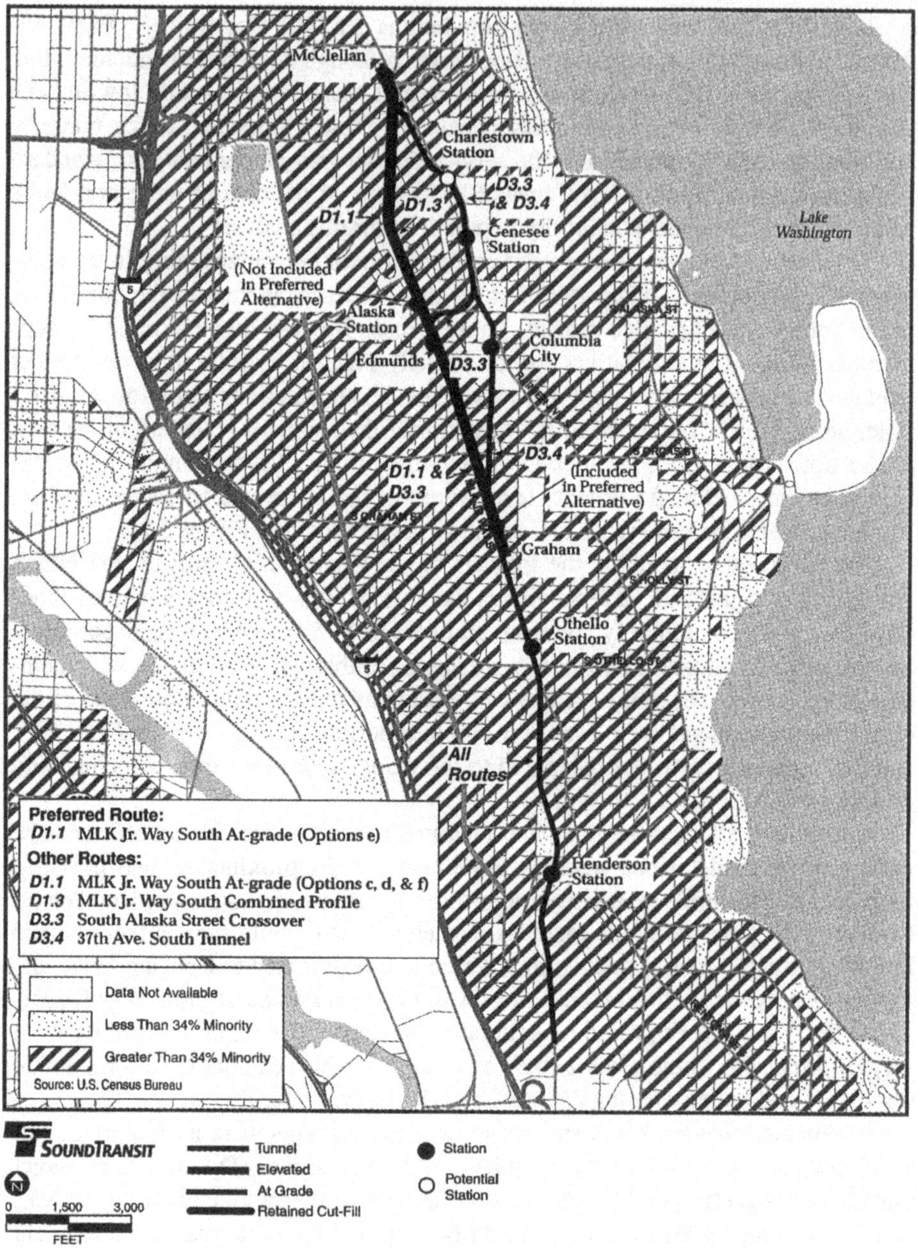

Figure 3.1 Localization of minority population areas within the Central Link Light Rail Project in Seattle

Source: USDOT (1998), *Central Link Light Rail Transit Project — Seattle, Tukwila and SeaTac*

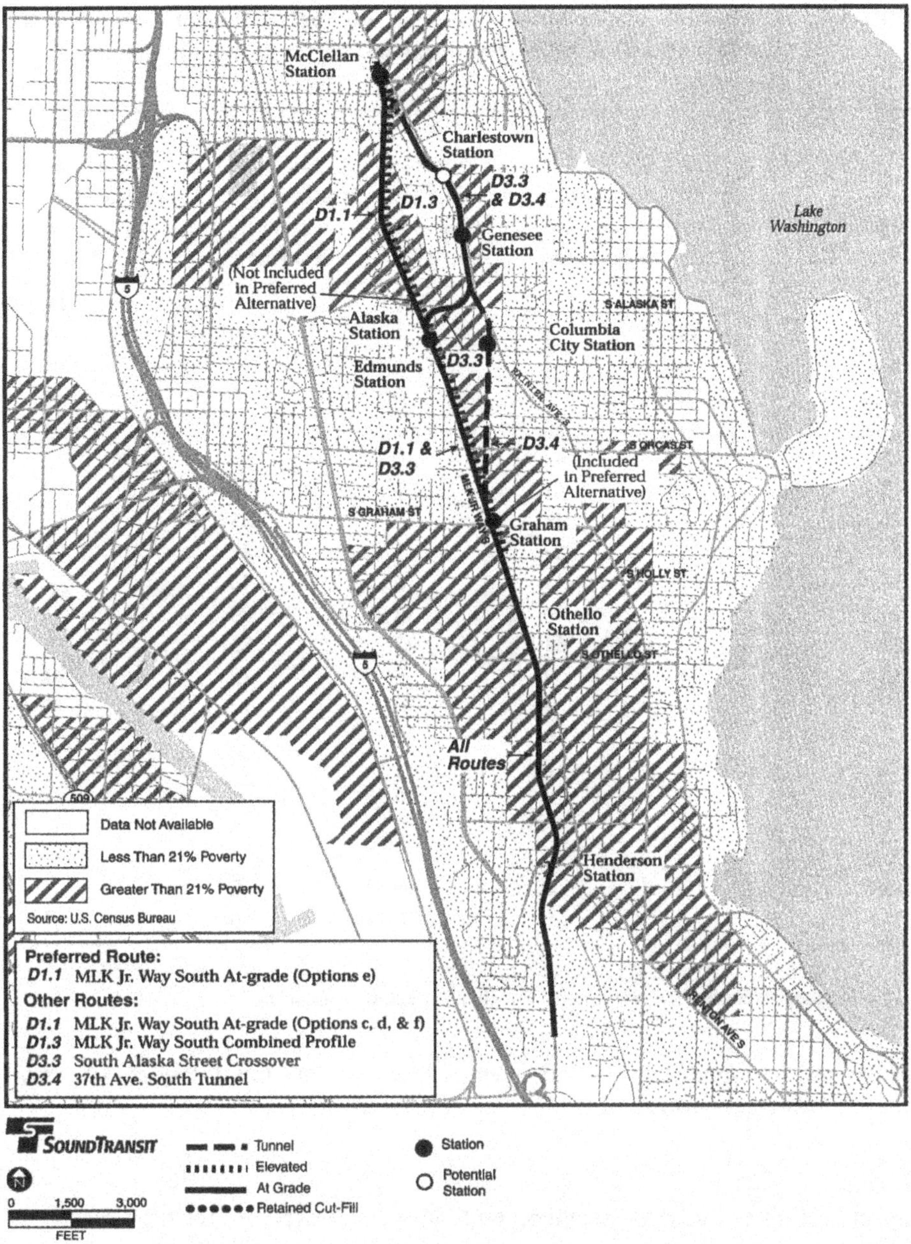

Figure 3.2 Localization of low-income population areas within the Central Link Light Rail Project in Seattle

Source: USDOT (1998), *Central Link Light Rail Transit Project — Seattle, Tukwila and SeaTac*

Table 3.1 Residential displacement impacts on minority and low-income populations (all significantly impacted segment alternatives)

Segment alternative	Total residential displace-ments	Probable minority residences impacted	Probable low-income residences impacted	Percentage of residences impacted that are minority residences	Percentage of residences impacted that are low-income residences
A2.1	8	1	1	13	13
B1	11	1	1	9	9
B2.1	41	7	4	17	10
B2.2	1	0	0	0	9
C2.3	11	10	1	91	0
C2.4	1	*nd*	0	*nd*	0
C3	14	11	1	79	7
D1.1c	53	44	17	83	32
D1.1d	32	27	11	84	34
D1.3	18	17	6	94	33
D3.3	112	93	33	83	29
D3.4	71	61	25	86	35
E1.1	8	2	0	25	0
E1.2	6	1	0	17	0
E2	2	0	0	0	0
E3	9	3	1	33	11
F1	3	0	0	0	0
F2.1	2	0	0	0	0
F2.2	2	0	0	0	0
F3.1	2	0	0	0	0
F3.2	2	0	0	0	0

nd = No data; Census data unavailable for this impacted population.

Source: Adapted from USDOT (1998), *Central Link Light Rail Transit Project — Seattle, Tukwila and SeaTac*

impacts. High and adverse neighborhood impacts are expected for the portion of the project which will be along surface streets south and east of downtown Seattle, where the major concentrations of low-income and minority populations live. Thus all three prototypes would disproportionately affect these groups.

Visual and aesthetic effects expected to remain after mitigation were treated by the Draft Environmental Impact Statement. Environmental justice assessment of these considered the affected population as those living in and adjacent to the zone of significant impact, since these people would be exposed for more time than would people who might travel through these zones. Several segment alternatives are ex-

Table 3.2 Disproportionate distribution of residential displacements on minority and low-income populations (three full-system scenarios)

Route scenario	Percentage of residences impacted that are minority residences	Threshold of dispro-portionality (minority)	Percentage of residences impacted that are low-income residences	Threshold of dispro-portionality (low-income)	Dispro-portionate?
Scenario 1	65 (72)	34 %	26 (28)	21 %	Yes (Yes)
Scenario 2	72 (72)	34 %	25 (25)	21 %	Yes (Yes)
Scenario 3	75 (75)	34 %	29 (29)	21 %	Yes (Yes)

* Values in parentheses are for the 45th to SeaTac variation.

Source: Adapted from USDOT (1998), *Central Link Light Rail Transit Project — Seattle, Tukwila and SeaTac*

pected to result in high and adverse visual impacts, as shown by Table 3.3, but those with the greatest disproportionality are again located along the southern corridor.

Recreation impacts were narrowly defined as project-related effects on local recreation facilities, after mitigation. In the absence of data on who uses these facilities, residents within a quarter mile radius serve as a proxy. Given the spatial distribution of affected parks, only one prototype for the full system disproportionately impacted minority populations.

Noise and vibration from both traffic and the light rail vehicles were mapped for significant impact zones. These were compared with the mapped low-income Block Groups and minority Blocks. While boundaries of impact zones do not always correspond to those for the Census areas, this comparison provides the basis for estimating whether the impacts are disproportional, both without (Table 3.4) and with mitigation (Table 3.5). High and adverse noise and vibration impacts, even after mitigation, are especially a problem along rail segments located at ground level along streets. Most of these segments are in the south corridor (Table 3.5), which is also the area with concentrations of low-income and minority populations. As a consequence, all three of the prototypes would have disproportionate impacts (Tables 3.6 and 3.7).

Transportation impacts focus on effects that the light rail project will have on local traffic patterns even after suggested efforts to mitigate these effects. As with recreation and visual impacts, it is difficult to assess the characteristics of the people affected, since they include both nearby residents and those traveling through an area. Again, impacted population was set as those residing within a quarter mile radius of zones of significant effect, the segment alternatives with the largest impacted populations were also in the areas south of downtown with concentrations of low-income and minority residents, and all three system prototypes had disproportionate

Table 3.3 High and adverse visual impacts on minority and low-income populations (all significantly impacted segment alternatives)

Segment alternative	Total population impacted*	Minority population impacted	Low-income population impacted	Percentage of minority population impacted	Percentage of low-income population impacted
A2.2	447	34	39	8	9
B2.1	1429	473	221	33	15
C2.3	276	226	47	82	17
C3	276	226	47	82	17
D1.3	2305	1940	623	84	27
E1.2	1706	453	257	27	15
E2	765	160	48	21	6
E3	305	34	35	11	11
F1	915	123	35	13	4
F2.2	94	2	8	2	9

* Population within Census Blocks adjacent to the zone of significant impact.

Source: Adapted from USDOT (1998), *Central Link Light Rail Transit Project — Seattle, Tukwila and SeaTac*

consequences, especially for minority populations.

Table 3.8 provides a summary of those segment alternatives that have high and adverse impacts on low-income and minority populations, after mitigation. This table includes each of the categories of effect that have been discussed. Scanning across these categories confirms that alternatives for the D segments have the greatest number of disproportionate effects; that is, represent the greatest environmental justice problems for the Central Link Light Rail Transit Project. As noted earlier, this is both a function of designs for this portion of the system being at grade along streets, and of this area south of downtown Seattle containing a concentration of low-income and minority people.

This description and discussion of the environmental justice analysis pursued for the Sound Transit light rail project illustrates the fundamental evaluation process outlined in the previous section of this contribution. But more importantly, it brings into focus a number of the problems faced in this process: in specifying impacted groups, in determining how low-income and minority populations should be defined, and in securing reliable and valid data to use in the evaluation. This case includes partial solutions to these issues that, while sometimes ingenuous, are each also sources of error. While the direction of this error — toward under or over estimation — is usually easy to assess, approximating the magnitude is evasive. These findings suggest kinds of data that are important to collect in the future if environmental justice ana-

Table 3.4 High and adverse noise and vibration impacts (without mitigation) on minority and low-income populations (all significantly impacted segment alternatives)

Segment alternative	Total population impacted*	Minority population impacted	Low-income population impacted	Percentage of minority population impacted	Percentage of low-income population impacted
A1.1	35	1	0	3	0
A1.2	149	19	11	13	7
B2.1	802	265	83	33	10
C2.3	3	3	1	100	17
D1.1c	4574	3702	1314	81	29
D1.1d	4574	3702	1314	81	29
D1.3	4914	4001	0	81	29
D3.3	4206	3269	1120	78	27
D3.4	3008	2323	778	77	26
E1.1	2719	505	307	19	11
E1.2	2645	493	281	19	11
E2	151	9	19	6	12
E3	849	386	100	45	12

* Population within Census Blocks in the zone of significant impact.

Source: Adapted from USDOT (1998), *Central Link Light Rail Transit Project — Seattle, Tukwila and SeaTac*

lysis is to be creditable. These findings also suggest topics that would be valuable to investigate, such as developing conventional operational definitions for population characteristics that validly address the concerns of social justice.

3.6 Conclusions

Every major investment or regulatory decision has social distributional effects. Environmental justice implications are a significant subset of these, and one that has received growing public attention. Executive Order 12898 and subsequent guidelines for carrying it out provide a framework for addressing this concern, and a policy mandate to federal agencies in the U.S. to assess and mitigate disproportionate impacts on low-income and minority populations. It is a unique effort by a government to address environmental equity issues.

In addition to describing this executive order and arrangements for implementing it, a fundamental evaluation methodology is proposed for meeting the objectives of this new requirement. This methodology can be employed in planning for new devel-

Table 3.5 High and adverse noise and vibration impacts (with mitigation) on minority and low-income populations (all significantly impacted segment alternatives)

Segment alternative	Total population impacted*	Minority population impacted	Low-income population impacted	Percentage of minority population impacted	Percentage of low-income population impacted
B2.1	484	224	76	46	16
D1.1c	388	357	116	92	30
D1.1d	388	357	116	92	30
D3.3	802	510	280	64	35
D3.4	179	148	8	83	5
E1.1	24	0	1	0	2
E2	101	3	13	3	13
E3	697	321	80	46	11

* Population within Census Blocks in the zone of significant impact.

Source: Adapted from USDOT (1998), *Central Link Light Rail Transit Project — Seattle, Tukwila and SeaTac*

Table 3.6 Disproportionate distribution of high and adverse noise and vibration impacts (without mitigation) on minority and low-income populations (three full-system scenarios)

Route scenario	Percentage of minority poulation impacted	Threshold of dispro-portionality (minority)	Percentage of low-income population impacted	Threshold of dispro-portionality (low-income)	Dispro-portionate?
Scenario 1	75 (75)	34 %	25 (25)	21 %	Yes (Yes)
Scenario 2	54 (54)	34 %	21 (22)	21 %	Yes (Yes)
Scenario 3	73 (74)	34 %	24 (25)	21 %	Yes (Yes)

* Values in parentheses are for the 45th to SeaTac variation.

Source: Adapted from USDOT (1998), *Central Link Light Rail Transit Project — Seattle, Tukwila and SeaTac*

Table 3.7 Disproportionate distribution of high and adverse noise and vibration impacts (with mitigation) on minority and low-income populations (three full-system scenarios)

Route scenario	Percentage of minority poulation impacted	Threshold of dispro-portionality (minority)	Percentage of low-income population impacted	Threshold of dispro-portionality (low-income)	Dispro-portionate?
Scenario 1	62 (62)	34 %	21 (21)	21 %	Yes (Yes)
Scenario 2	62 (62)	34 %	29 (29)	21 %	Yes (Yes)
Scenario 3	54 (54)	34 %	7 (7)	21 %	Yes (Yes)

* Values in parentheses are for the 45th to SeaTac variation.

Source: Adapted from USDOT (1998), *Central Link Light Rail Transit Project — Seattle, Tukwila and SeaTac*

opment, and in planning aimed at improving the existing environmental conditions faced by disadvantaged groups.

The proposed methodology integrates technical analysis with outreach and participation. The purposes of this integration are to seek important information for the analysis from the affected parties, and to work toward an agreement which is both ethical and has the political support that will improve its chances of being implemented.

A practical application of several of these ideas is provided by the environmental justice analysis for the light rail transit project in the Seattle area. While this case employs a reasonable methodology, it also points up the operational problems that confront planners in undertaking an assessment of this sort, and helps to identify data and definitional issues which need to be resolved to improve the creditability of this kind of analysis.

Table 3.8 Summary of high and adverse impacts after mitigation (all segment alternatives)

Segment alternative	Residential displacements			Neighborhoods			Visual			Recreation			Noise (without mitigation)			Noise (with mitigation)			Transportation		
	A	B	C	A	B	C	A	B	C	A	B	C	A	B	C	A	B	C	A	B	C
A1.1	–	–	–	–	–	–	–	–	–	–	–	–	×	–	–	–	–	–	–	–	–
A1.2	–	–	–	–	–	–	–	–	–	–	–	–	×	–	–	–	–	–	–	–	–
A2.1	×	–	–	–	–	–	–	–	–	×	–	–	–	–	–	–	–	–	–	–	–
A2.2	–	–	–	–	–	–	×	–	–	×	–	–	–	–	–	–	–	–	–	–	–
B1	×	–	–	–	–	–	–	–	–	–	–	–	–	–	–	–	–	–	–	–	–
B2.1	×	–	–	–	–	–	×	–	–	×	–	–	×	–	–	×	×	–	–	–	–
B2.2	×	–	–	–	–	–	–	–	–	–	–	–	–	–	–	–	–	–	–	–	–
C1	–	–	–	–	–	–	–	–	–	–	–	–	–	–	–	–	–	–	×	×	–
C2.3	×	×	–	–	–	–	×	×	–	–	–	–	×	×	–	–	–	–	–	–	–
C2.4	×	*nd*	–	–	–	–	–	–	–	–	–	–	–	–	–	–	–	–	–	–	–
C3	×	×	–	–	–	–	×	×	–	×	×	–	–	–	–	–	–	–	×	×	–
D1.1	×	×	×	×	×	×	–	–	–	–	–	–	×	×	×	×	×	×	×	×	×
D1.1D	×	×	×	×	×	×	–	–	–	–	–	–	×	×	×	×	×	×	×	×	×
D1.3	×	×	×	×	×	×	×	×	×	–	–	–	×	×	×	–	–	–	×	×	×
D3.3	×	×	×	×	×	×	–	–	–	–	–	–	×	×	×	×	×	×	×	×	×
D3.4	×	×	×	×	×	×	–	–	–	–	–	–	×	×	×	×	×	–	×	×	×
E1.1	×	–	–	–	–	–	–	–	–	–	–	–	×	–	–	×	–	–	×	–	–
E1.2	×	–	–	–	–	–	×	–	–	–	–	–	×	–	–	–	–	–	–	–	–
E2	×	–	–	–	–	–	×	–	–	×	–	–	×	–	–	×	–	–	–	–	–
E3	×	–	–	–	–	–	×	–	–	–	–	–	×	×	–	×	×	–	–	–	–
F1	×	–	–	–	–	–	×	–	–	×	–	–	–	–	–	–	–	–	×	–	–
F2.1	×	–	–	–	–	–	–	–	–	–	–	–	–	–	–	–	–	–	–	–	–
F2.2	×	–	–	–	–	–	×	–	–	–	–	–	–	–	–	–	–	–	–	–	–
F3.1	×	–	–	–	–	–	–	–	–	–	–	–	–	–	–	–	–	–	–	–	–
F3.2	×	–	–	–	–	–	–	–	–	–	–	–	–	–	–	–	–	–	–	–	–

A = Significant impacts remain after mitigation?
B = Impacted population over 34 % minority threshold?
C = Impacted population over 21 % poverty threshold?
× = Yes.
– = No.

nd = No data; Census data unavailable for this impacted population.

Source: Adapted from USDOT (1998), *Central Link Light Rail Transit Project — Seattle, Tukwila and SeaTac*

References

Bryant, B. (ed., 1995), *Environmental Justice: Issues, Policies and Solutions*, Island Press, Covelo, CA (USA).

CEQ (1998), *Environmental Justice Guidence Under the National Environmental Policy Act*, Council for Environmental Quality, Washington, DC (USA).

CEQ (1996), *Draft Guidance for Addressing Environmental Justice Under the National Environmental Policy Act*, Executive Office of the President, Washington, DC (USA).

Dryzek, J. (1990), *Discursive Democracy: Politics, Policy and Political Science*, Cambridge University Press, Cambridge (UK).

Federal Register (1994), 'Executive Order 12898, Federal Actions to Address Environmental Justice in Minority Populations and Low-Income Populations', *Federal Register*, Vol. 59, No. 32, p. 7629 (59 FR 32, February 16), White House Office, Washington, DC (USA). Also at http://www.epa.gov/history/topics/justice/02.htm.

Forester, J. (1993), 'Learning from Practice Stories: The Priority of Practical Judgment', in F. Fischer and J. Forester (eds.), *The Argumentative Turn in Policy Analysis and Planning*, Duke University Press, Durham, NC (USA), pp. 186-209.

Hillier, J. (1998), 'Beyond Confused Noise: Ideas Toward Communicative Procedural Justice', *Journal of Planning Education and Research*, Vol. 18, No. 1, pp. 14-24.

Kratch, K. (1995), 'Grassroots Reach the White House Lawn', *Environmental Solutions*, Vol. 8, No. 5, pp. 68-77.

Krimsky, S. and Plough, A. (1988), *Environmental Hazards: Communicating Risks as a Social Process*, Auburn House, Dover, MA (USA).

Kunreuther, H. and Easterling, D. (1996), 'The Role of Compensation in Siting Hazardous Facilities', *Journal of Policy Analysis and Management*, Vol. 15, No. 4, pp. 601-622.

Mier, R (1993), *Social Justice and Development Planning*, Sage Publications, Newbury Park, CA (USA).

Miller, D. (1980), 'Project Location Analysis Using the Goals Achievement Method of Evaluation', *Journal of the American Planning Association*, Vol. 46, No. 2, pp. 195-208.

Miller, D. (1985), 'Equity and Efficiency Effects in Investment Decisions: Multicriteria Methods for Assessing Distributional Implications', in A. Faludi and H. Voogd, (eds.), *Evaluation of Complex Policy Problems*, Delftsche Uitgevers Maatschappij BV, Delft (The Netherlands), pp. 35-50.

Miller, D. (1997), 'Dutch Integrated Environmental Zoning. A Comprehensive Program Dealing with Urban Environmental Spillovers', in D. Miller and G. de Roo (eds.), *Urban Environmental Planning*, Avebury Publishers, Aldershot (UK), pp. 165-178.

Miller, D. (2001), 'Evaluating Environmental Justice for Planning', in H. Voogd (ed.), *Recent Developments in Evaluation*, Geo Press, Groningen (The Netherlands), pp. 17-35.

Miller, D. and de Roo, G. (1999), 'Integrating Land Use Planning and Environmental Policy', in D. Miller and G. de Roo, (eds.), *Urban Environmental Planning*, Avebury Publishers, Aldershot (UK), pp. 1-12.

Miller, D. and de Roo, G. (1996), 'Integrated Environmental Zoning — An Innovative Dutch Approach to Measuring and Managing Environmental Spillovers in Urban Regions', *Journal of the American Planning Association*, Vol. 62, No. 3, pp. 373-380.

NEJAC (2004), http://www.epa.gov/compliance/environmentaljustice/nejac.

Ozawa, C. (1991), *Recasting Science: Consensual Procedures in Public Policy Making*, Westview Press, Boulder, CO (USA).

Sager, T. (1994), *Communicative Planning Theory*, Avebury Publishers, Aldershot (UK).

Seley, J. E. (1983), *The Politics of Public-Facility Planning*, Lexington Books, Lexington, MA (USA).

U.S. Department of Interior (1995), *Environmental Compliance Memorandum No. ECM95-3: National Environmental Policy Act Responsibilities Under The Departmental Environmental Justice Policy*, Office of the Secretary, Washington, DC (USA).

U.S. Department of Transportation (1997), *DOT Order to Address Environmental Justice in Minority Populations and Low-Income Populations*, Department of Transportation, Washington, DC (USA).

U.S. Department of Transportation (1998), Washington, Draft Environmental Impact Statement. *Central Link Light Rail Transit Project — Seattle, Tukwila and SeaTac*, Federal Transit Administration, DOT, Region X, Seattle, WA (USA).

U.S. Environmental Protection Agency (1996), *Guidance for Incorporating Environmental Justice Concerns in EPA's NEPA compliance Analysis*, USEPA, Office of Federal Activities, Washington, DC (USA).

White, A. L. and Ratick, S. J. (1989), 'Risk, Compensation and Regional Equity in Locating Hazardous Facilities', *Papers of the Regional Science Association*, Vol. 67, No. 1, pp. 29-42.

Williams, B. A. and Matheny, A. R. (1995), *Democracy, Dialogue and Environmental Disputes: The Contested Languages of Social Regulation*, Yale University Press, New Haven, CT (USA).

Williams, G., Thompson, J., Burdge, R. J., Fricke, P., Finsterbusch, K., Freudenburg, W. R., Gramling, R., Holden, A., Lewellyn, L. and Petterson, J. S. (1995), 'Guidelines and Principles for Social Impact Assessment', *Environmental Impact Assessment Review*, Vol. 15, No. 1, pp. 11-43.

Chapter 4

Issues in Transport Multi-Modal Choice — A Case Study in Wales

Christopher Yewlett

4.1 Introduction

Students of evaluation have classically identified two major different kinds: pre- (or prior) and post- evaluation. Post evaluation is concerned with the success and effectiveness (or otherwise) of programmes whilst prior evaluation, in contrast, is concerned with helping decision makers take difficult choices.

Prior evaluation is inevitably associated with decision making — where we are faced with a choice between options, which option is preferable? The development and application of appropriate methods to assist with this task has a long history in land-use and transport planning. Lichfield (1996; p. 209) identified some thirty methods in urban and regional planning, of which eleven were 'known to be used in transport evaluation', especially of road proposals prior to commitment to construction. However, as his case study indicated, the tendency was to adopt a narrowly road user focussed decision criterion.

Indeed, even during the recent planning 'dark age' in the UK during the 1980s, when Government enthusiasm for planning was so low that many planning authorities literally lost the relevant skills for positive planning (Crow et al., 1997; paragraph 4.3; Yewlett, 2001a; Yewlett, 2001b), transport (specifically traffic impact assessments) remained one of the few areas of relevant planning activity. Of course, evaluation prior to major expenditure, particularly by civil engineers (with economist support) remained a feature of transport investment, especially into new road construction.

Historical background

Evaluation in transport has a long history. The transport field is characterized as one involving substantial public expenditure, which then provides a mixture of benefits and, indeed, disbenefits. Some of these benefits are of a direct financial nature, either to private individuals or organizations, whilst others are indirect. This has therefore inspired an active interest in prior evaluation methods, so as to assist decision makers in selecting appropriate investments, whether competing opportunities within the transport field, or alternative fields of investment, taking into account the full range of factors.

Banister has traced this interest back to Dupuit's (1844) conclusion that more general benefits accrue to society from transport investment than are directly apparent in increased revenues. He comments that 'Early assessments were made on operational criteria such as whether it was physically possible for roads to accommodate traffic without unreasonable delay', also taking into account such matters as physical design standards, costs, and scale and timing of necessary improvements.

Subsequently, (from approximately the 1960s) the technique of Cost Benefit Analysis (CBA, or CoBA) has been developed to help formalize this. The pioneering early UK study concerned the proposed London-Birmingham Motorway (Coburn, Beesley and Reynolds, 1960). Here, for the alternative 'go' or 'no-go' decisions, the differences in aggregated travel times and in accident rates were estimated and costed into the overall decision. The Treasury was thus presented with the dual concept of 'Exchequer costs' and 'economic costs' (each with associated benefits). Exchequer costs include both direct expenditure and supposed direct savings (e.g. in NHS savings on treatment of accident victims) and thus the net impact on Treasury expenditures, whilst economic costs include wider benefits (e.g. fuel cost savings) which can be expected (and estimated) to feed back into the national accounts via taxation on enhanced income or profits. This kind of approach, extending the cost benefit analysis to the wider society (in contrast to typical internally focussed commercial investment appraisals) has, as it developed further, become known as 'Social Cost Benefit Analysis'.

This early pioneering work was subsequently developed into the 'COBA' cost benefit analysis method of appraisal (DoE, 1972). COBA adopted the standard UK assumed life of road works of 30 years, and thus discounted the costs and benefits of a new road over the 30 year period from the proposed opening date, to give a 'net present value' and a 'net present cost ratio', to help evaluate overall justifiability, and relative desirability, respectively. This was of course a purely economic methodology, utilizing savings in travel time; savings in vehicle operating costs; and savings in accidents, offset against capital construction and ongoing maintenance costs. The cost benefit analysis methodology has been developed over the years, and consolidated, with the developments of information technology, into a computer program (COBA), issued for the convenience of local authorities charged with forward planning of major road schemes (DoT, 1987).

COBA has attempted to broaden the basis of assessment. As well as the direct financial costs to the state (capital construction, maintenance, and operational), and the costs accruing to road users (expected to be negative in the form of benefits!), COBA has attempted to assess wider impacts, particularly those apparently quantifiable. Accident reduction has clear financial benefits, not only in savings to emergency services, hospital facilities etc., as well of course as the physical accident damage, but also in avoiding loss of productive careers within the economy. Reasonable estimates of such factors can be generated probabilistically. Harder to quantify was the value to individuals of savings in pain, personal suffering, and grief over deaths avoided. Although hard to quantify, saving of lives (and quality of life in nonfatal accidents) was clearly of political significance. At various times, decisions have either been made politically (leaving analysts to infer the value of a life post-hoc) or attempts made to determine a value through such methods as 'revealed preference' or 'stated preference'.

Two other major areas of concern were firstly the environmental consequences of proposed investments, and secondly the differential distributive costs and benefits. On the first, exploring the history of transport appraisal up to 1996 in an earlier volume in this series, Nash (1998) commented that 'Although a lot of effort has been put into valuation of environmental costs and benefits of road schemes in recent years, the view of DoT is that these valuations are as yet not sufficiently accurate to be used in practice' (Nash, 1998; p. 315). The significance of this to our current interest is that much of current UK transport policy (and indeed related land-use planning policy) was (and, in theory at least in 2003, still is) driven by global environmental concerns, most notably global warming (Yewlett, 1995). This reflected the increasing world-wide concern with the problem of global warming, as a consequence of the production of ever-increasing amounts of 'greenhouse gases', among which Carbon Dioxide (CO_2), an inevitable by-product of fossil fuels, was regarded as a major culprit (HMSO, 1990). Subsequently, the 1992 'Rio Conference' (UN, 1997) led to express UK commitments to take action (HMSO, 1994).

A second major factor necessitating a rethink of transport policy was the impact of increasing congestion on European cities, caused largely by the steady increase, (both absolutely and as a proportion) in daily private car commuters. The European Commission (as then was) specifically warned against attempts to alleviate traffic congestion by building new roads, and encouraged further relevant research (EC, 1992). To perpetuate the non-consideration of environmental impacts was thus likely to undermine these policy objectives, by disproportionately encouraging investments which would prove 'unsustainable' in the longer term.

Environmental imperatives

A second major problem with the approach to transport appraisal discussed above was the distinctly different approaches to evaluating investments in different areas of transport expenditure. Road schemes (barring limited tolls, until recently levied only to finance major bridges or tunnels) by definition involve direct Treasury expenditure, but indirect benefits, and therefore inevitably lead to the development of some kind of relative appraisal methodology, however crude, as the alternative, simple political decision, apart from 'value for money' investment issues, leads to a politically difficult situation which Ministers were reluctant to defend. In contrast, the (then nationalized) rail network had had to justify internal investment in profitable services (inter-city, bulk freight) on a purely commercial basis, including provision for funding infrastructure improvements out of returns generated. This was a major bone of contention to the industry and its supporters, as it was seen as a bias against intercity rail travel.

The non-commercial rail network (all other passenger services outside the major cities) on the other hand was funded on the basis of maintaining more or less the existing services at lowest possible cost. This in turn led to a dearth of investment, unless a local authority or other body was prepared to put up the money. In South Wales, for example, the former Mid and South Glamorgan County Councils funded a number of improvements to the greater Cardiff local network. In neighbouring Gwent, some of the surplus remaining at the winding-up of Cwmbran New Town Development Corporation was invested in a new station, since although on a main rail route, the original station had been closed in the 1960s, and Cwmbran had become the largest town in Wales without one! However, the entire process of rail support in this sector was highly political, and very hit and miss, with very limited explicit appraisal of potential changes.

The third element of rail passenger services, those providing local travel in major city areas (especially for commuters) came under a third different regime for appraisal of potential support. Bodies known as Passenger Transport Executives (as successors to the Metropolitan Counties) had control over local passenger rail service levels and fares, and could use social cost benefit analysis as a basis for appraisal.

Bus services had been deregulated from 1986, and subsequently increasingly privatized (with the remaining municipally owned operations required to operate as commercial undertakings in practice). However, local authorities retained powers to provide a subsidy for bus services fulfilling an identified social need (through competitive tendering). Although this provided a clear opportunity for social cost benefit analysis approaches, in practice this was rare, the more usual approach being to use accessibility standards to identify needed services (Nash, 1998).

London formed a unique situation, with London Regional Transport retaining powers to plan public transport in London, by directly controlling fares and services of privatized bus operators (who would then fill specified route requirements by competitive tendering), and by direct operational control of the Underground. This therefore allowed LRT to use social cost benefit analysis systematically (although even here the situation was muddied by the extensive role of local rail in London, especially for longer distance commuting).

There was thus a situation in which very different approaches were being used in different sectors, which were nevertheless potential competitors for transport provision. As Nash (1998; p. 311) described it, 'a highly differentiated and arguably totally inconsistent approach to transport appraisal was developing' in the late 1980s, with 'trunk (major) road schemes being subject to a fairly narrow cost benefit analysis, local authority schemes to a much wider multi-criterion approach and public transport typically to a purely commercial or accessibility based approach'. This is clearly not a situation which encouraged systematic consideration of alternative *forms* of meeting a particular transport demand (e.g. road versus rail; public versus private) rather than prioritizing the competing investments under the control of a particular local or sectoral agent. However, there were already indications of the evolution of a more integrated approach: the Common Appraisal Framework (DoT, 1994).

The Common Appraisal Framework

The idea of a Common Appraisal Framework arose from a number of directions: first, the recognized disparities in historic practices discussed above; and second, the specific problems with securing Government funds for urban public transport schemes, rather than road schemes. These problems in Birmingham and the wider West Midlands of England led Birmingham and Centro (the Regional Transport operator) to commission in 1991 the development of a 'framework which *would* allow for modes to be appraised on a comparable basis' (DoT, 1994; paragraph 2.1.8). The initiative was actively partnered by the Government, including finance and active publication of the report. This report, by going into considerable detail on the treatment of externalities, including distributional effects, as well as economic and financial issues, laid the groundwork for the later philosophy.

Third, by 1992 the Department of Transport had, in pursuit of the wider goal of integrating land-use with transport planning, accepted the principle of the 'package approach' to transport funding. This was a major political departure. Previously, different 'pots' of money were available for different activities: roads, public transport subsidy, rail support, etc.; and local authorities had to bid for their 'share' of each kitty. This meant that decisions about the balance of expenditure between different modes were taken centrally, and essentially politically, rather than by reference to any aggregation of local needs. In contrast, the 'package approach', flagged in PPG 12 (DoE and WO, 1992) and confirmed in PPG 13 (DoE, 1995) introduced the requirement that local authorities bidding for Central Government support had to provide a reasoned overall case for their transport expenditure, and could thus consciously seek to divert money away from roads towards public transport support. Other relevant inputs evolved from the pending need for more explicit appraisals of rail passenger support following privatization. (OPRAF, 1997).

Following the election of the ('New') Labour Government (May 1997), concern with the likely consequences of unbridled road construction, reinforced by extensive local and national public protest about several current proposals, led to a moratorium on trunk road construction pending a 'Strategic Review'. At the same time, a proposed overall 'Integrated Transport Policy' was under development, which appeared as the White Paper *A New Deal for Transport: Better for Everyone* (DETR, 1998a), a few days before the 'Roads Review' results (DETR, 1998b). Both emphasized a 'New approach to appraisal for transport projects'[1] (DETR, 1998a; chapter 4), stressing five key criteria: integration, safety, economy, environment, and accessibility. This was made more explicit in two further documents, the first subtitled *Understanding the New Approach to Appraisal* (DETR, 1998c) aimed at general readers (including local authority politicians and Chief Executives); and a second, subtitled *Guidance on the New Approach to Appraisal* (DETR, 1998d), aimed at a more technical audience.

The advent of 'Multi-Modal Studies'

Implementing this policy gave rise to the concept of the 'Multi-Modal Study'. The basic idea is that, whereas previously considerations had been restricted to a cost benefit analysis of a specific road proposal, now the intention was to look at a range of possible transport solutions to the perceived problem, and select the most appropriate overall strategy. Although some 'roads only' studies continued on localized problems, for the more strategic cases a programme of 'Multi-Modal Studies in which consideration would be given to problems and solutions affecting all modes of travel' was announced (DfT, 2000a; volume 1, paragraph 1.1.1). Here:

> The aim ... is to investigate problems on or with all modes of transport and to seek solutions to those problems. The output ... will be a number of different options ... Each option will consist of a transport plan, that is, a collection of quite specific and individual interventions. Analysis of options will need to be sufficiently detailed to ensure that robust decisions can be made. (DfT, 2000a; paragraph 1.1.3)

It should also be noted that devolution of Central Government powers to Wales (and Scotland) was in hand contemporaneously, in response to a different 'New Labour' manifesto commitment, and the powers being devolved included most transport matters. Partly as a consequence of this, as discussed below, Wales stole a march on England by commissioning the first, pioneering such multi-modal study in 1997.

4.2 Case study focus: The M4 Newport Multi-Modal Study

Setting the scene

The M4 Motorway is the key route from London to South and West Wales, and also forms the major part of the Southernmost of two Euroroutes[2] to Ireland. It also conveys heavy traffic to Bristol and the South West of England, which deviates immediately before the Severn Estuary. The route (see map in Figure 4.1) was in fact constructed piecemeal. It did not exist as a trunk route at all before the construction of the first Severn Bridge at Chepstow in 1966. At the same time, the stretch of the M4 which forms our focus was built around Newport, because, even then, the Usk river crossing in Newport was a notorious bottleneck. As a result, the relevant stretch of the M4, justified as a Newport bypass, became one of the first motorways to be constructed in the UK. It was originally constructed as a dual carriageway two lane route, and, because of its key bypass role, involved frequent junctions — some five over a 12 km stretch, to access both local Newport radial routes, and the main Birmingham route. It also provided relief for local traffic crossing the Usk in Newport itself.

Increasing traffic on the M4 to South Wales led to a decision to provide a Second Severn Crossing, and this was opened in 1996[3]. The new and old M4 routes converged some 10 km East of Newport. Increasing traffic also led to the widening of

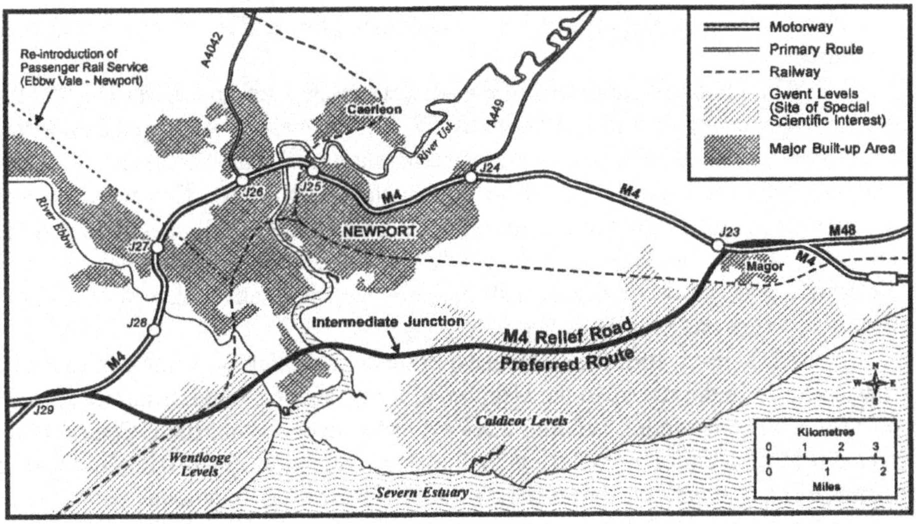

Figure 4.1 The Newport M4 bypass
Source: WAG (2002), *Trunk Road Forward Programme.* Courtesy: Welsh Assembly Government

the relevant stretch of the M4, wherever possible, to three lanes. However, the stretch immediately West of the Usk involved twin two lane tunnel bores, which could not readily be widened at all. After alternative river crossing routes for local traffic had been constructed, some slip road ramps were subsequently closed to divert this traffic. Despite this, by 1999, traffic in the tunnels had reached some 70,000 vehicles per day, with even higher flows on adjacent sections, and serious congestion at busy times.

As far back as 1989/90, the South Wales Area Traffic Study (SWATS) had been commissioned to look at the performance of the existing strategic highway network, forecast future traffic flows, and identify likely future capacity problems. The M4 Newport bypass stretch was identified as a priority potential problem and accordingly, under prevailing policies, in 1991 the Government included a new relief road around Newport in the future roads programme. Consultants (Ove Arup) were commissioned in 1992 to look at the options for such a road, including the possibility of widening the existing motorway. The Government subsequently concluded that the best option was a new road of some 24 km, skirting Newport to the South, and involving a major new downstream River Usk crossing (see map in Figure 4.1). The estimated cost was some £300 million. The chosen route had major environmental disbenefits, including adverse impacts on some five 'Sites of Special Scientific Interest' (or areas designated for special protection under UK environmental legislation), including significant areas of low-lying wetlands, a habitat category which has suffered particularly heavy losses in the UK. The proposed new route thus attracted considerable protest, particularly from environmentalists and more general anti-road lobbyists.

In 1997 a minor amendment to the route was announced, and in March 1997 the consultants were appointed to proceed to 'Stage 2', namely to work up the preferred route to a level of detail enabling the Government to make the necessary 'Statutory Orders' under the legislation to allow construction to proceed. However, this was a period of considerable political turmoil. There was a general perception that the incumbent Conservative government would lose the general election when called (it did in the event so do on 1 May 1997). This had important policy impacts, both locally in Wales and on UK-wide policy.

At the UK level, following extensive protests focussing on some controversial road schemes in the run up to the election, as noted above a moratorium was placed on new road construction pending a review. Moreover, at that time, Central Government administration in Wales (as in Scotland) had for several decades included a measure of administrative devolution. Topics controlled by 'functional' departments in London for England were controlled by a 'Welsh Office' headed by a Secretary of State for Wales. The range of topics so controlled had increased over the years; by the 1990s, the main exceptions were 'International Departments' (Foreign Office, Defence) and 'Law and Order' — including Home Office (Police and Prisons), as well as the Court system. Specifically, Transport (except rail and air matters, but including trunk roads) and Planning were devolved functions.

The Welsh Secretary was thus free to take an independent view on matters affecting Wales. However, he was also a member of the UK Cabinet, and as such could not be seen to deviate from UK policy principles, as opposed to meeting specific Welsh requirements. Therefore, on such matters as e.g. whether or not to continue a large-scale road construction programme, policy in Wales reflected that in England.

Second, there was a commitment to a referendum on a greater measure of Devolution, to a new National Assembly for Wales (NAW), in the Labour manifesto; the referendum was held (and carried) on 18 September 1997 (with the Assembly taking office 1 July 1999 after elections 1 May 1999). Amongst the matters to be devolved for determination by the NAW were Transport and Planning. The 'lame duck' Welsh Office ministerial team were devolution enthusiasts, and wished the NAW off to a flying start[4]. Therefore, as well as the 'Stage 2' development of the preferred route mentioned above, the consultants were also asked to undertake a multi-modal study of alternatives which would meet the same transport objectives. This exercise, which was to be carried out using the Common Appraisal Framework, turned out to be the UK's first, pioneering example of a Multi-Modal Study (Welsh Office, 1999; Good, 2000). The CAF study took place at a time of rapid change in transport policy, assessment and appraisal, as well as Governmental institutions. At this point, there was explicit commitment to an Integrated Transport Policy, (DETR, 1998a), leading to Parliamentary proceedings for the eventual Transport Act 2000 (applicable to Wales as well as England), but no detailed advice. Wales was thus going ahead, whilst in England there was little action, as official advice was still being determined. The M4 Newport CAF study therefore became a 'state-of-the-art' project, requiring the development of innovative methodology in many areas.

Possible alternative scenarios

The possible transport alternatives were to be considered against two objectives:

- To provide relief from the anticipated effects of increasing traffic on the M4 Motorway around Newport; and
- To appraise options on the basis of acceptable environmental, financial, economic and safety criteria.

The study explicitly set out to be a multi-modal appraisal of different forms of transport, including cars, public transport, freight, cycling and walking. Although the NAW powers related principally to roads, it was specifically decided not to restrict consideration to options under direct NAW control; nor, indeed, 'by any possible difficulties in promoting potentially unpopular measures' (Welsh Office, 1999; paragraph 7). Rather, the view taken was that implementation issues could be addressed once the conclusions were known. The approach adopted involved five main stages: first, to understand the travel patterns on the existing motorway; second, to develop transport models of the main movements; third, to define possible alternative transport scenarios; fourth, to assess the impacts of the alternatives; and fifth, to appraise the alternatives using a Common Appraisal Framework.

Existing travel patterns Analysis of traffic patterns showed very little local movement (less than three per cent), though a high proportion of through traffic either joined or left the motorway in the Newport area. Important components included South Wales – Bristol, and South Wales – Midlands, with a notable proportion of long distance traffic from further East on the M4.

Transport and traffic modelling From the established traffic patterns, a forecasting approach was developed which would: concentrate on the main travel patterns; represent the likely behavioural responses to possible transport initiatives, such as changing the mode of transport; and assess the effects of a wide range of policy, pricing and infrastructure measures.

Travel demand forecasting models were then developed for long distance and regional journeys, covering peak and off peak traffic; local movements were regarded as small enough to ignore. To undertake this modelling, the road user surveys already conducted as part of the road scheme development were supplemented by: public transport user surveys in the Cardiff and Newport areas (interviews with rail and coach passengers, and self-completion questionnaires for bus passengers — nearly 4000 in total); 'stated preference' surveys to provide information about the likely behavioural responses to various transport measures; and a survey of freight operators and shippers focusing on opportunities for switching freight from road to other modes.

Transport scenarios for testing A range of possible alternative transport measures was identified on the basis of current good practice and experience from UK and abroad, including consultations with the public sector, research organizations, rail and road passenger and freight operators, and other interest groups. The alternatives were then initially broadly evaluated against three key criteria to identify which might be appropriate for further consideration:

- The measures should potentially make a realistic contribution towards relieving the anticipated effects of increasing traffic on the M4 past Newport;
- Individual measures should be 'possible' — this was considered in terms of 'what' could be done, not the 'how' of implementation;
- Cost, judging whether the cost of a particular measure seemed commensurate with the likely impacts.

Following on from this initial evaluation, three basic transport scenarios were developed for testing: road building, enhancing public transport, and traffic/demand management. A fourth base case, do minimum, was also defined, to represent the likely future situation if current trends continued and no special measures were taken.

The term 'scenario' was used in view of the fact that the full introduction of certain combinations of measures was unlikely. Nevertheless, it was important to establish and appraise the impact of any particular strategy, if fully implemented. This information was then also used to develop a possible 'hybrid' scenario, utilizing elements from one or more 'pure' scenarios, to explore whether this might generate a more appropriate package of measures, with perhaps a more realistic prospect of implementation.

The scenarios elaborated

The *Road Building* scenario comprised the M4 relief road only (some 24 km of dual three lane motorway, due to open 2007). The capital cost was estimated at some £340 million (Welsh Office, 1999; paragraph 18).

The *Enhanced Public Transport* scenario comprised 'a range of measures to enhance alternatives to the use of cars and heavy goods vehicles, aimed at reducing traffic on the motorway around Newport' (Welsh Office, 1999; paragraph 19). Public transport proposals that were considered included the electrification of the London – Swansea main line, with a 'Newport Avoiding Line' to increase capacity; service improvements on routes; improvements to secondary main line services towards Bristol, Birmingham and Manchester, and to more local rail services; and specific proposals for key cities: a light rail system and Park and Ride facilities in Cardiff, and enhanced bus services for Bristol and Newport. As well as these public transport enhancements, to be reinforced by an effective ten per cent real reduction in fares for at least ten years, this scenario included measures to enhance cycling and walking opportunities, and freight measures to promote rail freight competitiveness and usage. The capital cost estimate was £930 million, although partly offset by increased revenue. Significantly, much of this capital cost would be incurred far from Newport.

The *Traffic and Demand Management* scenario was designed 'to make optimum use of the existing highway system and limit the demand, by means of a mix of infrastructure and policy measures' (Welsh Office, 1999; paragraph 20). Those considered comprised a mix of 'infrastructure and policy measures' (Welsh Office, 1999). Combined infrastructure and policy proposals included introducing road tolls on the entire stretch, and a variety of other measures: provision of High Occupancy Vehicle lanes; a reduced (50 mph)[5] speed limit; some ramp closures and ramp metering. (Intelligent vehicle and highways systems were also advocated, but recognized not to be effective over the study forecast period.)

On the wider policy front, increased car park charges (including workplace parking charges) coupled with urban road pricing was advocated for Cardiff, Newport and Bristol, reinforced by maintenance of the relative increases in fuel duty. More positively, travel awareness strategies (including 'Safe Routes to School' and 'Green Commuting Plans') should be reinforced by promoting greater telecommunications substitution: teleworking, video-conferencing and teleservices. The estimated capital cost was £176 million, again partially offset.

Following preliminary assessment of the Enhanced Public Transport and Traffic/ Demand Management Scenarios, a further *Hybrid Scenario* was also developed. This included most of the enhanced public transport scenario, but eliminating the new avoiding line, substituting 'tilting (diesel) trains' for electrification, and instituting a more modest package of traffic restraint measures, reducing the capital cost to £650 million, with again significant 'remote' expenditure.

Impacts and assessment

The transport scenarios generated were diverse. They were assessed against the primary objective of reducing (future forecast) Newport M4 traffic problems. However, they each implied a number of consequential effects, and these in turn were respectively evaluated in terms of: transport (travel, movement, accessibility); environment; and economic performance (Table 4.1). These overall criteria were disaggregated into some eight more detailed indicators of particular transport effects: relieve anticipated M4 traffic increase; avoid adverse traffic impact in and around Newport; reduce reliance on the private car; reduce growth in length of motorized journeys; improve safety for road users; promote accessibility (especially for those without a car); promote efficient and reliable freight movements; and improve journey time reliability.

All the scenarios tested showed a reduction in traffic on the M4 around Newport, compared with the 'Do Minimum' base, though clearly in different ways, and different amounts. See the Common Appraisal Framework Summary Table (Table 4.2) for details.

The scenarios were also assessed against (UK) National Transport policy objectives, as in the (DETR, 1998a) White Paper, especially: improving accessibility for people, improving integration between modes, and desire to reduce adverse impacts of heavy lorries. Overall, it was concluded, both public transport and hybrid scen-

Table 4.1 Costs and economic evaluation summary (million £, 1998 prices, discounted to 2003)

Indicator	Scenario			
	Road Building	Enhanced Public Transport	Traffic/ Demand Management	Hybrid
Total (undiscounted) capital costs	340	930	176	653
Attributed capital costs (undiscounted)	340	255	176	129
Attributed capital costs	312	240	162	125
Operating costs	17	183	303	395
Operating revenue	−43	370	4290	2178
Transport user benefits	578	1080	−3428	−352
Other benefits	11	−7	−90	−48
Accident savings	56	83	241	74
Economic NPV	273	1103	549	1332

Source: Adapted from Welsh Office (1999), *M4 Motorway between Magor and Castleton: Common Appraisal Framework Study Summary Report*

arios assisted, demand management was neutral, but road building did not.

The *Environmental performance* of the scenarios was assessed against some 14 environmental objectives, using appropriate performance indicators: traffic noise levels, total 'greenhouse gas' emissions, acidification loading, emissions affecting local air quality, adverse landscape impact, adversely affecting sites of national importance, adversely affecting 'irreplaceable' local sites, adversely affecting sites of cultural heritage, flood risks, community severance / inter-modal conflicts, demolition / land take, energy consumption in transport network, risk of construction disturbance to sensitive features, and support to transportation, land-use, planning, environmental, sustainability and health policies.

Lastly, *Economic performance* was assessed against a general objective of maximizing economic value, measured in terms of both financial indicators: capital costs, including construction, recurrent costs (operational, maintenance), and revenues (fares, tolls, and parking charges); and economic indicators, as used in more 'traditional' cost benefit analyses, including: accident cost savings, time and money benefits. These were discounted and aggregated in the usual way.

Findings

In all cases, it was established that there was little prospect of diverting much freight without major national policy changes; hence the analysis focused primarily on passenger issues.

Whilst the *Road Building* scenario would effectively remove congestion on New-

Table 4.2 M4 between Magor and Castleton Common Appraisal Framework summary table

Indicator	Objective	Road Building Scenario	Enhanced Public Transport scenario	Traffic/Demand Management scenario	Hybrid scenario
Transport: Local Issues i.e. relief to M4, avoid adverse impact on Newport	Optimize local impact (e.g. J25-26, 2007)	M4 objective achieved: 43% reduction. Minimal impact on Newport	M4 objective not achieved: 6% reduction. Small beneficial impact on Newport	M4 objective achieved: 77% reduction. Increase in traffic in Newport (11% by 2007)	M4 objective achieved: 58% reduction. Increase in traffic in Newport (24% by 2007)
Transport: Strategic Issues i.e. accessibility, integration, freight	Assist national transport objectives	Does not assist these objectives	Assists these objectives	Neutral to these objectives (due to lack of facilities for suppressed highway trips)	Assists these objectives
Environmental: Local issues i.e. noise NO_x emissions	Minimize adverse local impact	Local benefits to existing M4 corridor. Local adverse effects on the Levels	Improvement in local conditions, but some areas deteriorate	Complex effects on local conditions, some improvements, but adverse effects from traffic diversion	Complex effects on local conditions, some improvements, but adverse effects from traffic diversion, although less than T/DM
Environmental: Strategic issues e.g. greenhouse gas emissions, designated sites of natural importance	Minimize adverse strategic impact	Increase in CO_2 emissions (2% peak hour). Loss of 73 ha from SSSI	Reduced CO_2 emissions (4% peak hour). Loss of 22 ha from SSSI	Large reduction in CO_2 emissions (16% peak hour). No landtake from SSSI	Reduced CO_2 emissions (8% peak hour). Loss of 1.2 ha from SSSI
Economic: Local Issues	Maximize traveller benefits Maximize accident savings	Traveller benefits: £ 440 million Accident cost savings: £ 56 million	Traveller benefits: £ 1038 million Accident cost savings: £ 83 million	Traveller benefits: £−3556 million Accident cost savings: £ 241 million	Traveller benefits: £ −464 million Accident cost savings: £ 74 million
Economic: Strategic Issues	Maximize economic value	Net present value of: £ 273 million	Net present value of: £ 1103 million	Net present value of: £ 549 million	Net present value of: £ 1332 million
Capital Cost of scenarios* (undiscounted)					
Total**		£ 340 million	£ 930 million	£ 176 million	£ 653 million
Attributed		£ 340 million	£ 255 million	£ 176 million	£ 129 million

* The capital costs would be met from a variety of sources, and would, in some cases be off-set by revenue

** These costs are non-attributed and are likely to generate benefits elsewhere — these are an issue outside the scope of this study

Source: Adapted from Welsh Office (1999), *M4 Motorway between Magor and Castleton: Common Appraisal Framework Study Summary Report*

port's motorways, and would have economic benefits, it would not assist national transport policy objectives. Worse, it would adversely impact the environmentally sensitive Gwent Levels wetlands.

The *Enhanced Public Transport* scenario, whilst contributing to national policy objectives, would only remove small amounts of traffic from the M4. On the environmental indices, whilst providing strategic benefits, the new rail line would have similar disbenefits to the proposed road.

Traffic Demand Management would alleviate motorway traffic problems, but at the expense of worsening Newport's local traffic, with some localized disbenefits. However, whilst the revenues raised offered some economic benefits, there were major transport user disbenefits, given the lack of attractive public transport alternatives.

It was the major user disbenefits that led to the development of a *Hybrid* scenario. The particular Hybrid scenario investigated was forecast to reduce M4 traffic flows more than the Road Building scenario, but also to increase traffic in Newport. It would actually produce a greater transfer to public transport than simply enhancing public transport, and would also assist in achieving national transport policy objectives. On the environmental side, locally it would give rise to a 'complex array' of environmental benefits and disbenefits, but strategically, by omitting both the new Newport bypasses (road and rail) through the sensitive Gwent levels, it was clearly beneficial. Moreover, overall, whilst there were some transport user disbenefits, the increased revenue generated showed the highest economic value of all the scenarios.

This particular Hybrid scenario is of course arbitrary; other alternative 'mixed packages' could also be tried out. Therefore, following completion of the technical analysis in March 1999, the NAW consulted transport interests widely to establish what might be practicable in implementation terms. (These investigations were kept confidential for commercial reasons.)

4.3 Conclusion

The main interest in this study methodology arises from first the determination to compare different modes of transport as far as possible on an even footing; and second the attempt to widen the assessment into environmental considerations.

Earlier work on the (limited) use of formal evaluation methods in land use planning in British local government had suggested they were being used '… in a way which makes the plan preparation process more transparent, thus facilitating public scrutiny and debate…'; indeed, providing a '… valuable shift towards a "consequence display" approach…' (Yewlett, 2001a; p. 11). The present study is a further development in this desirable direction at a national level. The wider environmental issues were presented in some detail for consideration, reflecting what Rosenhead (1980) has described as the 'consequence display' philosophy. This approach is intended to allow the decision maker to compare and contrast the specific impacts of different possible courses of action on different interests. The 'economic' elements could be expressed in a common metric — financial units, as in the traditional cost benefit approach — but even here the various differential financial impacts were brought out explicitly for comparison purposes.

4.4 Envoi

Subsequently, the (English) Department for Transport embarked on a programme of some twenty-two multi-modal studies (MMS) (Mellor, 2002): eleven 'corridor' studies, nine 'area studies', and two 'orbital studies' (around London and Birmingham). By May 2003, some nineteen had reported (DfT, 2003; with another due in June). However, by January 2003, with seventeen reports in, a number of different conclusions seemed to be emerging, with some confirming road proposals, others emphasizing alternative 'soft' measures, and also concerns by Government about the affordability of some proposals. (LTT, 2003a). A further emergent political problem is how to resolve conflicts at an (English) regional level. The whole question of regional government is on the Government's agenda, whilst the issue of traffic constraint is itself a political hot potato. Right at the start of the process, Banister (2002; p. 253) pointed out that although the multi-modal studies are a desirable move away from 'single mode financing', there was (even then) 'an underlying suspicion that the outcomes will still result in more roads being built, rather than a truly integrated transport system being developed'.

Indeed, the Government's overall transport strategy is currently in some disarray, with a recognition that targets in the '10 year Plan' (DfT, 2000b) will not now be met, and, following resolution of the unsatisfactory national rail management structure, a recognition by the newly reconstituted Strategic Rail Authority (SRA) that many projects in the pipeline will have to be cut out for want of funding. On these wider issues, the House of Commons Transport Committee (2003) has published a report criticizing the Government for proceeding with road building schemes recommended by the multi-modal studies in England before deciding whether or not inter-urban road charging is to be introduced (LTT, 2003b), noting that different studies have adopted different — even mutually contradictory — approaches. Moreover, they pointed out that SRA seems to be undermining the MMS conclusions, by adopting different priorities, apparently without any evidence of a cost-benefit analysis in justification.

Ironically, back in Wales, two of the SRA's deleted projects have been re-instated following a Welsh Assembly Government (WAG) decision to underwrite the costs; one, the re-opening of the Ebbw Vale branch rail line in Newport's 'Western Valley' was a key component of the Public Transport scenario above.

An already committed new bridge and associated local roads to the South of Newport is currently under construction. However, no final decision has yet been taken on the proposed new 'M4 Newport Bypass Motorway' which sparked off the whole exercise. It is included in the Trunk Road Programme (WAG, 2002; paragraph 4.3.8-13) as a proposal in the long-term programme. The second Welsh Assembly election (1 May 2003) saw Labour win exactly half the 60 seats, in practice sufficient to replace the previous coalition WAG (which had included the Welsh Liberal Democrats) by a single party administration. The subsequent WAG restructuring saw Transport split off from the previous Planning, Environment and Transport portfolio, and merged with Economic Development portfolio (LTT, 2003c). This is expected to imply a 'more pro-business' agenda; i.e. less focussed on walking, cycling, and public transport, and potentially more sympathetic to road building. However, the newly appointed Welsh Minister for Economic Development and Transport promptly confirmed commitment both to the two rail projects, and to the M4 Newport relief road's status in the Trunk Road Programme (Davies, 2003); thus the longer term uncertainty remains.

Notes

1 'We are developing a new approach to the appraisal of different solutions to transport problems. This is designed to draw together the large amount of information collected as part of the appraisal of a transport problem and alternative solutions. This information is set against the five criteria which we have adopted for the review of trunk roads i.e. integration, safety, economy, environment and accessibility. It looks at the contribution of different forms of transport in developing alternative solutions and the potential effect of the new integrated transport approach, including the scope for and effect of demand management measures. It is our intention that this new approach, once finalised, will be applied to the appraisal of all transport projects, including proposals for all road schemes.' (DETR, 1998a; chapter 4).

2 Trans European Transport Network Roads.

3 The 'official' M4 route was re-aligned across the new bridge, leaving the original, as the M48, to serve as an access to Chepstow and minor routes.

4 There were a number of Ministerial personnel changes for unconnected reasons. However, the incumbent Welsh Secretary (by Labour Party arrangement) proceeded to become the new First Secretary (Premier) for Wales, whilst a junior minister was promoted to the new, much reduced, role of Welsh Secretary, now concerned primarily with securing finance, representing Welsh interests at Cabinet level, and overseeing necessary Wales legislation in the UK Parliament.

5 Editor's note: 80 km/h.

References

Banister, D. (2nd Edition, 2002), *Transport Planning*, E&FN Spon, London (UK).

Crow, S., Brown, A., Essex, S., Thomas, H. and Yewlett, C. (1997), *Slimmer and Swifter: A Critical Examination of District Wide Local Plans and UDPs*, RTPI, London (UK).

Coburn, T. M., Beesley, M. E. and Reynolds, D. J. (1960), *The London — Birmingham Motorway: Traffic and Economics*, Road Research Laboratory, Dept. of Scientific and Industrial research, Technical paper 46, HMSO, London (UK).

Davies, A. (2003), 'Ministerial Keynote Speech', in Institution of Civil Engineers (ed.), *Integrated Transport Delivered?*, Proceedings of the 3rd All Wales Transport Conference, Institution of Civil Engineers, London (UK).

Department of Environment, Transport and the Regions (1998a), *A New Deal for Transport: Better for Everyone*, DETR, London (UK), 20 July 1998.

Department of Environment, Transport and the Regions (1998b), *A New Deal for Trunk Roads in England*, DETR, London (UK), 31 July 1998.

Department of Environment, Transport and the Regions (1998c), *A New Deal for Trunk Roads in England: Understanding the New Approach to Appraisal*, DETR, London (UK), July 1998.

Department of Environment, Transport and the Regions (1998d), *A New Deal for Trunk Roads in England: Guidance on the New Approach to Appraisal*, DETR, London (UK), July 1998.

Department for Transport (2000a), *Guidance on the Methodology for Multi-Modal Studies (2 Volumes)*, DfT, London (UK).

Department for Transport (2000b), *Transport 2010: The 10 Year Plan*, DfT, London (UK).

Department for Transport (2003), Command Paper No. 5907 (Cm 5907) *Department for Transport Annual Report 2003*, Stationery Office, London (UK), May 15 2003.

Department of the Environment (1972), *Getting the Best Roads for Our Money: The COBA Method of Appraisal*, HMSO, London (UK).

Department of the Environment and Welsh Office (1992), *Planning Policy Guidance Note 12: Development Plans and Regional Planning Guidance*, DoE and WO, London (UK), February 1992.

Department of Transport (1987), *COBA 9 Manual: A Method of Economic Appraisal of Highway Schemes*, DoT, London (UK), May 1987.

Department of Transport (1994), *Common Appraisal Framework for Urban Transport Projects*, MVA Consultancy, Oscar Faber TPA and ITS Leeds, for the Department of Transport and the Birmingham City Council, HMSO, London (UK).

Department of Transport (1995), *Planning Policy Guidance Note 13: Transport*, in draft from March 1994, DoT, London (UK).

Dupuit, A. J. E. J. (1844), 'De la mesure de l'utilité des travaux publics', *Annales des Ponts et Chaussées*, p. , 2nd Series (1841-1850), Tome VIII (2nd semester 1844), pp. 332-375 translated in 1952 by R. H. Barback as *On the measurement of the utility of public work, International Economic Papers*, Vol. 2, p. pp. 83-110, cited in Banister (2002; p. 54).

European Commission (1992), *The Impact of Transport on the Environment: Sustainable Mobility*, EC, Bruxelles (Belgium), February.

Good, G. (2000), *The M4 South Wales Common Appraisal Framework Study*, Conference Paper, The Potential of Multi-Modal Transport Corridors, 26 January 2000, The Waterfront Conference Company Ltd, London (UK).

Her Majesty's Stationery Office (1990), Command Paper No. 1200 (Cm 1200), a 'Summary' is also available, which excludes detail on the planning system, *This Common Inheritance: Britain's Environmental Strategy*, HMSO, London (UK).

Her Majesty's Stationery Office (1994), Command Paper No. 2427 (Cm 2427) *Climate Change: The UK Programme*, HMSO, London (UK), January.

House of Commons (2003), *Jam tomorrow?: The Multi-modal Study Investment Plans, House of Commons Transport Committee, 3rd Report, Session 2002-03*, TSO, London (UK).

Lichfield, N. (1996), *Community Impact Evaluation*, UCL Press, London (UK).

Lichfield, N., Barbanente, A., Borri, D., Khakee, A. and Prat, A. (1998), *Evaluation in Planning: Facing the Challenge of Complexity*, Kluwer, Dordrecht (The Netherlands).

Local Transport Today (2003a), 'News — Darling: MMS teams should have been advised on affordability', *Local Transport Today* (UK), No. 358, 23 January 2003, p. 40.

Local Transport Today (2003b), 'News — MPs say DfT "wrong" to pursue MMS road plans before charging decision', *Local Transport Today* (UK), No. 363, 3 April 2003, p. 5.

Local Transport Today (2003c), 'News — Welsh strengthen transport and economy linkage', *Local Transport Today* (UK), No. 366, 15 May 2003, p. 40.

Mellor, C. (2002), 'Multi-modal study outputs leave DfT with a host of new challenges', *Local Transport Today* (UK), No. 350, 26 September 2002, pp. 11-13.

Nash, N. (1998), 'Developments in Transport Appraisal in Britain', in N. Lichfield et al., *Evaluation in Planning: Facing the Challenge of Complexity*, Kluwer, Dordrecht (The Netherlands), pp. 311-327.

Office of Passenger Rail Franchising (1997), *Appraisal of Support for Passenger Rail Services: Planning Criteria — an Interim Guide*, OPRAF, London (UK), November.

Rosenhead, J. (1980), 'Planning under uncertainty 1: the inflexibility of methodologies', *Journal of the Operational Research Society*, Vol. 31, pp. 209-216.

Welsh Office (1999), *M4 Motorway between Magor and Castleton: Common Appraisal Framework Study Summary Report*, Ove Arup and Partners, Cardiff (UK).

Wales Assembly Government (2002), *Trunk Road Forward Programme*, WAG, Cardiff (UK), March.

United Nations (1997), *The World conferences: developing priorities for the 21st century*, includes report of UN Conference on Environment and Development, June 1992, UN Department of Public Information, New York, NY (USA).

Yewlett, C. J. L. (2001a), 'OR in strategic land-use planning', *Journal of the Operational Research Society*, Vol. 52, pp. 4-13.

Yewlett, C. J. L. (2001b), 'Theory and practice in OR and town planning: a continuing creative synergy?', *Journal of the Operational Research Society*, Vol. 52, pp. 1304-1314.

Yewlett, C. J. L. (1995), 'Energy, Transport, Planning and Society: The case of the United Kingdom', in AESOP, *Planning for a Broader Europe*, Proceedings of the VIII AESOP Congress, İstanbul, 24-27 August 1994, Vol. 3, Yıldız Teknik Üniversitesi (Yıldız Technical University), İstanbul (Turkey), pp. 225-242.

N.B. Most of the UK Government documents cited are now also available on the web (often in sections with multiple addresses). No attempt has been made to list these here; entering the title into a suitable search engine (e.g. Google) is sufficient. Also, although apart from the onset of devolution in Wales, the name of the Department responsible for Transport in England has changed four times since 1996, the 'successors' have always maintained web access to the earlier material. For further details, please refer also to the List of Abbreviations at p. xvii.

Chapter 5

Evaluation of Urban Green Spaces[1]

Tüzin Baycan Levent and Peter Nijkamp

5.1 Introduction

Urban green may be seen as an important constituent of urban quality of life and the quality of urban green spaces as a key factor in making cities attractive and viable places to live in. However, urban green spaces are under a permanent pressure and the potential of green spaces is not always realized. Since current management practices are sometimes sub-optimal, it is of strategic importance to create an analytical and taxonomic framework for mapping out the importance of green space in cities. Such a framework needs to comprise a comparative evaluation device of urban green spaces as crucial public environmental goods.

The aim of this contribution is to investigate urban green spaces as a set of specific urban public environmental goods on the basis of a systematic assessment approach. The main question addressed is: 'Which types of evaluation approaches are appropriate for urban green spaces?' It seeks to approximate the intrinsic *value* of urban green on the one hand, while using the process, experience and output of the comparative European URGE project to review relevant evaluation techniques on the other hand. The next section is general in nature and will examine evaluation as a scientific methodology, its relationship with planning theory, emerging recent interests in planning and evaluation, and the use of different approaches in. section 5.3 is more specific and investigates urban green spaces from an evaluation perspective, while describing multi-faceted values of urban green. A taxonomy of values for urban green spaces based on ecological, economic, social and planning values of urban green is offered. section 5.4 evaluates process and experience of the URGE project by designing an interdisciplinary catalogue of criteria as an instrument for evaluation models. section 5.5 offers empirical results from several case studies conducted in parallel to the URGE project. The final section provides for some concluding remarks.

5.2 Evaluation — a review

Evaluation and planning

Evaluation is a transdisciplinary approach that is based on several methodologies used in social science research on complex decision-making. Trochim (2003) offers two definitions of evaluation:

1. Evaluation is a systematic assessment of the worth or merit of some object;
2. Evaluation is a systematic acquisition and assessment of information to provide useful feedback about some object.

The second definition emphasizes acquiring and assessing relevant policy information, because evaluation involves collecting raw data and testing their validity. Martinuzzi (2001; p. 20) defines evaluation as '... assessment of success — but in a wider context and understanding'. He emphasizes that evaluations are generally used to measure the success of projects, programmes and policies. Diez (2001; p. 41) defines evaluation from a policy evaluation perspective. According to her definition 'evaluation is an exercise directed towards understanding how policies function, why the changes observed are produced, in what circumstances and in what organizational or institutional context this happens, so as to be able to make recommendations that can improve policy design and generate new knowledge'. Next, evaluation must assess programmes, offer opinions and produce knowledge and recommendations that can contribute to improvement of current policy practice.

It is noteworthy that evaluation forms an important constituent of a planning process. Chadwick (1971) defines a planning process for both a problem and a system. This process involves the main stages of *formulation* and *modelling* the problem, *testing* the model and *implementation*. While every stage is based on testing, the process as a whole is based on feedback.

The stages of the planning process (such as the evaluation process) have been defined as a planning-evaluation cycle by Trochim (2003). This cycle is described in many different ways with various phases including both planners and evaluators. A planning process involves the following stages: *formulation* of the problem, *conceptualization* of major alternatives, *detailing*, *evaluating* the alternatives and *implementation*. Evaluation also involves several stages: *formulation* of the major objectives and goals, *conceptualization* and operationalization of the major components of the evaluation, *design* of the evaluation, *analysis* of the information, both qualitative and quantitative, and *utilization* of the evaluation results (Figure 5.1). The distinctive features between planning and evaluation are not always clear.

Value and valuation methods

The concept of 'evaluation' is frequently accompanied by the concept of 'valuation' and the related concept of 'value' which is concerned with an object of the valuation. Bingham et al. (1999) describe value as '... the general importance or desirability

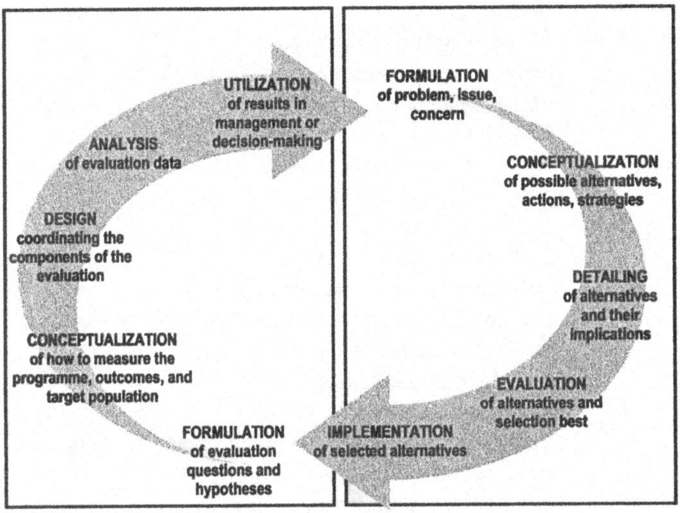

Figure 5.1 The planning-evaluation cycle
Source: Adapted from Trochim (2003), *The Research Methods Knowledge Base*

of something'. They also emphasize that it may not be possible to develop a single unifying definition of value. More precise definitions of value have evolved in different disciplines to meet different needs. Nunes, van den Bergh and Nijkamp (2003), for example, define value from an economic perspective focusing on welfare of humans. According to their definition, in an economic sense, '... value is the result of an interaction between humans and the object of valuation'. Therefore, valuation methods can be defined as methods which define and measure the importance or desirability of the object of valuation on the one hand, and results of the interaction between humans and the object of valuation, on the other hand.

In the last decades much interest in planning and evaluation has turned to environmental issues. The recognition of environmental degradation and the incorporation of environmental preservation in the set of goals of economic policy have led planners and others to develop methods to integrate the environment explicitly in the decision-making process. Valuation issues have been investigated and discussed in different approaches, but in particular in the context of new emerging disciplines, viz. ecological economics and environmental economics. While ecological economics has been seeking a wider system-focused perspective and related analyses of value, in environmental economics a preference-based value system prevails in which benefits of environmental gain or damages are measured by social opportunity cost or total economic value (Turner, Button and Nijkamp, 1999a). In this approach distinctions are made between use value (direct and indirect), option, quasi-option, and non-use value (bequest and existence). See also van den Berg (1999), Nunes,

Increasing complexity:
Multiple decision criteria;
Multiple effects;
Increasing scale of analysis

1. *Financial analysis*
   Financial profitability criterion;
   Private cost and revenues;
   Monetary valuation.
2. *Economic cost-benefit analysis*
   Economic efficiency criterion;
   Social costs and benefits;
   Monetary valuation.
3. *Extended cost-benefit analysis*
   Sustainable development principles;
   Economic efficiency and equity trade-off environmental standards as constraints;
   Partial monetary valuation.
4. *Environmental impact assessment*
   Quantification of a diverse set of effects on a common scale, but no evaluation.
5. *Multi-criteria decision methods*
   Multiple decision criteria, monetary and non-monetary evaluation.

Figure 5.2 A review of evaluation methods
Source: Adapted from Turner, Subak and Adger (1999b), 'Pressures, Trends and Impacts in Coastal Zones: Interactions Between Socioeconomic and Natural Systems'

van den Bergh and Nijkamp (2003), and Turner, Subak and Adger (1999b).

Economic valuation based on a functional approach should adequately map out the links between ecosystem structures, the characteristics of which provide society directly with extractive and/or non-extractive benefits (goods and services), and ecosystem processes providing indirect benefits to society. Economic valuation studies estimate the value of the flow of services assuming the sustainability of ecosystems and their interrelationships between themselves and the abiotic environment. At a generic level, a spectrum of evaluation methods and techniques can be distinguished (Figure 5.2) and used depending on the objective of the study. The more comprehensive the technique, the more information will be made available to assist in the appraisal of policy options from a societal perspective.

As mentioned above, the techniques in these valuation studies can be subdivided into two major groups: indirect and direct methods (van den Berg, 1999; Navrud, 1989; Nunes, van den Bergh and Nijkamp, 2003). The indirect methods assume either that private goods are complementary to environmental goods, or that environmental quality is incorporated in private good. The most important class of indirect methods are the Travel Cost Method (TCM), based on travel costs to visit a recreational area, and the Hedonic Price Method (HPM), usually based on economic property values. The direct methods use interview techniques to make individuals express their subjective evaluation of the good in hypothetical markets. The most important direct method is the Contingent Valuation Method (CVM) that is based on 'willingness to pay' or 'willingness to accept'. Another distinction of the valuation of environmental goods and services has been made by Folmer and van Ierland (1989). They examined the valuation of environmental goods and services according to four categories: 1) direct market value methods, 2) contingent valuation methods, 3) hedonic pricing methods, and 4) methods based on observable changes in non-market behaviour of individuals as a consequence of environmental changes. Finally, Turner, Button and Nijkamp (1999a) evaluate all these methodologies and techniques for the foreseeable environmental change impact categories and propose a set of valuation methods that are appropriate for assessing welfare gains/losses.

While studies in environmental economics focus on economic value and valuation, some studies examine value and valuation from alternative perspectives, e.g. philosophy, policy, planning and architecture (Brooks et al., 1995; Diez, 2001; Rolston, 1999). For example, Rolston (1999) distinguishes seven meaning levels of value in a philosophically-oriented analysis. This value taxonomy comprises: individual preference value, market price and individual good value, social preference and social good value, organismic and ecosystemic value. He criticizes economic valuation efforts to price these values. Brooks et al. (1995) on the other hand, focus on the economic and social value of the conservation of historic buildings and areas from a perspective of 'static' and 'dynamic' meanings of conservation. While the static meaning of the term conservation refers to unchanged conservation, the dynamic use refers to positive change. Diez (2001) criticizes the approaches of many of the evaluations that take the form of value-for-money studies from a policy evaluation perspective. Her criticism is focussed especially on three issues. First of all, it is not possible to appreciate and identify in a comprehensive way the extent of the effects of new policies on their beneficiaries and their economic and social impact; the intangible effects are not easily reduced to a single variable as required in value-for-money studies. Second, value-for-money studies concentrate on impact evaluation, without exploring the mechanisms that make it possible to produce effects (the so-called 'black-box' of evaluation). Third, value-for-money studies do not contribute to improving our understanding of the working mechanisms of the programmes and clarifying the role of stakeholders, as well as the context in which their actions and decisions unfold.

5.3 Evaluation of urban green spaces

A taxonomy of values for urban green space

By urban green spaces we understand public and private open spaces in urban areas, primarily covered by vegetation, which are directly (e.g. active or passive recreation) or indirectly (e.g. positive influence on the urban environment) available for the users (URGE, 2003). To describe the values of urban green spaces is important in order to define and measure their contributions to urban quality of life. It is also important to propose appropriate valuation methods for different values and from several perspectives, viz. ecological, economic, social and planning.

Several functions of urban green spaces such as utilization, production, employment, education, regulation, and preservation form the basis for the determination of dimensions, criteria and indicators that are relevant for the assessment. We offer here a taxonomy of values for urban green spaces which is stemming from their functions: 16 types which are based on ecological, economic, social and planning dimensions (see Figure 5.3). The importance and impact of each value as an input or output for other dimensions is shown with arrows. For example, the ecological values of urban green spaces provide resources for economic production such as wood, fruits, compost and energy. Life support value on the other hand, contributes positively to urban climate and as a result to society by absorbing pollutants and releasing oxygen. Economic values are interrelated with the society in terms of production and employment. The preferences of the society, on the other hand, affect economic values and impacts of urban green spaces in terms of a hedonic function.

In developing this classification we refer to the taxonomy of economic valuation of urban green spaces (Rodenburg et al., 2001). Therefore, we aim to describe relevant evaluation methods on the basis of economic valuation as far as they fit to our taxonomy; otherwise, we have to look for another kind of evaluation method deriving from social or policy evaluation. We have used here the taxonomy of values that Rolston (1999) developed for wildlands as a framework. This taxonomy provides us with a very useful framework due to the common values of wildlands and urban green spaces. Therefore, most of the types of urban green space values defined here are rather consistent with the Rolston's wildlands values. However, urban green spaces do not only represent the natural environment, but also the built environment; and hence, some different values of urban green spaces than the wildlands values, especially deriving from its planning dimension, are incorporated in the taxonomy. The translation of Rolston's wildlands values to urban green and the new ones that we insert is described below according to the classification given in Figure 5.3.

Values of urban green spaces

Ecological values

1. *Intrinsic natural value*. Urban green spaces have an intrinsic natural value for a healthy ecosystem. The biological diversity that the urban green spaces offers, contributes to ecological cycles, while a spatial continuity of urban green spaces enables a spatial movement of wildlife. The intrinsic natural value of urban green spaces constitutes an *existence value* from an economic valuation perspective.
2. *Genetic diversity value*. Urban green spaces can be a genetic reservoir while providing habitats for a diversity of urban wildlife (such as birds and insects) and preserving a diversity of urban resources (such as trees and plants). This preservation function is explicitly present in urban green spaces such as botan-

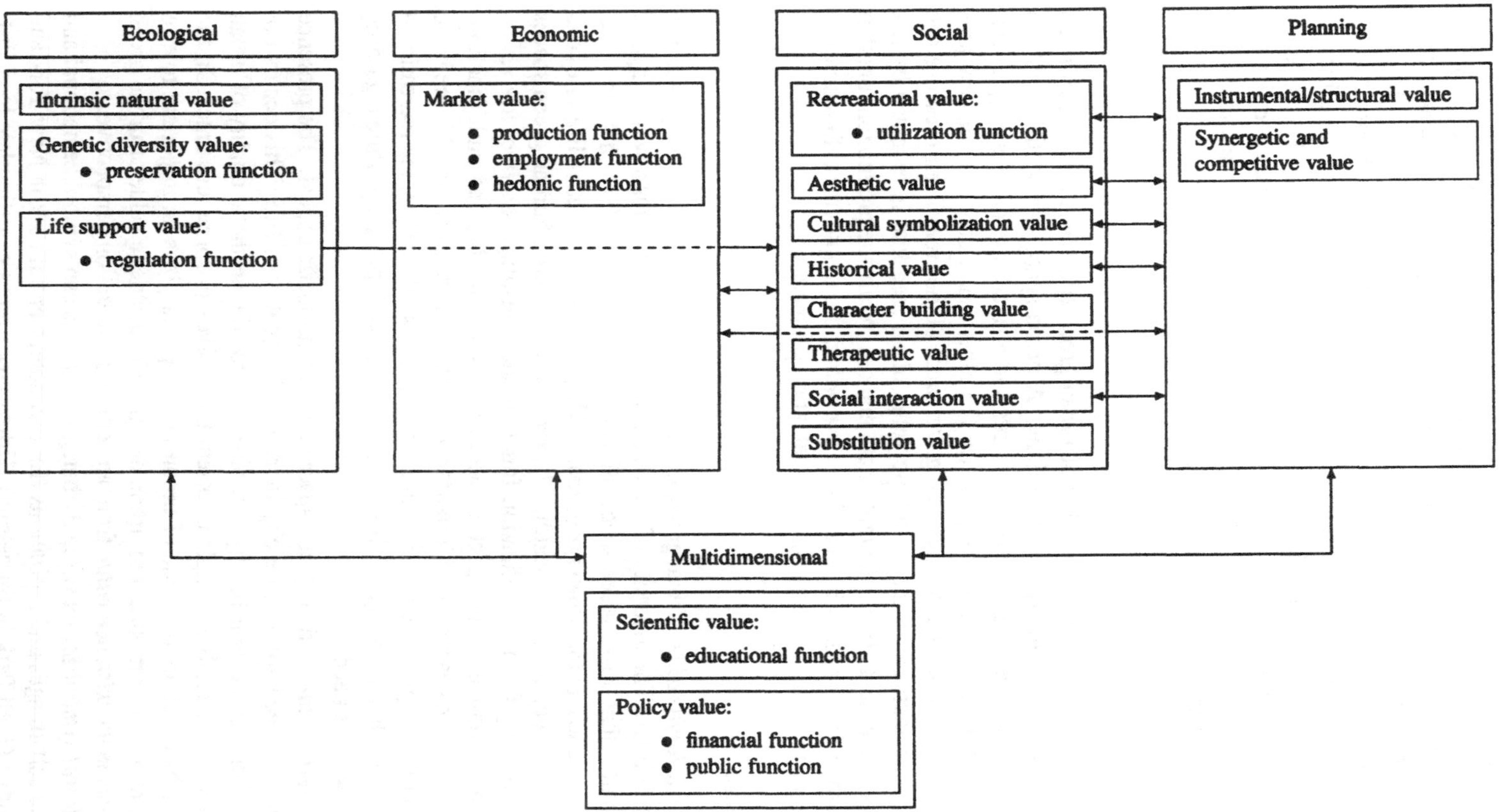

Figure 5.3 Taxonomy of urban green space values
Source: Adapted, in part, from Rolston (1999), 'Valuing Wildlands'

ical and zoological gardens. The preservation function of urban green spaces and the genetic diversity value is a ***bequest value***, especially in terms of benefits for future generations.

3. *Life support value.* Urban green space moderates the impact of human activities in absorbing pollutants and releasing oxygen and improves the urban climate. This purification ability that we call a regulation function of urban green space has an important contribution to the ecological processes and life support systems. The regulation function of urban green spaces is an *indirect use value* from an economic valuation perspective.

Economic values

4. *Market value.* The market value of urban green space is stemming from its production and employment functions. A green space is essentially able to deliver products such as wood and fruits and also compost and energy as elements of urban green production. On the other hand, they provide new jobs for development, maintenance and governance of the area. Their presence can create an increase in the economic value of an area that is reflected by hedonic prices and affects the real estate market. While the production function of urban green spaces is an *indirect use value*, the employment function is a *direct use value* from an economic valuation perspective.

Social values

5. *Recreational value.* Urban green spaces are valued for sports and sight-seeing possibilities. The diversity of land uses and opportunities for a wide range of activities that urban green space offers can create a pull effect on society and attractiveness to the urban green space. They help to foster active lifestyles and can be of real benefit to health. The recreational value of urban green spaces is stemming from its utilization function and constitutes a *direct use value*. From the utilization perspective, accessibility, availability and multifunctionality of green spaces are of importance. These factors constitute also the basic principles of planning in terms of urban facilities. Therefore, the recreational value of urban green spaces is a common value with planning while regarding the society's needs.
6. *Aesthetic value.* Urban green spaces have an aesthetic appeal. The presence of urban green spaces in a city increases the quality of life. This occurs not only because of their beauty, but also because the aesthetic quality of urban green spaces enables people to orient themselves in space and time. On the other hand, aesthetic value of urban green spaces plays an important role in planning as a component of urban design. The aesthetic value of urban green spaces is an *existence value* from an economic valuation perspective.
7. *Cultural symbolization value.* Urban green spaces can symbolize national and local self-images and aspirations (for example, Central Park in New York and Gaudi's Guell Park in Barcelona). Urban green areas can stimulate local cul-

tural moods and sense of belongingness and identity. They enhance cultural life by providing venues for local festivals, civic celebrations and theatrical performances. This symbolization value constitutes, on the other hand, one of the main values to be conserved from the planning perspective. The cultural symbolization value of urban green spaces can be seen as an *existence value*.

8. *Historical value*. Urban green spaces provide natural and cultural historical values. They also provide a pronounced historical museum and contribute to our sense of duration, antiquity, continuity, and identity. Urban green spaces preserve the natural and cultural local heritage for the future generations and its preservation function forms a pre-condition for sustainable development. The historical value of urban green spaces depending on the preservation function is a *bequest value* from a perspective of sustainable development. This value constitutes also one of the main values to be conserved from the planning perspective like cultural symbolization value.
9. *Character building value*. Urban green spaces can be used by organizations that encourage the human spirit to value the challenge of self-competence, preferences for teamwork or alone. Urban green spaces can help to teach one to care about his or her physical condition and also to calculate risks, to learn the instability of the weather, to lose and find one's way, to remember over success and failure. The character building value of urban green spaces can be seen as an *indirect use value*.
10. *Therapeutic value*. The use of urban green spaces can be a semi-therapeutic recreation while relaxing, walking and sporting. They can provide also a setting to treat psychologically disturbed persons, while offering the evolutionary course to need challenge, adventure, exertion and risk. Urban green spaces may provide a 'niche' that meets psychosomatic needs. On the other hand, urban green spaces provide safe play grounds for children and contribute to children's physical, mental and social development. Therapeutic value of urban green spaces depending on the utilization function can be seen as an *indirect use value* from an economic valuation perspective.
11. *Social interaction value*. Urban green spaces can contribute to social justice by creating opportunities for people of all ages to interact. They emphasize the diversity of urban areas by reflecting the different communities they serve and meeting their varying needs. Therefore, they contribute positively to a multicultural society. The social interaction value of urban green spaces can be seen as an *indirect use value*.
12. *Substitution value*. Urban green spaces can be seen as 'positive' and 'negative' alternatives for shortcomings in other fields. They can be a positive alternative for low-income groups without access to (sporting) clubs or without financial opportunities to go on vacation, car-less people and flat-dwellers without gardens/balconies, etc.. They can be seen also a nice place to sleep for the homeless and for doing illegal businesses as a 'negative' alternative. This value of urban green spaces stemming from the substitution and safety functions and they constitute a *direct use value* from an economic valuation perspective.

Planning values

13. *Instrumental/structural value.* Urban green spaces form the landscape and townscape structure of towns and cities. Urban green spaces are of importance in urban planning process as a technical instrument. Sometimes they can be used as a noise barrier or visual screening. They can increase the quality of neighborhoods by their windbreak and camouflage abilities. They can contribute to energy reduction by providing shelter for buildings. They can also function as buffer zone between parts of the city and can help to control the city growth or to soften the impact of development. As a technical instrument, this planning value of urban green spaces may have an impact on society and economic activities. This instrumental and structural value of urban green spaces constitutes an *indirect use value.*
14. *Synergetic and competitive value.* This value of urban green spaces is related to its quality. The quality of green spaces helps to define the identity of towns and cities, which can enhance their attractiveness for living, working, investment and tourism. Therefore, urban green spaces can create a synergy among different types of land use, their presence can increase the economic value of an area and also they can contribute positively to the competitiveness of cities. The synergetic and competitive value of urban green spaces can be seen as an *existence value.*

Multidimensional values

15. *Scientific value.* Urban green space can be seen as a laboratory for the pursuit of science. Urban green space can be an object of academic study and research in the areas of genetics, geology, biology, medicine, agriculture, forestry and evolutionism. This scientific value of urban green space enables society to better understand natural environment and appreciate applied science, which enables to manage and rebuild the environment. On the other hand, urban green spaces play an important role in the basic education of schoolchildren with regard to environment and nature. The scientific value of urban green spaces can be seen as a part of education function and constitutes an *indirect use value.* This scientific value refers to all dimensions of urban green spaces.
16. *Policy value.* Urban green spaces are of importance, not only in the urban planning process but also in urban policies. This value is reflected in the level of budget and the actual expenditures of urban authorities on green spaces. Policy value of urban green spaces is related to public authorities as policy makers on the one hand, and the financial function that is also connected to public function with the amount of green taxes or tourism taxes the people or visitors have to pay. Sometimes an entrance fee for some special green spaces such as botanical gardens can be also another financial instrument. The policy value of urban green spaces can be seen as an *indirect* and also an *existence value.* While urban policies have important impacts on all dimensions of urban green spaces at the local level, the policies deriving from each of the

environmental, economic, social and planning dimensions at both the national and the international level affect urban policies. Therefore, it can be said that the policy value is the most critical common value in this taxonomy.

This classification of urban green values offers a comprehensive evaluation framework for urban green spaces from several perspectives at a conceptual level. However, it is obvious that the evaluation should focus on well-chosen and transparent criteria and indicators according to evaluation needs.

Evaluation models and methodologies

In this section, we describe possible valuation methods to evaluate several values of urban green spaces (see Table 5.1). This framework offers a systematic assessment approach, when the complex and multidimensional structure of urban green spaces is taken into consideration. To offer a rather integrated evaluation framework, we prefer to discuss possible valuation methods for each dimension/category such as ecological, economic, social or planning aspects.

Ecological values As can be seen in Table 5.1, the ecological values consist of intrinsic natural value, genetic diversity value and life support value. Ecological valuation methods for ecological values are based on ***monetary valuation*** and ***non-monetary valuation***. Ecological valuation methods are aimed at assessing diversity and rarity of species on the one hand and the complex interactions between the biotic and abiotic environments on the other hand. The measurement of biological diversity is undertaken through the use of genetic, species and ecosystem richness or variety indices (Nunes, van den Bergh and Nijkamp, 2003; Turner, Button and Nijkamp, 1999a). The measurement of genetic diversity is based on valuation of ***genetic difference*** and ***genetic distance*** and also ***phenotypic trait analysis***. The valuation of species diversity is based on a catalogue of species (Red Data Books) which is known as ***biodiversity index***. To evaluate ecosystem diversity ***keystone processes***, ***health index***, ***ecosystem resilience and stability analysis***, and ***hierarchical structure*** is used. ***Population viability analysis*** and ***eco-regions*** or ***eco-zones*** classifications are also among the methods of valuation. While these valuation methods constitute ***non-monetary valuation*** from an ecological perspective, some ***monetary valuation*** methods are also described from an economic perspective. Among the monetary valuation methods for ecological values ***cost-benefit analysis***, ***travel cost method***, ***replacement costs***, ***tourism revenues***, ***production function*** and ***contingent valuation*** can be mentioned. Economic valuation of bio-technology and still undeveloped medicines, crops, pharmaceuticals products and other products and amenities that may never come to light constitutes also important aspects of economic valuation of ecological values.

Economic values Economic valuation methods for economic values are based on ***monetary valuation***. Among the monetary valuation methods for market values ***market analysis***, ***production functions***, ***financial analysis***, ***cost-benefit analysis***, ***travel cost method*** and ***hedonic price method*** can be mentioned.

Table 5.1 Types of urban green space (UGS) values and valuation methods

Values	Valuation methods
Ecological values: • Intrinsic natural value (existence value) • Genetic diversity value (bequest value) • Life support value (indirect use value)	*Monetary valuation:* cost-benefit analysis, travel cost method, replacement costs, tourism revenues, production function, contingent valuation. *Non-monetary valuation:* species and ecosystem richness indices, genetic difference, genetic distance, phenotypic trait analysis, biodiversity index, keystone processes, health index, ecosystem resilience and stability analysis, hierarchical structure, population viability analysis, eco-regions or eco-zones.
Economic values: • Market value (direct/indirect use value)	*Monetary valuation:* market analysis, production functions, financial analysis, economic cost-benefit analysis, travel cost method, hedonic price method.
Social values: • Recreational value (direct use value) • Aesthetic value (existence value) • Cultural symbolization value (existence value) • Historical value (bequest value) • Character building value (indirect use value) • Therapeutic value (indirect use value) • Social interaction value (indirect use value) • Substitution value (direct use value)	*Monetary valuation:* travel cost method, tourism revenues. *Non-monetary valuation:* contingent valuation.
Planning values: • Instrumental/structural value (indirect use value) • Synergetic and competitive value (existence value)	*Monetary valuation:* cost-benefit analysis, contingent valuation, hedonic price method. *Non-monetary valuation:* geographical information system (GIS) method, multi-criteria decision method.
Multidimensional values: • Scientific value (indirect use value) • Policy value (indirect use/existence value)	*Monetary valuation:* financial analysis, cost-benefit analysis, cost-effectiveness analysis, tourism revenues, taxes revenues. *Non-monetary valuation:* performance analysis, multi-criteria decision method, meta-analysis, value transfer, rough set analysis, fuzzy set analysis, content analysis.

Social values Social values require both *monetary valuation* and *non-monetary valuation* from social, economic and planning perspectives. Since social values reflect the individual and social preferences, the basic and common valuation method is *contingent valuation* for all of the social values. *Travel cost method* and *tourism revenues* on the other hand, are the most important monetary valuation methods for social values.

Planning values Planning values are based on competitiveness among the different land uses on the one hand and technical planning instruments on the other hand. Therefore, while *monetary valuation* is important for the competitiveness function of urban green spaces, *non-monetary valuation* plays a crucial role in physical planning process. To evaluate synergetic and competitive values *cost-benefit analysis*, *contingent valuation* and *hedonic price method* constitute the relevant monetary valuation methods. On the other hand, *multi-criteria decision methods* can be a relevant approach to evaluate synergetic and competitive values from a non-monetary valuation perspective. For non-monetary valuation, geographical information and geography-based analysis and methods are of importance. Geographical Information System (GIS) methods are the most important evaluation methods for spatial aspects.

Multidimensional values The multidimensional values refer to all dimensions/categories and it requires an overall evaluation. While the financial function and public policy is based on *monetary valuation*, the scientific function needs a *non-monetary valuation*. However, the need for an overall evaluation and the characteristics of the multidimensional values require the use of qualitative valuation methods. For monetary valuation of financial policies, *financial analysis*, *cost-benefit analysis*, *cost-effectiveness analysis*, *tourism revenues* and *taxes revenues* can be relevant methods. Among the non-monetary valuation methods *performance analysis*, *multi-criteria decision method* and *meta-analysis* can be mentioned. Particularly, meta-analysis can play an important role to evaluate the scientific values of urban green spaces while providing *value transfer*. Alternative analyses that are based on qualitative study findings can be *rough set analysis*, *fuzzy set analysis* and *content analysis*.

The next step is to collect relevant data on all these criteria in order to undertake a comparative evaluation study of findings in different cities with a view to the identification of lessons on urban green management. The instrument used here is the 'spider' approach. In terms of visualization, the spider model can offer a relevant method for a better understanding of the relationships among the factors and also developing and evaluating 'hypothetical scenarios' for planning and management. Our experiences have shown that the spider model can be used as an effective instrument in comparing availability of urban green spaces in several cities and city groups. The results of these case study researches are offered in section 5.5. To offer a consistent database for this experiment, we will first describe in the next section the structure of the so-called criteria catalogue.

5.4 Experiences from the evaluation of urban green spaces

The URGE project aims to provide helpful methods and measures for green space development and management in cities. One of the tasks is to design an Interdisciplinary Catalogue of Criteria (ICC) for the evaluation of urban green spaces. The ICC is based on the elaboration of sets of disciplinary criteria in the fields of ecology, economics, sociology and planning. The ICC consists of three tools: 1) a *city profile template* which characterizes the structure of a city with a special focus on urban green spaces, 2) the cities' *goals and demands* for green space planning, 3) *interdisciplinary criteria at the city level and at the site level* which serves for the analysis of the green structure of a city (URGE, 2003).

In the applications of the ICC, six thematic groups of criteria were distinguished, both for the analysis of the entire city situation as well as of single sites in the city. Criteria group No. 1, called *Quantity and continuity of green spaces*, focuses on the most important, quantitatively well-definable physical features of urban green spaces. In the second criteria group *Biodiversity and protection* mostly qualitative ecological aspects (e.g. species and habitats diversity) of urban green are analysed. Criteria group No. 3 *Environmental quality* contains criteria referring to the environmental situation of a city and of the surroundings of a green space. In the next criteria group (No. 4) different kinds of *Use of green* are investigated. As it is well known, the active use is the most important function and value of green for the urban population. The diversity of use is also reflected by the complexity of this group. Criteria group No. 5 *Public involvement* concentrates on the degree of citizens' participation in processes of urban green space development and planning. Increasing involvement of possible users in the planning process can contribute to the aim that the future development of urban green meets the requirements of the local inhabitants better. In the last criteria group *Planning, development and management* mostly practice oriented criteria are incorporated, which enable green planners to take into account the legal, planning, financial and managerial aspects of urban green spaces. Detailed descriptions of criteria groups, including criterion, sub-criterion and indicators for city level, are given in Table 5.2.

Table 5.2 Criteria and indicators of urban green

1. Quantity and continuity of green spaces
   - 1.1 Fragmentedness
     - 1.1.1 Surface area of urban green
       - Simple ratio of green area divided by total urban area size of urban green
     - 1.1.2 Largeness, extent of edge effects
       - Average shape index
     - 1.1.3 Isolatedness from other green patches
       - Average of inter-patch distances
     - 1.1.4 Connections to other green patches

- Average distance of green patches to each other

1.2 Soil sealing

1.2.1 Extent of disturbance to water dynamics

- The proportion of soil surface in each of the soil sealing categories

1.3 Availability

1.3.1 The area of urban green available to a person

- Area of urban green space per resident
- Number of visitors of urban green spaces as a percentage of the total urban population

1.4 Internal/external integrated system

1.4.1 Internal/external integrated system

- Existence and effectiveness of instruments capable to implement an integrated green system

2. Biodiversity and protection

2.1 Heterogeneity

2.1.1 Species diversity

- Number of species

2.1.2 Biotope diversity

- Number of biotopes

2.2 Preservation

2.2.1 Level of protection

- Proportion of protected areas from the total green area of the city

2.2.2 Protection of cultural and natural heritage

- Annual discounted future savings of costs for protection of urban wildlife and urban resources per km^2 urban green space
- Presence of botanical gardens/children's farms related to the total green area of the city

3. Environmental quality

3.1 Pollution and air quality

3.1.1 Amount of impurities in urban air

- Values of SO_2, CO, NO_2, O_3, dust and smog according to the guidelines of the European Union

3.1.2 Effectiveness of urban green tp remove pollutants and provide humidity

- Volume of vegetation

3.2 Regulatory effects

3.2.1 Moderating the (negative) impact of human activities on e.g. air quality

- Amount of the massive vegetation in urban green spaces, surface area of water and unsealed soil

3.3 Aesthetical and cultural aspects

3.3.1 Way of planning to preserve local identity of cities

- Existence of the aesthetical and cultural component in the context of the planning of urban green

3.4 Physical and emotional well-being

3.4.1 Physical, emotional benefits derived from urban green spaces

- European/government guidance regarding health. Pursuit of policies to promote health, particularly their integration with green space provision needs of all age groups. Environment specific indicators, such as the frequency of different 'urban illnesses'

3.4.2 Retreat against pace of urban life

- Presence of policy statements for providing appropriate urban environments, provision of sites with this remit, holistic approaches to quality of life

3.5 City identity

3.5.1 Importance of urban green areas to the residents

- Greater involvement of citizens

4. Use of green

4.1 Production

4.1.1 Production of products as woods and compost

- Number of products delivered by urban green space per km^2 urban green space
- Total 'green' profit as a percentage of the total 'urban' profit

4.2 Energy source

4.2.1 Use of natural resources to produce energy, to be used both within the green and the surrounding areas

- Presence of exploitation of energy resources within green areas

4.3 Employment

4.3.1 For maintenance of urban green, catering or education

- Number of 'green' jobs per km^2 urban green space
- Number of 'green' jobs per visitor of urban green
- Contribution of the total salary costs of 'green' jobs to urban income

4.4 Quality living and working conditions

4.4.1 Serve and meet users varying needs

- Existence of a wide range of user groups

4.4.2 Daily recreational needs

- Frequency of use

4.4.3 Life strategies

- Statements from users

4.5 Recreation

4.5.1 Creating pleasant environment

- Size of green areas
- Connectivity of green sites of the city (green system)
- List about the forms of the recreational use of urban green

4.5.2 Community events

- Actual use of sites, examples and case studies of such use and their respective methods of support and organization

4.6 Sports facilities

4.6.1 Multiple use

- A common feature of local authority site provision but examine whether there is adequate local provision

4.7 Substitution

4.7.1 Alternative for e.g. flat dwellers without gardens, or low-income groups without access to (sport) clubs

- Price and rent differences between houses/companies per m^2 with and without gardens/balconies
- Number of captive visitors as a percentage of the total number of visitors of the urban green space
- Distribution of income of the visitors of the urban green

4.8 Safety

4.8.1 Green as a safe place
- Annual number of incidents in green areas compared to the annual number of urban incidents

4.8.2 Fear of crime
- Annual costs of crime prevention and control with regard to urban green compared to the total costs of crime prevention in the city

5. Public involvement

5.1 Community ownership

5.1.1 Promote and encourage community ownership
- Proportion of community owned green spaces from thr total area of urban green

5.2 Citizen's involvement

5.2.1 Citizens involvement in green planning and management process
- Existence of effective instruments to involve citizens in the planning and management process of urban green spaces

5.3 Inclusion in Local Agenda 21-plans

5.3.1 Measures undertaken to include the urban city policy in the context of the Local Agenda 21
- Presence of an Agenda 21, and the green planning as an integrated part of it and number of people (classified by categories) involved in the Agenda 21 process

5.4 Education

5.4.1 To obtain insight in the interaction between humans and nature for user groups
- Total number of environment-related lessons in the age group of 6-18 years
- Costs of education and research projects with regard to (urban) green per km^2 urban green space (Euro/km^2)
- Area of children's farms in the city as a percentage of the total area of the city
- Total hours of (practical) education spent per year on green issues at elementary and grammar schools as a percentage of the total hours of education per year

5.4.2 Educational resource
- Physical and mental performance

5.5 Understand urban environments

5.5.1 More balanced understanding of the concept of sustainability
- Physical and mental performance

5.5.2 Exploration natural world
- Physical and mental performance

6. Planning, development and management

6.1 Legal and planning aspects

6.1.1 Urban green policy and its legal context
- Existence and impact of legislation, at the international, national, regional, local levels, on the planning and management processes of urban green

6.1.2 Planning and guidelines
- Existence and impact of planning instruments at the international, national, regional, local levels, on the planning and management processes of urban green

6.2 Urban green planning in relation with other kinds of planning

6.2.1 To verify the real fruition of urban green, provided to facilities and infrastructures
- Co-ordination between urban green planning and other kind of planning

6.3 Responsibilities within the administration

6.3.1 Definition of the roles played by the institutions involved in planning and managing urban green

- Level of performance
- Adequacy of the number personnel/extension of territory

6.4 Integrate private green

6.4.1 Measures to involve private green in the urban green system

- Presence of a plan and/or other administrative instruments to involve private green

6.5 Public authorities

6.5.1 The importance of urban green to the public authorities

- Green space related costs from the total city budget
- Number of hours planned/spent on urban green policy as a percentage of total hours planned/spent on policy
- The amount of budget per green job

6.6 Finances

6.6.1 Budget for urban green

- Annual cost of the green space maintenance (Euro/m^2/year)
- Distribution of funding (representative, intensive, extensive) in %
- Amount of budget/expenditures for development per km^2 urban green space
- Amount of budget/expenditures for maintenance per km^2 urban green space
- Amount of budget/expenditures for revitalization per km^2 urban green space
- The height of green taxes and tourism taxes

6.6.2 Management and provision of money for urban green spaces

- Identification of appropriate budgets, examine funds available at local, national and European levels. Consider partnerships

6.6.3 Activities to create income

- Existence of initiative to enable urban green to create income

6.6.4 Fund raising capacities

- Existence within the public administration of the capacities to raise funds for urban green

6.7 Management regimes

6.7.1 Urban governance

- Employment of staff with appropriate expertise, links with, and use of groups and organizations with this social remit, such as groundwork and conservation groups

6.8 Street green and road maintenance

6.8.1 Measures to preserve and maintain street green through the definition and co-ordination of rational maintenance procedures

- Existence of adequate measure to properly maintain street green

6.9 Waste management

6.9.1 Co-ordination between the selective waste collection and recycling, treatment of organic components and urban green

- Existence of plans and/or procedures to co-ordinate the urban green policy and the waste management plan

Source: Adapted from URGE (2003), *Development of Urban Green Spaces to Improve the Quality of Life in Cities and Urban Regions*

The most important conclusions that can be drawn from the design of ICC are the need to: 1) clarify criteria and indicators in an operational way, 2) compress and shorten the ICC, 3) eliminate overlap and duplication in the indicators and methods, 4) describe more exactly the relevant methods in the respective criterion, 5) refine the ICC towards an easy-to-handle 'express catalogue' for the analysis and evaluation of the green areas, and 6) provide a collection of 'best practices' especially relevant for the planning criteria where each city has its own specific legal and planning system.

The experience from the evaluation process of the URGE project has shown us lessons in evaluating urban green spaces at the application level. The first problem is to collect relevant data. The difficulties in collecting data do not only stem from a lack of data, but also from the classification categories or different measures that the cities used. These different classification categories make a comparison among the cities not an easy task. Besides, this experience has also shown us the need for a simple and clear set of indicators and methods for application, and a collection of 'best practices' from several specific legal and planning systems in European cities. This experience has provided an opportunity to develop a common language among the different disciplines in green planning and management which may be the most important contribution or lesson to be learned from this evaluation process. We will now turn to the empirical part of our study.

5.5 Some empirical results — Lessons from experiences

The need for an informative database and a more integrated approach requires comparative analyses in order to better understand the similarities and differences among cities and city groups. From this need we have conducted some empirical researches that aim to compare the similarities and differences in and between European and Dutch cities, especially to point out the availability of green spaces per inhabitant in cities. In this section we will offer the empirical results on European cities of several case studies. For these comparative case studies we deploy here the spider model as a methodology. The spider model enabled us to visualize the relative scores of different cities and city groups in terms of availability of urban green spaces.

A previous factor-analytic approach in terms of urban green spaces in European cities has shown that a strong relationship exists between urban green areas-built-up areas and urban green areas-water (Baycan Levent et al., 2002a). The results of this study indicated that the availability of 'urban green' is relatively high in metropoles and big cities, whereas the availability of 'natural green' such as forest and agricultural area is relatively high in medium-sized and small cities (Table 5.3).

An empirical comparison of green spaces in European cities brought to light that similar structures in terms of built-up area and urban green spaces can be observed in big and medium-sized cities (Baycan Levent et al., 2003). Cities having higher scores on built-up areas have also higher scores on urban green spaces. Similarly, higher scores on urban green spaces implies also having higher scores on water in the same city groups (Figure 5.4). The results of this study demonstrate that there is an order from small cities to metropoles in terms of available green per inhabitant, where metropoles constitute the most disadvantaged city group.

Table 5.3 Availability of natural and urban green in European cities

Metropoles > 1.000.000 inh.		Big Cities 500.000 ÷ 1.000.000 inh.		Medium-Sized Cities 100.000 ÷ 500.000 inh.		Small Cities < 100.000 inh.	
Berlin (D)	U	Birmingham (GB)	U	Antwerpen (B)	–	Alphen aan de Rijn (NL)	–
Budapest (H)	U	Kraków (PL)	N	Bern (CH)	–	Freiberg (D)	–
İstanbul (TR)	N	Genova (I)	–	Chemnitz (D)	N	Görlitz (D)	–
Wien (A)	U	Helsinki (FIN)	U	Dresden (D)	N		
Warszawa (PL)	U	Łódź (PL)	N	Edinburgh (GB)	U		
		Torino (I)	–	Espoo (FIN)	U		
				Leipzig (D)	N		
				Montpellier (F)	–		
				Salzburg (A)	–		
				Sarajevo (BIH)	–		
				Tallinn (EE)	–		
				Zürich (CH)	–		

U: Urban Green, N: Natural Green

Source: Adapted from Baycan Levent et al. (2002a), 'Urban Sustainability and Green Spaces'

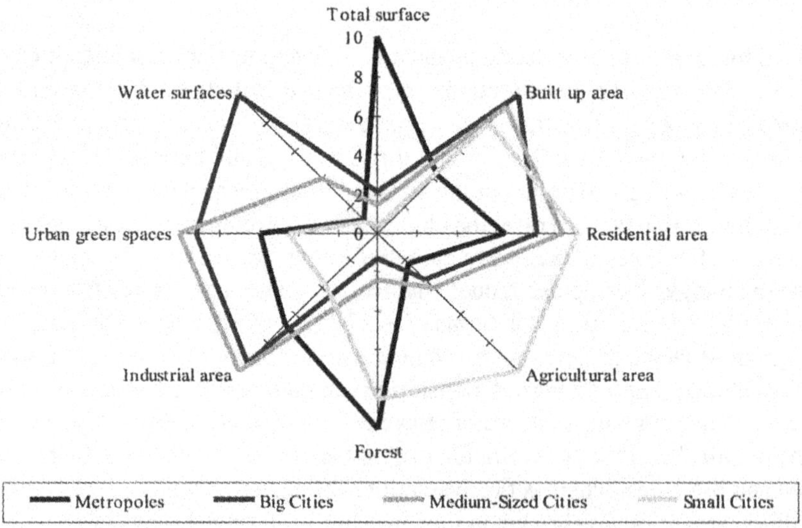

Figure 5.4 General land use within the four European city groups
Source: Adapted from Baycan Levent et al. (2003), 'Development and Management of Green Spaces in European Cities: A Comparative Analysis'

Table 5.4 Availability of urban green in Dutch cities

Big Cities		New Cities		Intermediate Cities		Peripheral Cities	
Amsterdam	U	Almere	L	Breda	–	Deventer	–
Rotterdam	U	Alphen aan de Rijn	L	Ede	S	Den Helder	S
Den Haag	U	Zaanstad	L	Eindhoven	U	Emmen	S
Utrecht	U	Zoetermeer	U	's-Hertogenbosch	L	Middelburg	–
				Leiden	–	Roermond	L
				Nijmegen	L	Enschede	S
				Tilburg	–	Groningen	–
				Zwolle	–	Maastricht	–

U: Urban Recreation Areas, S: Structural, Long-term Recreation Areas, L: Daily Leisure Areas

Source: Adapted from van Leeuwen, Rodenburg and Nijkamp (2002), 'Urban Green and Integrative Urban Sustainability: Concepts and their Relevance in Dutch Cities'

Complementary comparative case studies on green space in Dutch cities show also interesting links and patterns for different city groups such as big cities, new cities, intermediate cities and peripheral cities in the Netherlands (van Leeuwen, Rodenburg and Nijkamp, 2002; Rodenburg, van Leeuwen and Nijkamp, 2002). A comparative factor-analytic approach (Table 5.4) shows that Dutch big cities have a high score in terms of urban recreational factors, whereas new cities have higher scores on the daily leisure factor, and peripheral cities tend to have high scores on the structural, longer-stay recreational areas (van Leeuwen, Rodenburg and Nijkamp, 2002).

A similar comparison shows that large Dutch cities have the lowest scores on the availability of different types of urban green (Rodenburg, van Leeuwen and Nijkamp, 2002). They accommodate less green spaces, especially less natural green spaces, not only as a percentage of the total land use, but also concerning its availability per inhabitant (Figure 5.5).

A final comparison by means of spider model was applied to European and Dutch cities jointly (Baycan Levent and Nijkamp, 2002b). The results of this comparison show that small cities in both Europe and the Netherlands have better conditions in terms of urban green and non built-up area. A high population density goes together with a low availability of total recreational and urban green areas. While European and Dutch big cities have a relatively higher population density and lower total recreational and urban green areas, European and Dutch small cities have higher total recreational and urban green areas and a lower population density (Figure 5.6). This comparative framework shows once more that a sufficient availability of urban green spaces is more problematic for big cities.

These experiences from several case studies have helped us to understand different relationships that exist between urban green spaces and relevant background factors.

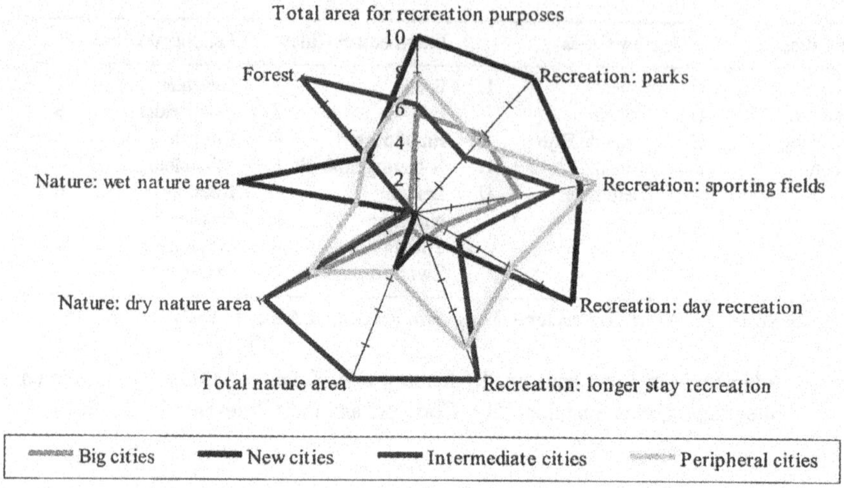

Figure 5.5 Green land use within the four Dutch city groups
Source: Adapted from Rodenburg, van Leeuwen and Nijkamp (2002), *Environmental Assessment Indicators for Urban Green Spaces, A comparative study on Dutch cities*

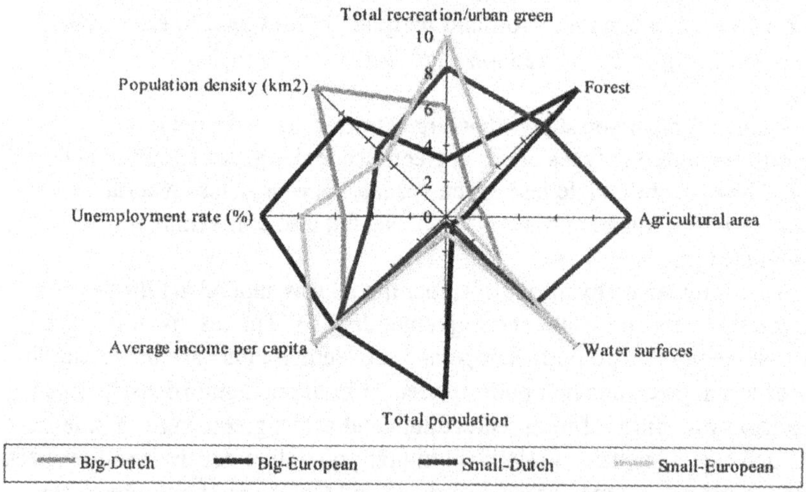

Figure 5.6 Availability of urban green spaces in European and Dutch cities
Source: Adapted from Baycan Levent and Nijkamp (2002b), 'Planning Urban Green Space: A Comparison of European and Dutch Cities'

5.6 Concluding remarks

The complex and multidimensional structure of urban green spaces requires integrated and new approaches for planning, development and management of green spaces. Evaluation of urban green spaces in the framework of these new and more integrated approaches is needed, as well as the design of a more integrated set of relevant methods deriving from several perspectives such as environmental, economic, social, or policy valuation.

Our experiences from the evaluation process of urban green spaces have shown us some difficulties such as a lack of relevant data, different measures and classification of data, administrative structure of cities and personnel capacities (in terms of number and expertise) of planning authorities, in evaluating of urban green spaces at the application level. Besides these restrictions, these experiences brought to light the need for a simple and clear set of indicators and methods for application. More comparative case study investigations and experiences of different cities in terms of planning and management of urban green spaces will be very helpful to better understand the relevance of the methods and measures adopted. These experiences will be also helpful in developing relevant policies at both the national and the local level.

The most important contribution or lesson to be learned from this evaluation process is that these experiences have provided an opportunity to develop a common language among the different disciplines in green planning and management. This process has shown that for analysis and evaluation of urban green spaces an active interdisciplinary dialogue is necessary, with emphasis on the complex interface between natural and social science approaches.

Note

1 This contribution stems from experience of EU project on *Development of Urban Green Spaces to Improve the Quality of Life in Cities and Urban Regions* (URGE). URGE aims at improving the provision of urban green spaces, thus raising the quality of life of the urban population and contributing to a sustainable development of European cities. The main question of the project is how urban green spaces can be developed from ecological, economic, social and planning perspectives, and which tools and instruments are helpful in this respect. A main target is to enlarge the knowledge about complex interactions between nature, economy and social activities in urban environments as a condition to develop and implement modern management strategies for planning of urban landscapes (URGE, 2003).

References

Baycan Levent, T., van Leeuwen, E. V., Rodenburg, C. and Nijkamp, P. (2002a), 'Urban Sustainability and Green Spaces', *Structural Change in Europe*, submitted.

Baycan Levent, T. and Nijkamp, P. (2002b), 'Planning Urban Green Space: A Comparison of European and Dutch Cities', *Australian Journal of Regional Science*, submitted.

Baycan Levent, T., van Leeuwen, E. V., Rodenburg, C. and Nijkamp, P. (2003), 'Development and Management of Green Spaces in European Cities: A Comparative Analysis', in J. Colman and E. Beriatos (eds.), *Urban planning and the pulsar effect: coping with peaks, troughs and repeats in the demand cycle*, ISOCARP, forthcoming 2003.

Bingham, G., Bishop, R., Brody, M., Bromley, D., Clark, E. T., Cooper, W., Costanza, R., Hale, T., Hayden, G., Kellert, S., Norgaard, R., Norton, B., Payne, J., Russell, C. and Suter, G. (1999), 'Issues in ecosystem valuation: improving information for decision making', in R. K. Turner, K. Button and P. Nijkamp (eds.), *Ecosystems and Nature: Economics, Science and Policy, Environmental Analysis and Economic Policy: 7*, Edward Elgar, Cheltenham (UK).

Brooks, C., Cheshire, P., Evans, A. and Stabler, M. (1995), *The Economic and Social Value of the Conservation of Historic Buildings and Areas*, The University of Reading, Reading (UK).

Chadwick, G. (1971), *A Systems View of Planning, Towards a Theory of the Urban and Regional Planning Process*, Pergamon Press, Oxford (UK).

Diez, M. A. (2001), 'New Approaches to Evaluating Regional Policy: The Potential of a Theory-Based Approach', *Greener Management International*, No. 36, pp. 37-49.

Folmer, H. and van Ierland, E. V. (1989), 'Valuation Methods and Policy Making in Environmental Economics: Relevance and Scope', in H. Folmer and E. V. van Ierland (eds.), *Valuation Methods and Policy Making in Environmental Economics, Studies in Environmental Science: 36*, Elsevier BV, Amsterdam (The Netherlands).

van Leeuwen, E. V., Rodenburg, C. and Nijkamp, P. (2002), 'Urban Green and Integrative Urban Sustainability: Concepts and their Relevance in Dutch Cities', *European Journal for Spatial Research*, submitted.

Martinuzzi, A. (2001), 'Introduction', *Greener Management International*, No. 36, pp. 20-26, Theme Issue: Evaluating Sustainable Development Policy.

Navrud, S. (1989), 'Estimating Social Benefits of Environmental Improvements from Reduced Acid Depositions: A Contingent Valuation Survey', in H. Folmer and E. V. van Ierland (eds.), *Valuation Methods and Policy Making in Environmental Economics, Studies in Environmental Science: 36*, Elsevier BV, Amsterdam (The Netherlands).

Nijkamp, P., Rietveld, P. and Voogd, H. (1990), *Multicriteria Evaluation in Physical Planning*, North-Holland Publishing Company, Amsterdam (The Netherlands).

Nunes, P. A. L. D, van den Bergh, J. C. J. M. and Nijkamp, P. (2003), *The Ecological Economics of Biodiversity: Methods, Values and Policy Applications*, Edward Elgar Publishing, Cheltenham (UK), forthcoming.

Rodenburg, C., Baycan Levent, T., van Leeuwen, E. V. and Nijkamp, P. (2001), 'Urban Economic Indicators for Green Development in Cities', *Greener Management International*, No. 36, pp. 105-119.

Rodenburg, C. A., van Leeuwen, E. S. V. and Nijkamp, P. (2002), *Environmental Assessment Indicators for Urban Green Spaces, A comparative study on Dutch cities*, Book in memory of Hans-Jürgen Ewers, Springer, Berlin (Germany), submitted.

Rolston, H. (1999), 'Valuing Wildlands', in R. K. Turner, K. Button and P. Nijkamp (eds.), *Ecosystems and Nature: Economics, Science and Policy, Environmental Analysis and Economic Policy: 7*, Edward Elgar, Cheltenham (UK).

Trochim, W. M. K. (2003), *The Research Methods Knowledge Base*, The Research Methods Knowledge Base Web Site, Cornell University, Ithaca, NY (USA), http://trochim.human.cornell.edu/kb.

Turner, R. K., Button, K. and Nijkamp, P. (eds., 1999a), *Ecosystems and Nature: Economics, Science and Policy, Environmental Analysis and Economic Policy: 7*, Edward Elgar, Cheltenham (UK).

Turner, R. K., Subak, S. and Adger, W. N. (1999b), 'Pressures, Trends and Impacts in Coastal Zones: Interactions Between Socioeconomic and Natural Systems', in R. K. Turner, K. Button and P. Nijkamp (eds.), *Ecosystems and Nature: Economics, Science and Policy, Environmental Analysis and Economic Policy: 7*, Edward Elgar, Cheltenham (UK).

Urban Green Environment (2003), *Development of Urban Green Spaces to Improve the Quality of Life in Cities and Urban Regions*, The URGE Web Site, Hamburg and Dresden (Germany), http://www.urge-project.org.

van den Berg, J. C. J. M. (ed., 1999), *Handbook of Environmental and Resource Economics*, Edward Elgar, Cheltenham (UK).

Chapter 6

Contextual Knowledge Generated by a Decision Support System for Brownfield Development — The Case of Porto Marghera (Venice, Italy)

Domenico Patassini, Paola Cossettini, Enrico De Polignol, Markus Hedorfer, Chiara Paneghetti, Enrico Rinaldi [1]

6.1 Introduction

The purpose of this chapter is to reflect upon the communicative use of the ELGIRA Decision Support System (DDS) which is currently in the phase of testing as a part of the CORILA research project[2]. Thanks to specific evaluation functions, and by assessing localized and widespread effects, the ELGIRA DSS aids strategy management in the reclaiming of polluted land within the redevelopment programme for the industrial area of Porto Marghera in Venice[3]. This methodology has been designed and tested to operate specifically for the industrial port area. However, the area is situated in a crucial urban and environmental position, because industrial waste has been deposited on landfill in casks and buried between the Mestre and the lagoon areas.

This critical state of affairs has been acknowledged by the land reuse scenarios proposed over the last few years and taken into consideration again by the Revised City Master Plan of 1999 and the Reclamation Master Plan of 2002. Important issues have been raised in these documents which this chapter addresses, and answers are sought to the question whether this DSS could be instrumental in overcoming the isolation of this area and reducing the stigma with which it has long been associated[4]? Also, as far as investors and local communities are concerned, would the DSS help them in getting to know and then to regain control of a territory that has been for far too long, and with dreadful consequences, under the domain of national governmental provisions? The following sections propose a course of action that, starting with the design of the DSS itself, reflects upon the knowledge that it generates, and on its ability to integrate with plans, programmes and projects for redevelopment.

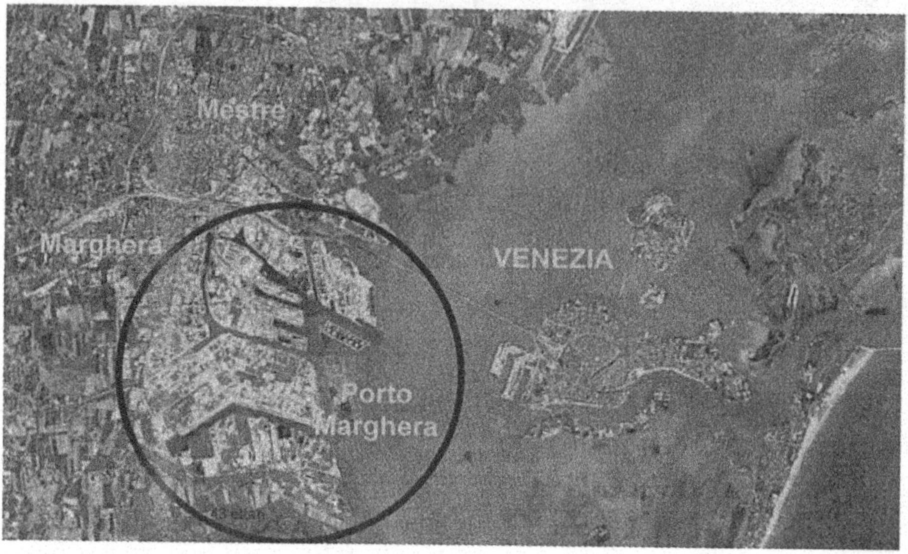

Figure 6.1 **Venice and Porto Marghera**

6.2 A mega brownfield site

Marghera is a national brown field site as stated by the Ministry of Industry decree 468 of 2001[5] (*mappa dei siti italiani*, i.e. 'map of Italian sites'). It is also one of the main planning issues for Venice as indicated in the Revised City Master Plan of 1999 and in preliminary documents of the Strategic Plan (Pugliese, 2003; Barbiani, 2002). The site, along the south-western coastal zone of the lagoon, comprises about 5000 hectares, divided into three zones. The first one includes surface lands that were artificially created with waste soil extracted during the maintenance of industrial and urban canals in the period from 1920 to 1960, and then partially occupied by factories of basic industries. The second refers to an industrial zone where the lion's share is occupied by commercial port infrastructures of chemical and related industries. The third zone covers a strip of near lagoon and port canal water surface. Therefore, the perimeter of the site includes mainland and surrounding waters located between the marvellous historical centre of Venice and the post-World War 2 urban sprawl. The site is further divided into thirteen macro-areas, out of which nine are industrial and four still natural but with very high soil and water pollution.

6.3 Master Plan 2002 within a local planning frame

The Master Plan (MP) of 2002 for the brownfield redevelopment, together with other local planning instruments, aims at leading Porto Marghera towards a safe and sure

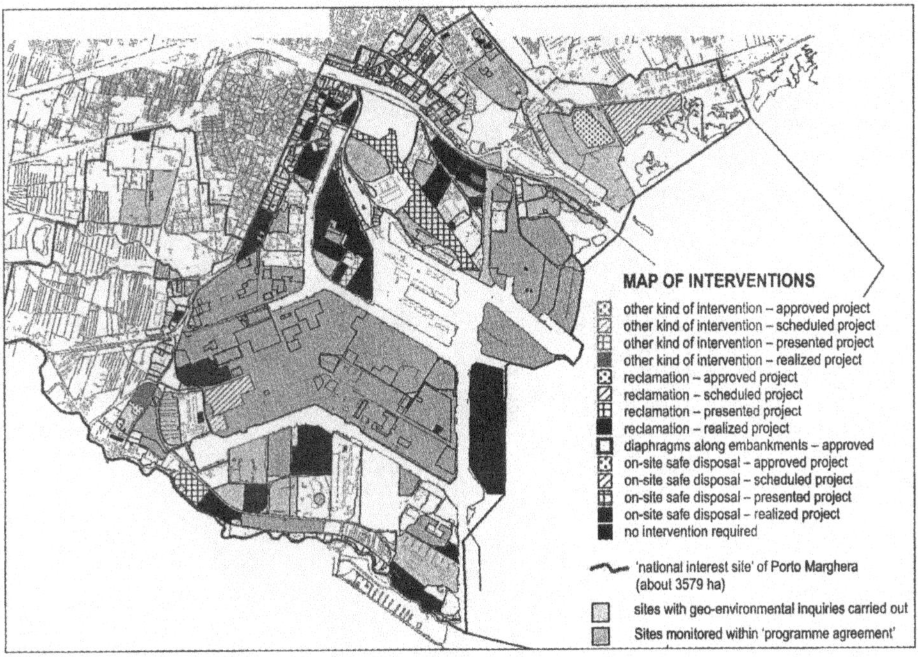

Figure 6.2 Porto Marghera 2002. Situation

future[6]. The new design is however not as yet visible either in the brownfield plan or in the Revised City Master Plan since the proposed scenarios of land use have not been completed. The new preliminary design includes manufacturing, logistic, and seaport functions. Porto Marghera has considerable infrastructures (Pugliese, 1996) and logistic potential, but suffers because of current land uses[7] from numerous problems of integration with the surrounding areas. Regional planning instruments have revealed many uncertainties as regards this aspect, while the traffic management in the area worsens despite a wealth of projects.

The Master Plan is a new instrument for the articulation of required actions and is of particular value as regards the size, the position and the history (often dramatic) of the area involved. Porto Marghera bears contradictory evidence to the waning of the long economic cycle of the chemical industry and its political role in Italian industrial history — particularly in that of the Veneto region. It highlights the defeat of those who claimed that just compensation was possible and payable on the environmental, health and social balances which have been concealed for years. The Master Plan also underlines the impossibility of increasing the amount of traffic on the road network, and the amount of negative external effects on the surrounding inhabited and natural areas.

The main aim of the MP is to pave the way for restoring the environmental quality and the reconversion of the industrial zone with a compatible mix of functions; by

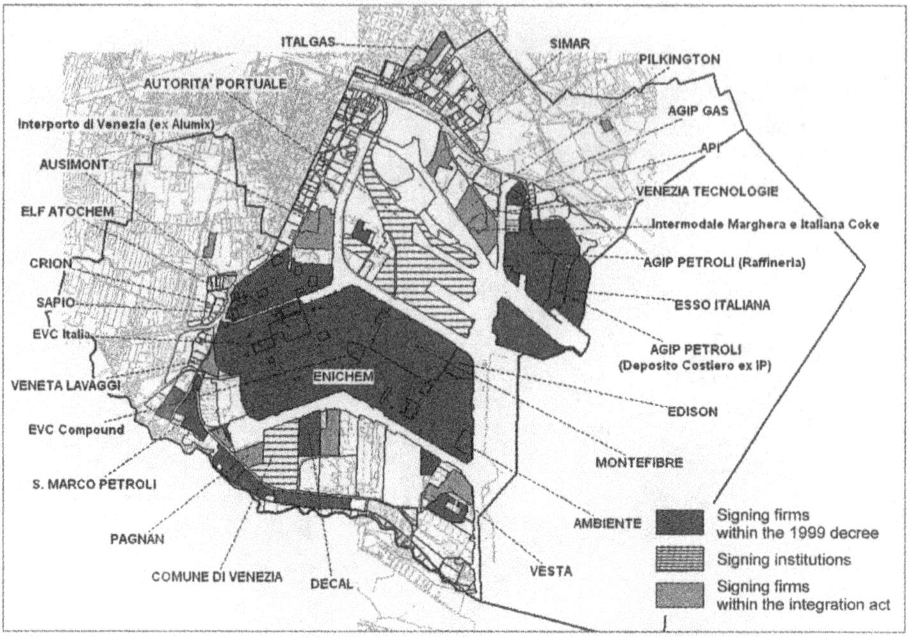

Figure 6.3 Enterprises and institutions signing Porto Marghera Agreement on Chemistry

putting abandoned areas, and those in the process of being abandoned, back onto the real estate market — with a new series of regulations and guarantees; by ensuring that a reduction in the stigma attached to the area increases the demand for land (which otherwise, in some cases is a demand for freight handling use of little value[8]), considering the inherent value of the location and general social benefits. In order to achieve these goals, the MP foresees the use of several different redevelopment operations in a fragile and changing environment.

The adoption of the MP by the Committee for the Observation of the Chemical Programme Agreement (*Comitato di Sorveglianza dell'Accordo di Programma per la Chimica*) was planned by the end of March 2003. The MP thus became the Director Plan (*Piano Direttore*) that defines intervention strategies, timing and costs of environmental reclamation in Porto Marghera, as stipulated in the Supplementary Act (*Atto Integrativo del DPCM*) of 12 February 1999, drawn up jointly by the Veneto Region and the Municipality of Venice. Once the assigned period of public review is over, the MP will be approved by the Service Conference for the Chemical Programme Agreement. The Prime Minister's office will then issue the necessary official decree for the Plan's adoption.

The unified management of the reclamation and redevelopment process of the industrial zone will be effected through the creation of a joint public-private man-

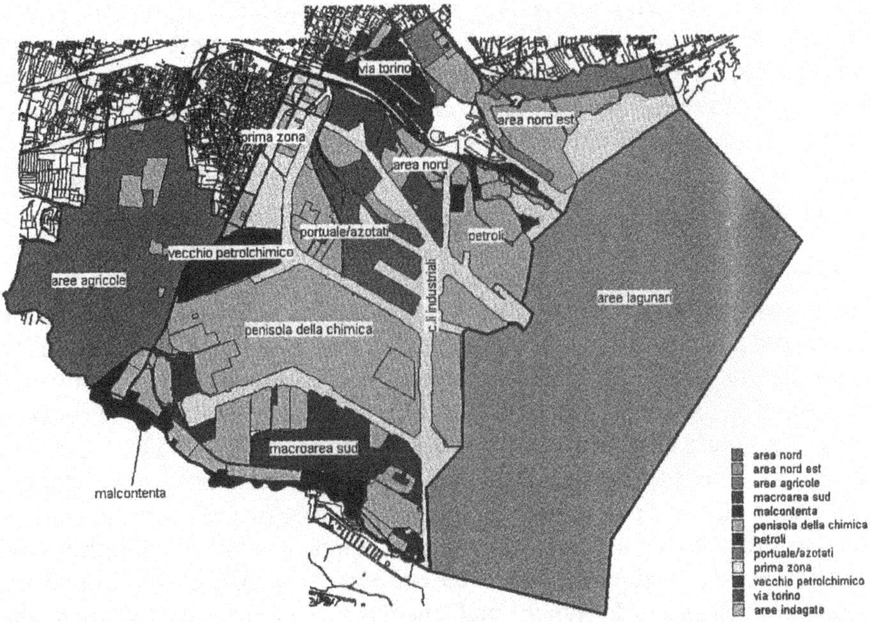

Figure 6.4 Master Plan macro-areas

agement committee, with the controlling interest belonging jointly to the Veneto Region and the Municipality of Venice, but with investment open to all the industries present on the land designated for reclamation, either directly or through associated companies. With this in mind, the Veneto Region has prepared a draft bill for establishing the 'ecological area' of Porto Marghera (in accordance with Article 26 of the DL (Decree-Law) 112 of 1998 and Article 41 of the Regional Law 11 of 2001). The management committee will be able to develop plans for reclamation and redevelopment, transformation and commercialisation of single areas (in accordance with Article 120 of the DL 267 of 2000). The controlling and joint interest in this case also will be held by the Region, the Province, and the Municipality. Participation will also be open to those with vested interests in particular reclamation projects.

6.4 ELGIRA — Towards compromise scenarios

ELGIRA is an acronym of Électre, Giuditta, REC, and AuReS (and recalls a phrase in Venetian dialect[9]): four analytical and evaluation models that constitute a DSS prototype that is now in the final testing phase (Patassini et al., 2003). In fact, the design of ELGIRA is still a 'work in progress' with its main aim being to find, for the actors of the redevelopment and development of Porto Marghera (be they promoters, producers, or consumers), acceptable compromises between economic costs, environmental merit, and the amount of total risk generated over a conventional life cycle period of 30 years. There are three main intervention strategies that the various techniques may undertake: the destruction or alteration of the polluting agents, their extraction or separation from the site, and rendering the pollutants inert. The fact that ELGIRA is still being developed and tested after a year and a half and that it is not a closed model justifies its use as an instrument to improve understanding rather than for decision-making. This does by no means devalue its usefulness, of course.

There are still very many mysterious legacies present in the industrial zone and in the surrounding areas, the latter deserving of as great attention as those sites in the industrial zone itself. One recent example of such 'left-overs' is the case of the former *Casarin* quarries in Viale Don Sturzo, which were used for the extraction of material then used in the nearby brickworks, until the beginning of the twentieth century. The quarry itself remained operative until the end of the 1950s. A historical examination of the site reveals how the abandoned quarries then became manmade lakes in the park area to the east of the *Margotti* daycare (nursery school), and how in 1964 an ordinance by the prefect allowed the dumping of various industrial waste material to be used to raise the height of the bed of the lake. Another more recent and dramatic example has to do with the problem of the disposal of sludge from digging and dredging of canals, considered by some to be resolvable with the creation of new waste dumps on the lagoon front. Further excavations in Porto Marghera or Mestre lead to more and more discoveries of cases like these.

Very little is known about these 'legacies', as with regard to the environmental characterization of the contaminating agents is very inadequate their combined effects, as well as their propagation in the ground, in the water, and in the air. Lack of knowledge is a difficulty also in assessing the effectiveness of plausible reclamation techniques for Porto Marghera (either single or combined), threshold values for health hazards, and information on the economic costs, which are not easy to standardize even for tried and tested techniques. These uncertainties are also shared by the concept of residual risk.

ELGIRA is designed for the construction of reclamation scenarios (but also for the evaluation of their plausibility) by combining various types of scientific, technical and ordinary knowledge. ELGIRA is the name given to a local knowledge generating procedure, based on a multi-objective evaluation model, aimed at brownfield reclamation and redevelopment. Given input development scenarios and environmental characterization, the procedure seems to be effective in finding a compromise among conflicting evaluation criteria such as financial and economic costs, environmental merit and the residual risk of selected clean-up processes with information on health hazard to the population exposed.

The procedure is organized into the following six modules (the last works as import module):

1. *Soil characterization* on a contaminant grid at the surface level, with actual and estimated[10] concentration values.
2. *Screening on- and off-site reclamation technologies* that might be applied

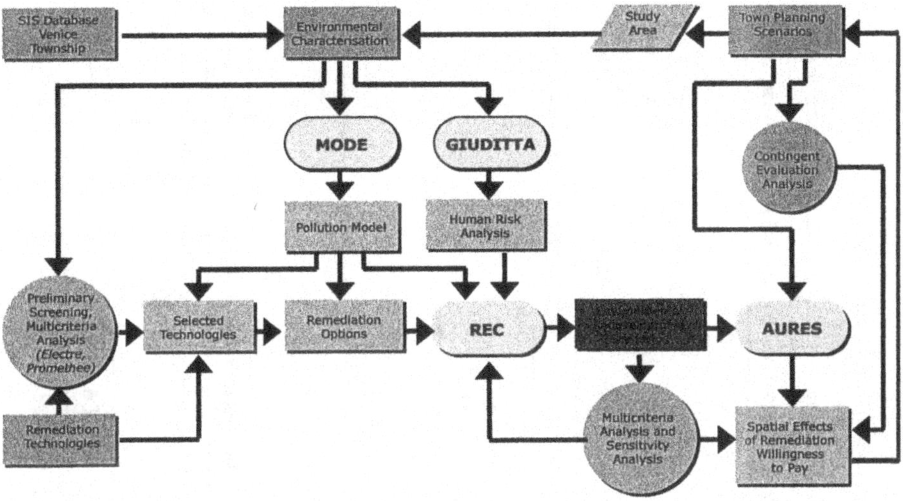

Figure 6.5 ELGIRA's rationale

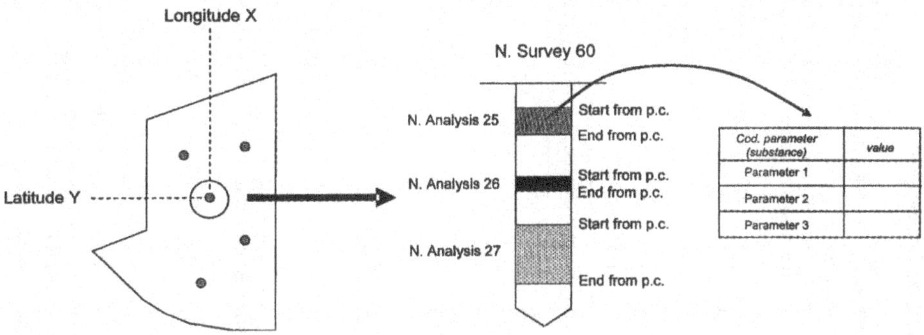

Figure 6.6 Environmental characterization

within the area according to selected redevelopment scenarios. An interactive multi-criteria analysis[11] is employed to find plausible ranking and possibly combine single technologies in sequence, using general criteria such as market availability of the technique, clean-up effectiveness, procedure impact (inconvenience and disturbance), financial return and so on. The criteria are weighted by experts[12] whose knowledge might be usefully combined with local knowledge, preferences, and perception of risk by main city and industrial users (second module).

3. *Estimation of health hazard index* for populations using or living nearby the industrial area. Value index changes with population exposure (third module, Giuditta[13]).

Table 6.1 Preliminary screening of reclamation technologies

Contaminant classes identified in the '43 Hectares' area		Bioreactors – slurry phase		Thermal desorption		Incineration		Vitrification		Soil washing		Solvent extraction		Capping + confining		Waste disposal		Solidification/ stabilization	
Fixed parameters	**weight**	value	score	value	score	value	score	value	score	value	score	value	score	value	score	value	score	value	score
Market availability	0.10	A	4	A	4	B	3	A	4	A	4	A	4	A	4	...	2	A	4
Area required for treatment plant	0.05	B	2	A	4	A	4	A	4	A	4	A	4	A	4	A	4	A	4
Environmental impact	0.10	B	3	C	1	C	1	B/C	2	B	3	B	3	B	3	C	1	C	1
Area available	0.15	A	3	A	3	A	3	A	3	A	3	A	3	A/B	2	A	3	A	3
Treatment time	0.10	L	2	M	4	R	5	R	5	R	5	L	2	R	5	R	5	M-L	3
Total fixed parameters	0.50	—	1.45	—	1.55	—	1.55	—	1.75	—	1.85	—	1.55	—	1.70	—	1.45	—	1.45
Variable parameters by pollutant	**weight**	value	score	value	score	value	score	value	score	value	score	value	score	value	score	value	score	value	score
PAH: Return (%)	0.30	78	2	98	5	99.9	3	99.9	5	91	3	96	4	...	3	...	5	/	/
Cost (€/t)	0.20	60	5	80	4	500	2	200	2	90	4	280	2	20	5	205	3	/	/
Total variable parameters	0.50	—	1.60	—	2.30	—	1.90	—	1.90	—	1.70	—	1.60	—	1.90	—	2.10	/	/
Mercury: Return (%)	0.30	/	/	/	/	/	/	/	/	85	3	/	/	...	3	...	5	...	1
Cost (€/t)	0.20	/	/	/	/	/	/	/	/	90	4	/	/	20	5	125	4	60	5
Total variable parameters	0.50	/	/	/	/	/	/	/	/	—	1.70	/	/	—	1.90	—	2.30	—	1.30
Metals: Return (%)	0.30	/	/	/	/	/	/	...	5	81-96	3	/	/	...	3	...	5	...	1
Cost (€/t)	0.20	/	/	/	/	/	/	200	2	90	4	/	/	20	5	125	4	60	5
Total variable parameters	0.50	/	/	/	/	/	/	—	1.90	—	1.70	/	/	—	1.90	—	2.30	—	1.30
Sums of fixed and variable param.	**weight**	value	score	value	score	value	score	value	score	value	score	value	score	value	score	value	score	value	score
PAH	1.00	—	3.05	—	3.85	—	3.45	—	3.65	—	3.55	—	3.15	—	3.60	—	3.55	/	/
Mercury	1.00	/	/	/	/	/	/	/	/	—	3.55	/	/	—	3.60	—	3.75	—	2.75
Metals	1.00	/	/	/	/	/	/	—	3.65	—	3.55	/	/	—	3.60	—	3.75	—	2.75

Legend:
... Value not quantifiable
— Value not computable
/ Value or score not applicable

Please note that the weights reported along with the intermediate totals of fixed and variable parameters correspond to the sums of weights $\sum$(weight) of the single parameters, while the corresponding total scores are weighted sums computed by $\sum$(weight × score). On the contrary, the total scores in the three bottommost rows are simple sums of the corresponding intermediate totals.

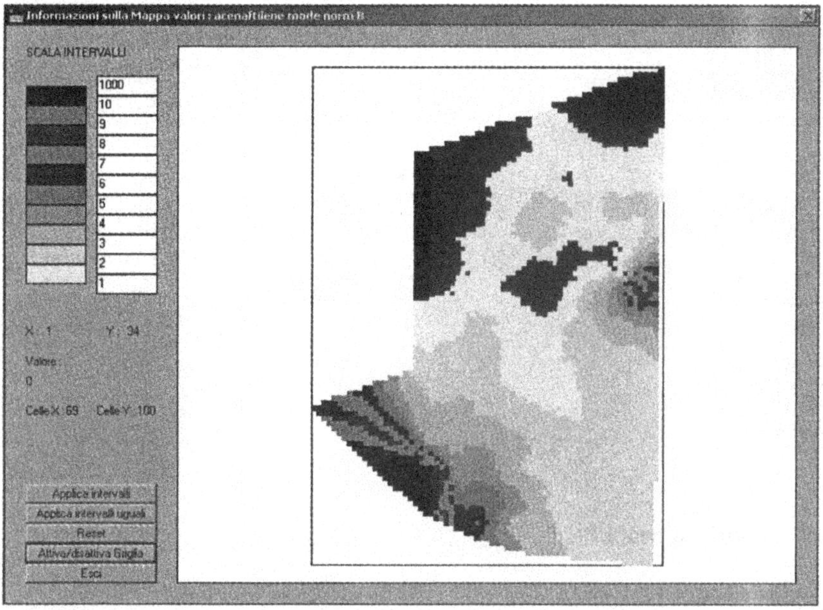

Figure 6.7 Threshold map after the legal limit for B-type sites (acenaphthylene)

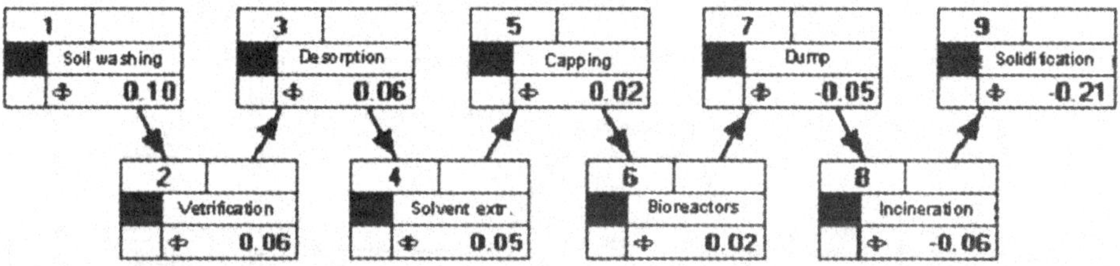

Figure 6.8 Prométhée outranking

4. *Calculating final performances*; namely, financial cost, environmental merit, and risk reduction according to each reclamation process under evaluation (fourth module, REC[14]). In the end, each reclamation process is described by the three min-max criteria.
5. *A cellular automata model* is designed with appropriate rules to capture spatial effects such as change of prices/rents on the market, urban quality indexes, land use opportunities and alike (fifth module, AuReS[15]).
6. *Information for a social cost-benefit analysis* transforming, whenever possible, financial costs into economic costs, based on correction factors[16], and estimating social and environmental benefits with the help of a contingent evaluation

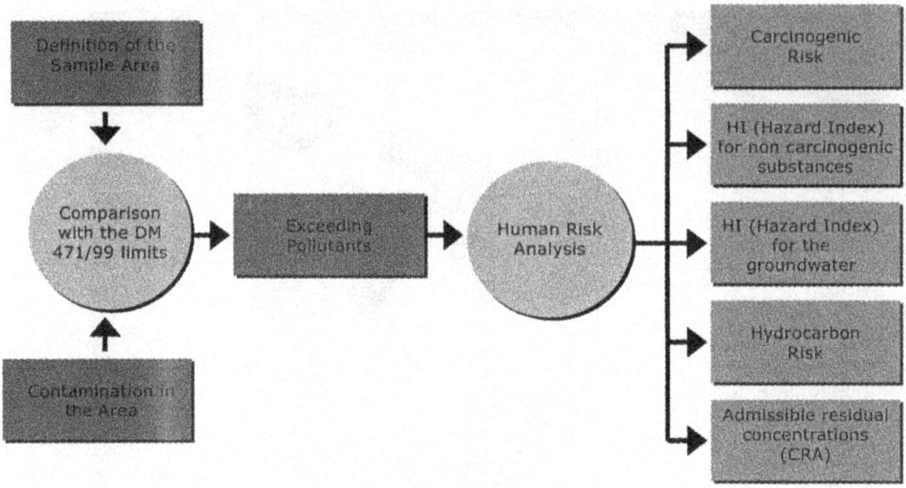

Figure 6.9 Giuditta module

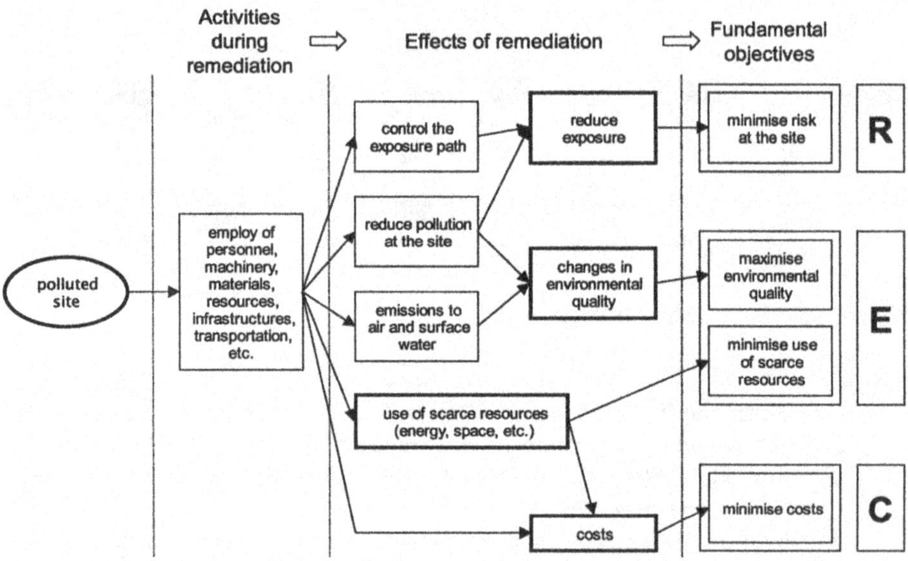

Figure 6.10 REC module

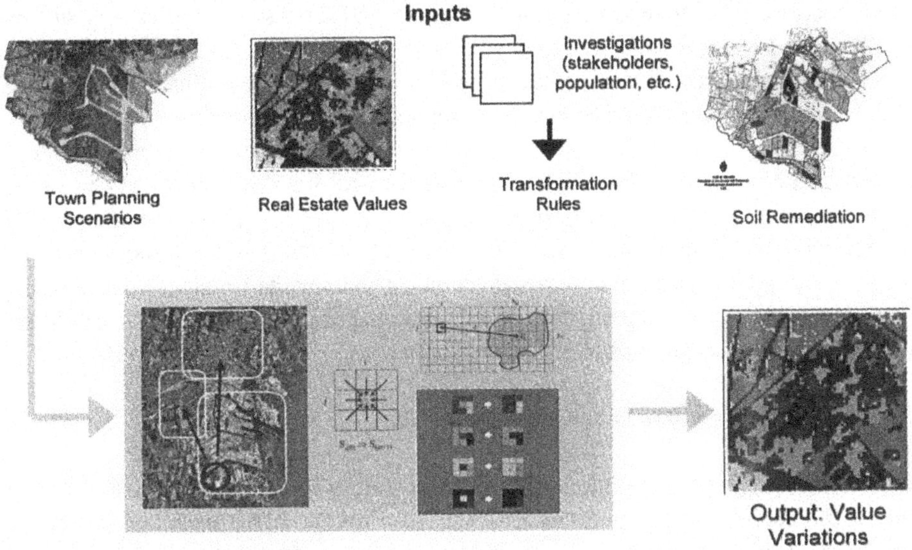

Figure 6.11 AURES module

analysis[17] on urban population and economic investors.

The first four modules have already been tested in a sample area of 43 hectares (the so-called *43-Hectares* area) with environmental characterization data provided by the Municipality of Venice and the 2002 Master Plan under discussion. The fifth module (AuReS) is still in the design stage, while the full implementation of the last (sixth) one depends upon the outcome of planned contingent analysis.

The procedure and its uses

ELGIRA uses and produces information for the selecting of reclamation techniques that would be effective in the specific context, elaborating via scenarios of future activity use of the site and the presence of polluting agents, the multi-objective functions that would bring about compromise solutions acceptable to the stakeholder. The basic information produced by the DSS is fundamental to the way in which the multi-objective functions are assessed, purpose for which the CORILA research project was designed. This process generates additional information, however, and it is on this information that we will now direct our attention, emphasising how evaluation produces not just mere judgment values, but knowledge (i.e. intangible assets) that is decisive in the construction of effective redevelopment strategies for the area.

Up till now, access to information regarding Porto Marghera has been limited so as to conceal facts that recent legal reports have only in part revealed (Benatelli, Favaro and Trevisan, 2002), and to defend privileges and positions within the monopoly of the reconversion strategies (Bettin and Danese, 2002). Two examples may suffice to illustrate the point: the availability of the matrices of environmental characterization that were created partly with surveys conducted by the polluters themselves, and the uncertain effectiveness of reclamation technologies, both on-site and off-site. Information regarding these matrices and technologies can easily be manipulated, thus obstructing a clear definition of regulations and liabilities necessary in order to guarantee acceptable thresholds of environmental merit and the construction of the brownfield development market. ELGIRA, albeit with much approximation, attempts to create a transparent course of action by opening the frequent 'black boxes' that are present in this type of procedure, and enabling simulations that would be useful in the reconfiguration of announced scenarios.

From evaluation issues to knowledge assets

One of the values of ELGIRA lies in the opportunity it creates to discuss, contextually, the usefulness and pertinence of the information that it uses and produces. The context itself is created through the effort made to render the procedure transparent, through comparison with instances and knowledge pertaining to fields other than those industrial, and through the spreading of the scenarios to include natural and inhabited surrounding environments.

Actions that create knowledge assets originate in the information domain of the model, and concern the following aspects in particular:

1. The construction of reconversion scenarios and urban redevelopment policies;
2. The plausibility of the reclamation processes, especially as regards multi-actor sharing and environmental merit;
3. The meaningfulness of the environmental characterization matrix, its control and updating;
4. The construction of a land information system able to carry out dynamic monitoring of the state of the environment, preferably in 3D;
5. The analysis of health and environmental hazards; clarifying meanings and implications of residual risk;
6. The creating of regulations of behaviour and liabilities that are comprehensible to the developing market;
7. Feedback on the input scenarios that activate the risk thresholds and reclamation processes;
8. Relations between localized and widespread effects;
9. A definition of the benefits of reclamation, including not only monetary, but local. Social and general benefits;
10. The risks connected to decriminalisation of environmental crimes;
11. Engagement between various disciplines, risk perception, and trust in the reclamation and development processes.

The construction of reconversion scenarios and urban redevelopment policies

The Master Plan seems unable to rid itself of the 'dead wood' of the past, and this is due not so much to the industrial-logistic choices, but rather to the lack of two fundamental considerations. The first lies in a careful study of the city in its entirety: the implications of a bi-polar structure as proposed by the Benevolo MP[18]; the danger that Venice might 'slide towards the sea'; the implications of when Mestre realizes the role it could play and abandons its hitherto role imposed by the industrial growth of Porto Marghera and the exodus of industries and families from the lagoon area; relations within the metropolitan area and so on (Andriolo and Patassini, 2000). The second consideration concerns the scenarios. Since the MP does not utilize scenarios as instruments of urban design, it is deprived of the possibility to hypothesise along the lines of 'what would happen if ...?', of recognizing where points of view may meet or diverge.

B. Secchi (2002) offers a synthetic but effective definition of scenario. 'Scenario is a polysemic and overall term which has acquired different meanings throughout both the history of the theatre and of weather forecasting. It is often used in a very approximative way and has become the term with which one refers to a more or less certain future, be it good or bad. Some of these images, immersed in and overtaken by differing forms of rhetoric, claimed by varying groups of actors, constructed with participant or technocratic procedures, have connotations of possible and evasive "*escape routes from the present*". Other images tend to be mere representations of current trends and yet others of documented courses which are then proposed to both small and large collective groups. Some indeed assume the features of visions, of representations which often allude to all the demands and wishes that pervade society, at one level or another. And finally there are those that are actual scenarios, those that really attempt to answer the question "what would happen if ...?". In this case the enquiry is into what would happen should these phenomena reach their extreme or probable consequences and future images are created — scenarios — which are partially incompatible with each other. It is this very incompatibility that renders them interesting, however'[19]. If the scenario is a compromise between projection, forecast and wish, then it becomes possible to recognize the stability, the uncertainty, the under- or over-determination.

The future of Porto Marghera may be evoked by many images: an industrial city in a post-Ford era, a city of the sciences, an open city, a city of new, contemporary mixes, and the return of the natural environment via courageous land renovation[20]. The MP seems to keep these aspects in the twilight, however, due to its sectorial nature; and neither does it seem to engage with the Urban Transformation Charter (Carta delle trasformazioni urbane)[21] or the construction of the new Strategic Plan. An effort must be made to amend this — and ELGIRA would be a beneficiary, since it is activated by reclamation scenarios which are anchored to destined land use and therefore allows for comparative analysis and interventions on multiple evaluation parameters.

Through analyses of sensitivity and robustness, and taking into account the feasible compromises between cost, risk, and environmental merit, ELGIRA is able to redefine the scenarios themselves, and it could act as a bridge between the MP and the Strategic Plan. Integration of these plans brings about further opportunities: a) redevelopment thus becomes a sort of 'compensation' (albeit overdue) for the territories and populations that have been damaged for so long; b) it is of help in the choice of reclamation strategies (either preventive or parallel) in that it aids relations between the territorial, municipal, sectorial, and political plans proposed by the administrations[22].

Plausibility of the reclamation processes

The plausibility of the reclamation processes addresses two objectives: one as concerns the direct and indirect effects on stakeholders, and the other from the point of view of environmental merit — a proxy (that can be improved) of sustainability. These objectives may be in conflict. Reclamation processes are complex activities of strategic significance, as can be identified in the ELGIRA procedure. Specific interventions of reclamation are enacted alongside regeneration and development processes within which it is possible to negotiate the interests of public and private investors via the use of operative scenarios of the plan. Several issues are thus raised, such as: how should reclaim strategies be assessed, internalizing the expectations of the investors and the scenarios of the plan, and therefore going beyond the criteria of technique screening? What should be the course of action when moving from small sites to mega sites?

The MP indicates how the type and the concentration of the polluting agents in Porto Marghera reduce the range of applicable technologies to those illustrated in Figure 6.8 at p. 97. The table describes a possible complete system[23] of techniques as suggested in the MP, related to the fixed and variable criteria of the polluting agents. The first criteria refer to the market supply of the technique, to the surface type of the sort of work necessary and to the availability of the area, to the timing of treatment and to the environmental impact. The second or variable criteria refer to operational costs and the effectiveness of pollution reduction. The symbol Φ indicates the outranking flow: if positive, it expresses how much each alternative is outranking the others (the higher, the better); if negative, it expresses how much each alternative is outranked by all the others (Brans and Mareschal, 1994; p. 301). The environmental merit of usable techniques varies, and indicates to what extent the compromise between costs and residual risk can be pushed.

Meaningfulness of the environmental characterization matrix and its updating

In the tests carried out to date, no geological ground model, fundamental to the study of the propagation of pollutants, has been used, and neither has the reliability of the environmental characterization been verified. The characterization matrix reveals, however, some uncertainties that influence the plausibility and effectiveness of the reclamation scenarios.

Taking into consideration just the sample area where ELGIRA was applied (the 43-Hectares area), the following problems came to light: partial coverage, time-limited application and limited reliability of surveys, varying effectiveness in two- and three-dimensional representation (though tri-dimensional representation was not carried out), inability to gather information regarding relations between the concentration and propagation of the polluting agents, and differing interpolation methods for the estimating of missing data. The application of the procedure to other areas that are less homogeneous and more strategic could reveal further problems. At a first, and extremely concise glance, the main limitations appear to be:

- The lack of system in the gathering of statistical data;
- The variability of the logs in terms of data on polluting agents , depth, etc.;
- Difficulty in following the propagation effects, due to the hydro-geological characteristics of the terrain;
- Reliability of collected data;
- The lack of a three-dimensional and integrated model of the ground;
- The lack of a protocol for the gathering of statistical data and continuous monitoring.

Dealing with these points calls for interpolations created with the cellular automaton MoDe, the values of which should anyway be treated with caution. This mode could be improved, even in this set up, in that:

- Reducing to 2D is useful (though may be made more efficient) before passing on to 3D;
- Vertical interpolation may be anchored to average or maximum (conservative) values or to more precise stratigraphic data;
- Geo-statistics may enable analysis of spatial correlation and relative tests[24].

Under these circumstances the subject of validation of characterization data may be taken into consideration, and an answer found to the question: how may risk analysis be detached from characterization?

Construction of a land information system capable of dynamic monitoring of the state of the environment and the conditions of risk

The current Land Information System (SIS — Sistema Informativo dei Suoli) is a starting point as regards a description of the area and management of the reclamation processes and their results. ELGIRA utilizes the SIS data as input, but may supplement it with intermediate and final output that, within a general-purpose geo-spatial information system, could modify the design and functioning of the SIS.

Analysis of health and environmental hazards — the meanings and implications of residual risk

Health hazards are assessed using the Giuditta module, and environmental risks are evaluated via REC (Risk; Environment; Cost). It is already possible to make a strategic risk analysis by working on the reclamation options and the stakeholders' objectives. This sort of analysis would be made easier, as would the zoning of risk (in terms of reclamation scenarios, regeneration, and development) by placing ELGIRA in a GIS environment and linking it to plans and programmes.

The first results show a great deal of difference in risk between industrial and residential hypotheses in proportion to the prescriptive environmental quality thresholds in Italy. These differences in effect individuate the variation intervals that are reduced to mixed redevelopment scenarios, and this is what would happen in the hypothesis that Porto Marghera opens up to the city and the lagoon. The test results also suggest other considerations.

No reclamation process can be completely risk-free, and no scenario is either; not even that which limits the naturalness of the lagoon area restoration to how it was at the beginning of the twentieth century[25]. In the words of U. Beck (2002): 'as for the ecological risks … we must reflect on the way in which trust between the industries and the consumers, laypeople and experts, science and critical public opinion can be renewed; for instance, via a "transparent chemistry" that lays its cards on the table of public opinion. It will be essential to recognize the difference (of immense political importance) between calculable risk and non-calculable uncertainty. Thus the following question is raised: who must decide, and with what authority, if no-one knows for sure the consequences of a decision, but can intuit that the bases of life and cohabitation will be touched by it?' Beck, by acknowledging the opportuneness of a '*culture of uncertainty*' that breaks with the taboo of the '*culture of residual risk*' on the one hand and a '*culture of certainty*' on the other, sees in uncertainty an element of freedom. 'This presupposes that there is willingness to debate and reform openly and publicly the bases of our approach to risk … The choice is between differing risk situations, often also … between alternatives that are of different dimensions and values and therefore difficult to compare' (Beck, 2002).

Virilio, in his 'Unknown Quantity' (2002) seems to approach the idea of the culture of uncertainty, in that he shows how in every invention is implicit the catastrophe that it could cause, and how that catastrophe is an invention as much as the invention that brings it about. A cultural attitude of this kind necessarily suggests a more prudent use of analysis of health and environmental risks, control over the analytic procedures and assessment of the sequential modules in Giuditta and REC, and more generally, of the use of the word 'sustainability' and of the evaluation syntheses themselves.

The creating of regulations of behaviour and liabilities that are comprehensible to the redevelopment market

Reclamation in itself, and the market for reclaimed land should be cause for reflection regarding the plans for the land along the lagoon, and more generally, on the reconversion of abandoned areas and the use of the territory for industrial purposes. Programmes and strategies for rehabilitating contaminated real estate are quite rightly focussed on transaction modality and relative costs, equity participation, clean-up standards and verification, reclamation loans and grants, assurances, eligibility and liabilities, financial assistance, and the like. These are all factors that play a crucial part in putting back on the market a resource that has hitherto been stigmatised and that risks being otherwise destined to a 'poor' use. The Porto Marghera area needs more, however; a design that is capable of accommodating mixes, and is willing to accept new settlements in the lagoon area, as indeed has happened elsewhere.

The good functioning of ELGIRA depends on how the reclamation and redevelopment programmes are managed; in other words, it is not limited to producing systems of techniques based on monetary or non-monetary performance, but aims at responding to the questions raised by an expanding market, wherein few subjects still operate who are capable of keeping together the planning and design of reclamation interventions. Amongst the problems that weigh most greatly on the design and functioning of ELGIRA at Porto Marghera, three seem to have most importance: a) the so-called operative technological sequence; b) costs; and c) the integrated management of the reclamation plan for redevelopment, affording the possibility of forming STUs, i.e. *Società di Trasformazione Urbana* (Urban Transformation Companies).

The operative technological sequence is created in response to the queries: Who is going to pay? Who is going to plan? Who is going to carry it out? As shown in the PRUSST (Urban Redevelopment and Sustainable Development Projects)[26] experience in Bari, 'the plan for the area destined for reclamation and all that is necessary for the clean-up operation obviously go well beyond the possibilities and the duties of the proprietor and the municipality; one could start with the responsibilities for the approval of the planning stages, as set out by law, which lie with the Ministry of the Environment', which in turn interacts with the specific Region, and the ministries of Industry, Trade, Artisan Industry, and Health (Pagliata, 2002). Special evaluation must also be made of the 'keys in hand' procedures, as well as the possibility that engineering firms specialized in reclamation[27] might operate on a prime contractor basis, then subcontracting out specific tasks.

Listed below are some of the more desirable operative conditions, as highlighted by the urban redevelopment programmes in Milan in 1997.

1. 'Carry out the reclamation work as soon as possible so that building may start within the time stipulated by the financing agreements, both public and private; otherwise the risk is to lose economic interest in the project and not achieve complete recovery' (Raimondi, 2002; pp. 48-49).
2. Present a detailed town plan that takes into consideration potential contamination from previous activities.
3. Avoid conflict between reclamation planning and town planning (avoid planning for green areas in the most contaminated areas, which would involve the risk of necessary variations and a lengthening of the whole project; ensure, where possible, that foundation works are carried out on sites that have been partially excavated for reclamation works; ensure that reclamation works and building works are concurrent).
4. Juxtapose, if possible, the two work yards. There are 'cases in which avail-

able financial resources for land reclamation are directly linked to the timing and the phases of the operations. Reclamation operations are often instigated by a private owner, who perhaps has bought the land in question aware of his/her obligation to carry out reclamation, but who does not in fact have any legal responsibility for the contamination of the area. Legislation has produced differing interpretations, in fact, on the questions of reclamation duties and owner obligations in contaminated areas, and these variations at times result in conditioning the positions taken by the local administrations and the private owners'(Raimondi, 2002; p.48). An interesting case in point is the experience of Rho-Pero[28] in the area of the former *Agip Petroli* refinery, where the new Milan Trade Fair site will be built. 'On the basis of detailed planning documents, indispensable information has been acquired which affords an evaluation of the possible juxtaposition of the two work yards, thus guaranteeing efficiency in the work of reclamation and monitoring, while at the same time ensuring conditions of safety for the workers on the building site. Fiera Milano[29] and Agip Petroli have identified the direct and indirect interferences of the two yards, and proposed the most suitable mitigation and compensation activities through the adoption of a series of executive expedients, such as realization techniques, management plans for the reclaimed land, protocols for the safeguarding of the environment and personnel' (Raimondi, 2002; p.49).
5. Management of excavated material.

Another important question of course is that of costs. The 2002 MP for Porto Marghera is a basic request document for public funding. As established by Law 426 of 1998, state funding for reclaim projects can cover up to 50 per cent of the costs. The average hectare cost has been estimated in the MP as 1.3 million euros, whereas the average price per hectare of industrial land is 1 million euros (100 euros per square metre). The difference between the two sums ids of obvious advantage to the industrial investor. The problem, however, lies in verifying the economic (and not only financial) return on mixed investments, both in the destinations and in the investors, as happens in integrated processes of redevelopment.

The test on the 43-Hectare site, carried out in 2003, highlights the costs for the five reclamation techniques shown in Table 6.2, where values are expressed in euros with relative confidence intervals. The MP is effectively responsible for initiating the management process and poses the problem of 'what manager, or managers?' Should the single managing entity be the preferred choice, then the STU (Urban Transformation Company) model could be adopted[30]. This is a model of mixed ownership — both public and private — based on the French SEM (*Societé à Economie Mixte*, Mixed Economy Companies) model. Being a particular social concern, this could become a single managing entity in keeping with the explanatory circular, for the following reasons.

1. The mega-site comprises an area between the historical centre and a large part of the mainland post-war urban expansion.
2. The characteristics of the town planning scheme of the area; the strategic rel-

Table 6.2 Cost estimates for reclamation options within the first ELGIRA model run (€, 2002 prices)

Reclaim Technique	Cost	Variation
Capping	5,322,300	± 155,800
Thermic desorption + soil washing	20,387,100	± 682,200
Soil washing (one line)	20,558,700	± 693,200
Soil washing (two lines)	20,558,700	± 693,200
Disposal	45,589,900	± 1,578,200

evance of the foreseen interventions within a territorial context, and not only of the Venetian area; the crisis situation requires (and has requested) variations of the town and regional planning tools; the adoption of specific operational methods for the plan, including agreements, partnerships, service conferences, and so on.

3. The project is particularly complex and of great economic scale, and the public administration intends to include private partners in the scheme both for supplementary financing purposes and for the wealth of knowledge and experience that has been created over the years; the MP refers to a planning agreement (for the chemical industry) drawn up amongst several different subjects.
4. Interventions of re-composition of the fabric of the city, restructuring, recovery of abandoned areas, building and reclamation are all necessary.
5. Ordinary town and regional planning does not have the necessary specific instruments at its disposal (the planning process started in Venice utilizes various instruments, not just those of town and regional planning). The crucial point is the relationship between transformation interventions (which are dictated by the 2002 MP) and ordinary instruments, particularly the MP, which in this case has Revised MP approval. The Urban Transformation Companies can carry out interventions with the use of current town planning instruments although they may not be the appropriate ones. They work at an operative and not structural level, in the disciplinary meaning of the term. Porto Marghera amply satisfies the minimum requisite for urban recovery aimed at remedying the lack of public spaces and services.
6. Given the size, the unitary costs should be less than the costs incurred in other, smaller sites.
7. The ground ownership is not fragmented. The Urban Transformation Companies could unite the owners (especially if they are involved in economic transformation which are both advantageous and of sustainable town planning characteristics) and the building contractors, real estate agencies and banks — and from a viewpoint of project financing, also public and private operators who are interested in buying.
8. The plan should include the building of public residential complexes, the fund-

ing of which should not be less than ten per cent of the total financial resources, both public and private, of the transformation programme (a fundamental consideration for admission to the financing programme)[31]. This requisite would orient the redevelopment project towards a mix of functions that are both productive and logistic, as would emerge from the Revised MP and the MP.

9. Evaluation criteria acknowledge Porto Marghera as an eligible project for the town planning and economic relevance, the presence of abandoned areas, for the public partners and banks involved, and for the amount of private investment in relation to public.

It should be remembered that it is possible to compete in the bidding with an established Urban Transformation Company so that the decision-making board may 'fully perceive the nature and the entity of the interests of the private categories mostly involved, as well as the capabilities and the necessary experience of the economic management of the Urban Transformation Company' (Marraffa, 2002).

Feedback on scenarios of input that activate risk thresholds and reclamation processes

At the end of the ELGIRA procedure, redefinition of the input scenarios can become one of the possible results of the dynamic compromise between cost, risk, and environmental merit. The procedure may take on an interactive nature via the construction of progressive scenarios and the activation of technological sequences. One example of interesting feedback might be that which addresses the query: is the health and risk assessment related to specific land use, or to the total value of the land[32]?

Relations between localized and widespread effects

For ELGIRA, being able to capture the widespread effects of the immediate surroundings of the reclamation area is of great importance, the main reasons being a reduction in the stigma attached to the area, the recovery of the site in question, and urban development and environmental safeguarding — all of which are implicit objectives in establishing perimeters for this Site of National Interest which measures 5,000 hectares — over double the surface area of Porto Marghera itself. The process used is, for the moment, uni-directional; i.e. from the lot to the context. Stated and revealed preferences, willingness to pay for shared scenarios and regulations for the propagation of the effects (for instance, the effects on the market values or on the indicators of environmental impact) could lead to the procedure becoming bi-directional, but this depends on the intelligence of the cellular automaton (AuReS) and the control of typical biases in the contingent analysis. This latter consideration refers in particular to the effects of conditioned response, such as the tendency towards hidden replies, the hinting at values at stake, the indeterminate nature of the contingent scenario (Mitchell and Carson, 1989). This exercise allows for more general reflection on the possibility and the sense of capturing spatial effects or the external effects of localized interventions in an urban context.

A definition of the benefits of reclamation, including not only monetary, but local, social, and general benefits

Given the complex history of Porto Marghera and its cycle that is 'independent' of the context, stigma reduction is clearly one of the most important objectives of the reclamation policies. Stigma reduction would consist of the creation of new opportunities, not restricted to a merely local level. These opportunities would entail the enriching of contextual understanding, and the benefits, only partially calculated by ELGIRA and not of a monetary nature, that may be transformed with the aid of contingent analysis and analysis of the preferences of the developers. The end result could produce an SCBA (Social Cost-Benefit Analysis) balance, with differentiated cash flow à la CIA/E (Community Impact Analysis/Evaluation).

The risks connected to the decriminalisation of environmental crimes

The results that emerge from ELGIRA are directly linked to legal indices and parameters, which, if modified, change the performance of the reclamation strategies. A comparative analysis of the results at an international level (keeping all the rest unchanged) may highlight how risk perception limits and criminal or administrative sanctions could change.

With appropriate adjustments, ELGIRA would be able to evaluate the effects of decriminalisation as proposed by the Italian Minister for Justice at the beginning of 2003. The proposal is in countertendency as regards the European Union in that the Council of Ministers and the European Commission declared in January 2003: 'an effective penal sanction, be it proportional or dissuasive is indicative of social reprobation which is qualitatively different from administrative sanctions or civil rights compensation mechanisms'. Crimes cited in the text of the 'decision staff' of the European Council of Ministers that are criminally culpable include the dispersal of life-threatening toxic substances, illegal elimination of dangerous waste that may provoke serious damage to persons, fauna and territory, and the illegal operating of plants that carry out dangerous activities. All member nations, furthermore, have undertaken to introduce crimes against the environment into the penal code within two years. With the use of ELGIRA, an evaluation is possible of how, despite decriminalisation, the crime may be rendered non-remunerative at a social and not just 'individual' level.

Different disciplines and the difficulty in engaging and encounter

ELGIRA combines various disciplines, mostly at a technical level, that have knowledge to contribute. Within the town and regional planning project, there will be an increase in the occasions for confrontation and dialogue among these disciplines. It is, in fact, 'to be hoped that the variables due to the choice of technical reclamation instruments are integrated into the planning process; variables such as those relating to the ground regeneration processes' (Alonzi, 2002). The main points of contact between reclamation techniques and territorial planning would seem to be the following:

- Ground regeneration by means of reconfiguration of the physical structure, in such a way that the landscape may become the principal object of transformation produced by the reclamation operations and that the 'contemporary' characteristic of a heavy industrial landscape may be thus enhanced;
- Wide scale redesigning, prevention of high risk production processes, management of the reclamation processes, and monitoring (these four actions should be linked);
- Spatial experimentation, with the formation of new landscapes (a synergy between reclamation techniques, industrial landscapes, and mixes).

Flexibility

ELGIRA, being an instrument of knowledge and orientation, increases its explorative and evaluation usefulness when it has a certain degree of system flexibility. Each module has its own flexibility, especially when the knowledge required is not standardized. It highlights conflictive points of view or works out uncertain parameters. It deals primarily with the construction of reclamation scenarios referring to town and regional planning instruments and the Strategic Plan, to the Master Plan and its suggested course of action, to the investors, and to the city user. ELGIRA does not utilize only fixed scenarios; it can modify and update them whenever necessary.

A second variable factor is that of the technologies deployed and their usage. It might be reasonably easy to assess the compromise between cost, risk, and environmental merit for a single reclamation technological method, but when there is a combination of technologies a revision of the entire process may be necessary, along with an updating of many parameters and evaluation criteria. The effectiveness and the efficiency of a technological train might lead to synergies that otherwise would be impossible.

A third flexibility component refers to value functions behind costs, risks, and merit; these vary according to contingencies, expectations, and stakeholder strategies.

6.5 Conclusion

ELGIRA, on first testing, has proved to be a valuable instrument of cost/benefit analysis to do with reclamation and redevelopment projects. It offers reliable input (albeit open to improvement) for research into prescriptions that can become the basis for compromise. Apart from its instrumental use, however, ELGIRA aids reflection on the plausibility of reclamation operations, the acceptance of these operations by the institutions and the communities involved, and on the problems of configuration of a new property market — at least in Italy.

Notes

1 Translation from the Italian: Judith McGrath.

2 CORILA Research Project 2000-04, Line of research 1.1 *Economic evaluation of environmental heritage*, Project: *Economic evaluation of environmental safeguarding and protection in the Venetian lagoon.* Main contractor DSE-UNIVE, Workpackage 3 (IUAV-DP), *Cost-benefit analysis of reclaim activities in the polluted sites.*

3 Editor's note: see Note 3 at p. 200 (Fusco Girard, Cerreta and De Toro, here) for details on Italian case studies.

4 Re. the economic self-sufficiency of Porto Marghera see G. Ernesti (2001; in particular pp. 52-69), 'Venice From the Land, Venice From the Sea. City and Port in the Industrial Age'. As regards the role of Petrolchimica from a historical perspective, also see L. Pes (2002), 'A History of Venice. The last forty years 1961-2001'. On the beginnings and the development of the port and the urbanization of Marghera see also G. Zucconi (2002; ed., in particular pp. 19-72), 'Greater Venice. An incompleted metropolis between the nineteenth and the twentieth centuries'; S. Romano (1979), 'Giuseppe Volpi. Industry and finance from Giolitti to Mussolini'.

5 The national environmental clean-up and rehabilitation programme concerns fifty sites, the so-called *Siti di Interesse Nazionale* (Sites of National Interest). Among the most interesting ones, there are Venice, Taranto, Brindisi, Sesto San Giovanni (near Milan), Turin, Bari, La Spezia, Naples, Gela (Sicily), and Manfredonia (Apulia). See also P. Colletta, R. Manzo and A. Spaziante (2002; eds.) 'Planning of the territory and technological risk — The DM of 9 May 2001. Urbanization control in areas subject to major-accident hazard'.

6 It has been calculated that the probable investment in a ten-year period would amount to 1,550 million euros, as of when the plans and consequent interventions for landscape redevelopment actually come into effect.

7 Porto Marghera developed as a closed pole, containing much of the supplier-client productive cycle, infrastructures for the providing of basic commodities, the port, the production of energy; see P. Costa (1972), 'The port in Venetian economics today'.

8 When the destination is that of mere warehousing and movement.

9 In Venetian dialect 'el gira' means 'it works'.

10 Where necessary, survey values are interpolated with the MoDe cellular automaton.

11 Électre II was utilized (a technique based on tests for sub-classing) and then compared with Prométhée, which has more severe response functions. The two systems do not present substantial differences.

12 Delphi, nominal group techniques, and alike could be easily applied to test properties of criteria set and their weighting.

13 Giuditta is a program for IT-driven management of environmental tolerability. The software has been co-produced by the General Department for the Environment (soil, subsoil, and industrial risk office) of the Milan Province Administration and the local branch of the international engineering and consulting company URS Dames & Moore. Other procedures are also available, such as ROME, RBCA, and alike. See also the Giuditta (http://www.provincia.milano.it/ambiente/bonifiche/giuditta_deng.shtml), ROME (http://www.sinanet.anpa.it/aree/Geosfera/Suolo/ROME2.asp), and RBCA Tool Kit (http://

www.gsi-net.com/software/RBCAtoolKitForChemRelease.htm) web sites for details.

14 REC, or RMK in the original version in the Dutch language, deals with three aspects, each of which is marked by one of the three letters that make up the acronym of the model: 'R' for risk reduction, 'E' for environmental merit, and 'C' for financial cost of soil reclaim.

15 AuReS is a self-produced cellular automata software useful for the simulation value transformation of land, real estate, environmental quality, opportunities, and preferences in both bordering and neighbouring polluted areas.

16 A correction factor is a ratio between economic and financial price of cost or benefit item.

17 A contingent analysis has been designed and will be implemented during 2004.

18 The 1999 Revision of the Mestre City Master Plan had been co-ordinated by L. Benevolo, Architect, hence it is often also referred to as the *Benevolo MP*.

19 See also L. Vettoretto (2001), 'Scenarios: an introduction, some cases and some perspectives'.

20 On land renovation and methods for territorial planning, see P. L. Cervellati (2000), 'The art of city care'.

21 The Charter contains and describes 'programmes and projects which due to their importance are destined to produce transformations in territorial uses and functions, and provide the communication and monitoring of those spin-offs which have effects on the territorial and urban organization'.

22 In Venice there are numerous town and regional planning instruments, both ordinary and complex. In other contexts, reclaim is a component of PRUSST (*Programmi di Riqualificazione Urbana e di Sviluppo Sostenibile del Territorio*, Urban Redevelopment and Sustainable Development Programmes), PRU (*Piani di Recupero Urbano*, Urban Renewal Plans), or planning agreements (*accordi di programma*).

23 The system is built with *Decision Lab 2000* software from Visual Decision Inc., Montréal, Québec (Canada), which develops an interactive decision support system based on the Prométhée and Gaia methodology. See J. P. Brans and B. Mareschal (1994), 'The PROMCALC & GAIA decision support system for multicriteria decision aid'.

24 See *Spacestat* software, developed by L. Anselin, University of Illinois at Urbana-Champaign, USA.

25 According to this scenario, the work group led by P. Leon from CLES at Rome estimated that compensation for environmental damage caused by the Porto Marghera industries to the quality of water, underground tables, the ground, wildlife, the lagoon sediment, and air quality would amount to 71,000 billion Italian lira (about 35 million euros). It has been estimated that the Montedison group, proprietors of Petrolchimica from 1971 to 1981 will be asked to pay 11/25 of the total compensation sum. M. Cartosio (2001), 'How much does Porto Marghera cost?'.

26 See Note 22.

27 Category G3 (ex S22).

28 Rho and Pero are two towns located respectively at 14 and 9 km west of Milan.

29 Translator's note: *Fiera Milano* is 'a group of several companies which runs exhibition areas, organizes shows and conferences, and supplies all promotional and fair services'. Citation from the Fiera Milano web site (http://www.fieramilano.it).

30 Article 17 (59), Law 127 of 1997, Explanatory Circular of Article 120 DLgs 267 of 18 August 2000, Public competition announcement attached to the Ministerial Decree of 6 June 2001 'Promozione delle Società di tasformazione urbana' (Promotion of Urban Transformation Companies).

31 Article 5 on procedures.

32 Total value includes use, exchange, option, and bequest values.

References

Alonzi, S. (2002), 'Tecniche di bonifica tra sapere scientifico e progetto di paesaggio' (Reclaim techniques within the frameworks of scientific knowledge and landscape planning), in S. Alonzi and A. Marin, *Bonifica dei suoli contaminati e progetto di paesaggio*, (Contaminated ground reclaim and landscape planning), *Urbanistica Informazioni* (Town and Regional Planning Information), No. 186, p. 41.

Andriolo, C. and Patassini, D. (2000), 'Elementi per la costruzione di scenari di mobilità nell'area metropolitana veneziana' (Elements for the construction of mobility scenarios in the Venetian metropolitan area), in P. Pedrocco (ed.), *Un sistema di trasporti metropolitani per Venezia: verso quale futuro?*, (A metropolitan transport system for Venice: a move towards what kind of future?), Centro Provinciale di Studi Urbanistici di Venezia, Ateneo Veneto, Venezia (Italy).

Barbiani, E. (2002), *Cantiere Venezia. Piani, progetti, realizzazioni, imprese* (Building site Venice. Plans, projects, realizations, enterprises), Insula, Marsilio, Venezia (Italy).

Beck, U. (2002), 'Il nuovo terrorismo inaugura la società mondiale del rischio' (The new terrorism inaugurates the world society of risk), *La Repubblica* (Italy), 13 December 2002.

Benatelli, N., Favaro, G. and Trevisan E. (2002), *Processo a Marghera. L'inchiesta sul Petrolchimico, il CVM e le morti degli operai. Storia di una tragedia umana e ambientale* (The Marghera trial. The Petrolchimico enquiry, the CVM and the deaths of the workers. The history of a human and environmental tragedy), Edicilo Editore, Portogruaro (Italy).

Bettin, G. and Danese, M. (2002), *Petrolkiller*, Feltrinelli, Milano (Italy).

Brans, J. P. and Mareschal, B. (1994), 'The PROMCALC & GAIA decision support system for multicriteria decision aid', *Decision Support Systems*, Vol. 12, No. 4-5, pp. 297-310, Elsevier BV, Amsterdam (The Netherlands).

Cartosio, M. (2001), 'Quanto costa Porto Marghera?' (How much does Porto Marghera cost?), *Il Manifesto* (Italy), 29 June 2001, pp. 7.

Cervellati, P. L. (2000), *L'arte di curare la città* (The art of city care), Il Mulino, Bologna (Italy).

Colletta, P., Manzo, R. and Spaziante, A. (eds., 2002), *Pianificazione del territorio e rischio tecnologico — Il DM 9 maggio 2001. Il controllo dell'urbanizzazione nelle aree a rischio d'incidente rilevante* (Planning of the territory and technological risk — The DM of 9 May 2001. Urbanization control in areas subject to major-accident hazard), Celid, Torino (Italy).

Costa, P. (1972), 'Il porto nell'economia veneziana, oggi' (The port in Venetian economics today), *Urbanistica*, No. 59-60, p. 109.

Ernesti, G. (2001), 'Venezia da terra, Venezia da mar. Città e porto nell'età dell'industria' (Venice From the Land, Venice From the Sea. City and Port in the Industrial Age), in AA.VV. (various authors), *Venezia: guida al porto*, (Venice: A Guide to the Port), Autorità portuale di Venezia (Venice Port Authority), Marsilio, Venezia (Italy).

Marraffa, R. (2002), 'Le Società di trasformazione urbana dalla prima alla seconda selezione' (Urban Transformation Companies — first and second selection), *Urbanistica Informazioni* (Town and Regional Planning Information), No. 186, pp. 69-71.

Mitchell, R. C. and Carson, R. T. (1989), *Using Surveys to Value Public Goods: The Contingent Valuation Method*, Resources for the Future, Washington, DC (USA).

Pagliata, A. (2002), 'Il PRUSST e l'amianto' (PRUSST and asbestos), *Urbanistica Informazioni* (Town and Regional Planning Information), No. 186, p. 47.

Patassini, D. et al. (2003), *El.Gi.R.A. A knowledge support procedure for the Porto Marghera brownfields (Venice), Methodology and Application of the '43 hectares area' (version 7.6, April 2003)*, CORILA, Venezia (Italy).

Pes, L. (2002), 'Storia di Venezia. Gli ultimi quarant'anni 1961-2001' (A History of Venice. The last forty years 1961-2001), in M. Insenghi (ed.), *Storia di Venezia. L'Ottocento e il Novecento*, (A History of Venice. The eighteenth and nineteenth centuries), Tomo III, *Il Novecento*, Istituto dell'Enciclopedia Italiana, Roma (Italy).

Pugliese, T. (ed., 2003), *Piano strategico città di Venezia, documento n. 10 (bozza)* (Strategic plan city of Venice, document no 10, draft), Comune di Venezia (Municipality of Venice), Italy.

Pugliese, T. (ed., 1996), 'La pianificazione urbanistica come strumento di politica industriale. La Variante al PRG per Porto Marghera' (Town and regional planning as an industrial policy. The Revised Master Plan for Porto Marghera), *Urbanistica Quaderni* (Town and Regional Planning Essays), No. 9, COSES, Venezia (Italy).

Raimondi, P. (2002), 'Bonifica e riuso nel milanese' (Reclaim and re-use in the Milan area), *Urbanistica Informazioni* (Town and Regional Planning Information), No. 186, pp. 48-49.

Romano, S. (1979), *Giuseppe Volpi. Industria e finanza tra Giolitti e Mussolini* (Giuseppe Volpi. Industry and finance from Giolitti to Mussolini), Bompiani, Milano (Italy).

Secchi, B. (2002), 'New territories: Scenari' (Scenarios), *IUAV — Giornale d'istituto* (IUAV — Institute's journal), No. 14.

Vettoretto, L. (2001), 'Scenari: un'introduzione, dei casi e alcune prospettive' (Scenarios: an introduction, some cases and some perspectives), *Quaderno del Dottorato di Urbanistica* (Doctorate Essays in Town and Regional Planning), No. 1, December, IUAV-DU, Venezia (Italy).

Virilio, P. (2002), *Ce qui arrive* (Unknown Quantity), Galilée, Paris (France). English edition by *Ce qui arrive* (Unknown Quantity), Thames & Hudson, London (UK), 2003.

Zucconi, G. (2002), *La grande Venezia. Una metropoli incompiuta tra Otto e Novecento* (Greater Venice. An incompleted metropolis between the nineteenth and the twentieth centuries), Marsilio, Venezia (Italy).

PART II
METHODOLOGICAL APPROACHES: NEW STRATEGIES

Chapter 7

Towards Social Value for Money

Nathaniel Lichfield

7.1 Introduction

The market is a mechanism for facilitating the exchange of goods and services for money. As such, the transaction identifies a money figure for the price which the seller is offering and the purchaser is accepting. In this each side is seeking 'value for money' in his terms. By definition the market price indicates what each of the parties to the transaction accepts as 'value for money'. But by definition, the market price ignores the externalities in the transaction, namely those costs to others which the buyer need not take into account and the benefits which he cannot enjoy. These costs and benefits exist outside the transaction, and are commonly termed social costs and benefits. Their addition to the direct cost and benefit creates the concept of 'social value'. This chapter focuses on the identification of such social value in practice.

The need to take into account natural and social resources when valuing human well being and evaluating related development strategies seems to question traditional approaches to valuation of assets and valuation of actions. A still dominant focus on market inter-actions and the parallel neglecting of non-market ones, seem to hinder our understanding of the complex paths of development as well as the role of human physical resources in this context. While the contributions to this book discuss the issues outlined here assuming different perspectives, this contribution employs an economic perspective.

Why is social value for money important?

The reason for pursuing value for money in economic analysis was classically formulated by Lionel Robbins (1932) when describing economics as the 'science which studies human behaviour as a relationship between ends and scarce means which have alternative ends'. This is predicated on observations of economic life, which show that in it 'ends' (socio-economic objectives) are, in contemporary culture, seemingly illimitable in terms of human needs and desires. And yet in each case there are only scarce means for satisfying them with the resources typically available to the individual, organization or government. In this sense 'scarce resources' are not necessarily seen in absolute terms (e.g. in land), but in the sense of resources not being sufficient to satisfy all the 'ends' with which the particular decision maker is faced. The decision maker would have to use what resources are available to provide for those 'ends' that maximize human welfare. Within this context, socio-economic analysis is employed to examine the relationships between the value of the output which will be achieved by any particular decision, against the costs of the input needed to achieve that output. The aim is to find the best possible, or the optimal, amongst the options. By definition this should achieve the maximization of human welfare.

Whereas this approach can be applied to socio-economic analysis of all entities in the economy, not all decision making units will have the same approach to the benefits and costs that result from that decision. At one extreme will be the individual, be he or she a producer or consumer, who is concerned with direct or private costs and benefits to himself or herself, but not with the indirect or social costs and benefits to others, which are implicit in that decision. These are the externalities, or spill overs. But a family man might decide also to take into account the benefits and the costs falling on all his family as a result of his decision, for example in the use of the one family car as between himself and his wife. Going further, a local authority could also take into account, in considering a new swimming pool, the direct value to be derived by the swimmers (including pleasure, health, etc.), and the indirect value of keeping children off the streets, as against the direct costs to be incurred which are distributed throughout the local authority area, through taxation. And equally well, central government would extend its concern to the national economy, thus taking into account benefits to the nation as a whole against the costs via taxation.

Thus the meaning of 'value for money analysis' may vary as its content varies in relation to the context of the decision takers and the benefits and costs they choose to include in their calculus. For the purpose of this contribution we use the term *private value for money* for a private individual or private organization and *social value for money* for that which falls on wider groups in society.

7.2 Exploring the difference between private and social value for money

This exploration could take place by way of theory and principles. But instead we explore it here by reference to a highly pertinent exercise which was carried out by the British Treasury around the end of the year 2002, when reviewing its practices on Central Government appraisal and evaluation of public expenditures. Taking current practice as a starting point in the Treasury *Green Book* (HM Treasury, 1997), they put forward in 2002, following consultation, an amended version with the aim of producing what has been referred to as a *magenta* book. Following is an account of the writer's contributions to the consultation. The paragraph references relate to the documents mentioned:

3. *What are the Green Book and Consultation Draft aiming to do?*

    1. The purpose of the Green Book is to ensure that no policy, programme or project is adopted without first having the answer to the question: 'is this

objective worth the resources which would be spent on it?' The guidance emphasizes the need to take account of the wider social costs and benefits of proposals, and the need to ensure value for money (p. 4, paragraph 2).

2. This is achieved through: identifying other possible approaches which may achieve similar results; performing an economic assessment of the costs and benefits for relevant options; and, wherever feasible, attributing money values to all impacts of any proposed policy, project and programme (p. 4, paragraph 3).
3. The Green Book process of appraisal and evaluation assesses the economic, social, environmental and financial impacts of a policy, programme or project and combines these to provide an overall assessment of how they meet Government objectives (p. 2, paragraph 3).
4. An economic appraisal analyses and measures whether the proposal is worthwhile. The best way to do this is through Cost-Benefit Analysis (CBA), which can be contrasted with Cost-Effectiveness Analysis (p. 7, paragraph 2.1.1).
5. Cost-Benefit Analysis: a term used to describe an analysis, which seeks to quantify in monetary terms as many of the costs and benefits as feasible, including items for which the market does not provide a satisfactory measure of economic value (p. 7, paragraph 2.1.2). The Consultation Draft does not include the Green Book amplification (p. 96) that 'the expression is sometimes confined to these costs and benefits alone and sometimes used to describe an analysis of the welfare costs and benefits' and (p. 100) 'welfare cost or benefit is defined as any effect on human well-being'. But perhaps this is covered in the following in the Consultation Draft (p. 30, paragraph 4.5.5.3):

   'In principle, appraisal should take account of all benefits and costs in the economy. This means that, ideally, as well as taking into account the direct effects of interventions, the wider effects on other areas of the economy aside from those immediately targeted by the policy or project should also be considered. These wider effects can have an impact both on costs and on benefits. It is, however, generally difficult to be accurate about the size of these effects.'
6. Depending on its nature, there may be a need to analyze a proposal to determine whether it may have a differential impact on sections of society. This type of impact is known as a distributional impact (p. 13, paragraph 2.4.4).
7. Options are ranked on the basis of a valuation of their expected net benefits. Ranking identifies a lead option, (that is, the one which most closely matches government objectives (e.g. economic, social, environmental etc.) and provides the required benefits, not simply the lowest cost option) (p. 25, paragraph 4.4.2.1).
8. Cost-Benefit Analysis seeks to identify the overall benefit or cost to society which would be derived from implementing a specific proposal.

It achieves this by measuring and then valuing benefits as well as costs and then subtracting one from the other (benefits minus costs) to obtain an estimate of the net benefit. This value is then discounted to determine present value and is referred to as the 'Net Present Value', or NPV (p. 26, paragraph 4.5.1.1).

9. CBA is the only method of appraisal which is able to show whether a proposal is economically worthwhile and is accordingly the preferred method of appraisal (p. 27, paragraph 4.5.1.8).
10. The main stages in trying to attribute a monetary valuation to impacts are to determine whether:
    A : impacts can be measured, and
    B : prices can be determined from market data
    (p. 27, paragraph 4.5.2.1).
11. Market data must be used to determine values wherever feasible. However, in nearly all assessments, there are impacts, such as environmental, social or health impacts, that have no market price, but which must be included, as they will have an impact on the sustainability of a proposed policy (p. 27, paragraph 4.5.2.2).
12. If prices cannot be readily determined from market data, use 'Willingness To Pay (WTP) for a benefit' (revealed preference). If this does not determine value for a benefit then ask people for stated preference or, in the case of costs, identify Willingness To Accept (WTA). If these techniques cannot be used, can other techniques such as multi-criteria analysis help? (p. 28, Fig. 12).
13. The impacts which cannot be given a monetary value must be listed, with some indication of their scale. If possible, quantitative measures, (such as levels of noise or air pollution) must be included. For example, there are a number of quantitative indices based on loudness, duration and variability of noise levels. (p. 29, paragraph 4.5.4.4). If some costs and benefits remain unvalued, this must be particularly stated and the basis of their appraisal must be in terms of their Cost-Effectiveness (p. 34, paragraph 4.5.5.15), i.e. the comparison of the cost of alternative ways of producing the same or similar outputs which are not given a monetary value (p. 7, paragraph 2.1.2.).
14. An option must be analyzed to determine whether impacts would differ by socio-economic groups. An analysis of the impacts would reveal the degree to which different socio-economic groups in society are, or will be, affected, and whether there is any significant distribution shift in cost and benefits between them, and within, these groups. (p. 48, Section 4.12.1 and 4.1.2.2).

4. *Some limitation in the method of what the Green Book and Draft is aiming to do*

   1. Despite the importance of quantifying the costs and benefits in money

terms only a proportion of valuations are based on market data while the remainder need to rely on non-market data, such as by revealed or stated preferences.

2. The unavoidable result is that a sizeable part of the actual benefit must be described in qualitative terms and separately listed.
3. Because of this limitation, for the time being at least (pending improvements in valuation techniques), there can be no monetary valuation of all benefits, and therefore of overall value for money.
4. It is therefore salutary to ask what is the real worth of the monetary values which will be generated under the Consultation Draft, following the schema in Section 4.5.3, Figure 12. This is an amalgam of value of many different kinds (market data, revealed preference, stated preference, WTA, multi-criteria analysis). This amalgam enables the prime objective to be achieved, namely to derive monetary expression for a summation and conclusion for net benefit.

5. *Overcoming the limitations of the revised Green Book via an improved social cost benefit analysis*

   1. The critical reason for dwelling on the limitations just described is the concern with the consequence of not being able to value in money terms all the benefits, at this stage of current knowledge of monetary valuation techniques. The result is that the benefits valued in money terms, and those not, must be handled separately. Only limited credence can therefore be given to statements about the valued benefits achieving value for money, or about overall value for money.
   2. This weakness can be overcome by using a method devised by the writer named Community Impact Evaluation (CIE). Although termed evaluation this method covers ex ante evaluation (appraisal in the language of the Green Book), and also interim and ex post evaluation.
   3. The essence of the method is to embrace all the costs and benefits which come within the Green Book definition on p. 96, including the welfare costs and benefits. For this reason the method has been described as 'true social cost benefit analysis'.
   4. Before proceeding to describe the method it should be pointed out that it has evolved since first being conceived in 1956 (Lichfield, 1956) under the title of Planning Balance Sheet Analysis and has been worked on since in terms of theory and application to case studies. A summary of forty years' work in these terms is found in Lichfield (1996)[1]. In the Appendix to the book are set out some fifty case studies using the method on actual problems, mainly as consultancy work.
   5. While the book was published in 1996 it refers to case studies which may have been carried out any time between 1966 and 1996. Thus, in addition to the change in title, there could be differences in the terminology used in the studies. For example, the early reference to 'instrumental

objectives' has been replaced by 'sectoral objectives'.

6. *Features of CIE which could overcome the limitations in Section 4*

1. The consultation draft says (4.5.2.1): 'The main stages in trying to attribute a monetary valuation to impacts are to determine whether:
A : impacts can be measured; and:
B : prices can be determined from market data.'
However, the term 'impact' is not defined either in the Green Book or in the Consultation Draft. Furthermore, in the general background literature the term 'impact' has no standard meaning. See for example Morris and Therival (1995; p. 298), Wathern (1988; pp. 7-8). It is here that CIE makes its contribution by the distinction between effects and impacts. (p. 61, pp. 120-122).
2. The effects are identified prior to the evaluation itself and are derived from the 'effect assessment' which is called for under Government Directives, the core of which is the Town and Country Planning (Assessment of Environmental Effects) Regulation 1988. Such effect assessments are conventionally and confusingly called impact assessments. Instead, one ought to differentiate between effects at source, effects at the receiving end (which may for example be diminished through distance), and the true impacts. Impacts are the changes in the way of life of people, that occur as a consequence of the effects. It is this which should be the subject of the impact assessment and the subject of the valuation. To illustrate, there is no disutility in noise per se unless the effect of the noise has repercussions on people's way of life, e.g. having to provide double glazing or having to move house.
'Effects' are thus defined as the objective elements of the conventional so called 'impact assessment', which can be and are measured scientifically (Morris and Therival, 1995), whereas the impacts are the consequences of the effects on people which may lead to a change to their way of life. It should be noted that a given effect may have different impacts on different people as, for example, where their sense of hearing is sharp or impaired.
We refer as 'sector' to all those people who experience a similar impact, on which the sector's valuation can be based (p. 124). This impact can be objectively measured and the approach to its valuation would be in the direction of value in use, use value or utility. Value in use is attached to a bundle of characteristics or attributes which collectively have the capacity to satisfy human needs, wants and desires, and thus have the potential to make a difference to their lives. The use value to the individual of any bundle equals the utility from its use minus the disutility of the use (p. 186).
3. Since the utility or disutility in the minds of the impacted person is entirely subjective, the valuation is helped by imputing a 'sectoral object-

ive' by which each impacted community sector is assumed to perceive and judge their preferences of the expected utilities, on the basis of the impacts in question. The definition of the sectoral objectives can be helped by some kind of 'market research' or public consultation in respect of specific types of impacts.

7. *Value of the CIE display. The references are: Community Impact Valuation 1996*

    1. The singular product of a Community Impact Evaluation is a display of the results of the evaluation in a standardized tabular form, with its supporting information. The display presents impacts caused by all the effects of the proposed project or policy etc., comprising both those which are capable of being valued in monetary terms (using the traditional methods explained in the consultation draft) and those which are not (e.g. Table 7.12, p. 132). The display is supported by a report which describes each and every one of the constituent entries and how it has been derived.
    The overall display shows the distribution of impacts amongst the population by reference to sectoral groups (Table 7.12). To facilitate the inclusion of all the relevant groups they are divided into owners and producers/operators on the one hand, and 'active'/'passive' consumers on the other. In the display there is an attempt to pair sectors in the first group with the relevant sectors in the second group.
    Tracing the progression of effects and side effects, and the distribution of their impacts amongst the different sectors of the population (Figure 7.2), is thus a ready vehicle for facilitating exploration of the features mentioned in the consultation draft, such as local equality and local justice (4.12.2). It is also the first step towards mitigation of adverse effects and compensation for people suffering adverse impacts.
    The open display of the distribution of all the impacts is a useful way of promoting accountability. It can in certain cases demonstrate that a decision which causes suffering of the few is justified by far greater and wide spread benefits to the wider community, but equally well it can expose a biased decision in favour of the few.
    2. Cost benefit analysis recognizes the need to examine the costs and benefits in a first order, second order and third order situation, where practicable, and not simply those of first order. CIE facilitates this approach by the concept of 'impact chain' (Fig. 7.4, p. 125). This not only provides a conceptual framework for the analysis but makes for a more methodical practice, in the way it proceeds through the first, second and third round stages. This is assisted by its distinction between effects and impacts (Table 7.10, pp. 126-127). The process is described on p. 129.

8. *Drawing Conclusions from the Display*
From the preceding it is apparent that in CIE the drawing of conclusions will

be more difficult than in the Green Book or the Consultation Draft, to the extent that they produce figures for net benefit. The CIE has greater complexity, handling at the same time the non-valued intangibles as well as the valued intangibles, and comparing utility in terms of distribution amongst diverse groups of people, recording the number of people impacted and the intensity of the impacts. But experience of the case studies has shown that conclusions can be comprehended and made (chapter 8). They are facilitated by following certain guidelines:

- The display would not show absolute measurements or valuations for different schemes or 'options' but rather the differences between them leading to ordinal ranking.
- Conclusions from the display can be tested by interviews of households, businesses, community groups etc. for validation or modification of the CIE findings.
- A series of probing questions could be posed to the evaluation analyst, some standard (for example which of the options is to be preferred) and some specific to the particular study (pp. 147-149).
- In some cases, the display and report will be sufficient to form the basis of conclusions. But in other studies, the very results will raise further questions of a practical or ethical nature which ought to be answered if firm decisions are to be taken. This justifies the entry into and expense, of a second cycle of the study, which goes into further depth, to achieve greater clarification and defensibility of a conclusion.
- The display could be exposed to more detailed discussions with stakeholders or the community at large, in order to elicit questions which could throw up further issues for clarification. In this kind of communication the very format of the study is valuable, for it shows what the stakeholders and the public are primarily interested in, i.e. how the project will produce impacts upon themselves, that is changes in their way of life.

The display and its report may expose inherent value judgements by the analysts, or perhaps by the decision takers whose preference for a particular option implies the weight they give to impacts on particular sectors, giving rise to issues of ethics or public interest. It is on this that it is worth recalling an early informed view by informed cost benefit analysts (Nash, Pearce and Stanley, 1975):

> Although we have questioned the logic of some of the arguments used to justify particular procedures, ultimately each procedure can be justified with reference to some set of moral notions. Thus the choice between methods is in the end an ethical one . . .
>
> The implication of this is that cost benefit analysis will be most useful if results are presented in a disaggregated format, such as that of Lichfield's Planning Balance Sheet with instances of effects and methods of evaluation clearly stated. Then it is likely that the reader will be able to

adjust the results to conform with his own moral notions, and thus to reach an informal opinion on the desirability of the schemes. Indeed, in all value judgements, it is those relating to equity, known to be controversial, that it would be helpful if the evaluator himself conducts, and presents the results of, a sensitivity analysis on the effect on his results of varying the value judgements used. On the other hand, quoting a single net present value or rate of return figure will be of use only to those who are aware and agree with the value judgements used in the study.

Note

1 The page, table and figure references below are to this book.

References

Department of Environment, Transport and the Regions (2000), *Multi-Criteria Analysis: A Manual*, DETR, London (UK).

Her Majesty's Treasury (1997), *Green Book, Appraisal and Evaluation in Central Government*, TSO, London (UK).

Lichfield, N. (1956), *Economics of Planned Development*, Estates Gazette, London (UK).

Lichfield, N. (1970), 'Evaluation Methodology in Urban and Regional Plans', *Regional Studies*, Vol. 4, No. 2.

Lichfield, N. (1996), *Community Impact Evaluation*, Taylor and Francis Books, London (UK).

Lipsing, R. (1962), *An Introduction to Positive Economics*, Weidenfield and Nicholson, London (UK).

Morris, P. and Therival, R. (eds., 1995), *Method of Environmental Impact Assessment*, UCL Press, London (UK).

Nash, C., Pearce, D. and Stanley, J. (1975), 'An Evaluation of Cost Benefit Criteria', *Scottish Journal of Political Economy*, Vol. 22, No. 21.

Pigou, A. C. (1946), *An Introduction to Positive Economics*, MacMillan, London (UK).

Robbins, L. (1932), *An Essay on the Nature and Significance of Economic Science*, MacMillan, London (UK).

Wathern, P. (ed., 1988), *Environmental Impact Assessment: Theory and Practice*, Unwin and Hyman, London (UK).

Chapter 8

The Use and Abuse of Indicators for Evaluating Land Use and Environmental Planning — Experience from the UK

Barry Pearce

8.1 Introduction

How can we ensure public resources (tax revenues) are being well spent and that appropriate incentives are in place to achieve this? How can policy initiatives best fit problems needing public policy attention? How do we divine good ideas for policy? These are some of the questions that have long concerned planning and policy analysts.

In recent years, in the UK and elsewhere, there has been growing recognition of the role, in improving policy and policy decisions, of monitoring and ex post evaluation. And within this, there has been keen interest in the role of *indicators*, and a dramatic increase in their use. There has been a particular interest in, and use of, environmental or sustainability indicators, but interest in indicators is not unique to environmental planning. Indicators are now used in many different fields, for example to produce league tables of the best and worst schools, universities, hospitals and local authorities.

There are good reasons for this trend. Reduction in the cost of data collection, storage and analysis — with greater availability and use of computers — has been a big influence generally (Smith, 1995). In particular countries a range of specific factors have been important. In Britain, for example, a major influence was publication in 1991 of the 'Citizen's Charter' by the then Conservative Government; a promise to the public to improve the quality of local public services.

But what exactly is the role of indicators and how useful are they, particularly in the field of land use and environmental planning? What are their advantages and disadvantages? What are the potential traps into which the designer of indicators may fall? And can the indicators that are in use be improved upon, or should we instead be seeking better alternatives? This contribution offers some views on these issues, building on work in the UK to design indicators for use in evaluating the effectiveness of land use and environmental planning[1].

8.2 What are indicators?

First, exactly what are indicators? Various definitions have been attempted, but basically indicators are a way of organizing information to track the status and progress of what is usually a large and complicated system. They are selective bits of information, however: they tell us about the status of the system and how it develops over time by focusing on key or representative parts of it, without having to measure each and every part individually. As one author has put it 'they are a way of seeing the big picture by looking at a smaller piece of it. And they tell us which direction a system is going in: up, down, forwards or backwards, getting better or worse or staying the same' (Conlin, 1995).

A rather obvious point to make but one that is worth labouring is that indicators do just what they say: they only *indicate*. They do not in themselves provide a wholly definitive measure of the system they focus upon. Their role is rather to provide a *guide* to the system's status, in most cases as this changes over time; *without* having to go to the expense of a full and comprehensive measurement exercise (which in practice could only be done occasionally) and *without* having to tailor this exercise exactly to the system each time it is conducted. At least this is the position in theory. Some of the criticism of indicators in practice is that they do not live up to this ideal.

8.3 Different types, for different purposes

Indicators have been variously categorized. A favourite classification, devised to describe types of sustainability indicator, distinguishes pressure, state and response indicators (OECD, 1994). *Pressure* indicators refer to measures of contextual influences or driving forces[2] on the environment, like changes in population or economic activity. *State* indicators signify measures of environmental conditions (e.g. habitat change, pollution). Finally, *Response* indicators deal with interventions made (e.g. regulations, projects).

A slightly different classification of indicators, more useful for our present purposes, distinguishes between:

- Monitoring indicators (also called benchmark / yardstick / back-cloth / system or status indicators) — used to measure and monitor changes in (the health or condition of) a system and identify any needs or problems, for example to see if a problem is getting 'better' or 'worse'. These then may be used to develop policy or interventions.
- Performance (or effectiveness) indicators — used to measure, monitor and evaluate the implementation and performance of a particular intervention (e.g. a plan, policy or project) on that system and then put pressure on implementers to achieve better performance. Basic questions that this type of indicator are designed to answer are: has the intervention been carried out as intended — what level of compliance has there been; have its objectives been achieved; and how can performance be improved next time around?

It is the second kind of indicator that is focussed upon here[3]. Indicators have an educative and mobilizing role in that they raise awareness of issues and problems and of the likely need for some response to tackle those problems. However, in the end indicators are almost always used for some kind of evaluation and performance improvement. They are used to track how well parts of the system are doing, and especially how well particular agencies within it are doing. There is usually an implication, at least, of some standard or target to aim at — some acceptable or desired end state. In addition, there may be a suggestion of wanting to see what happens, or to make improvements, over some time scale, even if it is just that this year's indicator figure has to be beaten next year. Most especially, indicators are very often used as a control mechanism. For example, league tables are constructed from them to keep everyone on their toes, to encourage better performance across the board, and in particular to provide incentives to poor performers so that they make improvements.

Indicators cover a huge range of topics and measure a large number of different items. It is usual to have not just individual indicators but sets or packages of interrelated indicators. Attempts at even greater sophistication aim to produce *indices* of indicators, which become themselves indicators in their own right[4]. The UK, where the Government is at present very keen on indicators, offers a good example of the huge variety if indicator possibilities. Indicators are now used and recommended there at National, Regional, County and local District levels[5]. At national level, for example, there are at least three important indicator sets required by the government which impinge on environmental planning (examples from each are given in the Appendix at pp. 141-147):

- 'Best Value' Indicators — a set of 198 (for 2003-2004) indicators for measuring quality and efficiency of public services provided by local authorities.
- UK Sustainable Development Strategy Indicators — 147 'Quality of Life Count' indicators for monitoring the extent to which the UK is achieving sustainability (including 15 key 'headline' indicators representing a 'Quality of Life barometer') and another 15 regional and 29 local indicators
- Regional Planning Guidance Indicators — some 112 indicators for monitoring achievement of Regional Plan policies (principally national government instruments)

8.4 A syntax and glossary for indicators

Table 8.1 offers a syntax and glossary of terms useful for the design of performance indicators. The starting point for designing indicators is generally to list and clarify the objectives behind the policy being evaluated. These can have official recognition or they can be what might be termed hidden or unofficial objectives, for example if the indicators are presented by private sector bodies or NGOs. In addition they can be either explicitly stated or, as they often are, implicit.

Objectives generally relate to a 'policy object' which is in need of some change:

Table 8.1 A typology of performance indicators: based on key information

Information category	Type	Examples of policy or indicator 'object'
Objectives		
State: • intended standard of benefits • acceptable level of cost • the means by which the intention is to be pursued NB. Official vs. unofficial Explicit vs. implicit	*Standards* — (usually minimum) acceptable level of compliance, performance *Targets* — desired end state (usually by / at a particular time) Relate to policy objects — inputs, process / activities, outputs, outcomes, impacts	to *reduce* to *retain/ protect* to *improve* to *achieve* some given (physical or value) level of, e.g. *staffing, planning activity, landscape, urban growth, vitality, recycling, design*
Indicators		
Environment ⇊	Pressures Conditions	social, economic and environmental trends
Inputs ⇊	Financial capital Human capital (used to formulate and execute planning policies)	planning staff, finance
Activities (process) ⇊	Procedures Work tasks (within the planning system, which produce outputs)	development planning and control, urban design, projects, best practices
Outputs ⇊	Intermediate (products / services retained within the planning system) Final (products / services impinging on those outside the planning system)	planning advice (internal) development plans planning advice (external) planning permits
Outcomes (on pattern of land use / development) ⇊	Intermediate (attributable to all factors, incl. 'noise') Final (attributable to planning intervention)	new buildings changes of land use building / design improvements
Impacts (on socio-economic system)	Intermediate Final	new jobs, amenities extra jobs, quality of life

what Smith has termed the 'phenomenon of interest' (Smith, 1995; p. 169). They refer to or imply some desired state of the particular policy object — which can be a benefit but it may also relate to a cost — and may measure values (e.g. monetary worth) or physical quantities. Policy objects can be inputs, process / activities, outputs, outcomes or impacts and so indicators can be measures of each of these. If they measure inputs, activities and outputs, for example, they will be indicators of compliance, economy and efficiency. If they measure outcomes and impacts, on the other hand, they will be indicators of effectiveness. It makes sense, therefore, to talk of input indicators, output indicators, impact indicators and so on. Finally, it is useful to distinguish intermediate and final indicators, depending on whether they try to isolate out 'noise'. More of that later[6].

8.5 The perceived promise / advantages of indicators: why so popular?

Indicators have been recommended and used because they promise a number of advantages over other technocratic means of assessing performance — for example cost benefit analyses (incl. planning balance sheet) and cost effectiveness matrices (e.g. EIA or SEA[7]). In the context of a decentralized, devolved system of governance, they have also been seen to offer advantages over simply relying on 'market' information and intervention-specific research (e.g. on which are the best universities, hospitals, etc.)[8]. They promise a means of describing, tracking or evaluating a system — or the interventions made upon that system:

- Which is quick and cost effective (even cheap — using existing, low cost, information);
- That yields sufficient of the information necessary to produce high quality decisions (e.g. information that is reasonably 'objective'); and
- Which is readily understood and easily comprehended by decision making principals and their accountable agents[9].

They can also help give direction to policy (eg. clarifying and facilitating greater understanding of objectives) and are relevant to the evaluation not just of projects but also policies, plans and programmes[10]. A key point here is that indicators are not supposed to be as comprehensive as provided for by other evaluation methodologies (e.g. cost benefit analysis) but, rather like the use of models in comparison with theories, can achieve as many of the advantages of comprehensiveness with much less expenditure of effort and resources.

8.6 Problems with indicators: the challenge for indicator design

Designing, producing and making good performance indicators operational is, however, very difficult to achieve in practice and they have been heavily criticized in some quarters (Figure 8.1). Near the top of the list of criticism is that indicators

- high potential for misuse — managerial, hierarchical, top-down
  - generate distrust
  - impose a crushing administrative burden (e.g. information overload)
- unreliable data — inconsistent, subjective, out of date
- measure what they can rather than what is important, expensively
- unclear objectives —
  - indicators misrepresent priorities
  - indicators fail to reflect priorities
- over-simplification
  - ignore costs and possible side-effects
  - downgrade qualitative issues/ measures
- fail to 'indicate'/ represent
- use inputs to judge outputs and outcomes — and fail to measure value added

Figure 8.1 Some problems: the use and abuse of indicators

tend to be a part of and assist a centralized, imposed, managerial control or governance system, one that is hierarchical and bureaucratized. They tend to be associated with a system of sanctions: rewards for good performance and penalties for bad performance. Such a system denies the importance of trust between those with authority to impose plans and those called upon to implement them, and indeed often generates mistrust. It suggests a mechanistic or militaristic 'systems' approach to governance and management, where poor performance is named, poor performers shamed through such means as league tables, and there is over-control[11]. The result can be huge and damaging deterioration in the morale of those asked to meet indicator targets, and who suddenly feel turned into machines or automata. In the long run, the effect is damage to performance as administrators fail to implement programs as they are supposed to do.

As well as these 'political' problems, there are also some particular problems with indicators that are often regarded as more 'technical'[12]. Some of these are very familiar[13]. Five commonly found technical problems are data issues, unclear objectives, oversimplification, autocorrelation and lack of validity, and failure to measure value added by the policy or plan.

Data issues

The first kind of problem relates to difficulties over the quality of data. Often there is a lack of reliability of the data upon which indicators are based. Data may not be collected on a consistent basis, for example. There may be disagreement over how the item to be measured should be defined. Or the gap between change in the environment being recorded and the subsequent availability of data may be prolonged so that, when they become available, the data are out of date. The temptation is to use data that already exist, to measure things that can be measured because the information is already available, rather than what is important or significant.

Objectives unclear

The second difficulty is that statements of policy objectives, the very bedrock upon which the design of performance indicators is founded, are in practice not often in a form that makes indicator design and extraction easy or, indeed, possible. Objectives are often stated too generally, sometimes they are muddled or ambiguous, often deliberately so[14]. As a result, key assumptions have to be made, and objectives will have to be interpreted by the indicator designers, risking misinterpretation.

In order to produce adequate performance indicators, objectives need to be clear, precise and sufficiently detailed[15]. They need to be expressed so they:

- Are achievement orientated;
- Give a clear indication of the achievement that is intended;
- Contain at least some implicit statement about the means (instruments) to be used to achieve what is intended; and
- Make it possible to tell whether or not (or the degree to which) the objective has been achieved (by the appropriate means).

At the very minimum, objectives need to be stated in such a way that they enable comparison between the actual state of the policy object being measured and some comparator: some benchmark such as a desired end state or direction of movement, or the performance of another organization or system. For more sophisticated indicators, the respective priorities of different objectives, and the acceptable trade-offs between them are needed, though these are rarely stated or explicit. Attempts to achieve one objective may make it more difficult to achieve another because there is potential for conflict, yet rarely do indicators acknowledge these conflicts and the acceptable trade-offs between objectives[16]. The package of indicators should be able to make clear what level of gain or improvement against one objective would be acceptable for each level of loss against another[17]. Unfortunately, objectives are often unclear in defining exactly what is to be achieved. In addition, they often give an inadequate definition of the policy object, or fail to state by how much or over what time it is to change.

Figure 8.2 gives some typical 'objectives' of the UK land use planning system — and reveals some of the difficulties with which indicator designers are faced, including:

- The need to pin down and clarify the policy object;
- The need to be clear about the nature of the change to the policy object that is desired;
- The need to find a suitable measurement scale for the policy object; and
- The need to be sure about which instrument or means of planning is relevant to each objective and the roles that these planning instruments are supposed to

Example:
To assist in moving towards more sustainable patterns of urban development:

- The kind of result intended — 'assist' — unclear.
- What level of sustainability is acceptable?
- Policy object — 'development' — too general, abstract. Also 'sustainable' difficult to define.
- What is the role of planning vis. other policy initiatives?

Others:

Doubts about relevance and role of planning
To provide a range of different types of housing for a range of different types of households
To reduce the need to travel, especially by car

Definitional difficulties — of policy object
To ensure there are sufficient land and buildings available to meet the differing needs of industrial and commercial development

Definitional difficulties — desired standard/ result
To encourage economic activity and promote a wide range of employment opportunities in rural areas
To ensure new development in rural areas is sensitively related to the existing pattern of settlement and countryside

Figure 8.2 Examples of UK planning objectives for which design of indicators proved difficult

achieve with respect to changing the policy object, as compared with all other possible influences.

When the information about each of these requirements is not clear, the indicator designers have to make extra assumptions if they are to produce indicators. The difficulty is that such assumptions are usually not easily extracted from the statements which governments make of the purposes they have for land use. And yet without these assumptions indicator design proves difficult if not impossible. Figure 8.3 shows some of the logic used to try to develop indicators, in one case. Indicator designers have to tease out the assumptions behind so-called 'objectives', but these objectives are rarely adequately expressed.

Over-simplification

A third kind of problem with indicators is what may be termed the problem of over-simplification. Where there are multiple objectives it is unrealistic to believe that it will be possible to design single indicators. Usually an indicators 'package' is required. The intention is to produce as few indicators in the package as is consistent with achieving a high level of usable information. But simplification opens up the

Objective:
To safeguard the countryside from encroachment by keeping land in the green belt permanently open:

- being clear about type of policy object (intermediate outcome)
- working definitions of:
  - benchmark or desired result — 'safeguard' (no change of use) from encroachment (to urban development)
  - policy object — open countryside (agricultural land classification)
- define measurement scale (acres of land)
- identify instrument (development control in GB)
- measure loss of countryside to development in suitable 'control' area

Figure 8.3 Developing an indicator — an example

risk of losing comprehensiveness. And because of a lack of comprehensiveness, indicators often give a distorted picture of the health of the system they are intended to track. If poor performance is associated with real sanctions[18], then use of indicators risks distorting the decisions and behaviour based upon them, often in many ways producing unintended consequences or unfortunate side-effects:

- Since most objectives tend to relate only to desired benefits, and tend to ignore broad opportunity costs[19] and possible side-effects (e.g. higher property prices from a restrictive planning regime designed to protect the countryside), the indicators based upon them and used to measure performance against them, tend to do the same;
- Emphasis is also on what is measurable and quantifiable. Plans and their indicators become dominated by numbers. The intangible, qualitative issues that can not be presented in terms of figures tend to get ignored. How, for example, is it possible to measure changes in, or the level of success of a policy intervention with respect to the non-material, even spiritual, dimension of the environment where it is not so much the physical changes in the environment that is important or significant but the perceived value or meaning which people place on it (e.g. the quality of the urban environment)?

The issue of quantitative vs. qualitative is more complex than it seems at first. There are many attempts to measure quality, for example the value, meaning or significance that something has. Certainly, apparently qualitative data can often be represented in quantitative terms. For example, the number of people who feel satisfied with a service, or who believe that their environment or housing — have got better or worse are measures of qualities. Not all these attempts, however, are successful. It is difficult to ask questions that are revealing about people's real feelings. Moreover the quality and value of different types of goods or services are often incommensurable: they use inconsistent measurement scales. Cost benefit analysis has tried to reduce some of these problems by converting all benefits and costs to a standard numeraire: money. But this has not been to everyone's satisfaction. Indicators, seen as competitor approach to CBA, rarely use the CBA methodology in this respect.

Unless indicators are well matched to the objectives of the policies they are being used to track or evaluate, any decisions that stem from the information and analysis the indicators generate are likely to be distorted. In effect the use of indicators may lead to an organization's real objectives being supplanted by other, less suitable objectives — there will be goal displacement, with the extent of difference between the two depending on the degree of match between indicator and objective[20].

Lack of 'indication' and autocorrelation

A fourth difficulty is almost the opposite of the third. Some indicator packages are easily criticized for being *too* detailed and comprehensive. Many indicators fail to *indicate* or represent the system and the broad or overarching objectives for it. Two indicators that are highly auto-correlated suggest duplication and redundancy. In the UK a positive example of a valid indicator of sustainability is the population of bird species — and especially farmland birds[21]. High bird count is correlated with a high insect count and insects thrive on flora, etc. Altogether this provides a good indicator of the health of the natural environment[22]. Other indicators of sustainability have tried to measure critical natural capital. Unfortunately indicator designers tend to get carried away with their task and end up with too many indicators in their indicator package. This certainly seems to be the case now in the UK. Rather than solve the problem of information overload, the indicator designers have given us more information and increased information overload!

Measuring value-added

The fifth and final problem with indicators relates to the difficulty of measuring value added. Indicators usually focus on measuring inputs (which are often as expressed in terms of direct costs), process or, at best, outputs (and thus on compliance and efficiency). The belief, certainly the assumption, seems to be that these provide a good indication of outcomes or impacts. The difficulty is that they do not assess value-added or 'additionality': the difference made by an intervention. They do not distinguish the contribution of the intervention being assessed from other influences; that is the effects of the policy intervention such as planning, from the effects of other factors such as the state of the economy or the development industry or the property market. They do not distinguish between situations in which the policy is not in effect or 'off', versus those in which the policy is in force, or 'on'. They fail to distinguish between the counterfactual and the actual. The reason for this is that measuring inputs, activities and outputs is so much easier than measuring outcomes and, especially, impacts. But there are real risks of not going the full distance.

Figure 8.4 offers an illustration and reveals two types of error that we can call type 1 and type 2 respectively; that of ascribing to planning something which should

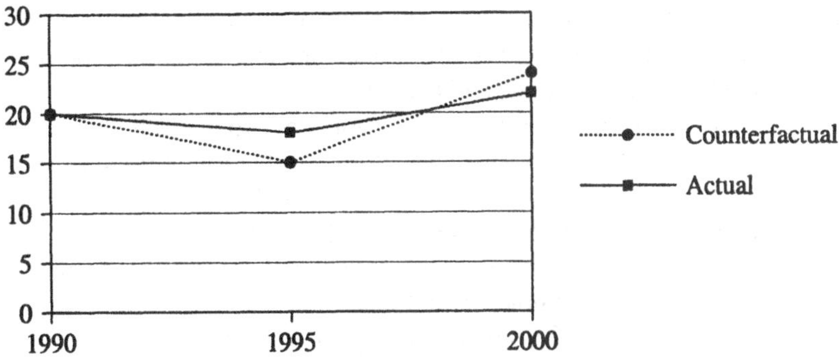

Figure 8.4 Actual vs. counterfactual

not be, and of not ascribing to planning something that should. The counterfactual is what would have happened without the policy initiative in place. In the diagram the policy initiative is introduced in 1990 to increase output, as measured on the vertical axis. From 1990-1995 the policy appears a failure since the indicator has gone down, but in fact is a success since it is better than would have occurred otherwise: a positive value added. From 1995-2000 the policy appears a success, because the indicator has gone up relative to both 1990 and 1995, but in fact is a failure in that the result is worse than would have happened without the policy initiative: a negative added value.

8.7 Criteria for indicators

So, where does all this leave us? It clearly leaves some very tight and restrictive criteria if we are to find the perfect indicator or indicator set. A number of authors have attempted to define some criteria for selecting indicators and indicator packages (Anderson, 1991; Morrison and Pearce, 2000; OECD, 1994). Here are the most common.

- Practical — data availability, reliability and cost: based on cheap / easily available and reliable (e.g. consistent, standardized) information. Collection of data should not impose a needless burden on those who provide it. The number of indicators should be limited.
- Clear — easy to understand, though without losing essential complexity. Each element of the indicator should be easy to define. The indicator package as a whole should be easy to understand, which usually means a limited number and complexity of indicators.
- Measurable — it should measure change in the 'object' of policy, or at least some reasonable proxy, in a standardized way.
- Holistic — covers the system, the policy vision / objectives, and each element, in a balanced way. Examines key elements of the system, providing a

representative picture of pressures, state, responses e.g. social, economic, environmental sectors. Deals with local and distant spatial scales; past, present and future time horizons; and costs and benefits.

- Necessary — whilst covering the system or vision, does so in a way that other indicators do not. Not highly correlated with or surplus to other indicators. Again suggests that indicator numbers should be limited.
- Vision orientated — orientated to a clear vision of what is desired.
- Resonant and significant — be meaningful, cogent and compelling. Each indicator, and the package as a whole, should strike a chord as measuring something significant in its own right, which will engage decision makers.
- Relevant — should enable assessment of the difference made by the policy intervention being focussed on.
- Speedily available — no lag between measurement and data being available.
- Comparable — between local areas, regions, countries. Also has geographical flexibility to be capable of being used to compare different geographical areas such as regions and local areas.
- Robust — changes in the objectives or instruments of policy should not make it easily redundant.
- Inclusive — generated through participation, employing a process accessible to a broad sector of the community, and of those whose work is being measured and assessed.

This is a pretty exhaustive list and shows that producing good indicators is no easy task. Indeed, one could very easily conclude that perfection is simply an unrealistic ambition. But does this mean that we should give up on trying to achieve perfection? The trouble with indicators is that there is virtually no alternative. There has to be some means of evaluating success and encouraging improvements. The only real alternative is better indicators (see Table 8.2).

8.8 Improvements to indicators

If there are real difficulties with the alternatives to indicators, such as cost-benefit analysis, and if it is true that in practice the alternatives are not in the ascendant in the way that use of indicators is, then what improvements can be made to indicators themselves? The previous analysis suggests a number of possibilities:

- Additionality indicators: indicators that measure value added. In the UK some attempt has been made to develop additionality indicators (Morrison and Pearce, 2000). Table 8.5 offers some examples.
- Informal Indicators. These are likely to address three issues (see Table 8.6).
    - Coverage of unstated objectives — Since performance indicators rarely mention the opportunity costs of achieving some desired outcome, because they focus on the desired benefits, informal indicators might be

Table 8.2 'New' types of indicators

Pros	Cons
Additionality indicators	
• Measure role / impact of the intervention. • Do look at performance.	• Difficult to produce — difficult to establish the counterfactual, little evidence of policy-off situation. Requires an intellectual leap, a 'model' or a 'control'. • Require lots of data and complicated analysis.
Informal indicators	
• Unofficial goals are usually clear — from critiques of planning. • Informal indicators can be developed by involving affected stakeholders (policy makers, implementers, impacted groups).	• Who decides exactly what these are?

devised to cover the costs of planning, beyond, that is, costs relating to inputs and activities.

- Coverage of 'unofficial' objectives — Indicators may be designed for 'external' stakeholders, as well as for internal management purposes.
- Support by policy implementers as well as policy makers — Management and organizational theory suggests that implementers and administrators are unlikely to buy into and support a performance indicators package unless they feel they have some ownership of its design. This raises the prospect of consulting and involving administrators and stakeholders, as well as the pubic, over which indicators to use. The ease with which indicators and their purpose can be understood is likely to be a big issue here.

• Keep the number of indicators small!

8.9 Conclusions

The promise of indicators is currently being experimented with and, indeed in many places, exploited to the full. There are many who support Osborne and Gaebler's (1993; pp. 138-165) homily: 'What gets measured gets done. If you don't measure results, you can't tell success from failure. If you can't see success, you can't reward it. If you can't reward success, you're probably rewarding failure. If you can't see

Example 1:

Objective: To prevent urban sprawl by keeping land in the Green Belt permanently open.

Indicator:

Compare
1. Area of land changing from rural to urban use in Green Belts as a percentage of the total Green Belt area, in England, with
2. Area of all land changing from rural to urban use in all peri-urban areas as a percentage of total peri-urban area*, in England.

* These areas could exclude Green Belt areas.

Notes:

This indicator compares the extent of urban sprawl inside Green Belts (policy-on) with similar areas where there are no Green Belts (policy-off). It indicates the difference made specifically by Green Belt policy.

Example 2:

Objective: To make full and effective use of land within urban areas for new housing development.

Indicator:

Compare
1. Percentage of all new housing built on brownfield* land, in England, with
2. Stock of all brownfield land used for new development, in England;
3. Percentage of households seeking to buy / let, looking for a city location.

* Land previously developed for urban use.

Notes:

1 shows the extent to which new housing is being built on recycled land and compares it with the extent to which recycled land is used for housing, 2. 2 and 3 provide likely explanations of changes in 1: a decline in 1 may be because the stock of brownfield land has diminished over time or because there has been an increase in demand for city locations. Comparing 1 with 2 and 3 thus allows for changes in 1 which are likely to occur due to other factors, unrelated to planning.

Other Examples:

Percentage of applications eventually securing permission: after all rounds (planning application, appeal, etc.).

Compare
1. Qualitative aspects of Permissions (e.g. compliance with plans re. public transport, energy efficiency, etc.) with
2. Qualitative aspects of developers original wishes (e.g. via survey).

Figure 8.5 Additionality indicators

success, you can't learn from it. If you can't recognize failure, you can't correct it. If you can demonstrate results, you are a winner!'

However, there is in some quarters perhaps a measure of over-confidence in the potential of indicators, and their risks and dangers are often underplayed. Certainly, there are very real challenges in the design and use of indicators. The apparent simplicity of indicators is a lure to their use but that simplicity may be deceptive. The process of designing appropriate indicators is actually rather complex.

Indicators that fail to make explicit the counterfactual or fail to try and isolate the effects of policy on what is being measured from all other possible influences,

Compare:

- Property prices (eg. housing), with
  Property prices in areas with similar construction costs and low restraint
  OR
- House prices, with
  Construction costs
  OR
- Land prices as a percentage of house prices, with
  Land prices as a percentage of house prices in areas of low restraint.

Figure 8.6 Informal indicators that 'cover' unstated objectives: examples

for example, will hardly provide satisfactory guides to performance. Moreover, the best indicators are likely to require data that are not currently collected and are rather difficult and expensive to collect. On the other hand, over use of indicators is likely to lead to information over-load, and the very purpose of having initially embarked upon the design and use of indicators will be negated.

Indicators can too easily become the principal objective of policy initiatives. By way of example, league tables have often become an end in themselves, distorting planning and decision making, with all resources channelled to recording apparent 'successes' at the expense of qualities that are not being measured and tracked. To put it very plainly, there is a big risk that indicators fail to indicate!

Finally, the biggest challenge of all is that achieving all these requirements at the same time can in practice be extraordinarily difficult. There is a very fine dividing line to be drawn between indicators that identify the value added of policy initiatives and those that are then so narrow that they risk distorting policy decisions.

Appendix 1: Examples of indicators from Britain

Best value indicators

Source: DETR (1999), *Quality of Life Counts: indicators for a strategy for sustainable development for the UK* and ODPM (2003), *Best Value Performance Indicators for 2003/4.*

1. Topics

   - Corporate Health
   - Education
   - Social Services
   - Housing
   - Environment
   - Cleanliness
   - Waste Management
   - Transport
   - Planning
   - Environmental Health and Trading Standards

- Cultural and Related Services
- Community Safety
- Community Legal Service
- Cross-Cutting Indicators

2. Best Value Indicators — Planning Topic
   - Percentage of new homes built on previously developed land
   - Cost of Planning Service per head of population
   - Number of planning decisions being departures from Development Plans
   - Percentage of minor applications determined in 8 weeks (minor) and 13 weeks (major)
   - Average time taken to determine applications
   - Percentage of applicants satisfied with the service received
   - Success rate (in per cent) on appeal
   - Percentage of decisions delegated
   - Existence of approved development plan adopted in last 5 years
   - Existence of one stop shop approach
   - Percentage of standard searches (re. planning applications) carried out in 10 working days by inquiring solicitors

UK sustainable development strategy indicators

Source: DETR (1999), *Quality of Life Counts: indicators for a strategy for sustainable development for the UK.*

1. Topics
   - Sustainable economy
     - Economic output
     - Investment
     - Skills
     - Employment
     - Resource efficiency
     - Economic stability
     - Sustainable production / consumption
     - Competitiveness
   - Sustainable communities
     - Poverty / exclusion
     - Education
     - Housing
     - Crime
     - Economic vitality
     - Employment
     - Health
     - Travel
     - Access
     - Quality of surroundings
     - Involvement and institutions
   - Managing the environment and resources
     - Road traffic
     - Wildlife
     - Land use
     - Waste
     - Climate change
     - Energy supply
     - Air quality and atmosphere

        - Freshwater quality
        - Seas oceans and coasts
        - Landscape and wildlife
    - International co-operation and development

2. Examples
    - Social progress
        - Numbers of population and households, by age group
        - Percentage of households in homes judged unfit to live in
        - Numbers reported crimes (vehicles, burglaries, robbery)
        - Percentage of population surveyed 'very worried' by crime
        - Percentage of householders saying there are problems in their area — vandalism, litter, noise etc.
        - Percentage of population exposed to high noise levels (30, 60 dB, etc.) outside their homes
    - Environmental protection
        - Emissions (Mt) of basket of greenhouse gases, CO_2 by end user (industry, etc.)
        - Cumulative reserves (Mt) of fossil fuels — gas, oil
        - Av. surface temperature (°C), mean sea level
        - Percentage of electricity produced from renewable sources — hydro, wind, sewage sludge, etc.
        - Number of days when air pollution is moderate/ high(urban/rural sites)
        - Road traffic levels (billion[23] vehicle miles) by mode
        - Percentage of children using different travel modes to get to school (car, bus, walk etc.)
        - Average journey length by purpose
        - Percentage of rivers (by length) of good or fair quality
        - Numbers of wild bird species — all, woodland, farmland
        - Waste arisings (Mt) — Percentage of put to landfill, recycled etc.
        - Percentage of new homes built on previously developed land
        - Number of vacant land and properties and hectares of derelict land, by sector
        - Square metres of new retail floor space in town centres and out of town
        - Percentage of buildings of Grade I and II at risk of decay

Regional planning guidance indicators

Source: ODPM (2002), *Monitoring Regional Planning Guidance: good practice guidance on targets and indicators*.

1. Topics
    - Biodiversity
    - The coast and rivers
    - Economic development
    - Housing
    - Minerals
    - Regional service provision
    - Transport
    - Waste
2. Examples
    - Housing
        - Annual rate of RPG housing provision compared to actual completions of new / converted dwellings by planning authority area (net and gross)
        - Percentage of new dwellings on previously developed land and through conversions of existing buildings by county

    - Percentage of housing provision built at less than 30 dwellings, 30-50 dwellings and above 50 dwellings, per hectare (net), by region and planning authority area
- Transport
    - Percentage of new development by planning authority area (housing, minimum 10 dwellings, industry and commerce and retail, minimum floorspace 1000 m^2) on sites complying with
        1. regional public transport accessibility criteria and
        2. car-parking standards, as set out in the regional transport strategy
- Economic development
    - Percentage of floorspace in schemes of 1,000 m^2 (gross) or more of land developed for industrial and / or commercial use (UCOs B1, B2), percentage of developed in preferred areas for development or regeneration, and percentage of each type of development on previously-developed land by planning authority area

Appendix 2: UK Government indicators for regional planning guidance

Source: ODPM (2002), *Monitoring Regional Planning Guidance: good practice guidance on targets and indicators*.

Housing (possible regional indicators, with primary objective on the left):

Objective 8	Indicators
Provide sufficient housing to meet likely housing need: overall level of provision and distribution to constituent structure planning authorities.	Number of additional dwellings provided for in Structure Plans and UDPs. Number of additional dwellings completed by Structure Plan and UDP area.
Underpin national target of 60 per cent of additional dwellings on brownfield land — taking into account the number of empty homes and the scope for converting redundant buildings to provide additional homes.	Proportion of dwellings completed on previously developed land or by reuse of existing buildings by LPA / County.
Provide advice and information on those factors local authorities should take into account in preparing their plans, informed by local housing need assessments.	Number of affordable homes provided for in Structure Plans and UDPs in the region. Number of affordable dwellings completed by LPA and County.
Set out principles of the phasing of land releases.	Housing completions for additional dwellings, by LPA by year. Planning permissions for additional dwellings, by LPA by year. Percentage of planning permissions given in accordance with the release policy (number of applications and number of dwellings).
Identify major areas of growth and determine where housing provision is to be sought by development plan area, taking account of assessed capacity.	Housing provision made in major growth areas in accordance with RPG provision, and the principles of sustainable development.

Create more sustainable patterns of development.	Number and/or square metres of completions per hectare by LPA / County. Number of car parking spaces per 1,000 new dwellings completed. Number of dwellings completed within *Y* metres of designated cycle path. Number of dwellings completed within *Y* metres of a public transport route of service quality *Z*. Energy efficiency of new housing development according to standard energy efficiency ratings. Energy efficiency of new development according to standard energy efficiency ratings. Number of developments completed within *Y* metres of designated cycle path. Number of developments completed within *Y* metres of a public transport route of service quality *Z*.
Create mixed communities and provide greater choice of housing.	Number of developments with a mix of housing types, sizes and affordable, with proportions specified in development plans. Number of completions of housing type *E*, *F* and *G*. Number of completions of housing size *H*, *I* and *J*. Number of completions by tenure type *K*, *L* and *M*.

Transport

Objective	Indicators
Public Transport accessibility criteria.	Percentage of completed development of type *C* complying with accessibility criteria. Number of authorities adopting accessibility criteria. Number of employment, retail, leisure and service developments (within designated areas) which are within *J* metres of a public transport stop with a service quality of *K*. Number of employment, retail, leisure and service developments (within designated areas) within *J* metres of a public transport stop with a service quality of *K*. Retail / leisure / business facilities on / off public transport corridors. Health / education services above specified size on / off public transport corridors or nodes.
Promote more sustainable transport choices.	Modal split of travel (*P* km) in the region. CO_2 emissions by transport mode. Noise levels (or contours) in city centres and along major transport corridors, mapped against population data.

Reduce the need to travel, especially by car.	New development over size *U* with density, which supports a public transport, service quality of *V*. Shopping trips by mode. Trips to health / education facilities by mode.
Set regional priorities for transport investment / management across all modes.	Transport investment. Transport management.
Provide a strategic steer on the development of railways, airports and ports.	Railway / airport / port development. Locations of major railway / airport / port development. Percentage of major ports and airport with environmentally acceptable means of surface access strategies.
Provide advice on the approach to be taken on off-street car parking standards.	Number of off-street parking spaces provided at new developments per dwelling or square metres of floor space.
Guidance on the strategic context for demand management measures such as congestion charging and levies on private non-residential transport infrastructure.	Percentage of Local Authorities who have implemented parking charges in LTPs in accordance with principles / scale of charges set out in RPG. Amount of revenue raised by workplace parking levies. Number of long stay parking spaces in town and city centres in sub-region *A*. Number of free parking spaces at out of town retail and leisure facilities. Level of charge at car parks in town and city centres in sub-region *Z*.

Economic development

Objectives	Indicators
Advise on general locations and criteria for strategic site selection. Identify the regional or sub-regional priority areas for economic development and regeneration.	Land taken up for economic development in areas identified for regeneration. Level of unemployment in priority areas. Percentage of inward investment to the sub-region and areas identified for regeneration. Number of new business start-ups In priority areas.
New development is compatible with the goals for transport policy.	Journeys to work by mode.

New development is compatible with the objectives of sustainable development including the re-use of previously developed land and clean air.	Percentage of development built on previously used land by sub-region. Public transport accessibility of new development sites measured in frequency, type and duration. Number of car parking spaces in new developments in relation to maximum car parking standards. Number of developments completed within *Y* metres of designated cycle path. Number of developments completed within *Y* metres of a public transport route of service quality Z. Public transport accessibility of new employment sites in UCOs *Y* measured in frequency, type and duration.
Realistic in assessment of the needs of business. Ensure there is sufficient land available, readily capable of development and well served by infrastructure. Ensure a variety of sites to meet different needs and facilitate competition between developers.	Area of land allocated for employment use that is well served by infrastructure. Area of employment land by type and location. Length of time for employment land to be developed by type and location. Area of land available for potentially polluting use.
Plan proactively to facilitate the establishment and expansion of innovative cluster areas.	Size and characteristics of identified clusters.
Provide long term spatial context for economic development by providing the regional physical development framework and an analysis of environmental constraints and opportunities. Should ensure regionally, or sub-regionally, significant housing, transport and other infrastructure proposals support the identified economic priorities.	Percentage of employment land incorporated into broader master plans.
Advise on general locations and criteria for strategic site selection to meet business needs while ensuring major 'greenfield' sites are not released unnecessarily as part of a competition between neighbouring authorities.	Number of strategic employment sites developed by sub-region.

Notes

1 Strictly speaking this contribution is concerned only with performance indicators used for ex post evaluation of policies and programmes. Some points will, however, be relevant to the design of other indicators, for example those used in project evaluation. In addition, the emphasis is on indicators for evaluating substantive planning policy and policy instruments, and not the planning system (the legal and institutional arrangements and processes set up to generate and achieve policy).

2 Driving Force indicators is a term used by the UN (1996).

3 The chapter also focuses on indicators of use for the ex post evaluation of policies, plans and programmes, rather than those used for evaluation of projects.

4 The Dutch National Environment Policy Plan, for example, produces an Aggregate Index

from indicators relating to six environmental 'themes', covering such issues as climate change, acidification, eutrophication. The United Nations has produced a Human Development Index that combines measures of life expectancy, educational standards and living standards.

5 It is apparently pretty much the same elsewhere.

6 The analysis presented here has influenced recent work in developing indicators for Regional Planning — see Appendix at pp. 141-147.

7 Environmental Impact Assessment and Strategic Environmental Assessment respectively.

8 The presumption here would be that the best will out-compete the less good — Darwinian 'survival of the "fittest"', and that there is no need for centrally imposed indicators (though the 'market' will presumably still collect its own information — the real difference being who collects it).

9 The pattern of accountability in the public and social sectors is more complex than conventional management theory, founded largely on an understanding of commercial organizations, has assumed. Accountability implies that the 'agent' gives an account of performance to the 'principal' and the principal holds the agent to account. The simple model of a single principal (the owner) and agent (manager) is inadequate to describe the range of stakeholders in public services (Smith, 1995). Stakeholders can include staff, users (e.g. local citizens) and other government agencies, both central and local.

10 By comparison, Cost Benefit Analyses:

- Offer comprehensive and consistent evaluation of projects, policies, etc.;
- Utilize relatively simple decision rules (e.g. NPV);
- Have high information requirements — are expensive;
- Have difficulties with intangibles, incommensurables;
- Generate complex technical issues which are difficult to understand; and
- Tend to be project specific.

11 Indicators need not be used in these ways, of course, but their relative simplicity means they usually are.

12 The critique here focuses on methodological issues. Criticisms of a more substantive kind, for example in relation to sustainability indicators, have argued that indicators tend to have a national and urban bias and pay relatively little attention to non-market or long-term economic issues, such as issues of social inclusion, social justice and participation. See e.g. Jackson and Roberts (2000).

13 Many of these are problematic for all approaches to evaluation.

14 Ambiguity may of course be deliberate: a way of resolving differences between the constituents who devised the objective, and who would otherwise be unable to agree. In some instances, especially in the public sector, the identification of objectives may not just be difficult but futile and even dysfunctional (Smith, 1995).

15 An alternative and often suggested rule is that objectives should be S.M.A.R.T — specific, measurable, achievable, realistic and timed.

16 Where indices or index indicators are used there is the particular problem of attaching appropriate weights to the individual items used to calculate the index. Attaching equal weights implies, for example in the UN's Human Development Index, that the indicators of life expectancy are of the same level of importance as those for living standards.

17 Land use or environmental planning objectives normally aim to reduce, improve, protect, retain or achieve some given level of, some aspect of the development process or physical environment (e.g. urban sprawl, town centre vitality, recycling of brownfield land, the level of house building, the quality of the countryside and other areas of natural beauty).

18 Sanctions can come in many forms, for example shame, punishment (reduction in resources) or rewards (increases).

19 Indicators do look at direct input costs — see below — but tend not to measure opportunity costs.

20 A number of different types of behaviour distortion from the use of indicators have been identified (Smith, 1995; pp. 171-172):

- Tunnel vision — managers ignore valued aspects of performance not encompassed or captured by the scheme of indicators;
- Suboptimization — managers pursue a narrow range of 'local' objectives at the expense of the objectives of the organization as a whole or of its partners;
- Myopia — managers neglect long term objectives at the expense of performance against current indicators;
- Measure fixation — managers focus on fixed targets and ignore the possibility of doing better;
- Misinterpretation and misrepresentation — managers manipulate data when this reveals poor performance, to suggest a different story than the one actually told;
- Gaming — managers deliberately underperform in order to avoid being set more demanding targets later ('ratcheting');
- Ossification — managers fail to change the indicator scheme when it should be changed, because it is costly and complex to do so.

21 Interestingly in many areas of Europe this would be a poor indicator from the point of view of representativeness, where cultural differences permit greater levels of shooting of birds.

22 This example shows how difficult it is to design indicators that enable good comparisons. In many parts of Europe, where shooting or birds for recreation is common measures of bird populations would be a very poor indicator.

23 Editor's note: one billion = 1,000 millions.

References

Anderson, V. (1991), *Alternative economic indicators*, Routledge, London (UK).

Conlin, R. (1995), 'Indicators of sustainable community: Seattle', in OECD, *Les indicateurs au service d'une politique de la ville, 3-4 avril 1995, Rennes*, (Indicators for urban policies), OCDE (OECD), Paris (France), proceedings of the Symposium ('Colloque') held at Rennes 3-4 April.

Department of Environment, Transport and the Regions (1999), *Quality of Life Counts: indicators for a strategy for sustainable development for the UK*, DETR, London (UK).

Jackson, T. and Roberts, P. (2000), *A review of indicators of sustainable development*, Scottish Enterprise, Tayside (UK).

Morrison, N. and Pearce, B. (2000), 'Developing indicators for evaluating the effectiveness of the UK land use planning system', *Town Planning Review*, Vol. 71, No. 2, pp. 191-211.

Office of the Deputy Prime Minister (2002), *Monitoring Regional Planning Guidance: good practice guidance on targets and indicators*, ODPM, London (UK).

Office of the Deputy Prime Minister (2003), *Best Value Performance Indicators for 2003/4*, ODPM, London (UK).

Organisation for Economic Cooperation and Development (1994), *Environmental indicators*, OECD, Paris (France).

Osborne, D. and Gaebler, T. (1993), *Reinventing Government — How the entrepreneurial spirit is trasforming the public sector*, Addison Wesley, Reading, MA (USA).

Smith, P. (1995), 'Performance indicators and control in the public sector', in A. J., Berry, J. Broadbent and D. Otley, (eds.), *Management Control: Theories, Issues and Practices*, Macmillan, London (UK).

United Nations (1996), *Indicators of sustainable development*, UN, New York, NY (USA).

Chapter 9

The Contribution of Strategic Impact Assessment to Planning Evaluation

Maria do Rosário Partidário

9.1 Introduction

Environmental Impact Assessment (EIA) evolved as an evaluation tool, in the early 1970s, precisely to address non-market values in project planning and development. It was conceived as an impact assessment tool that should operate *ex-ante* of any major public decisions on new regulations, plans, programmes or projects. Its main purpose was to ensure that environmental considerations were properly addressed in project evaluation, at the same level of economic and technical considerations, following a model similar to that already being performed by cost-benefit analysis.

Initally designed to mainly address ecological and physical issues, EIA soon expanded to include social and cultural issues, and later also health, technological, economic, institutional and fiscal consequences. The degree to which a wider scope of issues would be considered differed from country to country, as a function of the range of evaluation tools available to perform individual evaluations in each country.

In its first years EIA applied mainly to development projects, which are much more tangible and easier to address with respect to management of uncertainty and impacts prediction than are plans and policies of broader scope. The early 1980s would see its expansion to include programmatic, planning and policy-making levels of action and decision. This widening of scope required more flexible and less quantified methodological approaches given the inherent nature of policy and planning decisions. But it would also depend on the established decision-making system and its capacity to accommodate the rationality that characterizes the EIA model. Again countries have been responding differently.

In this process a new concept was generated. Originally known as EIA of policies, plans and programmes (EIA of PPP), it was subsequently named Strategic Environmental Assessment (SEA) to distinguish it as a new methodological tool. While loyal to the principles of EIA, SEA addresses levels of decision conventionally considered strategic, and consequently needs to perform differently than project EIA. SEA is adapted to the more comprehensive and multiple purpose, forward-looking and uncertain, nature of planning and policy-making.

Some argue it did this well. Others insist there is not much difference between EIA and SEA. Perhaps both views are fair. There is no single model for SEA and depending on the approach adopted, it may be more or less effective in meeting its intended purpose. A brief overview on different approaches to SEA, and how SEA is expected to perform, is offered in the next section. Subsequently, this chapter addresses the evolution from EIA to SEA as a planning evaluation tool, primarily dedicated to the assessment of non-market values at levels of policy-making and planning, and whether SEA is responding to the needs of strategic decision-making. It refers to the objectives of SEA and what distinguishes SEA from planning and other evaluation tools. It emphasizes the different interpretations that the term SEA has been receiving in different decision contexts, concluding by calling for the need to be pragmatic, and effective, in approaching impact assessment at strategic levels of decision-making.

9.2 What is SEA

SEA was initially conceived to assess environmental impacts at strategic levels of decision-making, including policies, plans and programmes. Defined by the International Association for Impact Assessment (IAIA, http://www.iaia.org) as an impact assessment tool, SEA shares original roots and common principles with EIA.

There are two major features that distinguish SEA in supporting decision-making. One is its capacity to facilitate the integration of environmental and social issues with development issues, supporting the design of more sustainable policies and plans at higher levels of decision-making. The other is its need to invite longer-term and larger-scale perspectives when considering development options, thus influencing and improving strategic decision-making performance and outcomes.

This means that SEA can help decision-makers in better visualizing possible future environmental and social consequences of development options, while they are still open, therefore ensuring early consideration of the negative effects, and opportunities of proposed development actions before they are planned, budgeted and approved, and also providing for an early warning of cumulative effects and large-scale impacts. In short, SEA can assist strategic decision-making to:

- Integrate environmental and sustainability issues in the policy-making and planning processes;
- Identify and discuss strategic alternatives while they are open;
- Promote environmentally sound and sustainable development options;
- Anticipate impacts that can occur at project level, therefore improving and strengthening project EIA;
- Facilitate strategic thinking and informed decision-making;
- Change the way decisions are made.

Over the years multiple forms of SEA have evolved. Some are founded on project EIA-based approaches, others on policy and planning methodological practices. Different models and approaches to the assessment of conflicts at strategic levels of decision-making have evolved. In some cases, SEA has streamlined assessment processes to look much like project EIA. In other cases, SEA have been fit to particular policy or planning processes (Partidário, 1996; Partidário, 1999). The need to have SEA approaches adapted to each economic, socio-cultural and political decision-making realities has led to multiple forms and shapes of SEA that can be observed around the world (Dalal-Clayton and Sadler, 2003).

There are basic features in impact assessment that are performed by SEA and shared by EIA. These include scoping the significant factors for assessment and decision, the analysis of an initial baseline situation, the need to consider alternatives in the assessment, the need to ensure public participation and make the decision public, and the monitoring or follow-up on implementation of the plan or policy. But the level of detail and the information available for SEA are significantly different than for project EIA.

In SEA, scoping should focus more on options that enable meeting the proposed objectives, and less on substantive issues that require extensive field work and observation. We often can only identify impacts, and at the best qualify them, but quantification is less possible; we work on best estimates. Except for detailed programmatic or major planning decisions, when sufficient time is made available for detailed technical and social analysis, or where reliable inventories or monitoring on the state of resources are available, there is normally no time or opportunity for detailed field work. Timeliness is a key factor in strategic decision-making. The moment to influence key options may have passed by the time fully adequate data has been collected. Follow-up, which means assessment based on monitoring and evaluation of evidence, is a challenge in itself, in part because initial policy or planning actions may account for only part of the outcome.

SEA is mostly about process management and collective thinking. It is about establishing a coherent framework for decision, that incorporates all dimensions of sustainability, to enable providing the right advice at key decision moments. SEA is about doing the right things, while EIA is normally about doing things right, or perhaps checking if things are being done in the right way. The next section will look at the influence that EIA has had on the development of SEA, and how that may be undermining the potential role of SEA as a planning evaluation tool.

9.3 From EIA to multiple approaches SEA

Methodologically EIA was created after the principles inherent to cost-benefit analysis, to extend its scope of concern into the environmental arena. With EIA the intention was that the positive and negative outcomes of a given development initiative on the environment — the environmental benefits and costs — would be adequately addressed. In practice, this proved to be a complex undertaking, even for EIA applied to project-level decisions, because of the non-market values involved in the assessment and also the multiple perspectives, and expectations, represented by different stakeholders. The limitations of employing the detailed quantitative analysis of EIA to broader decision making such as for policies and plans became even more pronounced, creating demand for more flexible approaches. Arguments in support of the new means of analysis provided by SEA have been advanced by a number of observers over the years (Lee and Walsh, 1992; Therivel et al., 1992; Wood and Djeddour, 1992; Sadler and Verheem, 1996; Therivel and Partidário, 1996; Partidário and Clark, 2000).

Because initial arguments in favour of SEA resulted from the need to improve the quality of projects (Lee and Walsh, 1992; Therivel et al., 1992; Wood and Djeddour, 1992), it is perhaps understandable that early forms of SEA would focus on policy decisions that just preceeded decisions on projects, employed project evaluation practices, and adopted an EIA-based model. One of the most outstanding methodological approaches reflecting this EIA-based model is the Programmatic EIA, developed in the USA as an original form of SEA, and still employing this terminology (Ann Miller, personal communication, after consultation of USEPA registry system in October 2002), even though its scope and methodological approach have become more strategic in nature (such as for example, in the case of the US Forest Service Roadless Area Conservation EIS, 2000, or even in the case of the USEPA Proposed Rule on EIA of non-governmental activities in Antarctica, Final EIS, 2002).

It is interesting to note that, in the late 1970s, the US Department of Housing and Urban Development (HUD) produced a methodology for assessing impacts at planning levels and for mainstreaming environmental issues in land-use planning. The Areawide Environmental Impact Assessment Guidebook (HUD, 1981) was one of the first operational statements for what is currently known as the Programmatic EIA.

The Netherlands is another important source of SEA based on the project EIA model. Indeed, the highly rationalized and structured physical and spatial planning in the Netherlands enabled an easy accomodation of the existing EIA-based model to the levels of programme and planning (Verheem, 1992). However, it did not achieve what was desired for policy making, and a specific tool was designed in 1996 to assist the development of government legislation and regulations, called the Environmental Test, characterized by a completely different reasoning and methodology (Verheem and Tonk, 2000).

More recently the European Directive 2001/42/EC of 27 June on the assessment of the effects of certain plans and programmes on the environment, commonly known as the SEA Directive (Therivel, 2004), prescribes use of SEA in a way that also follows an EIA-based model, arguably putting at risk expectations of making SEA a more planning and policy oriented evaluation tool in the European Union context. The essence of this Directive lies in the existing requirements for project EIA, as laid down in the 85/337/EC Directive, revised by the 97/11/EC Directive. While allowing for much discretion as to how member states will implement the requirements of the Directive, whether through project EIA, planning or any other kind of legal requirements, Annex 1 essentially defines the key information which, together with the specific focus on the preparation of an environmental report, in effect defines the discrete, highly structured, technically oriented EIA-based model.

However other forms of SEA exemplify the policy-making and planning practices have stronger influence over the methodological approach in SEA. Some follow very closely the European guiding requirements for the preparation of Structural Funds applications (EU DG Environment, 1998), which mostly affects Southern and Eastern European countries. Others adopt SEA forms that resemble more strategic tools, such as in Canada or in the Scandinavian countries (e.g. Denmark, Sweden, Iceland, Finland, Norway), where policy-making or a well-conceived planning process currently dominate the decision-making processes. This also would include the UK approaches to SEA, however in this case the British distinguish themselves by adopting different terminology. Here, what was initially called 'environmental appraisal of development plans' (DoE, 1993) was subsequently renamed as 'sustainability appraisal of regional plans' (DETR, 2000), with an enlarged scope to add on social and economic issues. Lee and Kirkpatrick (2001) have subsequently expanded the concept into the trade impact assessment arena. Figure 9.1 shows an array of different forms of SEA as currently implemented in different nations and institutional contexts.

But the need for SEA does not result only from the limitations of project EIA. As discussed, SEA offers the capacity to assist development of policy and planning practices by mainstreaming environmental issues into the policy and planning formulation processes, enabling a stronger environmental focus and ensuring that impact assessment takes place earlier, at the policy and planning levels. Consequently, SEA has a fundamental role in promoting sustainable principles and practices in policy and planning, offering an adequate scale, and decision context, to enable integrated approaches and the consideration of cumulative effects of decision options on important environmental concerns (Wood, 1995; Partidário, 1996; Sadler, 1998; Fischer, 1999; Goodland and Mercier, 1999; Partidário, 1999; Clark, 2000; Sadler, 2001). The objectives of SEA can thus be simply stated as:

- To contribute to more sustainable and environmentally oriented decision-making;
- To enable understanding environmental values in broader contexts and the cross-integration with social and economic issues;
- To improve the institutional and political contexts that surround subsequent decision-making, in particular those in which project EIA is carried out;
- To promote integrated decision making, which implies a new form of making decisions.

In summary, SEA is a decision support tool conceived to assess the impacts that visions, intentions or strategic proposals can have on the environment and on other factors that are relevant for sustainability, with the purpose of improving the quality of strategic decision making. It can be argued then that SEA must be adopted to act upon strategic initiatives, and not to play the role that EIA is expected to play (Partidário, 2000).

9.4 SEA — the risk of multiple interpretations

Paradoxically, however popular the SEA acronym has become, it has also created a variety of interpretations as to the meaning of the words *strategic* and *environment*. As shown in Figure 9.1 different extensions of the concept became visible as it developed in practical application, which is leading to the mounting confusion that can currently be observed with respect to the meaning and practice of impact assessment at strategic levels.

The term *strategic* in SEA was conventionally adopted to identify policies, plans and programmes all together, as opposed to projects. However, the notion of strategic implies a long-term perspective, with objectives set to be achieved in that long-range time period, the identification of a road map and the possible pathways that will enable achieving the objectives within the time set. It also implies a flexible process that enables reviewing and accomodating both pathways and objectives to changing contextual circumstances and evolving social, economic and political priorities. Following this reasoning, while a policy is undoubtly strategic, it is debatable whether some plans and programmes could be described as strategic, especially where they lack a long-term vision and objectives, a broad perspective, an underlying strategic decision culture and the necessary flexibility to enable the adaptation to unavoidable uncertainty.

With respect to the concept of *environment*, there are different interpretations. Some countries or regions limit its scope to only ecological and physical issues. Others consider the environment inclusive of social and cultural issues, yet others go even further to give it a larger interpretation that accomodates physical, ecological, social, cultural and economic issues. The latter represents the need to adopt an integrative approach to enable sound evaluation of development processes.

With the emergence of the sustainable development debate, a new platform is established to address integration. The concept of environment tends to become shortened to its most consensual notion, focused on physical and ecological issues, albeit with recognized links on to the social and economic dimensions.

This could mean a move away from the overriding debate of what fits under the term environment. The common notion of sustainable development is that it integrates the three dimensions: environmental, social and economic. However there are still difficulties in dealing with more than one dimension in an integrated way, reflected in the need to split up sustainable development into each of its three dimensions, and allowing these to be dealt with separately. Splitting the concept of sustainable development in this way is not only subverting the integrity of the concept, but making the advance of this new development paradigm more difficult, by cutting it into slices and allowing business as usual to continue.

This difficulty in interpretating what should be covered by the word *environment*, or instead by the term sustainability, is one key factor influencing the multiple SEA formats found in the literature and increasingly in practice, without reasonable and pragmatic methodological differentiations being made. This in turn leads to an array of different terms, including Strategic Environmental Assessment, Strategic En-

Policy SEA

- Policy Impact Assessment. Environmental assessment of policy proposals to Cabinet approval (Canada)
- Environmental-test. Assessment of government legislation proposals (The Netherlands)
- SEA of governmental proposals. Assessment of government legislation proposals (Denmark)
- Sustainability Impact Assessment of Trade. Assessment of sustainability impacts involved in WTO multilaterial trade negotiations (European Commission)

Regional and Spatial Planning SEA

- Regional EA. Evaluation of regional environmental and social implications of multi-sectoral developments in a defined geographic area, over a certain period (World Bank)
- SEAn (Strategic Environmental Assessment Analysis). Based on community involvement applies SEA in developing countries (Dutch Aid Agency)
- Environmental Appraisal of Development Plans. Assessment of planning policies at council level, with main biophysical insight (UK)
- Sustainability Appraisal of Regional Planning. Assessment of regional policy proposals, attempting a broader environmental sustainability approach (UK)

Sector Planning and Programme SEA

- Environmental Overview. Applies to the formulation stages of programmes, leads to early identification of environmental and social impacts and opportunities and incorporation of mitigation measures into programme redesign (UNDP)
- Sectoral EA. Evaluation of sector investment programmes involving multiple subprojects; integration of environmental concerns into long-term development; and investment planning or the evaluation of sector policies (World Bank)

Regional, Spatial, and Sector Planning and Programme SEA

- Strategic EIA. SEA applied to spatial plans and programmes using the project's EIA procedure (The Netherlands)
- Programmatic environmental assessment. Process of evaluating groups of actions related geographically or having similarities of project type, timing, media or technological character (USA)

Figure 9.1 Main forms of SEA applied to policies, plans or programmes
Source: Adapted from Partidário (2002), 'From EIA to SEA'

vironmental Impact Assessment, Programmatic Environmental Impact Statements, Sustainability Assessment and Integrated Assessment, all of them apparently prescribing similar principles but intending to represent different instruments, often resulting in too similar or, on the contrary, too different outcomes.

As a result, confusion is spreading across governments and institutions around the world as to the different instruments available to operate at the level of policies, plans and programmes, and how to distinguish between what they do, how they operate and what can be their expected outcomes. Worse than this, often it is hard to see the difference between SEA and EIA (in its traditional form as used at the project level), and consequently why would SEA be needed.

Notwithstanding, difficulties with applying EIA, designed for the detail involved in project development, to plans and policies where information and commitments are still quite abstract, are evident. Likewise, when adopting a strategic perspective in policy-making and planning, it becomes clear that a strategic approach to impact assessment is also needed and that an EIA-based model SEA is not appropriate.

The difficulty then is the choice of the right instrument, from the array currently being offered, that best suits the evaluation purposes. This choice is complicated by the fact that SEA share some general features of project EIA. These include the same principles of impact assessment (integration, participation, transparency, proaction, etc.); and similar methodological stages, generally organized in the same logic sequence: screening, scoping, alternatives comparison, impact assessment and follow-up.

9.5 The importance of strategic evaluation — the added-value of strategic IA to decision-making

The value of SEA is a function of the extent it influences, and adds-value, to decision-making (Partidário, 2000). As existing practice already demonstrates (Therivel and Partidário, 1996; Bina and Vingoe, 2000; Partidário and Clark, 2000; Fischer, 2001), SEA makes a significant contribution where spatial, or land-use, and sectoral planning failed to incorporate, in a systematic fashion, environmental and sustainability issues into the planning process, or where policy and planning failed to identify and compare feasible alternatives, based on broad, integrated criteria and accountable processes. Even where policy development and planning are already quite integrated and accountable, SEA can operate systematically as an *aide-mémoire* both as guiding and verification tool.

Despite all these acknowledged advantages, the professional community finds it difficult to understand the new and distinctive role associated to SEA. And this results largely from instances in which the term SEA is used, where the function of SEA is not applied. Many if not most of the cases currently identified as SEA can be questioned as to their actual strategic nature.

It can be argued that there is no reason for establishing new approaches, such as SEA, where situations could be supported by better planning, by EIA, by cumulative impact assessment, or by other forms of well-known impact assessment or planning. However if we want to be systematic about the identification and assessment of impacts likely to result from strategic options, that is if we want to use a guiding instrument that will facilitate that complex process, than we need an impact assessment tool that is designed to operate in a strategic context. We need Strategic Impact Assessment (IA).

While project EIA is often recognized as an administrative requirement that needs to be fulfilled to satisfy licensing / permitting processes, Strategic IA should be understood and employed more as a facilitator of sound, integrated and sustainable policy-making and planning. The incremental nature of strategic decision-making, to which Strategic IA applies, calls for this facilitating role, which runs in close articulation with the underlying process that is being evaluated.

As argued before (Partidário, 2002), there is a great demand on SEA capacities as it is expected to respond to needs at all levels of decision-making, from policy and planning to programme (see Figure 9.1). The impossibility of having a single SEA model or approach, that equally satisfies policy, planning and programme impact assessment requirements, is evident in the multiple SEA forms above cited.

The fact is that each of these levels of policy, planning and programme development are different, have different characteristics, different timings, different degrees of detail, and different purposes and outcomes. Programme development is probably as different from policy development as is project development. Planning, and especially strategic planning, is closer to policy and clearly different from more detailed approaches typical in programme development or project design. Programme development often is not differentiated much from project development. In fact, the impact assessment of project location alternatives, generally dealt with as a project issue, is treated by the Dutch as programmatic assessment (Verheem, 2000).

As previously argued (Partidário, 2002), while Strategic IA employs the principles of impact assessment, it is more useful to conceive of it as a framework that assists the policy, planning and programmatic decision-making process, to provide advice, information or public input at strategic moments, or decision windows. Such 'checking points in the policy-making process ... allow assessment and review of whether and how all relevant factors and concerns are effectivelly being integrated' (Partidário, 1996). Assisting decision-makers in this way can ensure that the principles of sustainability and impact assessment are fully integrated in future development decisions. When this happens, Strategic IA will be making a difference, adding value to sustainable decision-making.

9.6 Final remarks

Strategic Impact Assessment is designed to address issues raised by long-term and high-consequence decision making. That includes enabling more sustainable approaches in decision-making, better integration of environmental issues and satisfying other impact assessment needs that are not covered by EIA-based models. Acting at the strategic level means that information is often scarce and deficient. It also means that many alternative options are more political than technical (for example a decision on an emigration policy, or the preference between thermo power or hydro power where both options are technically feasible) which implies different and more flexible approaches, and that many times the analysis depends on qualitative evidence.

It can be argued that impact assessment, in its move from projects to plans and policies, implies moving from technical to a more political level of decision-making. And that means that Strategic IA must reflect that change with respect to more traditional forms of impact assessment such as project EIA or even more streamlined forms of SEA. By focusing on assessment activities that are introduced into the existing policy and planning processes, and are built into the existing decision frameworks, Strategic IA is seen as a facilitator for more sound and sustainable decision-making.

Even so, it is useful to seek opportunities to use other techniques of planning and policy development, along with Strategic IA, to maximize the complementary value of these instruments in improving decision making. This is especially the case when developing national sustainability strategies, national and regional environmental policy plans, environmental operational plans, sectoral and regional and local Agenda 21, and environmental municipal plans.

Likewise, the links between Strategic IA and existing policy and planning evaluation tools and procedures should be explored. Such existing evaluation mechanisms can provide methodological support for improving Strategic IA and in turn lead to broadening the range of concerns incorporated into these more specific tools and procedures.

References

Bina, O. and Vingoe, J. (2000), *Strategic Environmental Assessment in the Transport Sector: an Overview of Legislation and Practice in the EU Member States*, Final report, prepared by Environmental Resources Management for the European Commission, DG Environment, EC, Bruxelles/Brussel (Belgium).

Clark, R. (2000), 'Making EIA Count in Decision-Making', in M. R. Partidário and R. Clark (eds.), *Perspectives on Strategic Environmental Assessment*, CRC-Lewis, Boca Raton, FL (USA), pp. 15-27.

Dalal-Clayton, B. and Sadler, B. (2003), *Status and Potential for SEA*, Draft paper, IIED (Internationl Institute for Environment and Development), London (UK), http://www.iied.org.

Department of Environment (1993), *Environmental Appraisal of Spatial Development Plans* (GPG 15), ODPM, London (UK).

Department of the Environment, Transport and the Regions (2000), *Sustainability appraisal of regional planning guidance: good practice guide* (GPG 25), ODPM, London (UK).

European Commission – DG Environment (1998), *Handbook on Environmental Assessment of Regional Development Plans and EU Structural Funds*, DG Environment, EC, Bruxelles/Brussel (Belgium).

Fischer, T. B. (1999), 'Benefits arising from SEA application — a comparative review of North West England, Noord-Holland and Brandenburg-Berlin', *Environmental Impact Assessment Review*, Vol. 19, No. 2, pp. 143-173.

Fischer, T. B. (2001), *SEA in Transport and Land Use Planning*, Earthscan, London (UK).

Goodland, R. and Mercier, J.-R. (1999), *The Evolution of Environmental Assessment in the World Bank: from 'Approval' to Results*, Paper no. 67, Environmental Management Series, World Bank, Washington, DC (USA).

International Association for Impact Assessment (1998), *Principles of EIA and SEA*, IAIA.

Lee, N. and Kirkpatrick, C. (2001), 'Methodologies for Sustainability Impact Assessments of Proposals for New Trade Agreements', *Journal of Environmental Assessment, Policy and Management*, Vol. 3, No. 3, pp. 395-412.

Lee, N. and Walsh, F. (1992), 'Strategic Environmental Assessment: an overview', *Project Appraisal*, Vol. 7, No. 3, pp. 126-136.

Partidário, M. R. (1996), 'Strategic Environmental Assessment: Key issues emerging from recent practice', *Environmental Impact Assessment Review*, Vol. 16, No. 1, pp. 31-55.

Partidário, M. R. (1999), chapter 4 'Strategic Environmental Assessment – principles and potential', in J. Petts (ed.), *Handbook on Environmental Impact Assessment*, Blackwell, London (UK), pp. 60-73.

Partidário, M. R. (2000), 'Elements of an SEA framework — improving the added-value of SEA', *Environmental Impact Assessment Review*, Vol. 20, No. 6, pp. 647-663.

Partidário, M. R. (2002), 'Dalla VIA alla VAS' (From EIA to SEA), in L. Fregolent and F. Indovina (eds.), *Un Futuro Amico. Sostenibilità ed Equità*, (A Friendly Future. Sustainability and Equity), Studi Urbani e Regionali (Urban and Regional Studies), Franco Angeli, Milano (Italy).

Partidário, M. R. and Clark, R. (eds., 2000), *Perspectives on Strategic Environmental Assessment*, CRC-Lewis, Boca Raton, FL (USA).

Sadler, B. (1998), *Report on the International Seminar on SEA*, DETR, Lincoln (UK).

Sadler, B. (2001), *A framework approach to Strategic Environmental Assessment: Aims, Principles and Elements of Good Practice*, Proceedings of International Workshop on Public Participation and Health Aspects in Strategic Environmental Assessment, The Regional Environmental Centre for Central and Eastern Europe, Szentendre (Hungary), pp. 11-24.

Sadler, B. and Verheem, R. (1996), *Strategic Environmental Assessment — status, challenges and future directions*, Ministry of VROM (Ministry of Housing, Spatial Planning and the Environment), Den Haag (The Netherlands).

Therivel, R. (2004), *Strategic Environmental Assessment in Action*, Earthscan, London (UK).

Therivel, R. and Partidário, M. R. (eds., 1996), *The Practice of Strategic Environmental Assessment*, Earthscan, London (UK).

Therivel, R., Wilson, E., Thompson, S., Heany, D. and Pritchard, D. (1992), *Strategic Environmental Assessment*, Earthscan, London (UK).

United States Department of Housing and Urban Development (1981), *Areawide Environmental Impact Assessment Guidebook*, US Department of HUD, Washington, DC (USA).

Verheem, R. (1992), 'Environmental assessment at strategic levels in the Netherlands', *Project Appraisal*, Vol. 7, No. 3, pp. 150-156.

Verheem, R. (2000), chapter 13 'The use of SEA and EIA in decision-making on drinking water management and production in the Netherlands', in M. R. Partidário and R. Clark (eds.), *Perspectives on Strategic Environmental Assessment*, CRC-Lewis, Boca Raton, FL (USA), pp. 185-195.

Verheem, R. and Tonk, J. (2000), 'Strategic enviornmental assessment: one concept, multiple forms', *Impact Assessment and Project Appraisal*, Vol. 18, No. 3, pp. 177-182.

Wood, C. (1995), *Environmental Impact Assessment: a Comparative Review*, Longman, Edinburgh (UK).

Wood, C. and Djeddour, M. (1992), 'Strategic Environmental Assessment: EA of Policies, Plans and Programmes', *Impact Assessment Bulletin*, Vol. 10, No. 1, pp. 3-21.

Chapter 10

Problem Structuring Methods as an Aid to Multiple-Stakeholder Evaluation

Jonathan Rosenhead

10.1 Introduction

Evaluation is a word whose meaning has evolved. Certainly from an operational research perspective, forty years ago it would have had the connotation of the prospective quantitative assessment of the expected consequences of adopting alternative options. Today it is more likely to be used in the sense of the post-hoc assessment of the effect of implemented social policies or programmes. This migration of meaning itself encapsulates the experience of the intervening period. The notion that planning might, by use of models and measurement, identify the optimal way forward now appears as a distant utopian (or dystopian) fantasy.

The over-reaching ambition of the model-based planning practice that reached its peak with the US land use-transport studies of the 1960s laid the seeds of its own implosion (Lee, 1973). This was experienced not only in urban planning, but also in the private sector (Mintzberg, 1994). This retreat along a broad front from a rational comprehensive version of planning was paralleled by an active internal debate within operational research leading to a searching critique of its methodology and the assumptions that underlay it. See for example Thunhurst (1973), Ackoff (1974), Ackoff (1975), Chesterton et al. (1975), Rosenhead (1976), Checkland (1978), Ackoff (1979a), Dando and Bennett (1981), Eden (1982), Rosenhead and Thunhurst (1982), Jackson (1982), and Rosenhead (1986).

Arising partly from this critique, and also partly from tendencies already nascent within the profession, an alternative form of OR practice began to be articulated and practised. Sometimes called 'soft OR', it is best known as Problem Structuring Methods (PSMs). These methods constitute a family of approaches that offer a repertoire for providing model-based decision support for a variety of problem situations beyond the feasible range of traditional modelling approaches. It can, and will, be argued that PSMs can be considered as methods consistent with a communicative action approach to planning.

In this chapter I will first indicate the general characteristics of PSMs, and of the situations in which their use should be considered. Brief descriptions of some of the principal methods will be provided, as well as some accounts of their applications. Finally I will discuss the significance of this development in the context of planning, evaluation, and more generally.

10.2 The general nature of PSMs

Collectively, all of the methods that have come to be known as PSMs were developed independently, from the mid-1960s onwards. The principal methods were in being, though in their early forms, by the mid-1980s. These innovations accompanied, and to some extent preceded, critique of traditional OR referred to above. Broadly, OR was increasingly being seen as restricted to well-structured problems — that is, problems for which a consensual formulation can be stated in terms of performance measure or measures, constraints, and the relations through which action produces consequences. This limitation excluded whole categories of problem situation, and it was to these ill-structured problems that, in their different ways, the developing PSMs aimed to be relevant. Such unstructured problems are characterized (Rosenhead and Mingers, 2001) by the existence of: multiple actors, multiple perspectives, incommensurable and/or conflicting interests, important intangibles, and key uncertainties.

What could constitute decision support in such problematic situations? What each PSM offers is a way of representing the situation (that is, a model or models) that will enable participants to clarify their predicament, converge on a potentially actionable mutual problem or issue within it, and agree on commitments that will at least partially resolve it. To do this a PSM must:

- Enable several alternative perspectives to be brought into conjunction with each other;
- Be cognitively accessible to actors with a range of backgrounds and without specialist training, so that the developing representation can inform a participative process of problem structuring;
- Operate iteratively, so that the problem representation adjusts to reflect the state and stage of discussion among the actors, as well as vice versa; and
- Permit partial or local improvements to be identified and committed to, rather than requiring a global solution, which would imply a merging of the various interests.

The consequence of these requirements is that PSMs, although sophisticated in the way that they conceptualize and interact with the ongoing decision process, are relatively rudimentary in the mathematical or statistical apparatus that they bring to bear (in several cases they do, however, employ software to support the process of choice). Instead the methods tend to rely on graphical representations of complexity, systematic exploration of the solution space, comparison of discrete alternatives, and on uncertainty handled in terms of possibilities and scenarios rather than probabilities and forecasts. PSMs retain the core operational research element of the explicit modeling of cause-effect relationships. However their technically accessible characteristics enable the methods to be employed with facilitated groups, and indeed the workshop is the normal context of their use.

10.3 Some PSMs in outline

Different PSMs have their own particular ways of providing structure to the discussion of 'wicked' problems. Some are fairly general approaches, while others focus on more specific aspects of problem situations. Each has its own particular sequence or array of processes with associated tools or techniques. It may be helpful here to indicate their range by providing brief summary descriptions of some of the more widely used PSMs.

Strategic Options Development and Analysis (SODA) is a general problem identification method that uses cognitive mapping as a modelling device for eliciting and recording individuals' views of a problem situation. The merged individual cognitive maps (or a joint map developed within a workshop session) provide the framework for group discussions, and a facilitator guides participants towards commitment to a portfolio of actions. A more recent development, known as the Oval Mapping Technique, allows the joint map to be developed directly in a group situation.

Soft Systems Methodology (SSM) is a general method for system redesign. Participants build ideal-type conceptual models, one or more for each relevant world view. They compare them with perceptions of the existing system in order to identify possible changes each of which from at least one perspective appears to be advantageous. These are used to stimulate debate about what changes are both culturally feasible and systemically desirable.

Strategic Choice Approach (SCA) is a planning approach centred on managing uncertainty in strategic situations. Facilitators assist participants to model the interconnectedness of decision areas. A problem focus of a small number of decision areas is agreed, pro tem, based on their interconnectedness, urgency and importance. Interactive comparison of alternative decision schemes (each consisting of a set of options for each of the decision areas in the problem focus) helps them to bring key uncertainties to the surface. On this basis the group identifies priority areas for partial commitment, and designs explorations and contingency plans.

Robustness Analysis is an approach that focuses on maintaining useful flexibility under uncertainty. Alternative future contexts for the system under consideration are identified, and possible changes to the system are elicited from participants. In an interactive process, participants and analysts assess both the compatibility of alternative initial commitments with possible future configurations of the system being planned for, and the performance of each configuration in feasible future environments. This enables them to compare the flexibility maintained by alternative initial commitments across a range of possible future environments.

Drama Theory draws on two earlier approaches, Metagames and Hypergames. It is an interactive method of analyzing co-operation and conflict among multiple actors. A model is built from perceptions of the options available to the various actors, and how they are rated. Drama theory looks for the 'dilemmas' presented to the actors within this model of the situation. Each dilemma is a change point, tending to cause an actor to feel specific emotions and to produce rational arguments by which the model itself is re-defined. When and only when such successive re-definitions have eliminated all dilemmas is the actor's joint problem fully resolved. Analysts commonly work with one of the parties, helping it to be more effective in the rational-emotional process of dramatic resolution.

These descriptions are based substantially on Rosenhead (1996). For a fuller introduction to these methods, see Rosenhead and Mingers (2001). There are a number of other methods with some currency that have at least certain family resemblances to PSMs. These include critical systems heuristics, CSH, (Ulrich, 1994), interactive planning (Ackoff, 1979b), strategic assumption surfacing and testing, SAST, (Mason and Mitroff, 1981), Viable Systems Method (Harnden, 1990), System Dynamics (Lane, 2000; Vennix, 1996) and Decision Conferencing (Phillips, 1989; Watson and Buede, 1987).

There is clearly an extensive repertoire of methods available. In fact it is common to combine together a number of PSMs, or PSMs together with more traditional methods, in a single intervention — a practice known as multimethodology (Mingers and Gill, 1997). So the range of methodological choice is wider even than a simple listing of methods might suggest.

10.4 Range of applications of PSMs

The range of applications of these methods is extensive. Surveys are provided by Mingers and Taylor (1992) and Munro and Mingers (2002). The varied character of applications may be gathered from illustrative cases. An overview paper (Rosenhead, 1996) included descriptions of these cases.

Regional health planning: an application of Robustness Analysis to the planning of health services for Ottawa and the surrounding region of Ontario. Delphi analysis and cluster analysis were used in conjunction to generate alternative possible futures. Extensive consultation with health care deliverers, and with the public, were other features of the study.

Developing models to support a claim for damages: SODA was used to form a data bank of the experiences and judgements of an extensive management team, from which a system dynamics model was built. This served as the basis for a successful claim for costs due to delay and disruption against the Trans Manche Link company by one of its major contractors for the Channel Tunnel, the Bombardier group.

Contesting health strategy in a deprived inner city area: Strategic Choice was used by three citizens groups to oppose the closure of a local hospital. Using the methodology to elicit and structure information distributed over the participants, a strategy was found which proved successful in preventing the closure.

A recent applications survey paper (Mingers and Rosenhead, 2004) includes as examples short descriptions of three additional studies carried out by one of the authors:

Planning for a street festival: SSM, SODA and Strategic Choice were used to explore possible avenues for development for the Notting Hill Carnival in London, whose million plus participants were generating stress for the neighbourhood and growing risks. A follow-on study helped some 20 stakeholder organizations agree on a short-list for a new route for the procession.

Development planning for a third world country: a series of engagements in Venezuela using Strategic Choice both to study reconstruction after the flood disaster in Vargas state in 1999, and to develop participative methods for decision-making within 'special economic zones'.

Agreeing on a local paediatric care strategy: a series of three workshops with representatives of major hospitals and other health service stakeholders in an inner London area used Strategic Choice to agree on a consensual rationalization strategy in which two of the three local paediatric inpatient units would be closed.

None of these cases would be recognized by urban or land-use planners as falling within their remit. Yet many of them contain elements of context or content that parallel those encountered in planning.

10.5 Applicability of PSMs to planning

There have been relatively few uses of PSMs within the planning domain. The exception to this generalization is the Strategic Choice Approach (Friend and Hickling, 1997). This has been used quite extensively, especially in the 1970s by those counties that adopted a formal methodology to develop their land-use structure plans.

However this use of SCA pre-dated the recognition towards the end of the 1980s of this group of methods as members of a family with many common characteristics. Indeed over the intervening period there has been a dramatic growth in the number of methods available, and in their sophistication and capabilities. In 1989 these participative model-based approaches were commonly regarded by operational researchers as peripheral, or even as beyond the pale. For some time now they have been fully accepted as a part of the legitimate repertoire, and their use is becoming increasingly widespread.

There is reason to believe that these methods could be of relevance and use to the field of planning. This can be explored by reference to some identified dichotomies of problem types:

- *Messes* vs *problems* (Ackoff, 1979a);
- *Wicked* vs *tame problems* (Rittel and Webber, 1973);
- *Practical* vs *technical problems* (Ravets, 1971);
- *Hard* vs *soft systems thinking* (Checkland, 1978; Checkland, 1985).

These distinctions, drawn from the disciplines of operational research, design, history of science and systems, all point in the same direction. Problems for which there are uncontested formulations that can be specified in advance are susceptible to technical solution. But different methods, incorporating the engagement of human judgement and social interaction, are needed to make progress with problems for which these simplifying assumptions are invalid.

The RAND Corporation's work in New York City, as described by Greenberger, Crenson and Crissey (1976), produced examples of problems representing a range of complexity. In this work, RAND attempted to apply its cause-effect modelling and optimizing approach, honed on aerospace and defence problems, to the dilemmas of big city government. The results were very mixed. Success and implementation depended very much on the context. Traditional modelling methods worked well to the extent that the relevant city agency was structured as a quasi-military hierarchy, few of its staff were analytically sophisticated, the agency performed a well-defined task whose repetition generated reliable data suitable for quantitative manipulation, and priorities between alternative objectives commanded almost universal consensus. All of these features were in place for RAND's extensive work with the fire service. Diametrically opposite conditions held for the city's public health administration, and there RAND encountered comprehensive failure.

Broadly in land-use and urban planning the conditions for tame problems are present only for those separable issues that involve the routine performance of basic, non-controversial functions. For the rest, when only the traditional, technical methods were available, they have either demonstrated their unsuitability (a particularly egregious example is the attempt to simulate San Francisco's housing market) or left the field without analytic support. See Jacobs (1976), Little (1966), Robinson, Wolfe and Barringer (1965), and San Francisco Department of City Planning (1972).

The conditions under which planners and planning operate are more recognizably described in terms of the leading poles of the dichotomies arrayed above. For problem situations of consequence, there is no single decision-maker but rather numbers of players, and data is lacking as is a consensus on well-defined objectives. There are multiple perspectives, incommensurables, intangibles and uncertainties. These are the conditions (see section 10.2 above) for which PSMs were designed, and in which they have operated with some success.

10.6 Conclusions

Traditional operational research was the essence of rational comprehensive planning, itself in the direct line of modernist succession. There are some grounds for saying that Problem Structuring Methods constitute modelling's accommodation to post-modernism. If so, PSMs belong to the progressive strand of post-modernism, in recognizing the multiplicity of voices, but not in a way which disables collective action. In this respect these methods have an affinity with the communicative action school of planning theory (Fischer and Forrester, 1993). This too attempts to rescue an idea of rationality from the assault of post-modernism, and to devise a progressive planning practice after the collapse of those institutions (USSR, socialist parties and governments, trade unions) on whose maintenance and further strengthening the Political Economy school had been predicated.

In Communicative Action, people are not so much rational as 'reasonable'. They create understanding and design rational actions by talking and listening to each other. Instead of people understanding objects, people understand each other, and despite differences of perspective they agree on particular actions. There are thus no overarching objectives, but also no pluralist free-for-all. Planning practitioners need to construct 'free spaces' where democratic enquiry and debate can take place.

Problem Structuring Methods, by contrast with their modelling forbears, do not attempt to find some correct answer, but rather aim to assist a debate among the principals. Under the most testing of circumstances, where both the substantive issues and the tangle of interests are complex, PSMs attempt to make that debate more constructive by helping participants to build a representation of a mutual problem which is actionable. These methods may thus be seen as a modest contribution to the impossible task of creating Habermas's Ideal Speech Situation.

References

Ackoff, R. L. (1974), 'The social responsibility of operational research', *Operational Research Quarterly*, Vol. 25, pp. 361-371.

Ackoff, R. L. (1975), 'A reply to the comments of Keith Chesterton, Robert Goodsman, Jonathan Rosenhead and Colin Thunhurst', *Operational Research Quarterly*, Vol. 26, pp. 96-99.

Ackoff, R. L. (1979a), 'The future of operational research is past', *Journal of the Operational Research Society*, Vol. 30, No. 2, pp. 93-104.

Ackoff, R. L. (1979b), 'Resurrecting the future of operational research', *Journal of the Operational Research Society*, Vol. 30, No. 3, pp. 189-199.

Checkland, P. B. (1978), 'The origins and nature of "hard" systems thinking', *Journal of Applied Systems Analysis*, Vol. 5, pp. 99-110.

Checkland, P. B. (1985), 'From optimizing to learning: a development of systems thinking for the 1990s', *Journal of the Operational Research Society*, Vol. 36, pp. 757-767.

Chesterton, K., Goodsman, R., Rosenhead, J. and Thunhurst, C. (1975), 'A comment on Ackoff's "The Social Responsibility of Operational Research" ', *Operational Research Quarterly*, Vol. 26, pp. 91-95.

Dando, M. R. and Bennett, P. G. (1981), 'A Kuhnian crisis in management science?', *Journal of the Operational Research Society*, Vol. 32, pp. 91-103.

Eden, C. (1982), 'Problem construction and the influence of OR', *Interfaces*, Vol. 12, No. 2, pp. 50-60, April.

Fischer, F. and Forrester, J. (1993), *The Argumentative Turn in Policy Analysis and Planning*,

UCL Press, London (UK).

Friend, J. K. and Hickling A. (2nd edition, 1997), *Planning Under Pressure: the Strategic Choice Approach*, Butterworth-Heinemann, Oxford (UK).

Greenberger, M., Crenson, M. A. and Crissey, B. L. (1976), *Models in the Policy Process*, Russell Sage, New York, NY (USA).

Harnden, R. (1990), 'The languaging of models: the understanding and communication of models with particular reference to Stafford Beer's cybernetic model of organization structure', *Systems Practice*, Vol. 3, No. 3, pp. 289-302.

Jackson, M. C. (1982), 'The nature of "soft" systems thinking: the work of Churchman, Ackoff and Checkland', *Journal of Applied Systems Analysis*, Vol. 9, pp. 17-29.

Jacobs, A. B. (1976), 'Notes on the use and value of computer models in the practice of city planning', *Design Methods and Theories*, Vol. 10, No. 1, pp. 21-25.

Lane, D. (2000), 'Should system dynamics be described as a "hard" or "deterministic" systems approach?', *SRBS*, Vol. 17, No. 1, pp. 3-22.

Lee, D. B. (1973), 'Requiem for large-scale models', *Journal of the American Institute of Planners*, Vol. 39, No. 3, pp. 163-178.

Little, A. D. (1966), *Model of San Francisco Housing Market*, Technical paper No. 8, San Francisco Community Renewal Program, San Francisco,CA (USA).

Mason, R. O. and Mitroff, I. I. (1981), *Challenging Strategic Assumptions*, Wiley, New York, NY (USA).

Mingers, J. and Gill, A. (eds., 1997), *Multimethodology: Theory and Practice of Combining Management Science Methodologies*, Wiley, Chichester (UK).

Mingers, J. and Rosenhead, J. (2004), 'Problem structuring methods in action', *European Journal of Operational Research*, Vol. 152, No. 3, pp. 530-554.

Mingers, J. and Taylor, S. (1992), 'The use of soft systems methodology in practice', *Journal of the Operational Research Society*, Vol. 43, No. 4, pp. 321-332.

Mintzberg, H. (1994), *The Rise and Fall of Strategic Planning: reconceiving roles for planning, plans, planners*, Free Press, New York, NY (USA).

Munro, I. and Mingers, J. (2002), 'The use of multimethodology in practice — results of a survey of practitioners', *Journal of the Operational Research Society*, Vol. 59, No. 4, pp. 369-378.

Phillips, L. (1989), 'People-centered group decision support', in G. Doukidis, F. Land and G. Miller (eds.), *Knowledge-Based management Support Systems*, Ellis-Horwood, Chichester (UK), pp. 208-224.

Ravets, J. R. (1971), *Scientific Knowledge and its Social Problems*, Oxford University Press, Oxford (UK).

Rittel, H. W. J. and Webber, M. M. (1973), 'Dilemmas in a general theory of planning', *Policy Science*, No. 4, pp. 155-169.

Robinson, I. M., Wolfe H. B. and Barringer R. L. (1965), 'A simulation model for renewal programming', *Journal of the American Institute of Planners*, Vol. 31, No. 2, pp. 126-134.

Rosenhead, J. (1976), 'Some further comments on the social responsibility of operational research', *Operational Research Quarterly*, Vol. 27, pp. 266-272.

Rosenhead, J. (1986), 'Custom and practice', *Journal of the Operational Research Society*, Vol. 37, pp. 335-343.

Rosenhead, J. (1996), 'What's the problem? an introduction to Problem Structuring Methods', *Interfaces*, Vol. 26, No. 6, pp. 117-131, November-December.

Rosenhead, J. and Mingers, J. (2001), *Rational Analysis for a Problematic World Revisited: problem structuring methods for complexity, uncertainty and conflict*, Wiley, Chichester

(UK).

Rosenhead, J. and Thunhurst, C. (1982), 'A materialist analysis of operational research', *Journal of the Operational Research Society*, Vol. 33, pp. 111-122.

SFDCP (1972), 'The San Francisco Community Renewal Simulation Model', in I. M. Robinson (ed.), *Decision Making in Urban Planning*, Sage, Beverly Hills, CA (USA).

Thunhurst, C. (1973), *Who does operational research operate for?*, mimeo, Paper presented at Operational Research Society Conference, Torquay (UK).

Ulrich, W. (1994), *Critical Heuristics of Social Planing*, Wiley, Chichester (UK), first edition 1983.

Vennix, J. (1996), *Group Model Building: Facilitating Team Learning Using Systems Dynamics*, Wiley, London (UK).

Watson, S. and Buede, D. (1987), *Decision Synthesis: The principles and Practice of Decision Analysis*, Cambridge University Press, Cambridge (UK).

Chapter 11

Integrated Planning and Integrated Evaluation — Theoretical References and Methodological Approaches[1]

Luigi Fusco Girard, Maria Cerreta, Pasquale De Toro

11.1 Going 'beyond the market'

We live in an era in which market processes have become ever more pervasive and efficiency is sought at all costs, with an increase in social inequality and a decreased sense of community and the common good.

To go 'beyond the market' means facing issues regarding selection of goals and not just issues regarding the utilization of certain means to achieve given ends. It means recognizing that the basis for the values of exchange lies in ecological values and the cultural context (Schumpeter, 1954). To function properly, the market needs a cultural context endowed with values such as trust, transparency, respect, reciprocity, social norms and moral values; it depends on meta-economic values.

To go 'beyond the market' means recognizing the importance for development of human and social capital — non-economic values of trust, legality, cooperation, etc., which constitute real economic resources as they accelerate development processes.

To go 'beyond the market' means promoting a way of thinking that is richer than that offered by economics alone, transcending the sphere of personal interest and recovering the idea of the common good. It means going beyond the idea of purely instrumental value, by recognizing both the worth of a value in and of itself as well as the multidimensional rationality that integrates a 'mono-dimensional' way of thinking.

In terms of evaluation, this can be translated into moving beyond evaluating solely for efficiency towards evaluating in terms of social justice and the ethical dimension and facing the evaluation processes in the strategic and meta-strategic phases — thus moving beyond merely improving those processes in the decision-making and implementation phases — of urban or territorial transformation (Fusco Girard and Nijkamp, 1997).

Tied to social utility or the common good — meaning the selection of goals having value for the community at large — are evaluations of public commodities such as environmental and cultural ones. And, insofar as they distribute external effects, these constitute, at least partly, components of the common good and are characterized by social, historical, cultural, symbolic values.

Throughout human history, a dynamic equilibrium has existed between market and ἀγορά, between private and general interest; and this has been reflected in the city's very structure. Today we are witnessing a trend that sees the triumph of the market rather than the ἀγορά as market logic increasingly pervades the political sphere. The market guarantees efficiency in terms of resource use but it does not guarantee redistribution of opportunities. More precisely, unresolved issues regarding justice continue to multiply primarily for three reasons (Zamagni, 1994): the rules of democracy, the crisis in the welfare state, and the diffusion of new technologies. It occurs increasingly frequently that the rules/laws approved by the institutions of representative democracy do not express the common good but rather protect powerful interests advocated by the majority leading to the progressive exclusion of the poor, minorities, etc. . Thus, it becomes necessary to introduce mechanisms of participative/deliberative democracy that, by integrating the existing mechanisms of representative democracy, might help reduce the growth of inequalities (Fusco Girard et al., 2003).

Globalization and its associated migratory flows, along with the relocation of industry to countries with a lower-cost labour force, magnify this by multiplying social inequalities and conditions of injustice, thus leading to further conflict (real or potential) between the increasingly rich and the increasingly poor.

The resolution of the conflict between conservation and development cannot dodge this ethical dimension because it counters the well-being of *some* with the costs borne by *others*, in particular by future generations. On the other hand, this persistent conflict underscores the economy's inability to recognize the centrality of energy issues and the use of non-renewable resources produced by the economy from nature and consumed within the system of the human economy (Fusco Girard and Nijkamp, 2004).

There is no sustainable development if it cannot sustain human activities (residence, mobility, production, etc.) with new energy sources: geothermic/hydrogen, photovoltaic/hydrogen, wind/hydrogen.

11.2 Questions of justice and spatial planning in the European Union

Forms of material inequality regarding income, wealth, availability of assets, resources and means implicate inequality in the ability to make choices — and thus decreased freedom of choice. This leads to political inequality because the needs of the marginal/minorities are not included or represented in collective choices which, in their turn, increase material inequality.

Equal opportunity — meaning equal opportunity for access to resources — is closely tied to Europe's cultural roots and to the question of democratic institutions (representative, participative, deliberative). A relationship exists between the promotion of values and democracy and, thus, between evaluation and democracy. Societies promoting forms of participative and deliberative democracy, through which citizens are encouraged to discuss publicly alternative courses of action and development, tend to pay more attention to goals of equity and justice because they include the needs and the goals of all in their choices and preferences. So these societies are likely to achieve goals of redistribution in more effective ways.

It is the task of 'politics' and its 'tools' such as the city plan, the development plan, etc., to face the inequalities continually reproduced by the marketplace by redistributing opportunity in space.

Attention to redistribution does not only concern the analysis of differences between social groups in terms of occupation, income, resources, development, assets, decision-making ability, etc. — the inequalities between privileged groups and weaker and more marginalized ones. It concerns, above all, the possibility of taking these differences into account within the framework of processes of constructing collective choices in order to reduce them.

Paying attention to the satisfaction of the needs of those who are not involved in decision-making processes introduces aspects of justice into the process itself. Social justice and the sharing of collective choices are interdependent. In other words, the problem is not only to focus on the differentials of well-being between different social groups but, above all, to recognize how such differentials come about as the results of certain decisions. It is necessary to transform the decision-making process in order to reduce these differentials and create justice. 'Privatized' decision-making processes — in which partial interests prevail — reproduce and multiply social inequalities.

It is a matter of facing issues that have long been included in the notion of the 'good life' and common good. A good city is the city in which the common good is achieved, in which a community of citizens participates in the construction of collective choices. It is the city in which the fundamental virtue of the citizen is justice (Heller, 1987). A good city is an entire community that organizes/self-organizes in a decentralized way, making a series of choices that reflect the notion of 'good of the community'.

Diverse subjects contribute to the construction of the city's general interest by identifying specific unsatisfied needs and classifying priorities regarding needs and goals. The participation process helps to focus better on citizens' needs and goals, identifying the components of the general interest and, therefore, a community's common good.

Certainly, a willingness to cooperate, to coordinate choices, to rethink points of view must be present in order to activate participation. If the participative/deliberative process comes about in a coherent manner, it can produce not only specific decisions but also stimulate a particularly valuable public good: 'citizenship'.

In fact, choices are the fruit of evaluation and critical judgment regarding matters concerning the common good. Participation gives form to the interests, preferences, goals and values of the actors in the participative process when it contributes to defining the common good. In this way, therefore, participation promotes the transformation and the formation of the participants themselves. Preferences and values are not 'given' but are 'constructed' within a process of public discussion based on 'good reasons' evaluated in transparent ways. In the end, these preferences and values are opened to the common good.

In this light, the European Union has become aware of the necessity to go 'beyond the market'. Economic growth is indispensable for improving integration but it is not sufficient; it must be integrated with other goals/values which transcend those of exchange. In fact, the European Spatial Development Perspective, ESDP, (EC, 1999) recognizes the urgency to construct conditions of balance and justice in Europe.

Its point of departure is identifying the differentials of development in spatial terms — the existence and growth of inequalities in Europe between one area and another, between rich and poor regions; the reduction of poverty, social exclusion and marginality is one of its premises. Economic development alone can stimulate social inequalities, but, on the other hand, the preservation of the spatial order alone could increase the risk of stagnation and discourage modernization processes. In the same way, attention only to rebalancing might well weaken the potential for development in the most dynamic areas so the promotion of balanced spatial development becomes essential. In this sense, the ESDP underlines the importance of spatial planning, of pursuing the enhancement of the natural and cultural heritage that often characterizes remote areas, promoting economic development with a new capacity for attracting investment.

Sustainable Europe is a 'just' Europe in the sense that sustainability cannot be achieved if differences in levels of material, social, economic, environmental well-being are not reduced. Cooperation cannot be fostered among different subjects — along with cohesion, citizenship, shared responsibility, general interest — if inequality between one area and another continues to exist and worsens, and if goals of great equality and equity between people and generations are not achieved. It can be ascertained that inequality produces environmental decay — the antithesis of sustainability. Poverty and environmental decline are interdependent.

On the contrary, great homogeneity in income levels and in human/social capital leads to increased levels of natural capital. The ESDP document concludes by identifying an ethical/redistributive perspective seeking to promote territorial rebalancing: Europe takes the responsibility for the common good that is broadened to include remote areas and future generations.

If we diagram (Figure 11.1) the spatial dimension (from *local* to *global*) on a vertical axis and the ethical dimension (from *inequality* — as effect of only efficiency — to *equality*) on the horizontal one, the ESDP document can be interpreted as a tool to help move the centre of gravity of European development strategies towards quadrant IV.

The second quadrant represents the free market and the optimization of profits, economic growth addressing unlimited satisfaction of consumer needs, recognizing only individual rationality of *homo oeconomicus* who, by definition, maximizes utility in competition/conflict with all other subjects. It is this quadrant in which

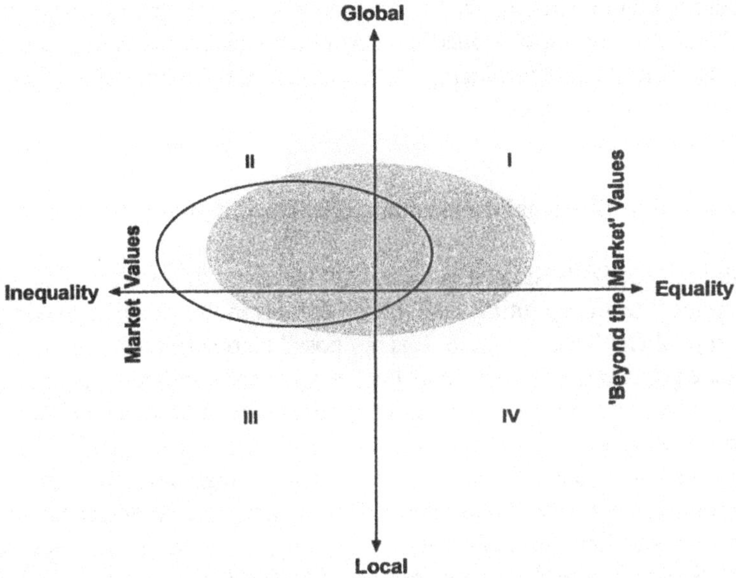

Figure 11.1 The spatial and ethical dimensions in development strategies

globalization is seen exclusively in economic terms in reference to the sole values of cost and market, the optimization of their difference independent of social or meta-economic values.

The development model with its centre of gravity in quadrant IV is, instead, centred on the local dimension, on its specificity, its particular identity, and seeks respect/conservation of the intrinsic value of its natural, historical and cultural capital, as well as their existence, option and bequest values. Thus, the non-use values coexist with those of exchange and cost and, therefore, with use values. Choice of a development model is a question of values characterized by a clear ethical dimension that are combined with other ethical values — such as social justice, equity, the common good, general interest, solidarity, cooperation, social utility — promoted by effective public institutions and by civil society.

Therefore, the ESDP proposes a vision of European space concretely shaped by economic values but also by non-economic and ethical ones. The same document can be read as an example of ethics applied to space which stimulates, in turn, a vision of planning as an exercise in spatial ethics (Healey et al., 1999; Faludi, 2000; Davoudi, 2002) directed towards achieving spatial 'equity' to improve conditions in Europe's various 'Souths' and in the different urban/metropolitan areas — according to a logic of sustainability. This could be made possible by improving Europe's internal areas, often rich in biodiversity as well as cultural landscapes, to achieve more balanced spatial development which might stimulate tourist development without jeopardizing resource quality. In practice, this means recognizing that the intrinsic value of 'nature' and 'culture' must be incorporated into decisions regarding spatial use. This might also contribute to producing a more immaterial, but important, form of development capital: *social capital.*

11.3 The ethical and institutional dimensions of territorial planning

To achieve a balanced spatial 'vision' it is generally necessary to promote innovation on the institutional level beginning with improvements in the decision-making process to support public/collective choice. It is not possible to believe in a return to former welfare-state policies which were, at all events, somewhat ineffective; nor is it possible that increasingly accentuated mercantile liberalism can promote conditions of greater justice.

It is necessary, then, to enhance the role of civil society through more widespread processes of governance and forms of public/private partnership. Civil society can, in fact, become the bearer of long-term general interest, which, within the institutions of representative democracy, tend to be subordinated to shorter term results. The crux of the matter is to include general interests in collective decisions by opening planning to the participative process.

Planning, in the global era, is increasingly introducing economic rationality into its choices. But the greatest challenge of our era is ethics. How, then, can we integrate economy and ethics? How can we go 'beyond' the economy?

Planning and evaluation could include the ethical dimension by enriching the deliberative process with the construction of consensus through participation by constructing choices based on the principle of general interest discussed in public arenas. Establishing what is preferable or good in the collective sense and what is of common interest or only of particular interest is, in and of itself, an evaluation process — a process of critical discernment. Economic and meta-economic values that shape the general interest are chosen; they express a shared vision of the local community expressed by the simultaneous presence of numerous differences.

Choices regarding the values/goals representing the general interest, and their priority, are the first instances in which ethical problems recognizing the rights of all — the poor and the marginal, immigrants, ethnic minorities, etc., as well as future generations — are set. With the activation of participative processes, priorities among values, goals, criteria can be defined especially regarding the reconciliation of: economic values and symbolic/ethical values; use values and non-use values; use values and market values.

Decisions regarding priorities are the result of an evaluation process during the strategic/meta-strategic phases of planning in which evaluations can go beyond the mercantile sphere by referring to the construction of desirable futures and to the consideration of different scenarios. They are characterized by a collective construction of meaning utilizing an inductive kind of logic which takes into account a plurality of points of view and actors. The decision-making process must, in fact, take into account an increasingly pluralistic context in which each person possesses an individual system of goals and priorities pursued with different strategies which can also be in conflict. In a context characterized by many points of view, a simple aggregation of preferences and utility is not sufficient to face up to such problems of choice.

The ethical dimension must also be considered in light of the needs/goals of future generations. It is not 'just' that quality of life can be improved today to the detriment of the unborn, leaving an environment whose air is more polluted, whose water is more poisoned, and whose ground is more contaminated.

While it is known that evaluation in terms of economic efficiency has been greatly explored and widely utilized (real estate analysis, financial analysis, cost-benefit analysis, etc.), and that environmental sustainability evaluation has also progressed over the last decade especially due to pressure by the environmentalist culture (environmental impact evaluation, contingent evaluation, travel cost method, etc.), it is clear that social equity evaluations have been much less explored. The problems presented by this type of evaluation are different and they range from the evaluation of a single resource to the evaluation of development and management plans/programs raising some of the following issues:

- How to evaluate projects/plans/programs while incorporating values of social equity?
- How to assess existence, option and bequest values, non-use values, and intrinsic value, which represent values which also reflect benefits for 'others' and are, therefore, characterized by a clear ethical dimension?
- How to assess a resource in terms of different social groups which can be in competition among themselves (rich/poor, today's/tomorrow's generations, direct/indirect users, potential consumers/non consumers, etc.)? How to aggregate these points of view?

For example, contingent valuation can attribute value to resources without a market (Bateman and Willis, 1995; Mitchell and Carson, 1989) given certain hypotheses. It is assumed that it is possible to render explicit a willingness to pay for a public good as if it were a private one. But the entire literature of humanist economics, from Genovesi (1765) to Ruskin (1871), to Hirsch (1976), to Etzioni (1988), has emphasized that human choices are not motivated on utilitarian bases alone.

11.4 Assessing value 'beyond the market' — intrinsic value and complex social value

An environmental/ecological resource disburses a flow of manifold services to different subjects: both consumers (direct, indirect, potential and future) and non-consumers. Thus, it possesses a social 'value'. To go 'beyond the market' means to study how to pass from its (possible) exchange value which expresses individual utility, to its social value, which takes into account the resource's social utility.

To assess resources from manifold, and possibly competing or conflicting, points of view and to aggregate such different values related to various types of consumers and non-consumers, it could be possible to adopt evaluation processes based on the idea of 'complex social value' (Fusco Girard, 1987).

The excellence of a place is an element that contributes to constructing the 'good life' of a community. A high-quality and beautiful environment can improve the feeling of well-being and can also create a sense of community, communicative networks, social capital, civic spirit. Beauty (seen as an aesthetic value) produces social identity and ethical values (Cold, 2001) spreading the perception that it is 'good' to take care of that place.

'Intrinsic value' is defined as an ability to go 'beyond' the private sphere, to transcend the value of private use, to recognize unity, the whole. Intrinsic value reflects the spirit of a place, its specific, unique and non-reproducible character — its particular identity that can create a sense of connection between community and manufactured capital, between community and cultural capital.

Intrinsic value exists when the inhabitants of an area recognize the bond with its past in certain qualitative values, in certain characteristics that express the sense of a place. But these values can also establish a bond between a place and its future.

Places with intrinsic value can create integration to reduce marginality and to overcome fragmentation. They are generally vibrant places having a public character as well as the ability to attract interest. They sustain, promote and regenerate life. And they promote the perception of a social dimension which is tied to the general interest and the common good stimulated in the past, as well as in the present and which will be stimulated in the future, transcending the culture of individual profit. Intrinsic value reaches beyond the individual dimension to the social one; it expresses a spiritual value as well, because it links individual and community, past and present, aesthetic values and use values, use values and non-use values, helping to express the profound unity between them.

Ecological economics takes into account symbolic and intrinsic values. Fromm (2000) distinguishes a resource's inherent value without which the services produced by an ecosystem would not exist; and a 'primary' value that reflects the capacity or ability to 'hold together' a resource's different components. Turner (1992) speaks of 'glue value' or primary value, defined as a set of interdependences that form ecosystemic integrity, guaranteeing resilience and reducing vulnerability to external pressures thus allowing 'adaptation' over time (Turner et al., 1993). This value expresses a system's organizational structure that also allows it to maintain its particular identity over time and is not represented only by the aggregation of the value of its single components (Turner, Bateman and Adger, 2001). For example, the integrity of a natural ecosystem allows it to secure solar energy (to be productive in the transformation of solar energy into chemical energy), to guarantee the decomposition of organic products as well as to procure nourishment; to assure a series of bio-geo-chemical processes within the water, air, carbon, nitrogen and phosphorus cycles.

This ecosystemic integrity which Costanza (1991) articulates as the product of productive ability, resistance and vitality expresses an autopoietic ability of the same system along with a heteropoietic one — an ability to sustain the life of human, animal and vegetation systems because, over time, it maintains the balance of atmospheric gases, utilizes waste, recycles nourishing substances, etc. To be able to evaluate this intrinsic value means to go 'beyond the market' and its values and to face ethical issues in evaluation.

Environmental economics accepts that the difference between overall ecosystemic value and total economic value is represented by primary systemic value, by cultural/symbolic value and by quasi-option value. These are different values from those expressed in willingness to pay evaluations and, therefore, are assessable in non-monetary dimensions. They express the spirit of a place, its roots, its particular soul, as well as the parts' interdependent relationships with the whole. Since they are values which are closely tied to place, they also express how they can be transformed by impacts of territorial transformation.

Intrinsic value, as recognized by the environmentalist culture, within a non-anthropocentric but rather eco-biocentric vision, expresses a resource's inherent value independently of its instrumental value, and appears congruent with the definition of primary systemic value.

It is a question of a value 'in itself' and 'by itself' that pre-exists human presence and reflects the recognition that the ecosystem, with all of its cyclical bio-geo-physical exchanges, exists and can continue to exist independently from human presence guaranteeing existence through biodiversity.

Since people cannot live without the biosphere but depend upon it, whereas the biosphere can also exist without people, evaluation of ecosystems cannot be conducted on a utilitarian base. Thus this kind of evaluation reflects the value of different ecosystemic services such as water and air purification, waste decomposition, soil maintenance, etc. Likewise, the symbolic/cultural/social value of a landscape, monument, coastal zone, etc., cannot be adequately expressed in monetary terms through an aggregation of private values. At the same time, we find producer/consumer behaviour that is combined in different ways with citizen behaviour which, on the other hand, recognizes general interest that goes beyond the private one.

The roots of this attention to general interest can be tracked down to the structurally social nature of human beings, with the recognition that they are interdependent and, therefore, feel the need to coordinate actions among themselves.

Intrinsic value is defined through a deliberative/participative process which assigns a value through public decision and consensus. It is a kind of deductive evaluation according to a constructivist approach (Berger and Luckmann, 1967; Patton, 1996; Healey, 1997), that includes an ethical dimension and expresses value that cannot be determined by economic calculation, insofar as it reflects utility for the community at large and not just for the single individual. It is a social value as well as a complex value because it goes beyond use value while also including other dimensions and their relationships.

The procedure of estimating complex social value is not, therefore, based solely on willingness to pay for goods having a public character. Rather what might appear effective is a procedure based on deliberative group processes (Jacobs, 1997; Coote and Lenaghan, 1997) using principles of participatory democracy and based on respective interpretations in order to reach a level of consensus within the general community.

A procedure analogous to contingent valuation can be used, with the difference that the defined value is a result of public discussion and does not represent a subjective value that expresses an individual willingness to pay. In other words, it focuses on the benefits that environmental/ecological/cultural resources are able to disburse to the overall community and their value is recognized by many points of view. Thus, benefits/advantages are not evaluated as simple aggregations of private/individual preferences.

Value and, therefore, willingness to pay, is not defined by individuals only as 'consumers' but in a public/participative context in which everyone finds himself/herself in the condition of a 'citizen' expressing his/her evaluation in dialogic-communicative-deliberative context founded upon the discussion of 'good reasons' (Habermas, 1984; Habermas, 1990). It starts from personal evaluations and proceeds to build consensus regarding the public good and finally reaches social evaluations that are not necessarily based on the use of monetary indicators but on multi-attribute methods.

In this way, an open process for building social evaluation is delineated within an informative framework that is richer and more collaborative than the one based solely on individual evaluations. The premise is that, to identify the value of resources of general interest, it is not possible to apply the same procedures used for defining the value from an individual point of view; rather different processes to reach the construction of social values should be encouraged.

11.5 Attention to redistribution in project evaluation methods

In the development strategies that envisage the city as the motor of economic growth in the globalized world and in the search for an ever increasing competitive edge, financial and economic evaluation techniques (financial analysis and cost-benefit analysis) become increasingly relevant.

With cost-benefit analysis, we have an aggregate analysis that confronts the sum of the benefits for those interested in a plan/project with the sum of the costs borne by subjects who 'lose'. Cost-benefit analysis (CBA) is based on the optimization of utility and transforms the real world's multi-dimensionality into a uniquely monetary dimension, providing information regarding the efficiency of a plan/project; but CBA is 'mute' regarding other dimensions (such as the ethical one) relating to the well-being of future generations and the excluded. Founded upon the concept of willingness to pay — which is greater for those with a more elevated income — cost-benefit analysis ends up favoring that group and certainly not the poor or future generations. Instead, multicriteria analysis seems to be able to include many points of view, including those of marginal subjects. It can stimulate participative processes within which to consider new goals and evaluation criteria which can reflect the interests of minorities, immigrants, young people, etc.; it is open to creating a process of deliberative-participative democracy through successive approximations in a cyclical way. For instance, the first applications of the cost-benefit analysis in the planning discipline clearly manifest interest in distributive aspects. The Planning Balance Sheet, PBS, (Lichfield, 1968; Lichfield, 1977; Lichfield, 1989) and the Goal Achievement Matrix, GAM, (Hill, 1973) are clear examples of spatial interpretations of CBA.

With multicriteria evaluation the distributive dimension is a structural one because it expressly focuses on how far a given goal is pursued in respect to others and, therefore, who is penalized or benefited because it assumes that a particular goal is important: it facilitates a distributive/ethical/social type of judgment.

In this light, it is clear that the preservation of a territory's quality is the task of spatial planning. This quality is not expressed only through values of market and use, but also through non-use values as well as through intrinsic and social/cultural values. Taking into account these values means to transcend the market when making land-use decisions by also considering the place's spatial characteristics.

To go 'beyond the market' allows us to safeguard values 'for others' (also for future generations) facing the ethical challenge of rebalancing. But this is possible only by encouraging real participation processes in spatial planning.

The following case study is presented as an example of how to go 'beyond the market' in the direction described above, integrating ecological with social/cultural values.

11.6 A project for sustainable mobility in the Sorrento Coast[2]

The Sorrento Coast is located in the Naples Province (Italy) and is afflicted with problems of mobility and accessibility. The zone is characterized by a dense built fabric distributed uniformly throughout its different municipalities; this 'sprawl', along with the lack of parking availability, generates intense traffic along with the correlated urban phenomena of congestion. The Sorrento Coast has a predominantly tourist-based economy which, in turn, creates sustained and continuous traffic movement throughout the year with important seasonal peaks.

With the goal of finding a solution to the mobility and accessibility problems in all the towns of the coast (Vico Equense, Meta, Piano di Sorrento, Sant'Agnello, Sorrento, Massa Lubrense and Agerola) and to propose a system of sustainable mobility, the following objectives were pursued:

- To explore possibilities for improving the connections of the Sorrento Coast with Europe, Italy, the Campania Region and the Naples Province[3];
- To transform most of the automobile and charter bus flows into an eco-compatible combination of collective and semi-collective means of transport (on land and sea, railway, roadway and cable);

- To identify alternative forms for the regulation and selection of the traffic not transferred to collective means;
- To define a system of non-invasive infrastructure;
- To plan pedestrian systems (also mechanized ones) of access to urban centers that broaden the influence of the collective means of transport.

To pursue the above-mentioned goals and, thus, to identify projects for proposal, the first action was the creation of the knowledge base regarding the current mobility situation. This described a transportation system composed of eight principal components:

- Private automobiles on road networks;
- Public road transportation;
- Public rail transportation;
- Charter bus services;
- Maritime transportation;
- Public elevators;
- Cable systems;
- Pedestrian routes and paths.

In particular, auto transportation uses the road network which, along the Sorrento Coast, is generally lacking in arteries and has inadequate geometric characteristics. Public road transportation is present within some municipalities and is entrusted to two private companies: the Circumvesuviana and SITA. Rail transport is the main component of public transportation in the area and uses the Circumvesuviana Napoli-Pompei-Sorrento line, characterized by 30 minute intervals. Charter bus connections are operated directly by tourist agencies: they greatly influence the area's traffic due to the great numbers of buses in circulation and their dimensions which often obstruct vehicular outflow. Maritime transportation is active especially during the summer and consists in connections with high-speed boats and small ferries between Sorrento, Naples and towns along the Vesuvio coast. Connections by cable are generally organized along the lines of maximum inclination, and include the Faito Mountain cable-cars and vertical elevators serving railway stations or private hotel structures. Finally, a network of footpaths, basically for tourist use, is of particular interest because these paths could be reactivated for use by low-impact vehicles.

Direct observation as well as interviews with representatives of the local communities evidenced that the current level of wintertime and holiday accessibility is barely sufficient given the system's infrastructural inadequacies: in particular road geometries, torturous curves, lack of maintenance, presence of road crossings, insufficient rail potential, lack of schedule opportunities, bad intermodal interconnections, distribution of rail stations located only in some towns. Furthermore, within this generally difficult situation, an important difference exists between coastal and interior connections. Problems of accessibility are concentrated during the tourist season but also during winter and spring holidays (weekend and weekday festivities).

One of the principal goals of the study was to improve the quality of mobility by managing its quantity — that is without increasing traffic, by offering public collective and semi-collective means of transport for the tourist traffic in order to substitute private automobiles and charter buses.

In fact, it can be observed that the quality of the urban context and the urbanized territory can also be determined by traffic conditions both in terms of infrastructure and networks. Thus, transportation systems can be considered as one of the tools with which to construct urban sustainability; they can play a critical role in offering economic opportunity and social benefits, but also in causing environmental decay, safety problems and congestion. It is important that project strategies take into account the interrelated economic principles and subsequent negative externalities (Camagni, 2000) along with the ethical principles and redistribuitve issues that influence the collectivity and clearly delineate the conflict between individual mobility and the collective interest. In order to define adequate choices within transportation planning it is fundamental to develop decision-making processes for complex environments, keeping in mind the implications of the relationships between the social, economic, technological and political aspects of development.

11.7 The methodological approach — a way forward based on evaluation techniques

In order to develop project strategies and construct choices for a sustainable mobility system on the Sorrento Coast, we utilized a methodology which conceives of evaluation as a dynamic learning process (Funtowicz and Ravetz, 1993; De Marchi et al., 2000), able to evolve according to possible changes and to adjust to continuous feedback from the different project phases, as well as from interaction and dialogue between 'common knowledge' and 'expert knowledge' (Nijkamp, Rietveld and Voogd, 1990). The evaluation method adopted is based on Multicriteria Decision Analysis, as an approach open to public participation, employing a set of techniques for ranking options by preference (Clemen, 1996; Keeney, 1992; Parruccini, 1994). In this way we sought to tackle complex problems with some degree of uncertainty and different types of data (monetary, non-monetary, quantitative, qualitative), in order to create a decision-making support tool by structuring a process for the evaluation of collective choices and activating participatory evaluation practices. This approach is multi-dimensional, in order to take into account the complex, heterogeneous and conflicting components of the target territory, including possible implications and different impacts (environmental, social and economic), and such as to allow reassessment of specific goals and review of the action plan on the basis of a cyclical evaluation process (Figure 11.2).

In drawing up each phase we applied suitable evaluation methods for interpreting, representing and managing the complex array of interests, goals and factors involved, and able to account for the different — at times conflicting — values.

Through the combined use of Problem Structuring Methods and Multicriteria and Multigroup Methods, and drawing on elements from scenario building and analysis (Gallopin et al., 1997; Khakee, 1999) we set up a decision-making support system

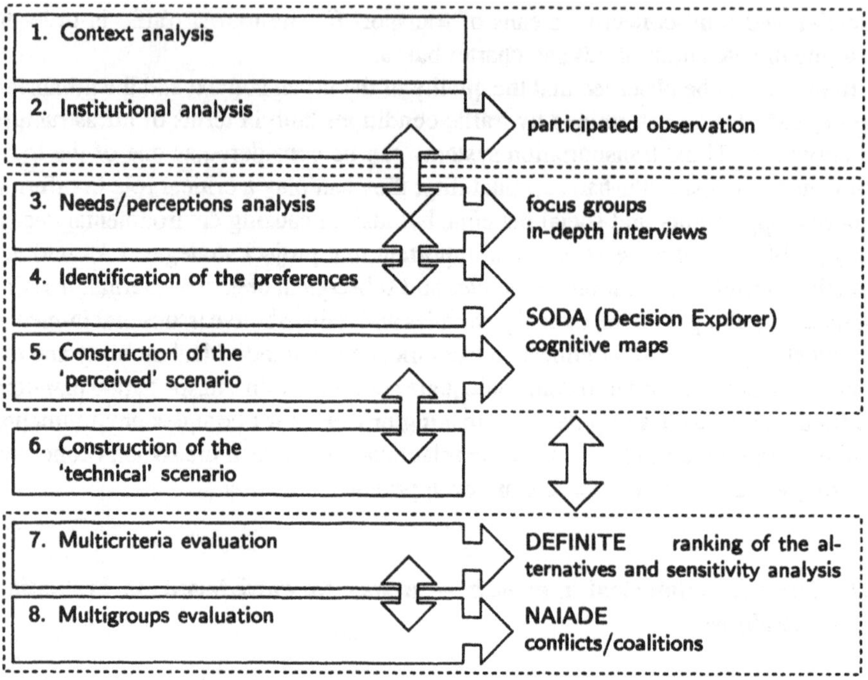

Figure 11.2 The methodology steps

based on an integrated approach, suitable for a flexible decision-making context. In particular, we adopted an institutional analysis method (De Marchi et al., 2000) to map out the actors and stakeholders involved in the decision-making process, and we used participated observation to understand the internal dynamics of community behaviour regarding the issue under consideration.

Institutional analysis enabled us to identify and analyze the endogenous human, social and environmental resources available, and to discover the community's social and economic perceptions. Indeed, performing an institutional analysis process implies defining the alternatives and highlighting the criteria which shape the preferences and mirror the hierarchy of interests of the various groups in the community. By giving our analysis this focus we were able to enlarge the cognitive framework and increase the number of tools available for the development of alternative scenarios in keeping with the various players and interest groups and their reciprocal relations.

We felt it was essential to identify the issues at stake by surveying the views and perceptions of the communities involved, taking into account the significant features of the area and the roles of the different users.

In general terms, we adopted two levels of interpretation: a 'macro' one, covering the larger area (the Sorrento Coast system), and a 'micro' one, which takes into account the reality, specific nature and values of each municipality involved. In this way we analyzed the issue of mobility in connection with ideas of local identity and liveability, acknowledging the vital role of communication and accessibility systems for improving quality of life on the coast.

Focus groups and in-depth interviews were conducted with representatives of the seven municipalities, industry (from the tourist, craft and farming sectors), civil society (cultural and environmental associations, private citizens) as well as the various categories of end users (residents, seasonal residents, students, commuters, workers, tourists grouped by area). This activity addressed several key issues, grouped into three main themes:

- Characteristics, conditions and potential of the Sorrento Coast area;
- Current problems and conflicts involving the various transportation systems;
- Alternative mobility strategies, including objective prioritization, alternative mobility solutions, benefits and opportunities.

Having identified the main issues for which we needed to elicit possible responses/reactions from key actors, we were able to highlight the key needs and problem areas, isolating the most significant perceived issues and needs. Analysis of the position of each stakeholder yielded a clear picture of each actor's views on traffic and congestion problems, and consequent suitable actions.

We found that the groups living and working in Sorrento Coast differ widely in their cultural models and life styles, mirroring their highly variable economic and social status. Also, these groups are often reluctant to identify commonalities or a shared ground for dialogue. Individualism and localism are an alibi for avoiding an otherwise possible integration process, and are one of the most frequent causes of conflict.

With the aim of identifying the different perceptions of issues and solutions by the municipalities involved in the decision-making process, we carried out needs analysis and preference identification based on Strategic Options Development and Analysis, SODA, (Eden and Simpson, 1989). SODA belongs to the class of Problem Structuring Methods, which enables modelling of data within a Decision-Making Support System, according to a communicative concept of planning (Rosenhead, 1996; Rosenhead and Mingers, 2001). With SODA we can address complex problems displaying soft, qualitative and unstructured data, with a focus on social and cognitive psychology components, which are reflected in social process management. This method enabled us to create a map of personal or group perceptions for use as a benchmark for the development of other, more far-reaching, analysis.

We used the *Decision Explorer*[4] software, which draws on the verbal format of an interview to plot cognitive maps, structure contents formally and methodologically, and appropriately analyses qualitative data. A cognitive map becomes the expression of a 'thought model', i.e. a system of concepts which express the nature of any given problem, and charts its meaning through their relations with other concepts. When needing to consider the views of several persons or groups regarding the problem, a 'strategic map' combining the individual maps can be plotted (Eden, 1986; Eden and Simpson, 1989; Rosenhead and Mingers, 2001). This is an effective tool for promoting negotiation among the group members in view of reaching a shared definition of

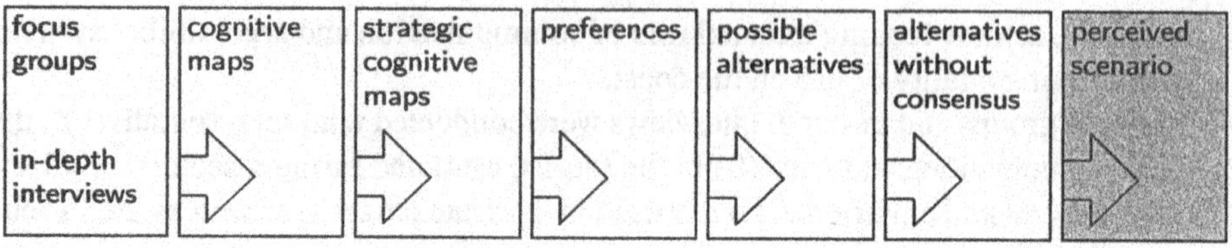

Figure 11.3 Steps in drawing up the perceived scenario

the problem and its possible solutions.

In particular, by constructing a map of ideas arranged in a coherent picture we can reach a better understanding of the situation, identify the real issues underlying the data, avoid data redundancy, deal with the conflicts among different opinions and options, broadening the field of arguments and reasons and identifying common ground. We can thus elucidate the structure of the reasoning process while preserving the wealth of data and managing complex information. Thus, flexible, concrete and acceptable solutions can be constructed, combining the options of the various persons/groups. According to this method, we reviewed the responses to interviews and the minutes of focus groups, regarding possible causes of traffic and congestion, the specificity of each municipality but also enlarging the vision to the whole Sorrento Coast, examining the causes of congestion and mobility-associated problems, viable solutions, solutions to be avoided or those without consensus. By plotting the conceptual chains for each map, we were able to pinpoint the expectations and possible solutions identified by each participant, thereby constructing a 'strategic map' representing interactions between the differing viewpoints of each municipality. By identifying the types of links in the strategic map, we analyzed the model and decided how to select the issues and solutions felt to be of primary concern. Consequently, through initial bottom-up evaluation, we defined the key components of the 'scenario as perceived' by the community (Figure 11.3) stemming from consultation with the 'laid knowledge'.

The outcome of these steps was used by 'experts' to develop technical choices. These were evaluated using the *Definite*[5] software (Herwijnen and van Janssen, 1988; Herwijnen, van Janssen and Nijkamp, 1992), having a multiple criteria approach, i.e. taking into account all known impacts (monetary and non-monetary, quantitative and qualitative) and listing the significant aspects of the planned choice together with its impact on the territory and the natural and built environment.

Last, we applied the NAIADE method — Novel Approach to Imprecise Assessment and Decision Environments method (Munda, 1995), for multigroup analysis of technical proposals to identify the possible consensus of the community involved, showing that group alliances can be fostered, thus making the proposed strategy truly feasible.

Combined application of different methods gave a multidimensional perspective to the evaluation process enabling it to accommodate the different demands and providing a foundation for concrete implementation of project options. This evaluation method allows analysis of spatial differentials in the target area, and full tapping into the potential stemming from the construction of shared collective values through a participative evaluation process.

11.8 From the 'perceived' to the 'technical' scenario

The characteristics and components of the 'perceived scenario' defined through a bottom-up approach and through the application of SODA methodology, sum up the needs and expectations of the communities involved in the decision-making process and, at the same time, identify alternative courses of action.

In particular, by comparing the different analyses ('domain', 'central', 'focus') we were able to infer a priority hierarchy and a preferability scale. Domain analysis lists concepts in a hierarchical manner based on the number of their links. Central analysis arranges concepts according to the complexity of their implication chains: the higher the complexity of relations for a given concept, the greater its central role. The two analyses complement each other, and comparison of their respective hierarchies makes it possible to evaluate which concepts play a key role for identifying guidelines for action. These two types of analysis allowed us to express preferences in terms of proposed solutions and, at the same time, to highlight the major causes — classified by user category — which contribute to worsen congestion and traffic. Finally, focus analysis enabled us to assign an order of preference for proposed solutions, by examining the solutions put forward by respondents and those considered inadvisable or without consensus. Thus we were able to draw up a priority list of the identified solutions, and to observe their basic coherence with the two former analyses.

These analyses indicate a clear need to create an integrated complementary mobility system able to meet a range of user requirements while improving quality of life. The output of analysis outlines the characteristics of the 'perceived scenario', which reflects the needs and wishes of the seven municipalities involved.

Drawing on the perceived scenario we were then able to define choices for the construction of a technical scenario, whose elements were arranged based on the know-how of the group of experts implementing the study. Thus, starting from the perceived situation, expert knowledge plotted alternative courses of action, setting in motion a continuous feedback process essential for technical evaluation of the identified solutions. In light of the input from the community, we identified several strategies referring both to existing transport systems and the introduction of new ones, namely (Figure 11.4):

- Upgrade railway service by means of an increase in commercial speed and frequency (11-minute intervals);
- Streamline and upgrade maritime services;
- Create an extensive local cable transportation system (cable railways and cableways) powered by photovoltaic energy to reduce environmental impact;
- Enlarge the footpath system, integrating it with the collective transport net-

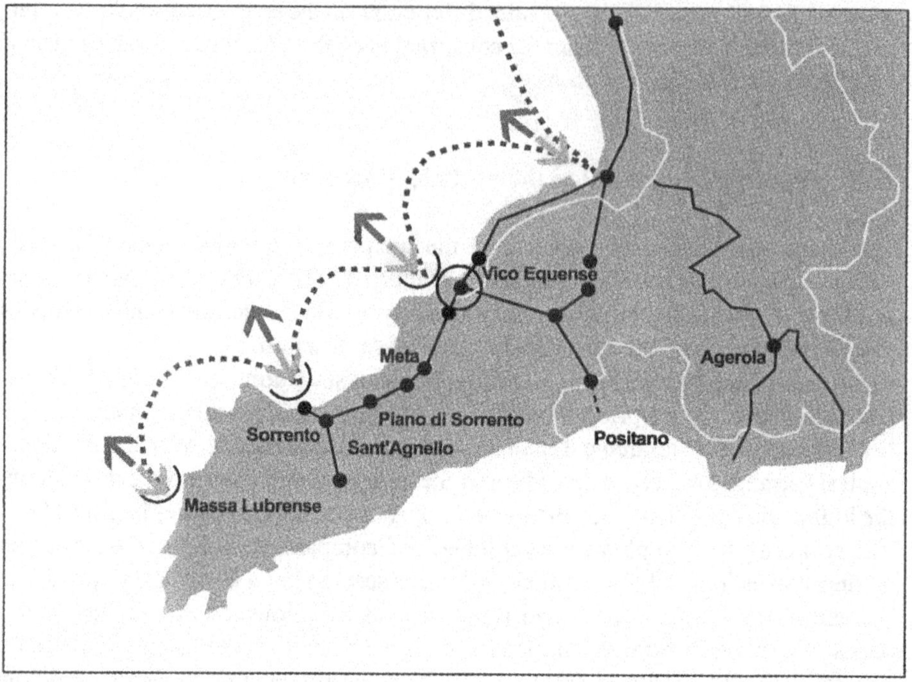

Figure 11.4 The new mobility system for the Sorrento Coast

work (railroad, maritime, cableways) and connecting it with the pedestrian areas of historic centres;

- Improve the local road system;
- Establish exchange nodes between the rail systems, city, inter-city and tourist bus routes, sea services and private transport;
- Create effective links with regional and national collective transport systems (intercity railway line, airport).

The proposed mobility system for the Sorrento Coast is based on a series of complementary actions, integrating the different transport modes (road, rail, cable, sea) in order to establish a comprehensive system which accommodates the elements that emerged from the perceived scenario. The technical proposal, due to the method followed in its construction, defines an overall project scenario as a significant alternative to the 'status quo' that can merge the requirements and wishes of the communities involved with economic and administrative feasibility, while respecting the territory's environmental and cultural values.

11.9 Multicriteria evaluation

External access to Sorrento Coast and its internal mobility may be improved by a set of actions regarding the road network, the rail and sea transport systems, and by streamlining administrative procedures associated with mobility management. Moreover, actions must target not only the efficiency and effectiveness but also social development, enhancement of the natural and built heritage, use of clean energy and saving of non-renewable energy sources — so as to maximize both the economic and the intrinsic values of the area.

With this aim in mind, we attempted to forecast the impacts of the proposed system on the different environmental components, comparing them with the effects of the present situation ('status quo'). The aim was to establish the cost/benefit ratio of the projects proposed, i.e. the amount of capital outlay versus the benefits (not only monetary) that would indeed accrue to the community — while ensuring full respect for the environment. In other words, we wished to ascertain if, and to what extent, project implementation would be preferable to sticking to the 'status quo'. Evaluation was, therefore, conducted by comparing two alternative scenarios: A (status quo) and B (project scenario).

The multicriteria method was used. We identified criteria, environmental components, recipient/receptors, objectives and indicators, taking into account the guidelines for Environmental Impact Assessment and Strategic Environmental Assessments (Table 11.1). We also established the 'positive side' of each indicator, i.e. whether its increasing weight represented a benefit to be pursued or a cost to be minimized (Table 11.2).

Bearing in mind that we were working within the framework of a territorial scale feasibility study, according to the types of information available some impacts were evaluated on a quantitative scale while others were assessed on a purely qualitative level. In particular, we used both the binary scale of a 'yes/no' type and the following ordinal, four-point scales: the first is of the type (− − −, −−, −, 0), for which level 0 (no effect) is the most preferable, followed by three levels of increasing negative effect, from right to left; the second is of the type (0, +, ++, + + +), where 0 (no effect) is the least preferable, followed by three levels of increasing positive effects, from left to right.

The first evaluation criterion refers to 'atmospheric protection'. It was shown that several environmental problems on a global and local scale alike are caused by emissions, a significant share of which comes from vehicular traffic. In particular, carbon dioxide emissions contribute to the 'greenhouse effect' and, consequently, to climate change. Other emissions are the major cause of acid rain and ensuing acidification of soil and groundwater, and still others have harmful effects on human health. Appropriate goals are the limitation of emission into the atmosphere of several of the most noxious pollutants: carbon dioxide (CO_2), nitrogen oxides (NO_x), carbon monoxide (CO), particulate matter (PM_{10}). In the short-medium term, our proposed scenario would halve CO_2 and NO_x emissions and reduce by one third CO and PM_{10} emissions compared to the current situation (status quo). In the long term,

Table 11.1 Identification of criteria and objectives

Sustainability criteria	Sustainability objectives	Symbol
Protection of the atmosphere	Limitation of greenhouse gases (CO_2)	O_1
	Limitation of acid emissions in the atmosphere (NO_x)	O_2
	Limitation of oxidizing agent emissions (CO)	O_3
	Limitation of particle emissions (PM_{10})	O_4
Conservation and upgrading of the quality of water resources	Limitation of changes in the direction of sea currents	O_5
	Mitigation of the effects of accidental pollutant spillages	O_6
	Limitation of the alteration of free water tables	O_7
	Limitation of the alteration of confined water tables	O_8
Conservation and protection of the characteristics of the soil and sub-soil	Limitation of the reduction of areas for agricultural and forestry uses	O_9
	Avoidance of changes to slope stability	O_{10}
	Avoidance of changes of coastal morphodynamics in beach systems	O_{11}
	Limitation of damage by strong vibrations	O_{12}
Conservation and upgrading of the status of wild flora and fauna	Limitation of the elimination of woodland vegetation	O_{13}
	Protection of the natural vegetation habitat	O_{14}
	Protection of species of cultural interest	O_{15}
	Protection of endangered species and habitats and conservation of biological diversity	O_{16}
Improvement of economic dynamics	Increased effects on the economy of the Province of Naples from the point of view of demand	O_{17}
	Increased effects on the economy of the Province of Naples from the point of view of supply	O_{18}
Efficiency and effectiveness	Reduction of road movements	O_{19}
	Increase in rail movements	O_{20}
	Increase in sea movements	O_{21}
	Reduction of travel times in road movements	O_{22}
	Increase in rail frequency	O_{23}
	Upgrading of vehicle parking systems	O_{24}
	Reduction in the use of non-renewable energy sources	O_{25}
	Reduction in noise level generated by vehicle traffic in the vicinity of inhabited areas	O_{26}
	Integration of varying transport modes	O_{27}
Cost of works	Minimizing of work costs	O_{28}

Table 11.2 Identification of indicators and units of measurement

Ob.	Indicators	Unit of measurement	Positive side
O_1	Emission of gas causing greenhouse effect (CO_2)	tonnes/year	min
O_2	Emission of acids in the atmosphere (NO_x)	tonnes/year	min
O_3	Emission of oxidizing agents (CO)	tonnes/year	min
O_4	Emission of suspended particles (PM_{10})	tonnes/year	min
O_5	Modification of direction of sea currents	yes/no	no
O_6	Mitigation of accidental pollutant spillage	yes/no	yes
O_7	Alteration of free water tables	(– – –, – –, –, 0)	max
O_8	Alteration of confined water tables	yes/no	no
O_9	Amount of lost farmland and woodland	(– – –, – –, –, 0)	max
O_{10}	Modification of slope stability	(– – –, – –, –, 0)	max
O_{11}	Modification of coastal morphodynamics in beach systems	yes/no	no
O_{12}	Presence of strong vibrations	yes/no	no
O_{13}	Elimination of woodland vegetation	yes/no	no
O_{14}	Natural level of vegetation formations affected	(– – –, – –, –, 0)	max
O_{15}	Protection of citrus fruit groves	yes/no	yes
O_{16}	Works in Bio-Italy Sites and/or integral reserves	(– – –, – –, –, 0)	max
O_{17}	Increment of effects on the economy of the Province of Naples from the point of view of demand	€	max
O_{18}	Increment of effects on the Province of Naples from the point of view of supply	€	max
O_{19}	Road movements	number of movements/year	min
O_{20}	Rail movements	number of movements/year	max
O_{21}	Sea movements	number of movements/year	max
O_{22}	Average travel time between Vico Equense and Sorrento	minutes	min
O_{23}	Frequency of trains	minutes	min
O_{24}	Creation of new vehicle parking areas	number of additional slots	max
O_{25}	Fuel consumption	tonnes/year	min
O_{26}	Reduction of noise level	yes/no	yes
O_{27}	Integration between varying transport modes	(0, +, ++, +++)	max
O_{28}	Capital costs	€	min

with the progressive introduction of more efficient engines and hydrogen-powered vehicles, pollutant emissions could be even further reduced.

The 'conservation and improvement of water quality' parameter is based on the principle that water is a renewable resource essential for human health and very existence; its availability and quality may be endangered by human intervention. It is therefore necessary to maintain the quantity and quality of existing resources and improve those already contaminated. The following goals were identified, regarding both surface and groundwater:

- Reduce alterations to the direction of sea currents;
- Mitigate accidental leakage of pollutants;
- Contain changes to free water tables;
- Contain changes to confined water tables.

The 'conservation and protection of soil and subsoil' parameter recognizes the fact that these are key resources for human well-being which may be endangered by inappropriate land use. It is therefore essential to preserve existing resources and improve degraded soils. We identified the following objectives applicable to the soil and subsoil:

- Curb the reduction of agricultural and/or forest areas;
- Avoid changes in slope stability;
- Avoid changes to the coastal morphodynamics;
- Limit damage caused by strong vibrations.

'Conservation and improvement of wildlife and vegetation' addresses the requirement to conserve and improve our natural heritage stock for the benefit of present and future generations. We identified the following goal applicable to vegetation cover, plant diversity and wildlife:

- Curb the destruction of woodlands;
- Protect wild flora and fauna;
- Protect species of special cultural relevance;
- Protect endangered species and habitats and conserve biological diversity.

The 'improvement of economic dynamics' parameter focuses on the economic impact of planned investments for upgrading the mobility system of the Sorrento Coast. Their benefits for the local economy and the whole province are considered, both in the short and long term. In particular, we used two types of indicators: the first covering the increase in demand for goods/services in the Naples Province the second covering the increase in terms of supply.

The 'efficiency and effectiveness' parameter, on the other hand, addresses the new opportunities opened to users by the upgrading of transport systems. In particular the following elements were considered: (1) reduction in car use; (2) increase in train use; (3) increase in maritime link use; (4) decrease in travel times; (5) increase in train frequency; (6) upgrading of vehicle parking facilities; (7) reduction in fuel consumption; (8) reduction in traffic-generated noise near urban areas; and (9) integration of different transport modes.

In particular, in the short to medium term, fuel consumption by vehicle traffic can be more than halved from current levels, a prospect linked to the recommended construction of cable railways and cableways powered by photovoltaic systems, which neither involve the consumption of fossil fuels nor contribute to environmental pollution. Solar panels can be mounted on the roofs of stations or adjacent service buildings: for example, a panel measuring approximately 130 × 70 × 45 cm (width × length × depth), weighing about 10 kg, produces 100 Wp (peak Watts) at 24 volts.

The proposed scenario also involves a significant increase in rail traffic per year, from the current 4.8 million trips to 8.4 million. Sea traffic would rise from 2.0 to 2.6 million movements, entailing a fall in road traffic trips per year (from 34.7 to 30.5 million).

The last evaluation parameter is 'works costs' which include the cost of land acquisition and compensation for property expropriation, as well as actual construction costs.

Once we had identified the criteria, objectives and associated indicators, both for the 'status quo' (Alternative A) and for the 'project scenario' (Alternative B) we assigned weights to the assessment criteria, grouping them under four headings:

- *Group I:* Atmospheric protection, conservation and upgrading of water resources, conservation and protection of the soil and subsoil, conservation and upgrading of plant and wildlife;
- *Group II:* Upgrading of economic dynamics;
- *Group III:* Efficiency and effectiveness;
- *Group IV:* Works costs.

Each group was assigned the same weight, that is 0.25 (yielding a sum total of one); this value was then equally divided among the individual objectives within each group. Hence, each of the 16 objectives in group I was assigned a weight of 0.015; the 2 objectives of group II a weight of 0.125; the 9 objectives of group III a weight of 0.028; the single objective of group IV a weight of 0.25.

All impact-associated data were shown in the evaluation matrix (Table 11.3) and were subsequently entered in the *Definite* software package. This made it possible to implement the following assessment methods: Regime analysis (Hinloopen and Njikamp, 1990; Nijkamp, Rietveld and Voogd, 1990), the Evamix method (Voogd, 1983), Concordance analysis (Roy, 1985; Roy, 1996), the Weighted Sum method. We chose *Definite* since it is a well-tested decision-making support tool, which has already been applied successfully to the planning of transport systems. The output of the multicriteria assessment system is a priority ranking for the two scenarios under consideration (Figure 11.5).

Each method used consistently showed the preferability of the project scenario. In particular, with the Evamix method, the two scenarios scored opposite values: A (status quo) scored −0.5, whereas B (project scenario) scored +0.5. Regime analysis yielded a preference probability for scenario A of 0.01, whereas that of scenario B

Table 11.3 The multicriteria evaluation matrix

Ob.	Indicators	Alternative A	Alternative B
O_1	Emission of gas causing greenhouse effect (CO_2)	53,000	25,000
O_2	Emission of acids in the atmosphere (NO_x)	47	27
O_3	Emission of oxidizing agents (CO)	740	280
O_4	Emission of suspended particles (PM_{10})	3	1
O_5	Modification of direction of sea currents	no	no
O_6	Mitigation of accidental pollutant spillage	no	yes
O_7	Alteration of free water tables	0	–
O_8	Alteration of confined water tables	no	no
O_9	Amount of lost farmland and woodland	0	–
O_{10}	Modification of slope stability	0	–
O_{11}	Modification of coastal morphodynamics in beach systems	yes	no
O_{12}	Presence of strong vibrations	no	no
O_{13}	Elimination of woodland vegetation	no	no
O_{14}	Natural level of vegetation formations affected	0	–
O_{15}	Protection of citrus fruit groves	yes	yes
O_{16}	Works in Bio-Italy Sites and/or integral reserves	0	–
O_{17}	Increment of effects on the economy of the Province of Naples from the point of view of demand	0	879,685,076
O_{18}	Increment of effects on the Province of Naples from the point of view of supply	0	1,674,000,000
O_{19}	Road movements	34,700,000	30,500,000
O_{20}	Rail movements	4,800,000	8,400,000
O_{21}	Sea movements	2,000,000	2,600,000
O_{22}	Average travel time between Vico Equense and Sorrento	20	8
O_{23}	Frequency of trains	30	11
O_{24}	Creation of new vehicle parking areas	0	3,650
O_{25}	Fuel consumption	14,100	6,300
O_{26}	Reduction of noise level	no	yes
O_{27}	Integration between varying transport modes	+	+++
O_{28}	Capital costs	0	350,453,150

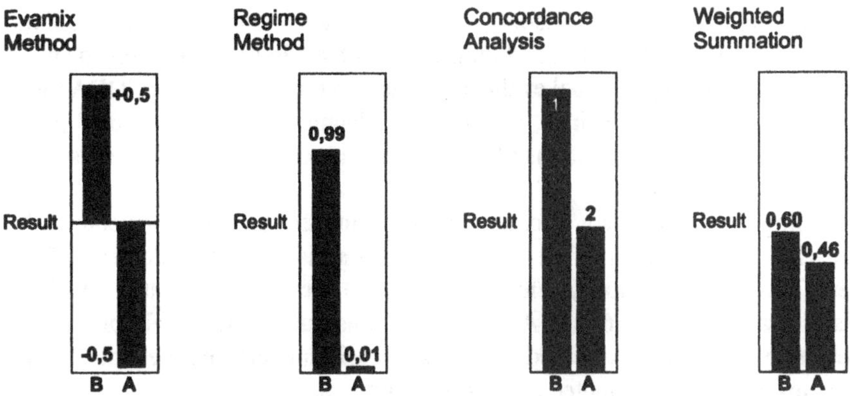

Figure 11.5 Evaluation result with the application of Definite

was 0.99 (in this case, since the method uses ordinal numbers, parameter weights were automatically converted by the software from cardinal to ordinal). Concordance analysis yielded a priority ranking with B (1) preferable to A (2), while the Weighted Sum method showed the difference between B (0.60) and A (0.46).

We can thus infer that the project scenario is preferable to the 'status quo' since estimated project costs are amply outweighed by the wide range of 'benefits' to the human, natural and built environment involved in the integrated mobility system project.

11.10 Multigroup evaluation

The project scenario, apart from being subjected to multicriteria evaluation, was also evaluated through the application of the NAIADE method (Munda, 1995), with the goal of identifying the degree of consensus — both at macro and micro levels — the various projects planned would generate among the communities involved. In particular, we identified the position of the seven municipalities regarding each component of the future scenario, verifying the concrete possibilities of setting up coalition relationships supporting the implementation of project objectives.

NAIADE is a discrete multicriteria method whose evaluation matrix can include both precise stochastic measurements and fuzzy measurements of the performance of different options, according to given evaluation criteria. Thus it is very flexible regarding its concrete applications. This method makes it possible to analyze contexts with a high degree of uncertainty and complexity, prioritize objectives, while also checking their impact on the communities in terms of stakeholder alliances. Ultimately, it enables the definition of a single defendable and equitable scenario supported by a fair level of consensus.

In this case, this method was applied for the construction of the equity matrix (local communities/proposed actions), through which we analyzed the conflicts between the different stakeholders and outlined possible alliances regarding the proposed works, formulating a verbal evaluation based on the output of the SODA tool. Using the judgments thus obtained, we drew up a 'dendrogram of coalitions' (Figure 11.6), which shows the positions of local communities regarding proposals contained in the project scenario.

Examining the dendrogram of coalitions we found that Piano di Sorrento (G3) and Sant'Agnello (G4) form a first coalition, a second is formed by Sorrento (G5) and Meta (G2). On the contrary, Vico Equense (G1) occupies an isolated position, whereas Massa Lubrense (G6) and Agerola (G7) constitute the last coalition. These alliances are based on the expressed positions of each municipality, i.e. the preferences and priorities they attributed to possible solutions.

The coalition between Piano di Sorrento and Sant'Agnello was the first to come about and reflects an attempt to reconcile the requirements of these two municipalities which are indirectly affected by the traffic and congestion revolving around Sorrento. On the other hand, Sorrento and Meta still need to define a common line of action so as to identify strategic choices for removing or controlling critical levels of traffic congestion. The likely reason why Vico Equense (G1) did not form alliances is that its main concern is establishing links between the urban area and the interior. An autonomous coalition is, on the other hand, emerging between Massa Lubrense (G6) and Agerola (G7), which share several issues and needs linked to the characteristics of their territory.

Our evaluation work showed that formal assessment tools can enhance understanding of the negotiation process leading to conflict resolution, improve the openness of the decision-making process and enable targeting of shared choices. The adoption of an evaluation-based approach to a decision-making problem marked by multiple conflicts of interest may, therefore, become the method of choice for opening a dialogue with the community: thus the process itself takes on a greater role than final choices.

11.11 Conclusions

From the construction of the preliminary investigation regarding the decision-making process, based both on analysis of the social, economic and environmental context and on institutional analysis, we performed multicriteria and multigroup evaluation of the scenarios drafted during the knowledge-building process.

Evaluation was conceived as a dynamic process, following the complex decision-making route right from the start. A key element for evaluation was the examination of the problems and conflicts between alternative mobility systems and their context, together with the expressed needs and preferences of stakeholders.

The output of the evaluation process made it possible to select, from a range of alternative accessibility and mobility strategies, the solution which best meets the requirements of an integrated and sustainable transport system, with the aim of

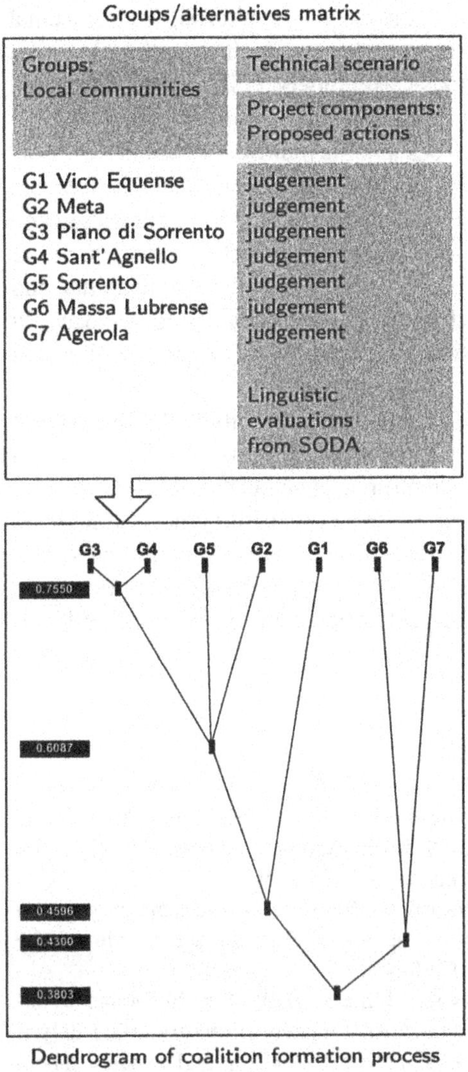

Figure 11.6 The dendrogram of coalitions with the application of NAIADE

fostering the enhancement and correct use of the existing territorial, environmental and cultural resources. At the same time, the output showed which options have the highest degree of consensus from the various stakeholders, pointing the way to the possible alliances that would be required in the subsequent implementation phase.

The ultimate goal was to plan an overall sustainable transport system for the Sorrento Coast, and to balance environmental protection requirements and development needs. In order to do this, we identified, in areas deeply altered by urbanization and human activity and marked by inadequate mobility and transport systems, a series of options compatible with environmental, spatial, social and cultural constraints, and we selected the most appropriate one based on an integrated evaluation approach. In other words, we attempted to draft a solution which would maximize overall social value.

A few months after the submission of this feasibility study to the Naples Province, steps were taken to include it in the Provincial Territorial Coordination Plan adopted on 6 February 2003. There is therefore a concrete possibility that, once adequate public and private funding has been secured, the infrastructure outlined will be created over the next few years. It is hoped that this will not only contribute to improving mobility on the Sorrento Coast but will also promote sustainable economic and social development, coupled with full respect for the area's rich natural and built heritage.

Notes

1 This contribution is the result of a collaborative effort: in particular Luigi Fusco Girard addressed the issues from section 11.1 to 11.5, Maria Cerreta those of section 11.7, 11.8 and 11.10, and Pasquale De Toro those of section 11.6 and 11.9.

2 Work carried out in the framework of the 'Feasibility Study covering the mobility system of the Sorrento Peninsula', commissioned by the Naples Province and coordinated by Prof. Marino De Luca and Engineer Fabio Ciuffini.

3 Editor's note: Italian administrative subdivision has essentially three hierarchically organized levels: regional, provincial, and municipal. Actually (February 2005) Italy is composed of: 20 regions with an average area of about 15,000 km^2 and an average population of about 2,850,000 inhabitants; 106 provinces with an average area of 2,800 km^2 and 540,000 inhabitants; and 8104 municipalities. Concerning their population of respectively 5.7 and 3.1 million inhabitants, the Campania Region and the Province of Naples (Napoli) considered in this contribution are located quite above these statistical means, while their areas (13,595 and 1,171 km^2) are not very far away from the average values or are even below them. It may also be interesting to report the figures of the other three Italian case studies presented within this book. The contribution of Patassini et al. (here) refers to the Veneto Region with an area of 18,391 km^2 and 4.5 million inhabitants, and to the Province of Venice (Venezia) which reaches 2,463 km^2 with 810,000 inhabitants. Instead the two cases cited in the contribution of Borri et al. (here) refer to the Apulia (Puglia) Region with 19,362 km^2 and 4.0 million inhabitants, and to the Province of Bari with 3,825 km^2 and 1.2 million inhabitants within its new administrative limits since 19 May 2004. All the surface and population figures of this note refer to the 2001

Italian general census of population.

4 Editor's note: software developed originally by academics at the universities of Bath and Strathclyde and now by Banxia Software Ltd., Kendal, Cumbria (UK). See http://www.banxia.com/demain.html for details.

5 Editor's note: software developed by Ron van Janssen and Marjan van Herwijnen at the Instituut voor Milieuvraagstukken (IVM, Institute for Environmental Studies) of the Vrije Universiteit (VU, Free University), Amsterdam, The Netherlands. See http://www.vu.nl for details.

References

Bateman, J. and Willis, K. (1995), *Valuing Environmental Preferences*, Oxford University Press, Oxford (UK).

Berger, P. L. and Luckmann, T. (1967), *The Social Construction of Reality: A Treatise in the Sociology of Knowledge*, Anchor, New York, NY (USA).

Camagni, R. (2000), 'Processi di globalizzazione e sostenibilità urbana. Nuova governance urbana e nuovi strumenti per l'infrastrutturazione finanziaria' (Urban globalization and sustainability processes. New urban governance and new financial infrastructuring instruments), in L. Fusco Girard and B. Forte (eds.), *Città sostenibile e sviluppo umano*, (The sustainable city and human development), Franco Angeli, Milano (Italy).

Clemen, R. T. (1996), *Making Hard Decision. An Introduction to Decision Analysis*, Duxbury Press, Belmont, CA (USA).

Cold, B. (ed., 2001), *Aesthetics, Well-being and Health — Essays within Architecture and Environmental Aesthetics*, Ashgate, Aldershot (UK).

Coote, A. and Lenaghan, J. (1997), *Citizens' Juries: Theory into Practice*, Institute for Public Policy Research, London (UK).

Costanza, R. (ed., 1991), *Ecological Economics: The Science and Management of Sustainability*, Columbia University Press, New York (USA).

Davoudi, S. (2002), 'Polycentricity — Modelling or Determining Reality', *Town and Country Planning*, Vol. 7, pp. 114-117.

De Marchi, B., Funtowicz, S. O., Lo Cascio, S. and Munda, G. (2000), 'Combining Participative and Institutional Approaches with Multicriteria Evaluation. An Empirical Study for Water Issues in Troina, Sicily', *Ecological Economics*, Vol. 34, No. 2, pp. 267-282.

Eden, C. (1986), *The Future Consultant-Finding the Multiplier*, School of Management, University of Bath, UK.

Eden, C. and Simpson, P. (1989), 'Soda and Cognitive Mapping in Practice', in J. Rosenhead (ed.), *Rational Analysis for a Problematic World*, Wiley, Chichester (UK), pp. 43-70.

Etzioni, A. (1988), *The Moral Dimension. Towards a New Economics*, The Free Press, New York, NY, USA.

European Commission (1999), *ESDP — European Spatial Development Perspective*, EC, Luxembourg.

Faludi, A. (2000), 'The European Spatial Development Perspective — What next?', *European Planning Studies*, Vol. 8, No. 2, pp. 237-250.

Fromm, O. (2000), 'Ecological Structure and Functions of Biodiversity as Elements of its Total Economic Value', *Environmental and Resources Economics*, Vol. 16, No. 3, pp. 303-328.

Funtowicz, S. O. and Ravetz, J. R. (1993), 'Science for the Post-Normal Age', *Futures*, Vol. 25, No. 7, pp. 739-755.

Fusco Girard, L. (1987), *Risorse architettoniche e culturali: valutazioni e strategie di conservazione* (Architectural and cultural resources: assessment and conservation strategies), Franco Angeli, Milano (Italy).

Fusco Girard, L. and Nijkamp, P. (1997), *Le valutazioni per lo sviluppo sostenibile della città e del territorio* (Evaluation for the sustainable development of the city and the territory), Franco Angeli, Milano (Italy).

Fusco Girard, L. and Nijkamp, P. (2004), *Conservazione delle risorse ambientali, territoriali ed energetiche e sviluppo economico. Le valutazioni integrate* (Conservation of the environmental, spatial and energy resources and economic development. Integrated evaluation), Franco Angeli, Milano (Italy), forthcoming.

Fusco Girard, L., Forte, B., Cerreta, M., De Toro, P. and Forte, F. (2003), *The Human Sustainable City. Challenge and Perspectives from the Habitat Agenda*, Ashgate, Aldershot (UK).

Gallopin, G., Hammond, A., Raskin, P. and Swart, R. (1997), *Branch Points: Global Scenarios and Human Choice*, Stockholm Environment Institute, Stockholm (Sweden).

Genovesi, A. (1765), *Lezioni di commercio e di economia civile* (Lectures on commerce and civil economics), Tipografia dei classici italiani, Milano (Italy).

Habermas, J. (1984), *The Theory of Communicative Action*, Polity Press, Cambridge (UK).

Habermas, J. (1990), *The Philosophical Discourse on Modernity*, MIT Press, Boston, MA (USA).

Healey, P. (1997), *Collaborative Planning-Shaping Places in Fragmented Societies*, MacMillan, London (UK).

Healey, P., Khakee, A., Motte, A. and Needham, B. (1999), 'European Developments in Strategic Spatial Planning', *European Planning Studies*, Vol. 7, No. 3, pp. 339-371.

Heller, A. (1987), *Behind Justice*, Basic, New York, NY (USA).

Herwijnen, M. and van Janssen, R. (1988), 'Definite', in A. G. Locket and G. Islei (eds.), *Improving Decision-Making in Organizations*, Springer, Berlin (Germany).

Herwijnen, M., van Janssen, R. and Nijkamp, P. (1992), *A Multicriteria Decision Support Model and Geographic Information System for Sustainable Development Planning of the Greek Islands*, VU, Amsterdam (The Netherlands).

Hill, M. (1973), *Planning for Multiple Objectives. Monograph Series, n.5*, Regional Science Research Institute, Philadelphia, PA (USA).

Hinloopen, E. and Njikamp, P. (1990), 'Quantitative Multiple Criteria Choice Analysis', *Quality and Quantity*, Vol. 24, pp. 37-56.

Hirsch, F. (1976), *Social Limits to Growth*, Harvard University Press, Cambridge (UK).

Ikelgami, J. (1994), *Intrinsic Value and Cultural Economics*, Witten University Press, Witten (Germany).

Jacobs, M. (1997), 'Environmental Valuation, Deliberative Democracy and Public Decision-Making Institutions', in J. Foster (ed.), *Valuing Nature? Ethics, Economics and the Environment*, Routledge, London (UK), pp. 211-231.

Keeney, R. L. (1992), *Value-Focused Thinking*, Harvard University Press, Cambridge (UK).

Khakee, A. (1999), 'Participatory Scenarios for Sustainable Development', *Foresight*, Vol. 1, No. 3, pp. 229-230.

Lichfield, N. (1968), 'Economics in Town Planning', *Town Planning Review*, No. 39.

Lichfield, N. (1977), 'Land Use Planning and Environmental Protection: Convergence or Divergence?', *Environment and Planning*, No. 9.

Lichfield, N. (1989), *Economics of Urban Conservation*, Cambridge University Press, Cambridge (UK).

Mitchell, R. C. and Carson, R. T. (1989), *Using Surveys to Value Public Goods: The Contingent Valuation Method*, Resource for the Future, Washington, DC (USA).

Munda, G. (1995), *Multicriteria Evaluation in a Fuzzy Environment: Theory and Applications in Ecological Economics*, Physica-Verlag, Heidelberg (Germany).

Nijkamp, P., Rietveld, P. and Voogd, H. (1990), *Multicriteria Evaluation in Physical Planning*, Elsevier, Amsterdam (The Netherlands).

Parruccini, M. (ed., 1994), *Applying Multiple Criteria Aid for Decision to Environmental Management*, Kluwer, Dordrecht (The Netherlands).

Patton, M. Q. (1996), *Utilization-Focus Evaluation: The New Century Text*, Sage, Thousand Oaks, CA (USA).

Rosenhead, J. (1996), 'What's the Problem? An Introduction to Problem Structuring Methods', *Interfaces*, Vol. 26, pp. 117-131.

Rosenhead, J. and Mingers, J. (2001), *Rational Analysis for a Problematic World Revisited: Problem Structuring Methods for Complexity, Uncertainty and Conflict*, Wiley, Chichester (UK).

Roy, B. (1985), *Méthodologie multicritère d'aide à la décision*, Economica, Paris (France).

Roy, B. (1996), *Multicriteria Methodology for Decision Aiding*, Kluwer, Dordrecht (The Netherlands).

Ruskin, J. (1871), quoted in Ikelgami (1994).

Schumpeter, I. A. (1954), *Capitalism, Socialism and Democracy*, Unwin, London (UK).

Turner, R. K. (1992), *Speculations on Weak and Strong Sustainability* (GEC Working Paper 92-26), CSERGE, Norwich (UK).

Turner, R. K., Bateman, I. J. and Adger, W. N. (eds., 2001), *Economics of Coastal and Water Resources: Valuing Environmental Functions*, Kluwer, Drodrecht (The Netherlands).

Turner, R. K., Folke, C., Green, M. and Bateman, I. (1993), *Valuation and Sustainable Management of Wetland Ecosystems: Three Case Studies* (Joint CSERGE/Beijer Institute Working Paper), CSERGE, Norwich (UK).

Voogd, E. (1983), *Multicriteria Evaluation for Urban and Regional Planning*, Pion, London (UK).

Zamagni, S. (1994), 'Global Environmental Change, Rationality and Ethics', in L. Campiglio et al. (eds.), *The Environment after Rio*, Graham and Trotnam, London (UK).

PART III
SCENARIOS AS AN EXPLORATORY APPROACH

Chapter 12

Analysis of the INTELCITY Scenarios for the City of the Future from a Southern European Perspective

Patrizia Lombardi and Steve Curwell

12.1 Introduction

INTELCITY is a one-year RTD (Research, Technological Development & Demonstration) roadmap project funded by the European Union Information Society Technologies (IST) Programme. It aims to explore new opportunities for sustainable development of cities through the intelligent use of Information and Communication Technologies (ICTs). It will integrate the knowledge of experts in Sustainable Urban Development (SUD) and ICTs to deliver a roadmap that relates the range of potential ICT development options to planning and urban re/development processes.

The partnership is led by the University of Salford, UK and includes: the Finnish State Technical Research Centre (VTT, *Valtion teknillinen tutkimuskeskus*); the German Institute for Technology Assessment and Systems Analysis (ITAS, *Institut für Technikfolgenabschätzung und Systemanalyse* of the Research Centre Karlsruhe (FZK, *Forschungszentrum Karlsruhe*); the Leibniz Institute of Ecological and Regional Development (IÖR, *Leibniz-Institut für Ökologische Raumentwicklung e.V.*), Dresden, Germany; the French Scientific and Technical Building Centre (CSTB, *Centre Scientifique et Technique du Bâtiment*); the Economic and Social Institute (ESI, *Economisch en Sociaal Instituut*) of the Free University (VU, *Vrije Universiteit*) at Amsterdam, The Netherlands; the Pierluigi Spadolini Department of Technology of Architecture and Design (TaeD, *Dipartimento di Tecnologie dell'Architettura e Design 'Pierluigi Spadolini'*) of the University of Florence, Italy; the Polytechnic of Turin (*Politecnico di Torino*), Italy; the *Napier University*, Edinburgh, UK; and the *University of the West of England*, Bristol, UK. The main objectives are to:

- Link ICT and SUD research groups in a thematic network to strengthen common understanding of the role of ICTs in urban planning, property, and management of cities;
- Identify a range of visions and scenarios for innovative use of ICTs to rethink the organisation of the city, and for planning and urban development processes that will aid more inclusive decision-making and support more sustainable

solutions across Europe;

- Identify social, economic, and technical barriers to implementing new ways of ICT working in urban re/development processes, in terms of knowledge and skills gaps, information overload and management, necessary to realise the potential of ICTs in SUD; and to
- Explore consensus over research opportunities with stakeholders in various European planning contexts, to identify integrated ICT-SUD research priorities.

In the first work package, the INTELCITY network has identified research challenges for future urban planning, design, and city management through the innovative use of ICTs. In particular, it has developed scenarios for the city of the future with a time horizon of 2030 during the first Workshop held in Oslo (24-25 September 2002). All the scenarios try to link ICTs use with Sustainable Urban Planning and Design activities.

This contribution is concerned with an evaluation of these alternative scenarios for the City of the future by using a multicriteria analysis (MCA), which provides a systematic process for trading off effects of various alternatives, synthesising individual contributions and values.

In this application of MCA, the evaluation criteria and weights are identified by the delegates of the INTELCITY Mediterranean Regions Workshop, held in Turin on 30 October 2002.

The structure of the contribution is the following: section 12.2 provides a short theoretical illustration of the MCA; section 12.3 illustrates the alternative scenarios established by the INTELCITY consortium; section 12.4 shows the application of the MCA to the case study; section 12.5 discusses the results obtained, providing a sensitivity analysis; and finally section 12.6 summaries the application and provides some conclusive remarks.

12.2 Multicriteria analysis and analytic hierarchy process evaluation methods

MCA is a decision-making procedure that uses utility theory to compare and rank alternative courses of action. It provides a systematic process for trading off effects of various alternatives to aid decision-making.

MCA takes into account all the aspects and values involved in a decision-making process, providing all the following benefits: a clear definition of the criteria used in the selection of an option from among alternative solutions; a weighting of the criteria to be used in the evaluation, in accordance with different points of view; a combination of multiple aspects which have different nature; a comparison between objectives, strategies of the various subjects involved, and available resources; a transparent and explicit evaluation approach.

Compared with cost-benefit analysis, in MCA the measure of benefits are not related to the concept of 'willing to pay' but to the 'goal achievement level', which involves the evaluation of performance against a number of criteria. Both performance and criteria can only be defined by a value-based judgement; they are not empirically verifiable. Indeed, the term performance must be a goal-oriented-behaviour, i.e. a behaviour rendered meaningful by the existence of a criterion that specifies when a goal has been attained (Francescato, 1991).

By taking into account different points of view and a weighting of the criteria to be used in the evaluation of alternative options, MCA methods provide the possibility to realise a meaningful and pluralistic evaluation of alternative scenarios, synthesising all the contributions of the different experts and the points of view of the actors involved.

Because of its flexibility, this approach has been successfully applied to military strategy, politics and companies, as well as to regional and urban planning for evaluating alternative courses of action and/or design solutions, assessing their impacts on the built and natural environment (Saaty and Vargas, 1981; Fusco Girard, 1987; Roscelli, 1990). In this last field, the evaluation process assumes the followings characteristics.

- A tool for *participation* and for *mediating between conflicts* because it takes into account the different objectives of decision-makers and preferences of people, in trying to reach one final solution.
- A tool for providing *information* on the environmental, social and economic consequences of a planning process or policy through time.
- A *forecasting* tool which includes all the relevant effects generated by urban projects on the natural, architectonic, spatial, functional, social, and economic environment, in the long term.
- A tool for *integrating* different evaluation methodologies, which are used to verify the environmental sustainability of urban projects.

Decision makers can express their views, assigning individual preferences to the various criteria of evaluation. Therefore, discussion and negotiations should be encouraged where exponents of different groups of opinion, political currents and lobbies, as well as the promoters and executors of the proposed actions, may be represented.

The research literature presents a wide range of MCA methods which can be grouped in families, as quantitative, qualitative and mixed (Voogd, 1983; Fusco Girard, 1987; Roscelli, 1990; Lombardi, 1995; Lombardi, 1997; Lichfield et al., 1998). These differ from each other in the nature of information they are able to manage, i.e. cardinal (hard), ordinal (soft), or mixed data.

The method named *Analytic Hierarchy Process* (AHP) is able to manage all three of the above mentioned typologies of information. It allows the investigation to reach a set of ratings for the decision alternatives by aggregating the relative weights of the decision elements. The procedure starts by breaking down the decision problem into a hierarchy of interrelated decision elements. At the top of the hierarchy lies the most macro decision objective, such as that of selecting the best alternative. The lower levels of the hierarchy contain attributes which contribute to the quality of the decision. Details of these attributes increase at the lower levels of the hierarchy. The last levels of the hierarchy contain decision alternatives.

In setting up the decision hierarchy, the number of levels depends on the complexity of the problem and on the degree of detail the analyst requires to solve the problem. Since each level entails pairwise comparison of its elements, Saaty suggests the number of elements at each level to be limited at a maximum of nine (Saaty and Vargas, 1981).

The input data for the problem consist of matrices of pairwise comparisons of elements of one level that contribute to achieving the objectives of the following higher level. Pairwise comparison data are collected for only half of the matrix elements: diagonal elements always equal one, and the lower triangle elements of the matrix are the reciprocal of the upper ones.

Pairwise comparisons give to the user a basis to reveal his/her preference by comparing two elements. Furthermore, the user has the option of expressing preferences between the two as *equally preferred*, *weakly preferred*, *strongly preferred*, *very strongly preferred*, or *absolutely preferred*, which are translated into pairwise weights of 1, 3, 5, 7, and 9, respectively, with 2, 4, 6, and 8 as intermediate values.

The technique of the AHP takes as input the above comparisons and produces the relative weights of elements at each level as output using the eigenvalue method. The eigenvector of each comparative matrix is the priority list, while the eigenvalue gives the measure of consistency in making the assessment or comparison. The synthesized eigenvector is the global sequence of the alternatives with respect to achieving the goal.

The eigenvector and the maximum eigenvalue of the comparative matrix are determined by solving the general problem of eigenvalues:

$$\mathbf{A}w = \lambda_{max}w \tag{12.1}$$

where $\mathbf{A}$ is the comparative matrix, w the eigenvector, and λ_{max} the maximum eigenvalue. In addition, the method includes consistency checks for input matrices by calculating first the *consistency index* (CI), which is given by:

$$\mathrm{CI} = \frac{\lambda_{\max} - n}{n - 1} \tag{12.2}$$

where n is the number of considered criteria. This value is then compared to the *average consistency index* (ACI) calculated from a large sample of randomly generated reciprocal matrices using the scale $\frac{1}{9}, \frac{1}{8}, \ldots, 1, \ldots, 8, 9$. The ratio of these two values is called *consistency ratio* (CR) of the matrix of comparisons:

$$\mathrm{CR} = \frac{\mathrm{CI}}{\mathrm{ACI}} \tag{12.3}$$

The resulting vector is accepted if CR is about 0.10 or less. Thus, for $n = 3$ CI needs to be 0.05 or less, for $n = 4$ it needs to be 0.08 or less, and so on as shown in Table 12.1. If the consistency ratio is not less than 0.10, the problem should be studied again and the judgments revised. It can be said that the AHP has a systematic procedure for better judgements (Saaty, 1980).

Table 12.1 Average consistency indices (ACIs) and corresponding maximum acceptable consistency indices (CIs) with consistency ratio (CR) equal to or less than 0.1 (after T. L. Saaty)

n	1	2	3	4	5	6	7	8	9	10
ACI	0	0	0.52	0.89	1.11	1.25	1.35	1.4	1.45	1.49
CI (truncated)	0	0	0.05	0.08	0.11	0.12	0.13	0.14	0.14	0.14

Source: Adapted from Saaty (1980), *The Analytic Network Process*

The last step of the procedure aggregates relative weights of various levels obtained from the previous step in order to produce a vector of composite weights which serves as ratings of decision alternatives in achieving the most general objective of the problem. The use of AHP is facilitated by the availability of a user-friendly decision-support supporting software: *Expert Choice 2000*[1].

The AHP method can be also used as a prioritising technique, for assigning the scoring and quantifying the weights of the evaluation criteria in other (quantitative) methods, such as in the *concordance-discordance method* (Lombardi, 1997).

12.3 The INTELCITY scenarios

In this study, AHP is used in the context of a Reality Check exercise. The aim is to evaluate a number of scenarios which were developed by the INTELCITY network for the city of the future in a Knowledge Society (KS).

Five alternative scenarios have been taken into consideration, aggregating and synthesizing those developed in the INTELCITY Workshop of Oslo (24-25 September 2002), as follows:

1. *e-Democracy City*
2. *Virtual City*
3. *Cultural City*
4. *Environmental City*
5. *Post-Catastrophe City*

A detailed description of the scenarios is illustrated in the following sub-sections.

Scenario 1: Electronic-Democracy City

Key dimensions Sustainable urban development: multi-functionality of buildings and spaces; stable physical communities. Knowledge Society: new platforms for articulation of interests; communication, education and enabling tools, e.g., automated translation; group decision support. e-Governance (electronic governance): effective transparency; new self-organising structures; effective participation and empowerment; effective leadership that is responsible and accountable; mediating conflicts of interest.

Summary description In this scenario ICT is seen as an enabling mechanism, changing peoples' opinions and behaviour patterns through information provision and empowerment. It provides new ways of decision making and negotiation through inclusiveness and accessible participation in the decision-making processes that affect the community. This would involve the deployment of a variety of tools such as hard set accessible web based group decision support for visioning, advanced visualisation tools, scenario planning and automatic translation as well as democratic participation tools such as e-voting and highly devolved decision making.

A peer-to-peer information system architecture is necessary, rather than client/server, that would seek to provide educational support to enable understanding of the socio-economic and environmental impacts of various options under consideration in a way that dissolves boundaries, e.g. between interest groups and between physical and virtual worlds. The electronic-governance characteristics include:

- Rethinking the role of community education and ways of opinion-forming;
- Creation of new platforms for articulation of interests;
- Decentralized, transparent and open decision making at all levels;
- Enhanced organisational capacity (structures, knowledge, resources, motivation) to enable an iterative two-way flow of information between the community and decision makers (public and private organisations); and
- That together will lead not only to better ways of making decisions, but also to better, more sustainable, community decisions through a more self-determined, informed consensus and more accountable leadership.

Thus the scenario is one in which self-determinism occurs within a socially cohesive community, respecting the wider community and the environment.

Assumptions A common value system based on equity, peaceful coexistence and an inclusive, integrated, multi-ethnic society that is motivated to seek more sustainable lifestyles. That a combination of technological progress and new ways of governance can together deliver the capacity to remove barriers to effective participation, e.g. lack of access, literacy, information overload, apathy, etc. and good governance, e.g. co-opting of rights and responsibilties. That e-governance will lead to more sustainable communities.

Scenario 2: Virtual City

Key dimensions Extensive tele-working. 'Smart' transport networks. Intelligent agents and buildings. Live anywhere mobile lifestyle (remote access). Intelligent environments ('lean, green, and smart') — city responds to individual behaviour to facilitate sustainable living. New infrastructures to support these features. Ambient provision of personalized, self-tailored information. Strong, progressive governance:

effective representation; empowerment; liberating — socially inclusive.

Summary description This scenario represents a knowledge society of networks and flows, where citizens are able to work and live anywhere in the city, supported by intelligent environments that are 'lean, green, and smart' (economically efficient and ecologically sound). Ubiquitous computing and tele-work lie at the centre of work and living, supported by 'smart' transportation and logistics networks. It also depends on the development of intelligent agents to provide personalized, self-tailored information to support a culturally rich, mobile lifestyle.

It is recognized that this will require major infra-structural development in the supply of utilities and that both the economic and environmental transformation which this predicates would also require 'strong' governance. This requirement, however, provides the opportunity to use the ICT's and 'smart' technologies both to empower citizens and make the corporate sector socially responsible (i.e. by taking on economic and environmental issues). New social support groupings are established such as local virtual village halls as well as more dispersed partnerships (e.g. pressure groups) across the whole city and beyond. Together this offers the potential for a more socially inclusive and therefore, progressive form of governance. If dispersed, virtual cities are to emerge, they need a stronger cultural basis and their socio-economic and environmental implications need to be more clearly articulated.

Assumptions Technological progress delivers the capacity to create a highly detailed model of the city (or larger region?) that is kept in real-time correspondence with the physical world through a dense array of sensors, using a wide range of technologies. The detailed, but anonymous, information available on every individual's consumption and behaviour patterns enables optimization of overall resource use and feedback to consumers either as information or through the price mechanism. Effective ways of managing security of information are established that are socially acceptable and so that individual privacy is ensured and the power of the network provider is moderated. Mass customization and accessibility for all citizens is available so that inclusiveness is achieved and inequalities in accessing or understanding information are eliminated.

Scenario 3: Cultural City

Key dimensions Social interaction: caring for people (ethical issue); equal representation of stakeholders (democracy); inclusive participation; lively, liberal, multicultural, tolerant, supports diverse value systems and spiritual integrity; learning — free and accessible education. Physical and technological characteristics: human scale; high quality, aesthetic environment (buildings and urban landscape); public spaces for interacting; invisible, but supportive technologies.

Summary description This scenario is underpinned by a strong social and environmental ethic. The principles of the cultural city define its social and political organization, emphasizing liberal democracy, equity, multicultural diversity, and cultural and spiritual integrity. It provides the ideal community environment where individual needs and well-being can be balanced with that of society in general.

Advanced technology is present although entirely invisible — it is embedded. This applies to all forms of technology, including mobility and communication technologies. In the cultural city the additional means and channels of communication that ICTs provide assist, imperceptibly and unobtrusively, in all aspects of life, work, education, art, leisure, and the democratic processes. It is particularly useful in the negotiation and mediation necessary for agreeing collectively, e.g. for urban re/development action.

The cultural city has a distinct physical form, which is human in scale. This is a high quality environment in which the buildings and landscape are predominant, rather than the mobility systems. The built heritage provides cultural symbols, a strong, sustainable, binding factor between the present and the past. At the heart there is a civic entity, space(s) for cultural and artistic exchange, and for democratic engagement. Thus it is framed and facilitated by a fundamentally democratic decision-making process. This commences with commitment to stakeholder definition of goals and objectives for a new sustainable future and its delivery according to a democratic expression of rights and responsibilities, individual, corporate, and governmental.

Assumptions A common value system based on equity, peaceful coexistence and an inclusive, integrated, multi-cultural society that is motivated to seek more sustainable lifestyles. That technological progress and change can deliver completely embedded technological systems and that the necessary information will be made available by all members of society. This also assumes entirely unobtrusive information, computing, and interfaces, e.g., through wearable, fully integrated, wireless nano-technology, which in turn can support all functions of life — education, a variety of communication needs and democratic decision-making. That a richer more democratic culture will, of itself, lead to more sustainable communities.

Scenario 4: Environment City

Key dimensions Most of the current (late 20th / early 21st century) environmental and social problems are solved through: greater density of habitation; more public transport; clean manufacturing and elimination of pollution; resilient service provision; more educated and informed citizens (knowledge society); full employment based on knowledge; universal access to broadband technology; disappearance of interface technology; resource use efficiency (no scarcity of land, green space, energy, clean air/water, etc.); better security and safety, reduced crime; and participatory/collaborative decision making.

Summary description This scenario is based on the realistic concept of incremental change in which all the current environmental and social problems are gradually addressed, solved, or ameliorated over the period up to 2030. ICTs would play an important part in this environmental transition through integration of these changes into society in ways that are both enabling and contribute to the quality of life.

In physical and ecological terms the environment city would be very resource efficient achieving 'factor 4' reductions[2] (at least). An important legal aspect supporting this is the requirement on all manufacturers to recycle/reuse at end of product life, thus closing liability loops, which in turn would reduce pollution to very low levels. Resource reduction targets would constrain the outward expansion of cities, with polycentric (internal) growth patterns to reduce mobility requirements and provide greater flexibility in use of space, and with a better balance in the investment in public and private spaces. Regeneration of the existing fabric would provide greater density of habitation, more effective and efficient public transport and local food production.

In economic terms full employment (in its wider sense meaning some form of rewarding all activity) would be stimulated through the adoption of a service economy where innovative means of extending product life would be sought. The value of 'public goods' would be rediscovered.

In social and cultural terms a multi-cultural, secure, and safe society will be achieved through a combination of governance measures and the application of ICTs. This would seek to increase 'self-organizing' capacities through better public information and participation in urban re/generation so that cities could become lively cultural places, which should tend to decrease current problems with crime and insecurity.

The environment city can be summed up as being of long life, low energy, and adaptable. This could be applied equally to the buildings and infrastructure as much as to the citizenry.

Assumptions A common eco-orientated value system, supported by 'green' economics and legal framework. That a combination of more resource efficient technologies, application of ICTs, access to information, and new ways of participative governance can together maintain high quality of life whilst avoiding current environmental consequences, through a co-evolutionary city re/development system. That effective monitoring and assessment systems will become available to enable the effective prediction of socio-economic and environmental consequences of re/development options and to manage unexpected external environmental, climatic or economic events.

Scenario 5: Post-Catastrophe City

Key dimensions This scenario is predicated on an environmental or natural catastrophe, that results in re-assertion and/or re-evaluation of: concept of finite resources; property rights; economic system effectiveness; social equity considerations; importance of environmental protection; government control over markets and corporations; and top down regulation, monitoring, and control of targets and consumption patterns.

Summary description This scenario is driven by the albeit small possibility of high impact events, such as a natural catastrophe, (e.g. very large volcanic eruption or a meteor strike), environmental catastrophe (e.g. serious global warming causing loss of ice cover at the poles with significant sea level rise), or global war, which may be sufficiently serious to also cause breakdown in the economic system and/or global trade. This would considerably alter the relationship between citizens and the state, and impact significantly on the freedom of choice of citizens. This might be exemplified by a crisis in the use of fossil fuel and its adverse impacts on climate and environment, and the possible imposition of a carbon tax or very large resource reduction quotas.

It is likely that wealth and quality of life would suffer initially with effective action being seen to be imperative in order to improve matters. Free market conditions would be unlikely to respond quickly enough to events or to respond sufficiently to alleviate the threat(s). Government(s) would have to impose regulations to control behaviour of markets, citizens, and industry, assuming for example that the cost of carbon misuse is sufficient to make it worth conserving this resource. Complexities and uncertainties in this situation are large. Means of encouraging rather than enforcing more sustainable behaviour would be relevant, e.g. trading carbon credits, giving interest on carbon accounts, etc.

Amongst these uncertainties information and communication technologies would be highly relevant to such new forms of rationing, i.e. in establishing social equity in allocation of resources. Clearly it can enable real-time monitoring of resource use, carbon in the example, by individual citizens, companies, and other organisations.

Assumptions A catastrophic event of sufficient seriousness that it disturbs the environmental and/or economic systems, and that resources are finite. That advanced ICT-based monitoring and assessment systems will be available to enable the effective prediction of socio-economic and environmental consequences of unexpected external environmental, climatic, or economic events.

12.4 Application of the analytic hierarchy process to the INTELCITY scenarios

The evaluation of these options requires a complex consideration of multiple aspects, including spatial and functional factors, environmental and social issues, financial and economical resources, and legal and juridical frameworks.

The selection of a relevant set of evaluation criteria and their weights is very crucial for the development of an MCA, as it directly influences the results (Voogd, 1983). In an evaluation process, this operation has a 'political' meaning because it provides the 'context' of the evaluation, while the operation of assessing the alternative options with regard to the criteria has a 'technical' meaning.

There are two possible approaches for selecting a set of criteria in an evaluation context: a deductive approach, starting from the characteristics of the scenarios or, alternatively, an inductive approach, starting from the personal view of decision makers and from their definition of sustainable urban development.

In this study, the experts and decision-makers who have been asked to identify the evaluation criteria and weights were free to adopt both of the approaches. They are the users of the INTELCITY Mediterranean Platform and the participants of the Regional INTELCITY Workshop held in Turin (30 October 2002). Therefore, the evaluation is characterized by having a Southern European perspective.

In terms of skills employed, the group of experts included planning authorities, civil and traffic engineers, architects, planners, economists, technical services, academics, and post-graduate students.

Planning authorities are in charge of achieving sustainable urban development and in need of new ways of working and new tools for reaching this aim. The workshop was particularly targeted at decision-making authorities at the local and sub-regional levels. Private planning consultants are in need of tools for the evaluation of existing situations, and of guidelines for new development. Members of the scientific research community are seeking new ways of working, new methodologies for finding solutions for complex problems of sustainable urban development, and the development of new ICTs in this domain.

In addition to the above group of experts, the workshop included a number of under-graduated students from the School of Architecture of the Polytechnic of Turin, and a group of non-European post-graduate students (architects and engineers) from Mexico, Colombia, Vietnam, and several African countries.

The workshop consisted of an afternoon of intensive, interactive activities where delegates were asked to identify: 'What are the attributes (issues or criteria) for illustrating their vision of the city of 2030 (less than seven)? What are the indicators/parameters or sub-criteria that can specify them? What are the priorities or weights of them?'

This exercise required participants to develop an explicit individual vision and definition of sustainable urban development and to discuss (eventually negotiate) it with the group. The time allocated for this exercise was about one hour. The delegates were then asked to return to a plenary session with a maximum of two sheets summarizing their criteria and weights.

The final discussion emphasized the variety of issues characterizing the city of the future in a South-Mediterranean knowledge society. However, it was possible to recognize some common issues among the participants, and particularly the strong emphasis placed on the social and cultural issues of sustainability and quality of life, on one side, and the limited role assigned to the information and communication technology aspects, seen simply as a transparent mean for innovation in the infrastructure and institutional sectors rather than a crucial factor of change for the urban scenario (e.g. Virtual City).

From a detailed analysis of the individual summary sheets (31 sheets in total)

Table 12.2 Frequency of the issues

Issues	Experts	Students	Non-EU	Only EU	Total
1. Ecological issue	11	4	4	15	19
2. Infrastructure efficiency	15	6	4	21	25
3. Social interaction	9	–	–	9	9
4. Quality of life	13	4	1	17	18
5. Institutional efficiency	9	5	3	14	17
6. Economical development	7	1	3	8	11
7. Spatial issue	3	1	3	4	7

filled out by the workshop delegates, the following set of common (more frequent) issues emerged:

1. Ecological issues. Includes environmental quality, greenery, pollution, etc.
2. Infrastructure efficiency. Refers to transport system, ICT, accessibility to services.
3. Social interaction. Includes social integration, multi-ethnical environment.
4. Quality of life. Refers to architectural quality, cultural life, urban security.
5. Institutional efficiency. Refers to governance, participation, democracy.
6. Economical development. Includes growth (occupation, GNP), equity (ending poverty).
7. Spatial issue. Deals with population and limitation of urban sprawl.

Table 12.2 shows the number of times the above issues have been indicated by the respondents in their individual criteria-identification sheet.

The individual sheets also made it possible to identify the importance order (or weight) assigned to the above issues. This weight differs markedly among the decision makers. In particular, the group of experts more frequently assigned high priority to the issues of ecology, infrastructure efficiency (transport, information, ICTs), and institutional efficiency; the students pointed out the importance of social interaction/integration and, finally the non-EU delegates emphasized the role of economy for the achievement of sustainable urban development, in terms of local resources, occupation, GNP. Table 12.3 shows the frequency with which each issue was chosen as the most important by each respondent.

Tables 12.2 and 12.3 show a different order among the issues (criteria), based on the more frequent issue, and on the frequency of the most important issue for each respondent. A comparison of the results obtained from the above two tables shows that:

1. Infrastructure efficiency is placed at the first position by all the three groups of respondents;
2. Quality of life is more important than the ecological issue only for the EU delegates in terms of frequency with which it is chosen (but it is less important

Table 12.3 Frequency of the first issue*

Issues	Experts	Students	Non-EU	Only EU	Total
1. Ecological issue	5	1	2	6	8
2. Infrastructure efficiency	5	2	1	7	8
3. Social interaction	3	3	–	6	6
4. Quality of life	2	–	–	2	2
5. Institutional efficiency	5	–	–	5	5
6. Economical development	1	–	2	1	3
7. Spatial issue	–	1	1	1	2

* The numbers refer to the frequency of each issue being chosen as most important.

than the ecological issue in terms of priority assigned by respondents, especially for the non-EU delegates);
3. Institutional efficiency is less important than the ecological issue for all;
4. Quality of life is more important than social interaction for all;
5. Social interaction is more important than economic development only for EU delegates;
6. The spatial issue is the least important issue for the EU delegates.

Clearly, the above results cannot be simply translated in a single list of weights. However, it seems realistic to start from a single vector and successively to carry out, first, a sensitivity analysis by varying the weights until the order of the criteria changes in order to test their stability, and, second, a number of changes in the 'critical' weights, which provide different evaluation 'contexts', reflecting the different views of the respondents illustrated above. The results from these operations will be illustrated and discussed in the next section of this chapter.

The weights vector used in the analysis is based on a normalization of the numbers in column 'Only EU' of Table 12.2 (see Figure 12.1).

The following step is the pairwise comparison of the five alternative options in relation to the evaluation criteria.

Using the Analytic Hierarchy Process (AHP) method (*Expert Choice 2000* package), seven matrices have been developed; each matrix contains the result of a technical evaluation based on pairs comparison of the scenarios with regard to each individual criterion, answering the following question: 'Which is more important between the two alternatives (a) and (b), with respect to this criterion? And by how much?'.

These comparisons are based on the nine-point measurement scale (Saaty's scale). In addition, the consistency ratio CR has been checked for each matrix as a value lower than 0.1.

Finally, the eigenvector from each matrix is automatically obtained which provides the ranking of the alternative scenarios in relation to each criterion, as illus-

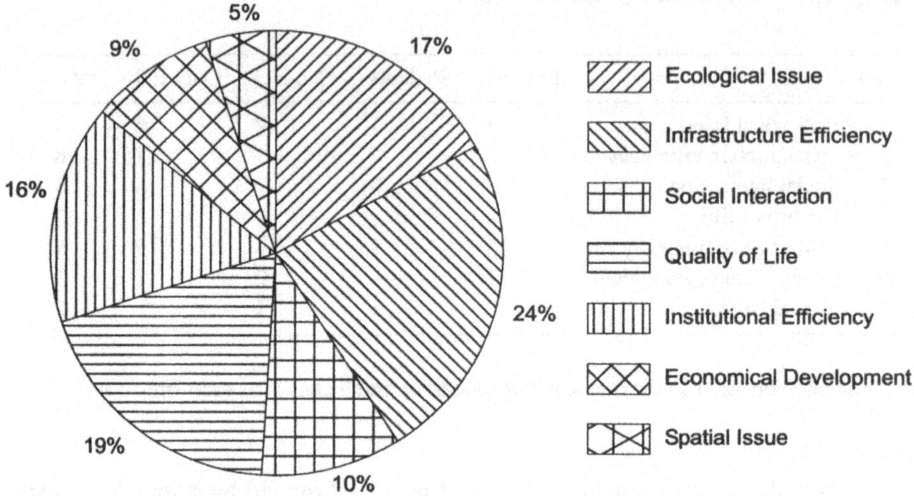

Figure 12.1 Criteria weight

Table 12.4 Relative weights of the five scenarios with regard to each criterion

Issues	1-Eco	2-Effi	3-Soc	4-Qual	5-Inst	6-Econ	7-Spat
e-Democracy City	1.2	2.5	1.9	1.5	4.2	4.3	1.0
Virtual City	1.7	4.8	0.4	1.2	1.8	2.4	4.8
Cultural City	1.8	1.4	5.1	4.5	2.5	1.6	1.3
Environmental City	5.1	0.8	1.7	2.6	0.7	1.2	2.4
Post-Catastrophe City	0.2	0.5	0.9	0.2	0.8	0.4	0.5

trated in Table 12.4.

Figure 12.2 provides a visualization of the performance of the scenarios illustrated in Table 12.4, employing a radial (spider) model.

The final vector of composite weights for the alternative scenarios, which has been obtained in the last step of the AHP application from the criterion weights, is illustrated in Table 12.5.

12.5 Discussion and sensitivity analysis

The final weights of the scenarios shows that the *Cultural City* receives the largest score, followed by the e-Democracy City, the Virtual City and the Enviro-City. The first three scenarios are quite close to each other in terms of final weights. This is mainly due to the high weight given by the Mediterranean respondents to three criteria: infrastructure efficiency, quality of life, and institution capacity.

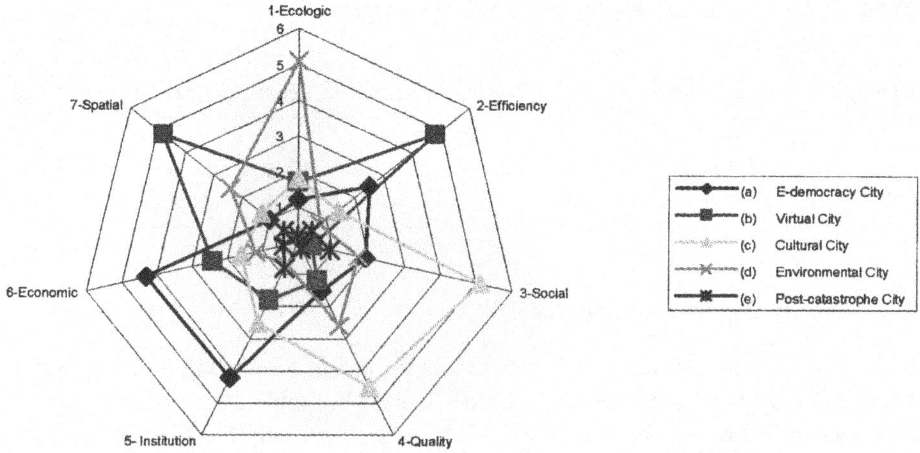

Figure 12.2 Radial graph of the performances of the five scenarios

Table 12.5 The final weights for the alternatives

Alternatives	Final weights
e-Democracy city	2.5
Virtual city	2.4
Cultural city	2.6
Environmental city	2.0
Post-Catastrophe city	0.5

In this section a number of changes are proposed in the weights of the criteria in order both to test the stability of the results, and to provide different evaluation 'contexts' which better reflect the different views of the respondents illustrated in the previous Tables 12.2 and 12.3. In particular, the following 'contexts' are proposed:

I a different order of the criterion weights, reflecting column 'Total' in Table 12.2;
II a different order of the criterion weights, reflecting column 'Total' in Table 12.3;
III a different order of the criterion scores, reflecting column 'Only EU' in Table 12.3.

The suggested three lists of criterion weights are illustrated in Table 12.5.

The results obtained from the MCA evaluation of the scenarios considering the above three sets of weights for the criteria (contexts) are the following:

1. Context I offers an equal weight at first position for the three scenarios of the Cultural City, the e-Democracy City, and the Virtual City;
2. Context II shows that the e-Democracy City wins against the Cultural City;
3. Context III shows that the Cultural City wins again, followed by the Virtual

Table 12.6 Suggested alternative criterion weights

Weights	1-Eco	2-Effi	3-Soc	4-Qual	5-Inst	6-Econ	7-Spat
I	18	24	8	17	16	10	7
II	23	23	18	6	15	9	6
III	21	25	21	7	18	4	4

City and the e-Democracy City.

In conclusion, the EU-delegates' view seems to lead to a selection of the Cultural asset of the city in both, the two contexts defined by Table 12.2, considering the frequency of all the issues, and Table 12.3, considering only the frequency of the issue judged as most important. However, if we include in the group of respondents also the non-EU delegates, the more important scenario seems to be close to an e-democracy urban asset. This is mainly due to the high priority given by the non-EU participants to the issue of economic development that includes GNP, occupation, and equity.

An additional comparison is proposed with the results obtained from a different MCA method. This exercise is developed in order to control what in literature is defined as 'uncertainty of the method' (Voogd, 1983), i.e. the dependency of the final results on the MCA method used. In this additional sensitivity analysis, a qualitative MCA method is adopted: the Regime Analysis (Fusco Girard, Nijkamp and Voogd, 1989). The Regime method is a qualitative, multiple analysis, developed in the area of soft econometrics. It is based on a combination of Kendal's paired comparison method for ordinal data and logit analysis. The method does not require cardinal data, but only a classification of the criteria in increasing or decreasing order of importance. This is the main advantage of the method that is in fact applied to contexts in which the planners or decision makers are uncertain. In this study the Regime method has been applied to the case study, using the evaluation matrix shown in Table 12.4 and all the four criterion weights vectors previously illustrated (see Figure 12.1 and Table 12.6). The results from this application of Regime analysis provide the following final ranking of the alternative scenarios.

First position: Cultural City.
Second position: e-Democracy City.
Third position: Virtual City.
Fourth position: Environmental City.
Fifth position: Post-Catastrophe City.

This ranking has proved to remain stable with the changing of the criterion weights.

12.6 Summary and conclusion

In this study an MCA application has been developed in order to select the more preferred scenarios of the city of the future from a South-Mediterranean perspective.

MCA is able to determine lists of priorities from a finite series of choice options (alternatives) which are assessed and compared in relation to identified characteristics of the problem (criteria), when that problem is appropriately broken down into its fundamental elements (Voogd, 1983).

The evaluation criteria adopted in this study are those selected by the INTELCITY Mediterranean Platform users. Different sets of weights are suggested in order to reflect the composition of the groups (EU-only respondents and total number of respondents including also persons from non-European countries). The results obtained show that the Cultural City scenario is preferred by the EU respondents in all the contexts provided in Table 12.2 (based on the frequency of the issues), followed by the e-Democracy scenario and the Virtual City. The e-Democracy scenario seems to be more important than the Cultural City for the total number of respondents only when the analysis takes into account only the most important issue (Table 12.2). In conclusion, this study indicates that South-Mediterranean people:

- Enjoy traditional cultural environments;
- Require efficiency in infrastructure, services, and institutions;
- See the role of information and communication technology as a transparent mean for innovation in the institutional sector (governance) rather than as a crucial factor of change in the urban scenario.

These results have been checked against the problem of 'uncertainty of method' and are confirmed in the final application of the Regime analysis.

Acknowledgements

Although this work is a joint effort of the two authors, Steve Curwell is responsible for the paragraph 'The INTELCITY scenarios' while Patrizia Lombardi is responsible for all the remaining paragraphs. The authors of this contribution wish to thank both the INTELCITY team and Think Tank who have participated to the first INTELCITY Workshop held in Oslo (September 2002) and the INTELCITY Mediterranean End-Users who have participated to the Mediterranean INTELCITYNET Workshop held in Turin (October 2002).

Notes

1 Editor's note: software produced by Expert Choice, Inc., Arlington, VA (USA). See http://www.expertchoice.com/software for details.

2 Scale of energy consumption reduction within an eco-oriented society.

References

Brandon, P., Lombardi, P. and Bentivegna, V. (1997), *Evaluation in the Built Environment for Sustainability*, Chapman&Hall, London (UK).

Curwell, S. and Lombardi, P. (1999), 'Riqualificazione urbana sostenibile: un'analisi comparativa Torino-Salford' (Sustainable urban regeneration: a comparative analysis Turin-Salford), *Urbanistica*, No. 112, pp. 96-103 (English version pp. 114-115).

Deakin, M., Mitchell, G. and Lombardi, P. (2002), 'Valutazione della sostenibilità: una verifica delle tecniche disponili' (Urban sustainability assessment: a preliminary appraisal of current techniques), *Urbanistica*, No. 118, pp. 28-34 (English version pp. 50-53).

Francescato, G. (1991), 'Housing quality: technical and non-technical aspects', in A. Bezelga and P. Brandon (eds.), *Management, Quality and Economics in Buildings*, E&FN Spon, London (UK), pp. 602-609.

Fusco Girard, L. (1987), *Risorse architettoniche e culturali: valutazioni e strategie di conservazione* (Architectural and cultural resources: assessment and conservation strategies), Franco Angeli, Milano (Italy).

Fusco Girard, L., Nijkamp, P. and Voogd, H. (1989), *Conservazione e sviluppo: la valutazione nella pianificazione fisica* (Conservation and Development: Evaluation in Physical Planning), Franco Angeli, Milano (Italy).

Lichfield, N., Barbanente, A., Borri, D., Kakee, A. and Prat, A. (eds., 1998), *Evaluation in Planning: Facing the challange of complexity*, Kluwer Academic Publishers, Dordrecht (The Netherlands).

Lombardi, P. (1995), 'Non-market and multicriteria evaluation methods for public goods and urban plans', in A. G. Meban, R. S. W. Shaw, W. J. McCluskey and I. C. Hanna (eds.), *Financial management of property and construction*, University of Ulster, Belfast (UK), 231-245.

Lombardi, P. (1997), 'Decision making problems concerning urban regeneration plans', *Engineering Construction & Architectural Management*, Vol. 4, No. 2, pp. 127-142.

Pearce, D. and Turner, R. K. (1990), *Economics of natural resources and the environment*, Harvester Wheatsheaf, Hemel Hempstead (UK).

Roscelli, R. (editor, 1990), *Misurare nell'incertezza* (Measuring under Uncertainty), Celid, Torino (Italy).

Roy, B. (1985), *Méthodologie multicritère d'aide à la décision* (Multicriteria decision support methodology), Economica, Paris (France).

Saaty, T. L. (1980), *The Analytic Network Process*, McGraw Hill, New York, NY (USA). Reprinted in 1996 by *The Analytic Network Process*, RWS Publications, Pittsburgh, PA (USA).

Saaty, T. L. and Vargas, L. G. (1981), *The Logic of Priorities — Applications in Business, Energy, Health and Transportation*, Kluwer-Nijhoff, Den Haag (The Netherlands).

Stone, P. A. (1989), *Development and Planning Economy*, E&FN Spon, London (UK).

Voogd, H. (1983), *Multicriteria evaluation for urban and regional planning*, Pion, London (UK).

Chapter 13

Scenarios as an Exploratory Evaluation Approach — Some Experiences from Southern Mediterranean

Angela Barbanente and Abdul Khakee

13.1 Introduction

In his review of notable planning disasters, Hall (1981) proposes two ways for avoiding future disasters: improve forecasting methods and refine evaluation criteria by explicitly ranking gains and losses in the near against distant future. In a turbulent age, the improvement of forecasting methods is quite problematic. Ranking near and distant futures requires images of alternative future developments.

The need for goals and/or specific notions of a not too distant a future — say five to ten years — have been vital premises in planning. However, the need of long-term knowledge with a time horizon of twenty or more years has become increasingly important as the society becomes more and more aware of possible long-term consequences of present decisions.

In particular, the field of urban and regional planning is challenged by ecological issues requiring long-term thinking. This creates a renewed interest in considering distant horizons in decision making. The current perspective, anyway, seems to be radically different from that of the traditional planning approaches, especially when it is associated with the idea of 'risk society'. From this viewpoint, an intrinsic uncertainty affects the future, since possible consequences of modern technology are indiscriminate, unpredictable and, in some cases, irreversible. Moreover, threats are not always visible or tangible to people especially when they do not appear to pose a threat in people's life span (Beck, 1995; p. 162).

Even though a broad scientific consensus exists about the potential serious damages implied by phenomena such as global warming, climate change, loss of biodiversities, degradation of a wide array of biological systems, and the problems of absorbing the array of new chemical compounds, the ability of scientists to predict outcomes and impacts of environmental transformations is inadequate. Popular worries and concerns are influenced as much by beliefs as by evidence. In the face of such unpredictability, the risks and unintended consequences related to taking the wrong kind of preemptive action in the face of some imagined 'collision' might be just as bad as not taking action in the face of imminent disaster (Harvey, 2000; pp. 216-217).

In planning practice, the recent surge of interest in visioning exercises has raised awareness of planners' role in shaping the future (Myers and Kitsuse, 2002), paralleled by a flourishing of collaborative approaches where the community of planners include a large array of stakeholders (Innes, 1996; Walzer, 1996).

The use of scenarios has been increasingly propagated as an approach useful to deal with the many long-term uncertainties that characterize contemporary society in many fields. Investigating the multiplicity of possible futures may provide essential knowledge for present decisions, assuming a perspective that, instead of looking for ways to reduce uncertainty, accepts it as an intrinsic part of the future and finds ways of living with it.

Functions of scenarios range from selection of strategies and identification of future possibilities, to making people aware of uncertainties, stretching their imagination and triggering learning processes. Interactive scenario building aims at promoting people's involvement for 'rehearsing' (Schwartz, 1991) a future that is inherently uncertain but that they may be able to influence and shape with their choices (May, 1996). At the same time long-term knowledge provides a basis for a wider discourse that is a prerequisite for citizen participation.

Evaluation with the support of long-term knowledge, even if it cannot promise to avoid disasters or predict surprise events, can contribute to judge our actions in a wider and more articulated picture of the future (Gordon, 1989). Thus, it can help us face developments with long-term consequences and prepare us for them.

One such development is the rapid technological transformation in the field of electronic communication and bio-technique with built-in surprise events e.g. the current disquiet with regard to the building of the Internet system and the subsequent decline in the information-technology (IT) industry and a general downturn in the economic growth. It is most likely that this development could have been met with a better preparedness if the policies leading to the expansion of IT-industries had been evaluated with the help of alternative visions of an IT-society.

The same can be said of the environmental problems facing the global and the local societies. Kenneth Boulding's (1966) vision of the coming 'spaceship economy' in face of the failure to make fundamental changes in waste production and waste treatment could have, for example, been used to evaluate national and international obligations. The failure to live up to the Kyoto Agreement and the World Climate Convention can be partly ascribed to inability to pre-judge political and economic obstacles with the help of the knowledge presented in the coming spaceship scenario.

The current paranoia that is exhibited by the US government and its allies with regards to international terrorism has largely to do with decisions in the field of arms sale. Scenarios portraying possible developments as a result of the collapse of the Soviet Union and the subsequent lawlessness in arms sales would have perhaps prevented current political malaise.

Globalization of economy and the control of world production by multinational companies is another development where an evaluation with the help of long-term knowledge might have been useful. A relevant question is if the current economic crisis could have been averted if the chain of events leading to the default of a small number of these companies, and the subsequent recession resulting in the world economy, could have been evaluated with the help of alternative scenarios of the globalization of the world economy and the management of large companies.

One of the main purposes of long-term knowledge as developed in scenarios is to influence ideas, preferences and desires. In this contribution we are limiting ourselves to one category of scenarios, namely desirable scenarios. We are not including possible and probable scenarios in which case probability theory can be used to evaluate choices made in the present. Limiting ourselves to desirable scenarios helps us focus on the question whether our choices are favorable or not in relation to these desirable scenarios. A desirable scenario is defined as a narrative of a state of affairs or development over time. The purpose of such scenarios is to help us understand how current decisions and preferences can affect reality as it is likely going to be at a distant future.

However future knowledge has a very tenuous relationship to current choices because scenarios consist of 'conjectural knowledge' (May, 1996). The use of scenarios to assess current preferences and ideas poses a major methodological and practical challenge for futurologists as well as planners and decision-makers. This contribution is a modest attempt to meet this challenge.

The contribution is made up of three major parts besides this introduction and a concluding section. In the following section the differences between conventional use of evaluation and evaluation based on scenarios are discussed. It also introduces the concept 'explorative evaluation' that is more appropriate when scenarios are used for evaluative purpose. The next section presents methodological aspects of using scenarios to evaluate current choices. In the third section the desirable scenarios developed in Tunis, İzmir and Rabat-Casablanca, in connection with the Concerted Action's program on agriculture and urbanization in southern Mediterranean countries, will be analyzed in the light of the proposed methodological approach. The concluding section discusses the usefulness of using scenarios to evaluate current choices and the need for further research.

13.2 Emerging vs. conventional issues on evaluation and scenarios

Evaluation is a crucial aspect of all planning and policy-making practice. Every planning or policy making act gives rise to option possibilities and the 'prospective' evaluation implies that the likely results of different way of acting are judged before a decision is implemented. The prospective evaluation helps judge which of the ways of acting is more worthwhile than others. Once a chosen plan or policy is implemented, 'retrospective' evaluation becomes necessary in order to assess the results of the implemented decision. Evaluation methods focus on costs or inputs e.g. in the case of threshold analysis, or on outputs or values as in the case of multicriteria analysis or on input as well as output e.g. in cost-benefit analysis. Both 'prospective' and 'retrospective' evaluations are accepted as integral parts of policy analysis and planning practice. However, these conventional uses of evaluation are not really applicable when assessing present preferences with the help of distant knowledge as produced in scenarios. Other approaches seem more coherent with this kind of knowledge.

As is well known, also in the planning field, many different ways of interpreting evaluation have been developed in the last two decades, which go beyond the conventional use of evaluation. Nevertheless, plan evaluation still involves the crucial divergence between rational analysis and a pragmatic approach: objectivity and precision, on the one hand, and embracing context and seeking values from diverse viewpoints, on the other. The divergence is also between the knowledge that aims at protecting us from contingency and surprise on the one hand, and knowledge that may prepare us to cope more clearly and effectively with unexpected difficulties, on the other (Hoch, 2002; pp. 54-55). The sharp distinction between perspective and retrospective evaluation is also under discussion. In this respect the need to integrate ex-ante, in itinere and ex post evaluation in planning practice has been highlighted (Lichfield and Prat, 1998).

Moreover, with the shift from a 'decision oriented' to a 'classification oriented' perspective (Voogd, 1983), evaluation is seen not only as a tool for choosing the preferred policy alternative but also as a process for organizing information and preparing arguments to support planning strategies. This implies the need for a more 'adaptive evaluation' (Faludi and Voogd, 1985), flexible enough to deal with changing circumstances during the decision-making process, and more sensitive to planning contexts.

In addition to the more conventional view of evaluation as a tool for comparing different alternatives before a decision is made and for assessing impact and value for money during and after implementation, evaluation has become increasingly an instrument for forming a judgement and providing evidence and about stimulating learning and understanding. The acknowledgement that evaluation is a social process that develops in mutable political contexts (Cronbach et al., 1980) has given rise to evaluation approaches that emphasize stakeholders' point of view in judgement for arriving at shared policy constructions (Guba and Lincoln, 1989). In such perspective, the creation of a learning environment for people involved in policy making and implementation may help them in their effort to reach desired goals. In participatory approaches, evaluation is considered to be a process people undertake as a formal, reflective activity for their own development and empowerment (Patton, 1990; p. 129). These approaches seem to be increasingly important in planning, as it moves away from 'blueprint plans' toward more action-oriented policies which require an aptitude to learn and act collaboratively.

A scenario is an outline of a set of hypothetical events with a view to focus attention on strategic decision points (Kahn and Weiner, 1967). It highlights major determinants that might cause the future to develop in one or another direction. There is a wide range of definitions of the term 'scenario' and consequently a broad diversity with regard to methodological approaches to construct scenarios (Bunn and Salo, 1993; Schoemaker, 1993). Approaches for generating scenarios vary all the way from highly structured probabilistic algorithms and causal simulation models, to less structured methods based on reasoned judgement and intuition in describing alternative futures; from methods that require a high level of expertise to interactive and participatory approaches that emphasize public discussion and shared decision-making (May, 1996; Bell, 1997). Regardless of what approach is used, there is always an underlying desire to improve present policy making in order to achieve a desirable future.

The participatory and normative concern in scenario-building and in futures studies more generally has gained strength since de Jouvenal's (1967) seminal work in the mid-1960s and the First International Conference in Futures Research. The emphasis then was to make use of scientific approaches to solve social problems and to democratize futures research so that it belonged to everyone. In the subsequent years the framework of representative government was considered more appropriate to satisfy participatory and normative concerns. There were, however, several well-known exceptions to this approach. For example 'Birmingham in Future' is a well-known example of futures studies in 1980s, where grassroots groups had the entire responsibility. Since the 1990s, a direct democratic approach has become all the more dominant because of issues related to sustainable development. The rise of extra-parliamentary initiatives in futures studies suggests the search for new forms of participation in designing a desirable future. The latter is expected to provide an impetus to think about the desirable future and to make it come true.

The use of desirable scenarios for evaluative purposes implies new methodological innovations both for scenario building and evaluation. Both of these activities are based on the crucial recognition that the future is unpredictable, but that present decisions will have implications for the future. Thus, the use of scenarios for evaluation allows us to avoid using the precise and detailed forecasts required in conventional evaluation, that have actually proved to be of little use (Palumbo, 2001; pp. 167-168). Moreover, participatory scenarios allow the production of shared knowledge frames useful to highlight stakeholders' knowledge paths and bents for action, but are hardly reliable for predictions. So what are the major differences between conventional and exploratory evaluation? These differences can be classified under three captions: functions, knowledge, and organization.

Functions

Conventional evaluation focuses on the choice of best possible decision or a set of decisions among several alternatives. The use of scenarios in evaluation aims to improve the background to decision-making.

Conventional evaluation is either prospective (forward looking) or retrospective (backward looking). Usually, in the former case the emphasis is on finding the best alternative to be implemented. In the latter case the focus is on assessing the results of the implemented decision in relation to goals in order to find out if they were fulfilled, and if not what needs to be done in order not to repeat the same mistakes. Exploratory evaluation is anticipatory in the sense that the values and preferences behind the current policy making are examined in relation to hypothetical knowledge generated in the scenarios. Exploratory evaluation combines both forward and backward looking aspects since the evaluators have to look back from a distant future to current policy making, but at the same time to assess present preferences in relation to a narrative of desired changes in the distant future.

Conventional evaluation is supposed to have an instrumental use. Exploratory evaluation has a conceptual use and symbolic use. The former is used for enlightenment and the latter for persuasion to form new views and perceptions (Weiss, 1998; Shulha and Cousins, 1997).

Knowledge

The most important differences between conventional and exploratory evaluation are found with regard to knowledge. A considerable degree of accuracy is a necessary requirement in conventional evaluation, even in the case of ex ante evaluation. Otherwise a decision would not obtain required legitimacy and necessary resources would not be made available for its implementation. Exploratory evaluation does not and can not have the same accuracy requirements, even if it helps to provide necessary indications in order to improve the background to policy making so that the desires expressed in the scenarios can be fulfilled. It may finally be questionable because of unforeseen events that may turn up side down all the premises of the preferred scenario.

Conventional evaluation focuses on finding out if proposed policies meet specific efficiency and effectiveness criteria. It is essentially a quantitative exercise with a varying input of qualitative judgement. The knowledge contents of conventional evaluation are rigorous and data-based with a view, in ex ante evaluation, to compare alternative policy proposals. By aiming at finding out a satisfactory way to alter current thinking, exploratory evaluation is a probing activity. In order to assess the degree of desirability of various ideas, exploratory evaluation can not be expressed in other terms than qualitative ones. Knowledge in scenarios as well as exploratory evaluation is intuitive and hypothetical. Images and visions can not be treated as anything but conjectural.

Conventional evaluation is fairly detailed and is either input or output focussed or both. In exploratory evaluation assessment of a set of desires and values can only be done in a very broad fashion. Since it is not a question of tangible resource input or output, exploratory evaluation has neither input nor output to reckon with.

Organization

Less crucial but nevertheless important is the way conventional and exploratory evaluations are organized. Conventional evaluation is the responsibility of policy analysts whether working as consultants or as experts employed by public agencies.

Even in the case of stakeholder-based discursive evaluation (e.g. the naturalistic responsive approach; Guba and Lincoln, 1989), the role of evaluator is vital as a facilitator of the discursive process. Conventional evaluation is closely related to an ongoing decision-making process in an agency or a community. Exploratory evaluation, on the other hand, focussing on the desirability of ideas can only be undertaken by those whose ideas and preferences in the present are to be altered. It is not explicitly related to a specific policy process. It is generic in the sense that the evaluation leads to preferred futures thinking among the broadest possible group of persons.

13.3 Methodological reflections

It would be wrong to suggest that all scenario-building exercises stop short of elaborating scenarios or writing narratives that constitute the scenarios. Though the use of scenarios as a base for evaluation is not included in well-established techniques and practices, there is always some kind of evaluative aspect in cases where those involved go beyond scenario elaboration to determine the implications of alternative scenarios for current decision-making. In planning, scenarios are usually considered as a rhetorical tool with important evaluative implications. In fact, they stimulate reflection about possible futures and suggest if/then arguments in a way that is more flexible than that based on true/false criteria (Patassini, 2001; p. 215). Before we present our approach for exploratory evaluation, let us briefly describe the evaluative elements in some scenario building cases.

In their comparison of the approaches in scenario analysis, (Huss and Honton, 1987) show that two of the four methods go beyond the scenario elaboration step to determine the implications of the scenarios. For example, SRI International analyses whether the scenarios provide support for current strategies or proposed decisions, if they imply changes in the design of particular strategies, what threats and opportunities the scenarios imply, and what factors and forces deserve monitoring in the light of information from the scenarios. In the case of the *BASICS*[1] methodology, scenarios were used to identify how well-positioned the agency was if the scenarios should occur and what strategies should be developed to take advantage of the opportunities presented while reducing potential threats.

In his review of the literature on scenario analysis, (Schnaars, 1987) does not take up the issue of the implementation of scenarios. His article deals mostly with probable scenarios for which he suggests the assessment according to the likelihood of the occurrence of developments outlined in the scenarios. In a more recent review of scenarios, May (1996) builds his approach on several approaches for preparing the scenarios and suggests an analysis of the consequences of the scenarios in order to identify robust decisions that would survive in different situations, and indicators that would help monitor changes as they occur.

Since the focus in our case is to evaluate the background to policy making with the help of interactive scenarios, evaluation is carried out as an interactive process. The discursive process has been succinctly described by Guba and Lincoln (1989).

Its main features are:

- Interactive and explanatory process involving a wide range of stakeholders, each with their own values and knowledge and own way of reasoning and judging;
- All stakeholders have their claims, concerns and issues that are brought forward during the evaluation process;
- It is as inclusive as possible so that all stakeholders have the opportunity to participate, and participants learn about the values and preferences of other participants and participate in a common attempt to achieve the desirable scenario;
- It does not aim to achieve specific goals; its aim is to foster mutual appreciation of challenges and opportunities in order to achieve a desired future.

Thus exploratory evaluation has to be organized in such a way as to develop a functional discourse, achieve an inclusive arena and promote a learning process which expedites mutual understanding about future development. For this purpose we propose the following criteria for exploratory evaluation:

- Desirability of preferences, values and aspirations (abbreviated henceforth as PREVA) ranging from most desirable to least desirable;
- Nature of PREVA ranging from romantic to sophisticated;
- Extent of shared PREVA — from generally shared to partially shared (including conflicts and convergences);
- Availability of catalysts in order to promote future understanding as an ongoing process;
- Robustness of PREVA in relation to current PREVA;
- Realism versus idealism.

13.4 How to use scenarios in policy evaluation — three case studies from Southern Mediterranean

Interactive scenario building for Metropolitan Tunis, İzmir and Rabat-Casablanca

In order to understand how scenarios can be used in policy evaluation, we will refer to three cases of interactive scenario building. They concern respectively three southern Mediterranean urban regions: Metropolitan Tunis, İzmir and Rabat-Casablanca. The focus was on the conflicts between agriculture and urbanization, originated by the pressure of urban growth on fertile peri-urban lands in Tunis, the impact of urbanization and tourism on coastal zones in İzmir, and the consequences of globalization on traditional production and subsequent urbanization in Rabat-Casablanca[2].

An interactive scenario-building approach was used in order to encourage stakeholders to create their own images of the future and outline strategies to realize these images. It was based on Robert Jungk's Future Workshop (Jungk and Mullert, 1997). This method includes the following essential features. First, it allows involvement of non-experts in designing the future because it does not need any specific expertise. Second, it has potentiality in terms of generating knowledge from interactive learning and of facilitating creativity among the participants. And third, it is rather flexible and easy to adapt to specific situations. Future Workshop starts with a preparatory step followed by three major phases, all involving interactive brainstorming sessions and dealing with critique, fantasy and implementation.

Here we are not going into details about the application of such a method in the three case studies. In brief, the modified version of Future Workshop that was adopted in all three cases included the following activities. In the critique phase participants began to investigate the issue at hand, focusing on problems and negative experiences stemming from the present situation, and selecting the issues of greatest concern by some system of voting. In the imagination phase, they were asked to forget practical limitations and obstacles of the present reality, and to generate future visions on the bases of PREVA with a time horizon of 30 years. In the implementation phase, the participating stakeholders were invited to go back to the present reality, with its power relations and constraints, and to single out obstacles and limits to the implementation of future visions and possible ways to overcome them. In the İzmir and Rabat-Casablanca experiences, some phases of the process were supported by the computer software *MeetingWorks*[3] (Barbanente, Khakee and Puglisi, 2002; Khakee et al., 2002).

Both the selection and involvement of stakeholders in interactive scenario building are crucial components of the process and for the subsequent exploratory evaluation. Evidently, contents and possible uses of scenarios are very much influenced by participants' personalities and interest in participatory activities. Thus, it is important, on the one hand, to ensure that the perspectives and insights of different interests and views are represented, on the other, that stakeholders' interest in the whole scenario building process is kept alive. Especially in Tunis, the attempt to involve a wide and varied range of key stakeholders was only partially fulfilled. Thus, while in İzmir the average number of participants present in all sessions was about 30, in Tunis and Rabat-Casablanca it was 20, mainly representatives of governmental institutions. In İzmir and even in Rabat-Casablanca, NGOs and corporations were represented. It is quite clear that the interest in specific policy issues influenced the level of commitment of different stakeholders. In particular, since many of the participants were public officials directly engaged in policy domains concerned with issues in the scenario exercise, their involvement might, however, be motivated by an interest in obtaining approval of their ideas by politicians or colleagues.

It is not easy to summarize the results of the three experiences. The results consist of more than two hundred statements for each case study. Most statements were generated during imagination and implementation phases. They include numerous, widely different images of future with a clear prevalence of positive, desirable, and sometimes idyllic pictures. The critique phases, however, were organized in such a way as to obtain a sufficient convergence of opinions on current problems and their priority order; thus, each of their results was composed of not more than fifteen priority problems.

The pictures generated during imagination and implementation phases clearly contrast with the concerns about current problems that were expressed in the critique phase. Nevertheless, they were strictly connected with them. In fact, a number of statements regarding the desirable future were largely a by-product of stakeholders' dissatisfaction with the current situation. On the other hand, both visioning and implementation activities induced participants to broaden enormously their 'cognitive boundaries': many issues that were absent among the problems identified in the critique phases emerged in the subsequent phases. Such results highlight the importance of focusing on the knowledge process rather than on the final results: how ideas developed from one phase onto another one is as interesting as the conclusions reached during each step.

The changeable nature of preferences, values and aspirations — enlarging evaluation perspectives

The difficulty in establishing ends and objectives, based on some kind of societal PREVA, is one of the crucial points in planning and policy making. It relates not only to possible divergences between real and articulated PREVA but also with regard to the aggregation of articulations into a collective expression. Since PREVA are alterable, they should be considered as outputs rather than merely inputs in planning and policy-making. There is a twofold relationship between actual PREVA and the world of imagination. People base current PREVA on what they already know, while they are not able to express future PREVA because they are not able to imagine them. If we can enlarge and enrich people's imagination about what may happen, we can change their perception about the future PREVA.

Evaluation criteria are often drawn from planning and policy ends and objectives, which in their turn are based upon some dissatisfaction about the present situation, and more-or-less well-defined interpretations of societal PREVA. Since people's perceptions of PREVA change when their space of imagination are altered, scenarios can be considered a powerful tool in order to broaden evaluation perspectives. In our experience of scenario building activity such an enlargement of views was conspicuous in the passage from the critique phase, that focus on problems and negative experiences of the present situation, to the imagination phase, that aims to stimulate stakeholders' creativity in envisioning imaginary futures.

For example in Tunis, during the critique phase, using three rounds of a questionnaire survey, stakeholders were asked to single out the most relevant problems connected with the relationship between agriculture and urbanization with a sustainable perspective. Close analysis of answers to questionnaires shows that most problems were perceived as directly related to inadequate land use management: 'illegal or partially controlled urbanization', 'land speculation', 'difficulty in controlling the land and real estate market' and 'difficulty in constituting land reserves' (see Table 13.1). Other answers were indirectly connected to the problem of land use control. In fact, informal and speculative housing, in stakeholders' views, were the main causes of imbalance between housing, green spaces, other infrastructure and

Table 13.1 Lists of problems ranked by priority level identified by stakeholders in the critique phase (Tunis case study)

Problems	Problem areas
1. Illegal or partially controlled urbanisation	Land use
2. Inadequate development management in agriculture	Agriculture
3. Land speculation	Land use
4. Difficulty in controlling land and real estate market	Land use
5. Inadequacy of public transport	Transport
6. Lack of green areas in the central urban areas	Infrastructure
7. Environmental degradation and pollution	Environmental
8. Unbalance between habitat and working places	Spatial organisation
9. Scarcity of space suitable for urbanisation and difficulty in constituting 'land reserves'	Land use
10. High rates of unemployment	Labour market
11. Difficulty of life in rural areas	Agriculture
12. Abandonment of rural areas	Rural life
13. Lack of future-oriented projects	Strategic development
14. Lack of urban amenities in peri-urban areas	Infrastructure

working places. Half of the problems have to do with deficiencies in land use management. It is worth mentioning that the İzmir experience showed similar and even clearer results. Ranking the problems that came out in the critique phase, a picture emerges in which six out of the ten problems to which stakeholders assigned higher priority were directly related to land use control (see Table 13.2).

In general, these initial outcomes reflect the dominant stakeholders' viewpoint, in which the perception of the institutional and regulatory dimensions prevailed over economic and social ones, and cultural issues were almost completely neglected. In addition, most problems were observed from a physical perspective. Stakeholders showed their deeply embedded mental models, on the basis of which they probably acted. The narrowness of such models highlights the importance of one of the intangible functions of scenarios, namely that of stretching existing mental models and thus triggering some form of learning.

The passage from problem identification to imagination and implementation phases brought with it an ensuing increase in stakeholders' perception about the multidimensional nature of the problems concerning agriculture-urbanization relationship in the Tunis case. This occurred after the immersion in the world of imagination by using the anticipatory approach starting from different visions of future as well as interactive brainstorming sessions. For example, by comparing the results of the critique phase with the list of problems produced by the Tunis stakeholders during the phase of scenario implementation, as summed up in Table 13.3, we observe that the understanding of problems had radically changed. New problem areas were introduced, which were totally neglected in the previous phase. In particular,

Table 13.2 Lists of problems ranked by priority level identified by stakeholders in the critique phase (İzmir case study)

Problems	Problem areas
1. Uncontrolled development of the coastal zone	Land use
2. Irregular and unplanned urban housing expansion	Land use
3. Irregular and unplanned industrial development	Land use
4. Uncontrolled immigration from the countryside	Demographic policy
5. Traffic congestion in the metropolitan area	Transport
6. Water and sea pollution	Environmental
7. Air and soil pollution	Environmental
8. Depletion of agriculture lands	Agriculture
9. Wasteful use of natural resources	Environmental
10. Weakness of land use and environmental planning and regulation	Urban planning

they were related to human, social and financial concerns. Interestingly, all three Tunis scenarios: the Eco-City, the Tower City and the Human City, implied a similar enlargement of perspective.

The participants in all three cases came out in favor of a more 'pro-active' approach, based on individual incentives, education and citizen involvement instead of the existing approach for controlled management of urbanization and agriculture. They also singled out possible cultural obstacles and constraints to the implementation of visions e.g. 'the mentality of the Tunisian ... that hardly accepts comprehensive development but prefers low density, single family housing'.

Some ideas, however, persisted during the entire scenario building process and across different scenarios. For example, notwithstanding the above-mentioned enlargement of stakeholders' perspectives and considerable differences in beliefs and values underlying each scenario, land use management reappeared as one of the key strategies in all three Tunis scenarios (see Figure 13.1). This reveals the existence of 'shared mental models', hinting at the dominant ways in which stakeholders interpreted driving forces for changes in environment.

As is well known, policy outcomes are influenced not only by formal empirical and normative suppositions that a public policy, or plan or program, rest upon, but also by participants 'program theories'. The evaluation should surface these theories, pointing out the assumptions embedded into the program (Weiss, 1972). Highlighting 'shared mental models' may be helpful for in itinere and ex post evaluation of plans, programs or projects, since they may reveal implicit intervention theories that are different from the 'formal theories' that officially justify them. The knowledge included in scenarios may throw light upon linkages in the causal path to the expected outcomes of a policy and may help single out assumptions that inform policy design and implementation. In addition, scenarios highlight stakeholders' knowledge paths and bents for action, which may turn into reliable predictions of policy

Table 13.3 Lists of problems related to scenarios (Tunis case)

Problem	Problem areas
Eco-City Scenario	
High cost of public management	Public administration
Low degree of public involvement	Political
Lack of economic means in public and private spheres	Economic
Brake in economic development	Economic
Waste generation	Environmental
Low yield	Social
Land fragmentation	Land market
Blocking of public projects (schools, hospitals, networks)	Infrastructure/economic
Water scarcity (irrigation)	Agriculture
Market failures	Economic
Insufficient supply of investments	Economic
Unregulated competition between economic operators	Economic/social
High maintenance costs of public works	Public administration
Lack of skilled labor	Educational
Rapid and anarchical urbanization	Land use
Human City Scenario	
Demographic pressure	Social
Land scarcity	Land market
Not possible for economically weak people	Economic
Lack of means to accomplish SDA of land development	Economic
Disrespect for town planning	Law
Improper use of space	Land resources
Low abidement of land use rules	Law
Building needs	Social
High social costs	Social
Lack of resources	Economic
More developed road network	Infrastructure
Lack of resources for investments	Economic
Tower City Scenario	
High costs of investments	Economic
Physical insecurity	Social
Concentration of job-seekers in the same environment	Labor market
Lack of basic infrastructures	Infrastructure
Low maintenance of green space	Infrastructure
Speculation on agricultural lands occupied for urban use	Land use
Air, water and land pollution	Environmental
Decrease in agricultural production	Agriculture
Rural exodus: producers become consumers	Economic
Development of rural and port infrastructure	Infrastructure
Human resource development	Education
Degradation of family structure	Social
Crisis of social values	Social
Rise in virtual communication	Infrastructure

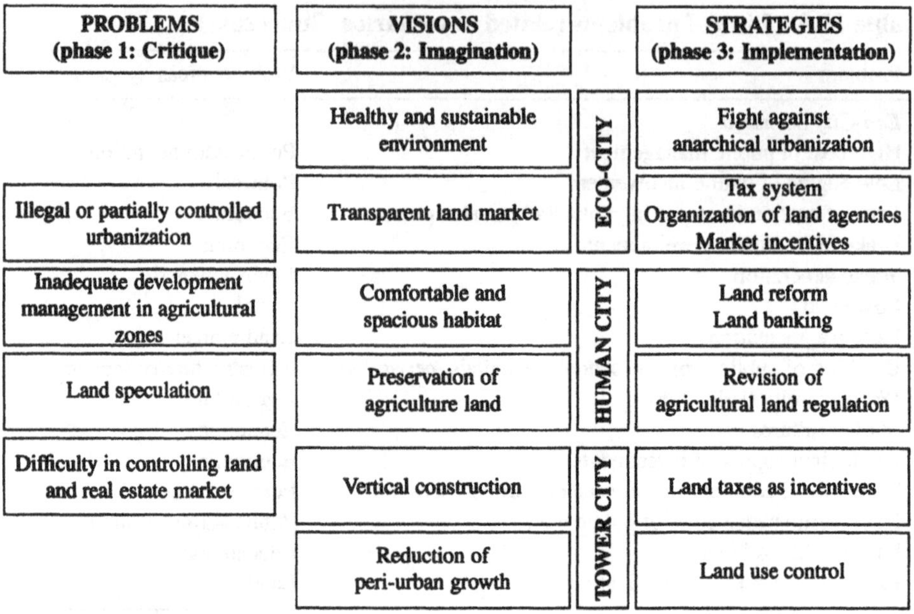

Figure 13.1 Permanence of issues across different scenerios and phases (Tunis case study)

developments, if the same stakeholders are involved both in policy formulation and implementation.

In the three case studies scenarios provided a link between desires and outcomes, and exploratory evaluation improved the insight in this link. For example, in the case of the World City vision for İzmir, the stakeholders presented a narrative where the urban region had no immigration at all (see Figure 13.4). This can be explained by the concern for the current uncontrolled immigration to the İzmir region from the rest of Turkey and its consequences on the provision of housing, social and physical infrastructure and environmental quality. In the implementation phase, an exploratory evaluation showed how current PREVA needed to be changed in order to obtain a better managed immigration policy.

By exposing underlying assumptions, scenarios extended the scope of exploratory evaluation. Once again the İzmir study provides a useful illustration. In the implementation of the Democratic City vision for İzmir the dominating underlying assumption was fundamental political change against the current disquiet in Turkish politics. During the implementation phase, the evaluative work made clear the shortcomings of the existing evaluative practices especially because the objective was to improve the political environment for making and implementing decisions.

In conventional evaluation, understanding why a policy 'works properly or not', it is usual to check if that policy reached its predefined goals, but in exploratory evaluation it is necessary to understand assumptions underlying the policy. Goals change during the period leading to a distant future. In conventional evaluation it is probable that only part of societal PREVA was represented, limiting the scope of evaluation. In exploratory evaluation a comprehensive view of PREVA emerges, extending the scope of evaluation considerably. For example, all the three case studies show not only that future images include cultural, social, political and economic aspects but, most importantly, the actions necessary to implement the desired vision embrace these aspects. Human beings, rather than physical, administrative and technical issues, are placed at the center of scenarios. Improving the quality of education and increasing public participation in decision-making in all three cases are considered crucial in order to achieve the desirable images of the future. The scope of evaluation becomes quite considerable.

Conventional evaluation pays limited attention to social justice by paying attention to equal participation and equal access to information. Despite the fact that in southern Mediterranean countries, stakeholders work under considerable political constraints, the interactive scenario building seemed to enhance stakeholders' consciousness of these issues.

Most of the stakeholders involved in the three case studies were public officials. The multidimensional framework that they constructed during the scenario building process might have some consequences on the way in which they would judge policies in their ordinary duties, especially in paying attention to expected and unexpected outcomes in a long-term perspective.

Possible implications of desirable visions

Useful insights for exploratory evaluation may come from scenarios if we turn our attention to the issue of desirability. As we have said before, major results of our scenario building activity were a number of desirable future visions of the three urban regions. Focusing on desirability can be relevant for a number of reasons.

First, it is significant with respect to a specific aim of the Concerted Action program, which is to help and promote a sustainable use of soil and water in southern Mediterranean cities. The task of developing evaluative criteria that incorporates the notion of sustainability is not only complex but also questionable. It is well known that there is no clear and agreed definition of sustainability. A number of global, national and local goals and related indicators have been defined with reference to this concept. What is more, 'such a diverse range of environmental, economic, social, political, demographic, institutional and cultural goals have been said to be part of "sustainable development" that most governments or international agencies can characterize some of what they do as contributing to sustainable development.' (Satterthwaite, 1997; p. 1668). From another perspective, sustainability can be viewed as a limitation rather than a goal (Marcuse, 1998), in the context of evaluating desirability. A measure that is not sustainable cannot be considered ipso facto undesirable, since there might be balances between the negative sides of the measure against the positive consequences that flow from it. The risk is to assume sustainable goals as

1. Diffusion of literacy skills among population
2. Enhancement of human capital as a basic resource for development
3. Development of regional transport infrastructures
4. Education in new technologies
5. Reduction of water shortage by new recycling technologies
6. Promotion of foreign investments
7. Improvement of urban transport system
8. Promoting wide spread use of information and communication technologies
9. Promoting Rabat-Casablanca as African capital in the field of information technologies
10. Promoting Rabat-Casablanca as the primary economic pole of Magreb

Figure 13.2 Ten most voted possible consequences of globalization ranked by desirability levels (Rabat-Casablanca case)

absolute values and to use them as an easy way out in conflicts arising in other policy areas. Many dilemmas arising from such an attitude exist in the cases studies.

Second, the dominant notion of sustainability, especially in Tunis and İzmir, assumed a narrow point of view, focused on problems of land-use allocation and physical development. Desirable visions played an important role in enlarging stakeholders' horizons about the possible implications of sustainability.

Third, the stakeholders had an active role in not only predicting but also shaping the future. For both purposes, quantitative techniques are usually applied to describe the most probable future (truth) as if it was the desired (ideal) one (Myers and Kitsuse, 2002). In all three case studies, reflecting on future scenarios helped stakeholders become more aware of the crucial distinction between predicted and desirable futures.

Last, focusing on alternative desirable scenarios rather than on one probable future, the stakeholders became aware of not overlooking the importance of norms and values in future development, and that such considerations were not confined only to some steps of the decision process.

There are several ways of dealing with the issue of desirability in scenarios. In order to define a sort of classification of aspirations, from the most to the least desirable ones, one can resort to some voting system. This method was applied with the help of the software MeetingWork in İzmir and Rabat-Casablanca. Conscious of the limitations of the mechanistic system of ranking as well as of the possible unstable and contingent character of their results, the process was improved by means of iterative and interactive procedures that were introduced. The results in Figures 13.2 and 13.3 show desires and aspirations with the highest level of consensus in Rabat-Casablanca and İzmir respectively.

Desirable visions in the case studies range from idealistic to sophisticated ones. This wide range of stakeholders' disposition towards the future reflects the difficulty in separating the rational sphere from the emotional one in normative activities such

Socio-cultural
1. Prioritizing human capital. New education system to establish this priority.
2. Cultural and environmental conscientiousness through school education.
3. More attention paid to adult education.

Economic
1. Save us from being a consuming society. Production-consumption balance be established.
2. Existing resources to be used in optimum ways. Come back to production.
3. Tax reform to generate tax paying and improved control of informal economy.

Political/institutional
1. National policies harmonizing according to EU standards. Local governments restructured to become more active. Experts control of public activities.
2. Improved electoral system. Elected representatives have well-educated and qualified facilitators.
3. Stop political patronage. Efficient public services.

Physical/environmental
1. Planning studies for strategic human and physical development.
2. Improve law implementation.
3. Regional management of environmental and physical problems.

Figure 13.3 Three most desirable actions to overcome socio-cultural, economic, political/institutional and physical obstacles to the implementation of the Democratic City vision (İzmir case)

as planning and policy making. Nevertheless, in the final scenario narratives, realistic desires prevailed over the visionary ones. This was due to the difficulty for stakeholders to detach themselves from the constraints of present situation. On the other hand, realistic visions seemed to prevail over the more visionary ones during the process. During brainstorming sessions, some stakeholders had difficulty in using arguments strong enough to support idealistic desires in the face of more realistic and sophisticated ones. However the interactive process resulted in some of idealistic visions being accepted, while the others were considered less relevant or discarded by the stakeholders.

In the İzmir case, for example, stakeholders were asked to distinguish between realistic and idealistic visions (see Figure 13.4). The former depicted a well-regulated and managed city: 'Land use and environmental plans cover all districts in the province, population growth is under control thanks to family planning and immigration regulation, air and water pollution are under control, socio-economic conditions have improved, people are more sensitive to the environment, recycling reduces the use of resources and there is an effective monitoring and control of environment'. It is clear that in this case, regulatory and physical dimensions once more prevailed over other considerations because they reflected strong affiliation to current policies. The latter was more concerned with political, social and cultural issues and suffused with a strong ethical/moral tension. For example, 'Opinions of the society are taken into consideration .... All members of the city council are ... honest ....

Municipalities are not sacrificing beautiful things in order to get more votes in the elections … . Municipalities stop worrying about their political futures and start to work enthusiastically … . There are no negative implementations of mayors in order to benefit money or votes … . Bribe and conspiracy are suppressed'.

The old problem of values

As is well known, futures research is thick with values (Fowles, 1977). This is evident, for example in the Rabat-Casablanca study, where the statements presented in Figure 13.1 are imbued with value judgements with regards to making the Moroccan society more technology oriented as a consequence of globalization. Similarly the three scenarios developed for Tunis, entitled Tower City, Eco-City and Human City, and the two scenarios developed for İzmir, entitled World City and Democratic City, reveal different values underlying stakeholders' visions. But differences in values concern also actions. Many aspects referring broadly to the well being and quality of life were felt to be threatened by market values that normally shape development models. For example, Figure 13.3 shows the three measures that stakeholders considered most important in order to implement the vision of 'World City'. Apart from the expected emphasis on education, economic measures were imbued with value-loaded expressions such as 'Save us from being a consuming society … . Production-consumption balances should be established'. The confidence in technical experts that had emerged in the critique phase find expressions in such statements as 'Activities are carried out and controlled by experts', 'The elected representatives make use of well-educated and qualified facilitators' among the most desirable political/institutional measures, and 'Planning studies considering future make use of qualified personnel' among the physical/environmental ones.

Explanations of values, desirability, worthiness and ethicalness are specific to a particular discourse group and social context. In this light, it can be useful to identify values of certain groups and make value judgements clearer. If we agree that 'when values lie unexamined, they are dangerous' (Lynch, 1981; p. 1), then scenarios can be beneficial to evaluation since they expose values. What is more, multiple visions of the future stress the intrinsic plural character of values and their variation in time, space and between individuals and groups. These multiple visions also reveal that policy makers and the subjects of policies dwell in different value settings, and that any exogenous way of defining policy goals and evaluation criteria may be severely brought into question by stakeholders.

Moreover, in the light of the varied and changeable nature of desires, hopes, and aspirations expressed by stakeholders, using scenarios for exploratory evaluation of near future policy options stimulates us to consider the intrinsically variable character of goals in relation to time, space and affected individuals and groups. This reminds us of the need, in the course of in itinere and ex post evaluation, to look beyond mere assessment of the achievement of objectives to include unexpected outcomes, which may correspond to PREVA that were neglected in policy formulation.

Our case studies include desires and aspirations that are substantially different,

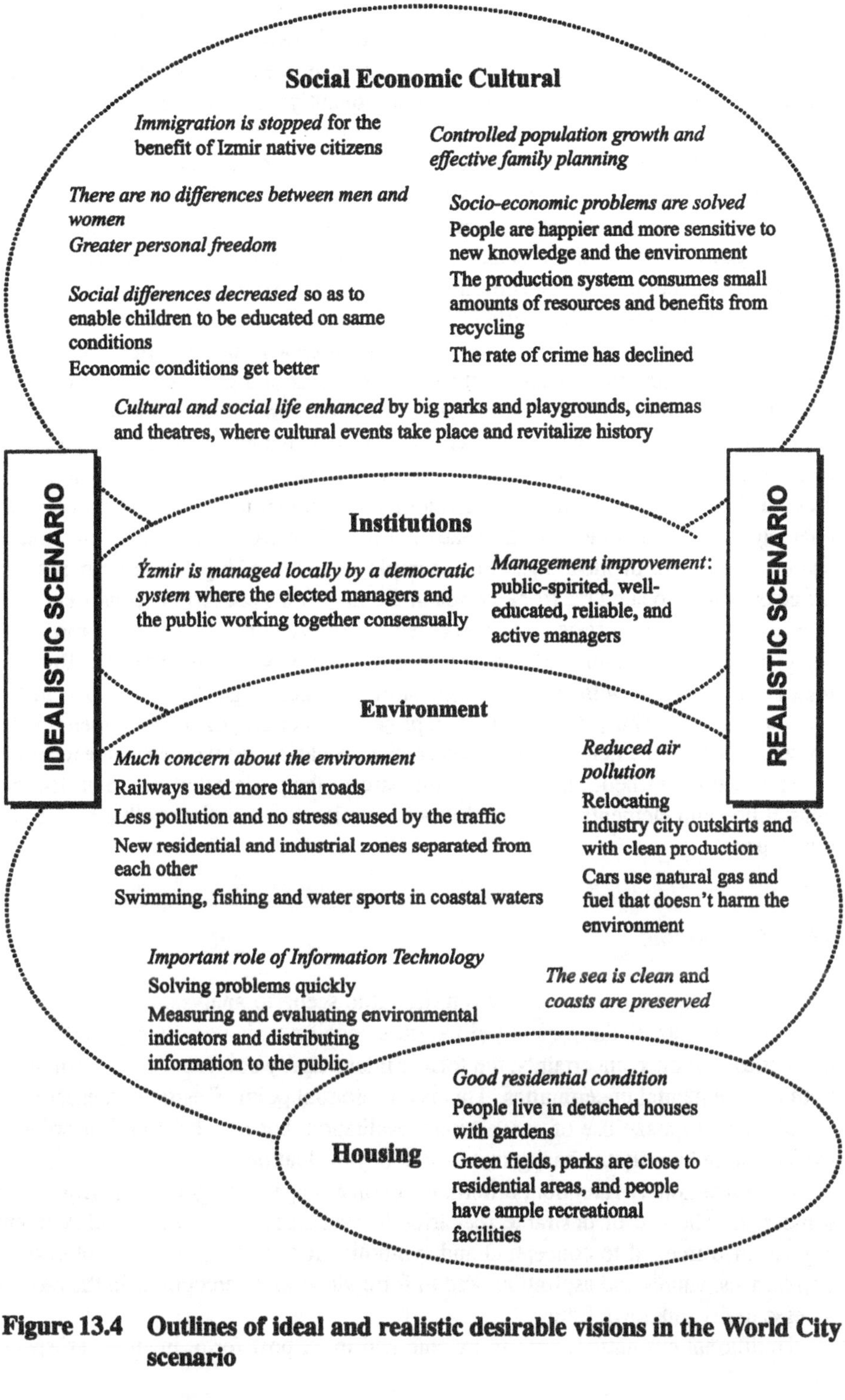

Figure 13.4 Outlines of ideal and realistic desirable visions in the World City scenario

reflecting conflicting experiences, concerns and values. For example, in the Tunis case, contrasting positions emerged very clearly between those oriented to environment conservation, and so willing to protect resources and ensure their renewal; and those oriented to modernization, and consequently wishing to promote 'modern' forms of urban development and economic production. Conflicts in values do not affect only the most abstract desires and aspirations in a sort of hierarchy that we could depict, but are reflected also in very simple ideas about spatial organization. For example, single-storey cottages with gardens and careful restoration of old buildings to serve as guesthouses in the coastal zone (in the Democratic City) contrast with the picture of big shopping malls and office buildings and parks and playgrounds, with cinemas and theatres (in the World City).

Scenarios can be useful in order to outline policies that may be more or less robust to the variation of values between individuals and groups. Of course, this does not solve the problem of variation of values in time. Moreover, scenarios are deeply dependent on current values. The only way to deal with such a problem seems to be to create plans and policies that are flexible enough to adapt to value shifts. Nevertheless thanks to the interactive, iterative, and sometimes reflective process that characterized the generation of alternative visions, this process led to the creation of shared framework of meanings. For example, the idea of big shopping malls and office buildings located far from the sea in the first Tunis scenario is consistent with that of 'coastal line forested and preserved' included in the second scenario. The high social and economic value of the coastal zone is widely recognized. But that idea is not coherent with that of 'single store cottages in gardens' included in the second scenario. Thus, if we evaluate a project concerning the development of the coastal zone with the help of the two alternative scenarios, we would be able to single out elements of resilience in relation to the parts of the project that aim to protect the coastal line and elements of vulnerability in relation to the activities that have to be developed.

13.5 Conclusions

One of the major differences between desirable scenario analysis and trend-based forecasts consists of the radically different stance towards uncertainty. While the latter tries to reduce uncertainty, the former intentionally confronts decision-makers with environmental uncertainties. This is an essential point. Desirable scenarios do not allow us to make use of conventional evaluation, but may be useful in order to explore more broadly the background for policy evaluation.

In conventional evaluation, criteria for choice range from goals to performance standards. The use of desirable scenarios in evaluation indicates an enlargement beyond instrumental to conceptual and symbolic: for the enlightenment of current preferences, values and aspirations and to form views and perceptions in the face of an essentially unknown future.

Traditional evaluation, both in ex ante and in ex post form, involves prospective and retrospective assessment of the impact of the measures that are undertaken. Scenarios, however, have a different perspective. They help to expose unquestioned assumptions of conventional evaluation by looking into the structure, the context and the underlying plural values, and thus enlarge the range of evaluation. Moreover, participatory scenario-building results in shared knowledge useful to highlight stakeholders' preferred use of knowledge and bents for action that may turn into reliable predictions. There is in this clearly a pragmatic dimension.

The weakness of visionary approaches, that has been singled out especially, is their lack of connection to feasibility aspects and subsequent high costs (Helling, 1998). In this study we argue that feasibility is not a primary criterion for judging the usefulness of scenarios for evaluative purposes. The scenarios are there to influence current PREVA. Moreover, our scenarios involve low costs not only in preparation but also in implementation. Their simplicity allows not only mental images of the world that stakeholders share but also use them as a frame of reference for action. Turning to Peter Hall's proposal to improve forecasting methods and refine evaluation criteria by explicitly ranking gains and losses in the near against distant future, our study shows that the use of scenarios for exploratory evaluation helps to avoid the imposing of one view of the world upon the future, and thereby to avoid 'the tyranny of future' (Fowles, 1977).

Notes

1 Editor's note: software developed by S. Millett from Battelle Memorial Institute at Columbus, OH (USA). Actually known under the name *IFS* (Interactive Future Simulations). See http://www.battelle.org/technicalnetworks/bco/policy.stm#forecast and http://www.battelle.org/news/98/49software.stm for details.

2 All three case studies are part of the Concerted Action on 'Agriculture and Urbanisation in the Mediterranean Region' financed by the European Union. Its general objective is to co-ordinate research efforts on sustainable use of natural resources, in particular land and water in the Mediterranean region.

3 Editor's note: software produced by Meetingworks, Seattle, WA (USA). See http://www.meetingworks.com/html/meetingworks_software.html for details.

References

Barbanente, A., Khakee, A. and Puglisi, M. (2002), 'Scenario building for Metropolitan Tunis', *Futures*, Vol. 34, No. 7, pp. 583-596.

Beck, U. (1995), *Risk Society: Towards a New Modernity*, Sage, London (UK).

Bell, W. (1997), *Foundations of Futures Studies — Human Science for a New Era: History, Purposes and Knowledge*, Transaction Publishers, New Brunswick, NJ (USA).

Boulding, K. E. (1966), 'The Economics of the Coming Spaceship Earth', in H. Jarrett (ed.), *Environmental Quality in a Growing Economy*, Resources for the Future, Johns Hopkins University Press, Baltimore, MD (USA), pp. 3-14.

Bunn, D. W. and Salo, A. A. (1993), 'Forecasting with scenarios', *European Journal of Operational Research*, Vol. 68, No. 3, pp. 291-303.

Cronbach J. L. et al. (1980), *Towards Reform of Program Evaluation: Aims, Mathods and International Arrangements*, Jossey Bass, San Francisco, CA (USA).

Faludi, A. and Voogd, H. (eds., 1985), *Evaluation of complex policy problems*, Delftsche Uitgevers Maatschappij BV, Delft (The Netherlands).

Fowles, J. (1977), 'The problem of values in futures research', *Futures*, Vol. 9, No. 4, pp. 303-314.

Gordon, T. J. (1989), 'Futures Research: did it meet its promise? Can it meet its promise?', *Technological Forecasting and Social Change*, Vol. 36, No. 1-2, pp. 21-26.

Guba, E. G. and Lincoln, Y. S. (1989), *Fourth Generation Evaluation*, Sage, Newbury Park, CA (USA).

Hall, P. (1981), *Great Planning Disasters*, Penguin, Harmondsworth (UK).

Harvey, D. (2000), *Spaces of Hope*, University of California Press, Berkely and Los Angeles, CA (USA). Published by arrangement with *Spaces of Hope*, Edinburgh University Press, Edinburgh (UK).

Helling, A. (1998), 'Collaborative Visioning: Proceed with Caution!', *Journal of the American Planners Association*, Vol. 64, No. 3, pp. 335-349.

Hoch, C. J. (2002), 'Evaluating Plans Pragmatically', *Planning Theory*, Vol. 1, No. 1, pp. 53-75.

Huss, W. R. and Honton, E. J. (1987), 'Scenario Planning - What Style Should You Use?', *Long Range Planning*, Vol. 20, No. 4, pp. 21-29.

Innes, J. E. (1996), 'Planning through consensus building: A new view of the comprehensive planning ideal', *Journal of the American Planners Association*, Vol. 62, No. 4, pp. 440-453.

de Jouvenal, B. (1967), *The Art of Conjecture*, Basic Books, New York, NY (USA).

Jungk R. and Mullert, N. (1997), *Future Workshops. How to Create Desirable Futures*, Institute for Social Inventions, London (UK).

Kahn, H. and Weiner, A. J. (1967), *The Year 2000: A Framework for Speculating on the Next Thirty-Three Years*, Macmillan, New York, NY (USA).

Khakee, A. (1988), 'Relationship between futures studies and planning', *European Journal of Operational Research*, Vol. 33, No. 2, pp. 200-211.

Khakee, A. (1991), 'Scenario construction for urban planning', *Omega — International Journal of Management Science*, Vol. 19, No. 5, pp. 459-469.

Khakee, A. (1999), 'Participatory scenarios for sustainable development', *Foresight*, Vol. 1, No. 3, pp. 229-240.

Khakee, A., Barbanente, A., Camarda, D. and Puglisi, M. (2002), 'With or Without: Comparative Study of Preparing Participatory Scenarios for Izmir with Computer-Based and Traditional Brainstorming', *Journal of Futures Studies*, Vol. 6, No. 4, pp. 45-64.

Lichfield, N. (1996), *Community Impact Evaluation*, UCL Press, London (UK).

Lichfield, N. and Prat, A. (1998), 'Linking Ex Ante and Ex post Evaluation in British Town Planning', in Lichfield et al., *Evaluation in Planning: Facing the Challenge of Complexity*, Kluwer Academic Publishers, Dordrecht (The Netherlands).

Lynch, K. (1981), *A theory of good city form*, The MIT Press, Cambridge, MA (USA).

Marcuse, P. (1998), 'Sustainability is not enough', *Environment and Urbanization*, Vol. 10, No. 2, pp. 103-111.

May, G. (1996), *The Future is Ours. Foreseeing, Managing and Creating the Future*, Praeger, Westport, CT (USA).

Myers, D. and Kitsuse, A. (2002), 'Constructing the Future in Planning: A Survey of Theories and Tools', *Journal of Planning Education and Research*, Vol. 19, No. 3, pp. 221-231.

Norse, D. (1979), 'Scenario analysis in INTERFUTURES', *Futures*, Vol. 11, No. 5, pp. 412-422.

Palumbo, M. (2001), *Il processo di valutazione. Decidere, programmare, valutare* (The evaluation process. Deciding, programming and evaluating), Franco Angeli, Milano (Italy).

Patassini, D. (2001), 'Valutazione delle politiche territoriali e ambientali in Italia: limiti di un processo di istituzionalizzazione' (Evaluation of spatial policies in Italy: Development of evaluation in Italy), in N. Stame (ed.), *Valutazione 2001. Lo sviluppo della valutazione in Italia*, (Evaluation 2001. Development of evaluation in Italy), FrancoAngeli, Milano (Italy), pp. 213-219.

Patton, M. Q. (1990), *Qualitative Evaluation and Research Method*, Sage Publications, Beverly Hills, CA (USA).

Satterthwaite, D. (1997), 'Sustainable Cities or Cities that Contribute to Sustainable Development', *Urban Studies*, Vol. 34, No. 10, pp. 1667-1692.

Schnaars, S. P. (1987), 'How to Develop and Use Scenarios', *Long Range Planning*, Vol. 20, No. 1, pp. 105-114.

Schoemaker, P. J. H. (1993), 'Multiple Scenario Development: Its Conceptual and Behavioral Foundations', *Strategic Management Journal*, Vol. 14, No. 3, pp. 193-213.

Schwartz, P. (1991), *The Art of Long View: Planning for the Future in an Uncertain World*, Doubleday Currency, New York, NY (USA).

Shulha, L. M. and Cousins, J. B. (1997), 'Evaluation use: Theory, research and practice since 1986', *Evaluation Practice*, Vol. 18, No. 3, pp. 195-208.

Voogd, H. (1983), *Multicriteria Evaluation for Urban and Regional Planning*, Pion, London (UK).

Walzer, N. (ed., 1996), *Community Strategic Visioning Program*, Praeger, Westport, CT (USA).

Weiss, C. (1972), *Evaluation Research: Methods of Assessing Program Effectiveness*, Prentice-Hall, Englewood Cliffs, NJ (USA).

Weiss, C. (1998), 'Have we learned anything new about the use of evaluation?', *American Journal of Evaluation*, Vol. 19, No. 1, pp. 21-33.

Chapter 14

Ethical and Moral Reasoning and Dilemmas in Evaluation Processes — Perspectives for Intelligent Agents[1]

Dino Borri, Grazia Concilio, Franco Selicato, Carmelo Torre

14.1 Introduction

Do planners consider ethical/moral arguments? When and how is ethical/moral reasoning used for evaluation in planning? Do planners feel responsible towards those people who will be affected by their actions? In what way do planners include moral responsibility in the decision process and its outcomes? What is ethical and moral in environmental evaluation (short-term vs. long-term benefits and/or costs) and is a planner allowed to consider long term benefits more relevant than short term costs? What about local vs. global dimensions in terms of behavioural rules and principles? Is choosing among evaluation methodologies and instruments an ethical and moral issue? How do planners use ethical and moral and/or technical evaluation: separately, parallel, shifting from one to another, consciously, recognizing the power associated to the one or the other?

The complex domain depicted through the above questions is investigated in this contribution within the perspective of designing intelligent artificial systems able to carry out moral reasoning and by discussing two case studies: one related to real estate market mechanisms and focusing on their ability to recognize, in prices, some urban dynamics raising ethical and moral issues; the other regarding environmental protection policies and any conditional boundary to action imposed by ethical and moral principles.

When considering the use of information technology (IT) based instruments dealing with the above ethical dilemmas, many basic questions arise. Does ethical and moral reasoning in spatial planning become necessary when conflict situations have to be faced? Is it useful when dealing with different ethical and moral frames? Does ethical and moral reasoning become necessary when ethical and moral dilemmas emerge? When can technical/ethical and moral dilemmas be easily overcome? Is ethical and moral reasoning context dependent? How relevant are the circumstances when deciding how to act/reason in a certain situation?

'Fields of tension' emerge when dealing with economic and moral responsibilities: are solutions built simply by choosing the one or the other? Are there universal ethical and moral values which structure decision reasoning?

Backgrounds of possible arguments for decision making can be characterized in economic (referring to cognitive instrumental reasons), strategic (referring to the advantage of the considered system in the long run), and moral (referring to normative reasons, especially moral values and responsibilities) terms: what about their needs and uses?

Moral arguments can be used to serve a technical goal in the long run: how is it possible to separate instrumental from non-instrumental ethical and moral reasoning? Is ethical and moral reasoning in planning more likely to be shared among in-group members than among out-group members? Planning interactions create exposure to the ethical and moral beliefs of 'significant others': how do decision makers use ethical and moral reasoning when dealing with pluralistic decisions?

Cognitive Moral Development (CMD) theory suggests that decision makers will allow ethical and moral considerations to constrain their economic/technical behaviour: is that true in spatial planning? How is self-interest relevant when dealing with environmental/real estate issues?

Starting from previous work by the authors, this contribution explores the most recent advances in artificial intelligence (AI) with regards to qualitative ethical and moral reasoning. By examining two case-studies of environmental planning for a natural park and of real estate price formation, we investigate the potential of having recourse to AI agents able to deal with the often overlapping knowledge-decision dimension in planning, becoming aware of the emergence of ill-structured moral and ethical reasoning in human-machine interaction. Our perspective is that useful artificial agents can be envisaged for supporting humans in the management of the intriguing frontier between technical and ethical and moral value-based reasoning, for instance by alerting humans of the changing reasoning environment and the related inadequacies of the machine, and/or giving advice to humans about the need in order to be effective — because of a changing environment — of shifting from monologic, monotonic, single, and simple reasoning to plurilogic, non-monotonic, collective, and complex reasoning.

14.2 The ethical and moral problem in planning

Over the last several decades, a view of the environment oriented towards the reconciliation of nature and history has taken strong root. This view entails harmonizing naturalist components with built spaces where the values of the settled communities are concentrated; or natural spaces with those where the human condition is more dominant; specificities with differences not only of historical-environmental but also of relational type, and urban environments with communities in a state of continual flux and evolution.

So the destinies of places are interwoven with those of the communities that have settled there, to such an extent that the places have gradually acquired a sense and value, not as specific, unique and unrepeatable realities but because they bear the imprint and significance — specific, unique and unrepeatable — of earlier places, customs, histories of the community, together with the overall aspirations and laws (often unwritten) that sustain a particular society.

For this reason, a new ethic has grown up, that highlights the need to fight the spread of a form of generalized passivity in facing environmental decay, and is now considered by many to be waging a true ethical battle for our times (Tagliagambe, 2000). This battle does not only aim to combat indifference and inertia but also to manage differences in views, values, beliefs and opinions.

The anthropocentric view consists largely of forms of indifference and/or environmental prevarication, but also of more targeted actions aiming to contain the perverse effects produced by human processes. For instance, there is an ethical dimension in the environmental issues that is renewing the anthropocentric view of human actions, this time no longer aiming — at least directly — to pursue useful and functional goals for man while totally neglecting their impact on the environment, but rather oriented towards the search for new forms of use of the resources, and for new behavioural styles. Thus, there is an attempt to identify new living opportunities, limiting and containing as far as possible environmental damage, but still within the perspective of guaranteeing the survival of the human species. Is not the threat of catastrophic scenarios for humanity the strongest incentive to build up a different environmental conscience? McHarg (1969) said that there are 'sinister reasons for optimism', and regarded the most recent failures as providing the strongest impetus for improving environmental planning.

There is, therefore, an 'environmental' ethic — no longer or not only a 'pro-environment' ethic — that attempts to focus mainly on the 'place of nature in the world of man and reciprocally, on the place of man in the world of nature' (McHarg, 1969; McHarg, 1996). The ethical change resulting from the new vision of ecological disciplines and the different conception of nature, overcoming the concept of man's dominion over nature and of nature as a 'unique script' (Scandurra, 1997), has overturned the traditional views that were consolidated until a few decades ago.

The environment, in any case, can no longer be assumed to be an external element, something that is there, but becomes a springboard against which human behaviour must be sounded, in other words the built or natural context within people operate and act with intentions based on their expectations; in practice a balanced synthesis of 'reality and possibility' (Tagliagambe, 2000). This means an ethic that finds its justification in its power to activate building processes featuring a new community awareness and sense of belonging to the place. And in this perspective new forms of mobilization of knowledge can be defined, within which the role of the planner takes on a new and special significance. In the same way as planners, evaluators are thus involved in active practice, being no longer impersonal practitioners insensible to the contextual conditions and 'pragmatic', as described by Schön (1983), or as 'negotiators', according to Forester (1989): they efficaciously project themselves towards the future in an effort to re-build a different relationship between population and place, community and living environment.

This means paving the way for a new way of operating, abandoning unconditional faith in technical expertise and stimulating critical reflection on the different knowledge fields that combine to delineate the overall environment. In this new way of operating, the planner is an actor armed with specific knowledge and ethical 'intentions' for the tasks of stimulating collective awareness of the environmental aspects that underlie the development of the human settlement and of fostering agreement over coherent decisions for the organization of the settlement space (Maciocco, 2000). This way of operating is therefore built on reflecting on the heuristics and ways of reasoning and acting, on learning about the history, micro-histories and salient stories of a place exploring specific expert fields.

It is clear that in all this, in building an environment-oriented plan and especially in commiting himself/herself to stimulating social interaction in order to foster agreement on the plan, the planner acts according to responsible intentions, therefore also according to her/his ethical responsibility. He/she cannot merely listen to the voices of the environment and settled communities, smoothing the path towards a destiny whose ultimate responsibility will belong to the community, but must act within the sphere of personal choices, with the ability to choose for good reasons, in full awareness of his/her role and limits. In other words, there is an assessment component in any plan that cannot be evaded, because there is always the need to take a stand on 'views' and 'different possibilities' that in any case require a definite decision to be made (Palermo, 2000).

Moreover, this responsibility does not only concern the social sphere, the decisions and actions which affect the living spaces of the communities, albeit in a collaborative context on which there is substantial agreement and convergence as to choices that are coherent with the environmental structure of the places. It concerns also and above all those same environmental components that have been the object of the prior expert studies; 'mute' components in whose favour all factors of uncertainty and the principles of prudence should be given priority over any abstract planning hypothesis.

A new ethic of responsibility is rising to the fore (Karlsson, 1997) dealing with globalization of environmental change and long-term effects of human decision-making processes and actions. Increased uncertainty and the consciousness of a 'continuous insufficiency of knowledge' should lead to a new sense of limitation and prudence towards the environment, as well as towards other individuals and future generations. In this perspective the relationship between nature and culture is destined to change. This new ethic of responsibility supports the development of a new local reflexivity (Giddens, 1984), refusing the presumption that it is possible to dominate nature and to postpone to future generations dramatic environmental risks, expressing its criticism against the 'Prometheic impetus' — to use Gottmann's famous expression about American history — of modern design, and involving an effort to care for and to collaborate with the land.

The evolution of an ethical vision of the built/natural environment poses new, hard questions and affects the planner's action, increasing the uncertainty of action and of evaluation. When dealing with environmental problems in planning, is it possible to adopt standard behaviours? Is the environmentalist, anti-anthropocentric view, an ethics which should lead to unique solutions in any context, to any issue? The fight for sustainability, for instance, embracing the principles of equity, welfare and cultural/environmental preservation, enhances the complexity of planning meanwhile making hard reconciliation of diverse goals and tasks.

Focusing on infra-generational equity, planners should promote consumption of resources to ensure the welfare of a wider sector of communities in the short term while, in the long term focusing on inter-generational equity, planners should fight against consumption of environmental resources.

Furthermore, decisions about uses of cultural and environmental capitals are in the hands of local and global decision makers who often have conflicting views. If the preservation of natural resources, landscape and built cultural environment is due to local communities which are the repositories of local knowledge, are the local communities also free to decide for consumption? Is sustainable development the only presently acceptable universal normative approach?

14.3 When and how does ethical and moral reasoning emerge in spatial planning evaluation?

The ethical and moral aspect in evaluation disciplines is traditionally represented in those issues which are the domain of public interest. The counter position between public utility and private utility, between public interest and private profit has accompanied many positions on planning theory and practices, consequently shaping evaluation approaches (Khakee, 1998).

Planning *per antonomasia* is finalized to pursue public interest. Economics supports planning by creating models that represent the public interest, following a given interpretation of the behaviour of people and society. Referring again to tradition, for instance, both liberalistic and Keynesian economies seek to satisfy public interest, and the diverging visions depend not on the final aim but on a different scale of value which has as its direct consequence the use of an evaluation approach to identify the 'most socially profitable choice'. The search for the most socially profitable choice passes through analysis of the convergence between public welfare and individual utility.

Speaking about individual utility and social values we could identify at least three distinct visions expressed by three different ways of considering the transition from individual values to societal values (Menzel, 1999):

- The social welfare function, represented by a complex function of various individual utilities;
- The social welfare function which depends on individual members' 'individual social welfare functions', being different from the traditional individual welfare functions noted above;
- The society's welfare as not always depending on the individual members' societal values expressed in either of the two previous definitions.

These three visions of welfare ethically shape economic models to represent social and individual choices. In Khakee's work, for instance, the statement that evaluation methods change as a consequence of a planning vision, can be reinterpreted in the form of the consideration that evaluation methods and planning approaches change as a consequence of economic visions, which can in turn depend on specific ethical and moral positions. This means, maybe, that when dealing with ethical and moral dilemmas in a planning context, the economic character of the decision as to which resources to use, actors to involve, environment to work on, always responds to ethical and moral scopes, and refers to different ethical and moral visions. Relating to this, it is difficult to believe that there is a precise level of complexity, or conflict, corresponding to the transition from non-ethical economic reasoning to uneconomic ethical reasoning.

If economic reasoning in planning is intrinsically ethical and moral — looking at the essential role of a 'final aim' in the plan — the state transition in a typical 'rational' means-ends plan can be considered from the standpoint of a context where opposing ethical and moral economic visions can coexist at different (low/high) levels of conflict, leading to relevantly different solutions or process directions. So an intriguing question is: in the case of high conflict, does the selection of a specific evaluation model mean that we are choosing a specific ethical and moral economic vision? In a sense, the question has already been posed by Funtowicz and Ravetz (1992), speaking about 'postnormality' in evaluations. They affirm that the higher the stake, the lower the degree of trust in the evaluators' answer. Moreover, as the relationship between conflicts and ethics increases, the difficulty in selecting an evaluation approach also increases.

Different evaluation methods shape action and solution spaces in different ways. The action space and the feasible space relevantly change because of even small reductions or extensions of points of view, criteria, values. For instance, as Forester (1989) reminds us, stressing the importance of deciding sometimes means evoking some higher ethical/moral principle that compels everyone to agree. How do different evaluation approaches correspond to different economic ethical and moral visions? How do we identify an increase in the 'field of tension' of organizational dilemmas (Nijhof and Fisscher, 1997) and derive a new ethical position?

Roughly, the use of cost benefit analysis (CBA) instead of Cash Flow Analysis (CFA) signals transition from individual profitability to social profitability. Even if the structure is substantially common in CBA and CFA, CBA considers monetary parameters to shape socioenvironmental effects, beyond the individual financial expenses and profits. This means we are supplying a methodological answer to the ethical and moral needs to take into account socioenvironmental effects. CFA, on the contrary, is coherent with the ethical and moral idea that individual profits shape society welfare and therefore only market effects matter and deserve our consideration. In the same way, the shift from CBA to multigroup analysis, e.g. CIE (Community Impact Evaluation), responds to the need to consider socioenvironmental/financial costs and benefits that are differentiated per social group, according to the ethical and moral assumption that no single group should have to bear unfair impacts deriving from a decision. In the CBA case an absolute ethical and moral economic vision is in force: socioenvironmental effects are considered relevant for the community as a whole. In the CIE case, the ethical and moral economic vision becomes more context-dependent: the distribution of socioenvironmental effects becomes relevant. Besides evaluation methods and procedures, according to the above represented model, are challenged by a problem of 'creativity'.

In order to better understand the concept of creativity in evaluation, Zeleny's (1983) classification of mono and multi-criterial methods and approaches can be considered. For him, *evaluation* is searching for a convenient feasibility space. It is the opposite of *exploration* that searches for a solution starting from a set of given criteria (points of view). Zeleny calls *intelligence* a dynamic process where alternatives and criteria do change continuously and freely in a continuous and unstructured process. Finally, if both criteria and solutions are given we have only to deal with *computation*.

Ethics can be conceived as a source of preconditions on points of view and alternative solutions: in this case, the constraints to the feasibility space are imposed at the same time by technical and ethical aspects (see the theory of Cognitive Moral Development). Consequently, ethics is an impulse that generates reduction or complexification in evaluation, through the decreasing or increasing of criteria and points of view. Intelligence leads to an increased range of solutions, thanks to the use of creativity, to respond to ethical and moral needs. In Zeleny's representation, the search for new solutions is implemented by looking for a reduction of trade-offs. In the same way, the economics literature on sustainable development, for instance, demands that planners be the reducers of trade-offs between socio-environmental and financial capital (Fusco Girard and Forte, 2000; Munda, 1995).

Further support is given from business management — see Graafland's (2002) model — which demonstrate that *ceteris paribus* profitable choice is given by ethical and moral solution, even in the private market, as long term profit is affected by the ethical and moral consumers' judgement on the behaviour of a firm (Hamilton and Rao, 1996; Daviss, 1999).

14.4 Recent advances in ethical and moral artificial reasoning

Traditional discussions combining ethical and moral principles and the spread of IT are carried out in terms of Computer Ethics[2]. They always involve familiar moral ideas such as personal privacy, harm, taking responsibility for the consequences of one's actions, putting people at risk, and mainly concern the proper use of information technologies — see, for example, Forester and Morrison (1993), in their discussion about moral issues in artificial intelligence. Recently, however, the term 'computer ethics' has acquired a broader sense, that includes applied ethics, computing sociology, technology assessment, computer law, and related fields. This broader kind of computer ethics examines the impact of computing and information technology upon human values, using concepts, theories and procedures derived from philosophy, sociology, law, psychology, and so on. Maner, the father of the term 'computer ethics', proposed considering this field as a separate domain from others (Maner, 1999), requiring dedicated theories[3]. The proposal by Floridi and Sanders (2001) to shift attention towards the concept of Information — rather than Computer — Ethics also tends towards this direction.

However, different approaches have to be taken into account if we consider IT as a participant in the human-computer interaction process. Fritz (1996), for example, discusses the ethics of artificial intelligent systems and suggests the opportunity for distinguishing an ethical action (in terms of adequate action) using a traditional additive model of traditional cost-benefit evaluation (he speaks of advantages and disadvantages): an action is ethical when the sum of all the different advantages and disadvantages computed for each of the components of the society in which the Artificial Intelligent System (AIS) operates is positive.

Far from being an effective model of ethical evaluation for action, Fritz's suggestion represents an attempt to introduce the ethical dimension in AISs. Firstly, with regards to the spatial planning domain, Fritz's proposal is largely limited by the obvious lack of complete knowledge about the consequences of the considered actions. Another relevant limit is the lack of a behavioural-procedural dimension in the action, concerning the way of exploring and selecting objectives, or considering 'what others' are 'significant' in the evaluation, or when an action has to be assessed in terms of ethical quality.

A different but still limited approach is presented by Tridle and colleagues (1995) for the implementation of an expert system making ethically critical judgments with regards to cancer treatments. Their prototype can distinguish three categories of treatment ethics and suggest to the doctors some possible initiatives; in some cases it can also supply them with the justification. Such a prototype, appearing as a sort of alerting system, is a highly specialized one and requires the recognition of different categories of ethical issues[4] which are treated differently by the system. Some questions need to be considered: is it possible to categorize ethical issues? Is it ethically correct? How many categories of ethical issues should be considered to cover a sufficient and acceptable set of consequent actions? Is alerting the best approach to ethical issues or should we prefer to leave such a task to humans with their ability to heuristically interact with the environment?

In a wider approach to the perspective of developing Ethical Artificial Reasoners (EAR), Colemann (2001) tries to summarize the recent debate on this theme on the basis of a 'virtue ethic'[5]. Speaking of 'computational agents' (CA)[6], Coleman accepts the traditional assumption that the ultimate end of computational agents is to serve humans; he discusses CAs' ethics in terms of how they serve humans in the achievement of ends humans chose. In order to contribute to the discussion about what a good computer is, Coleman focuses on categories of virtues, characterizing their ethical behaviour. He initially groups agentive, social and environmental virtues:

- *Agentive virtues* enable agents to function independently in a variety of environments and can be divided into proactive virtues (self-movement, self-regulation, autonomy, goal orientation, independence, self-sufficiency, agency, intelligence, reliability, efficiency and accuracy) and reactive virtues (flexibility, reactivity, adaptivity and autopoiesis);

- *Social virtues* enable agents to interact with other agents and include communicative virtues (communicativity, explicit and implicit responsiveness, veracity, accessibility, and character) and cooperative virtues (respectfulness, reliability, flexibility, adaptivity, and reactivity);
- *Environmental virtues* refer to agentive or social virtues for a specialized environment and comprise conservative virtues (moderation, tidiness, obedience, and safety) and informative virtues (identifiability, openness and inquisitiveness).

Moreover, Coleman introduces moral virtues in order to discuss computational agents' ability to deal with human ultimate ends, and divides them into two tentative subcategories: altruistic virtues and egoistic virtues. The former, 'which reflect the need to be concerned with others, include non-maleficence, freedom from bias, safety, vigilance, beneficence, and obedience and accessibility. Egoistic virtues, which reflect a need to be concerned with one-self, include self-protection and vulnerability' (Colemann, 2001; p. 258).

The 'android arête' discussed by Coleman draws up a list of the most important characteristics ('virtues') of what we would call an EAR. The attempt made to categorize the virtues starting from the world of artificial agents appears very interesting but, sometimes, seems to touch on the boundaries of science fiction in face of the complexity of the real world. In any case, it highlights the emerging exigency to discuss the ethical dimension of computer science, overcoming the traditional vision of computer ethics and exploring the complexity of ethical reasoning by artificial agents.

14.5 Considerations from two case studies

Ethical and moral dilemmas in urban rehabilitation: real estate market vs. social housing policies. Some rhetoric on gentrification

An emerging rhetoric in urban rehabilitation refers to the role of financial resources and the coincidence between social valorisation and the creation of high-rent estates. According to this rhetoric, strategies in urban rehabilitation are increasingly based on the financial-economic feasibility of interventions. Plans should be economically self-sustained and attractive for entrepreneurs and financial investors. A key field in evaluation is represented by economic assessments and forecasts regarding the real estate market and its dynamics as a consequence of rehabilitation policies. Even without forgetting the basic role of planning as market regulator, planners recognise the need to cooperate or at least to deal with real estate consultants in order to strengthen their purpose of implementing urban policies without loss of financial competitiveness.

On the subject of access to the housing market, the differentiation between users and producers creates supply and demand intervals which identify different economic value levels, favouring a complex market segmentation. In the case of real estate, *gentrification* means a change of market character, because the users of the real estate change according to its own *quality*: quality which in this case essentially means substitution of low income households by high income households. From this standpoint, the need to maintain a role for social housing policies can lead to some dilemmas which locate the decision context between the search for profitability and the search for social equality.

In the case of the degraded urban neighbourhoods of Madonnella and San Pasquale, in Bari,[7] such dilemmas assume a practical dimension, which is a far cry from some basic theoretical debates. Gentrification, for instance, has been considered a positive aspect of the urban rehabilitation process while it often represents a fine way to start a process of alienation of the weaker segments of the local community (as in the well known case of the tragic urban rehabilitation in the Bronx district, in New York City).

In our case study the analysis of real estate market values reveals the existence of a low-rent area, built in the middle of the 20th century and now located in between the ancient core of the city and the urban expansion of the 1970s and 1980s. Here the buildings are mostly owned by people who lack of the financial resources that are needed to start rehabilitation processes. Here, until now, no attention has been shown for the rehabilitation of the area by the entrepreneurs, who do not evidently consider the valorisation of the area as a profitable concern. In fact, in Bari, the pressure of the building market is still oriented towards building new complexes, as construction costs are lower than rehabilitation costs. Therefore, in our case study area, the real estate market is characterized by the existence of dwellings rented to low income people who generally pay amounts of money unregulated by law or contracts and who would not be able to find lodging in many other parts of the city because of the level of their income. A crucial point is the convergence of visions of planners and consultants, who respectively act as supporters to public and private decision makers.

The solution space for real estate consultants is represented by all alternatives which are able to create added financial value after the physical rehabilitation of the buildings. Evaluation in the consultants' domain aims at identifying solutions which maximize added value for entrepreneurs and owners. The planners' solution space, instead, covers all projects which offer better condition of life to low income residents. According to the planners' vision, gentrification may be ethically compatible with social rehabilitation if it is accompanied by compensating social policies.

The relevant trade-off between the creation of new market attractions and the public control of rents for social housing policies leads to a dilemma. A common solution space should provide an answer to the issue of rehabilitating the built environment without expelling old residents while creating attraction for investors. This solution seems to correspond to a vision shared by all actors.

The description of the context by the estate consultants identifies the following roles (the distinction being based on the character of the financial resources that each actor can provide): investors, promoters, high income house owners, low income house owners, high income renters, and low income renters. This view does not capture some qualitative aspects which create intergroup differences, such as the legal status of renters and owners and the different groups of renters. Low income renters for instance can be classified as migrants or as university students, or as households.

The estimation of real estate values is basically founded on the information deriving from official data on rents for households which often report, according to the registered contract, a lower rent than the real one. In fact, the first two groups 'do not exist' in the market, due to the illegal status of rents without registered contracts, and, furthermore, investors and promoters are interested only in households status. Therefore the real distribution of social resources throughout the real estate market does not emerge in this kind of financial analysis.

What will happen when the perception of the composition of the low-rent group changes, due to the constitution of a migrant community? The consciousness of the need to ensure popular priced dwellings to low-rent people may still not be shared by all social groups. A conflict can arise as to the possibility of building a priority list, favouring one against other ethnic groups. The question whether illegal migrants can represent 'significant others', in the same way as any other autochthonous poorest community group, imposes the need for resolving new ethical dilemmas. Information about the real estate market does not provide support for such a decision: a new hidden market is rising up and a new dilemma is emerging. Planners do not agree to the proposal to consider the migrants' needs among the objects that shape the social profitability of a popular housing policy.

After the question: 'Is it ethical to consider a better built environment for better citizens?' new relevant questions are rising to the fore: Is the postponement of rehabilitation until a social housing policy has been implemented a possible solution in order to safeguard low income households? Is a social housing policy supporting owners who are carrying on a policy of illegal renting of dwellings an ethically acceptable solution? Should the migrants' point of view be considered in a community impact assessment?

The consultants' behaviour in our case study illustrates the transition from technical and economic approaches to ethical and moral approaches. The valorisation of the area no longer appears to be linked only to the financial dimension, while in the consultants' reasoning the point of view of the social actors appears as a precondition of the decision to invest in the area. This is coherent with Rutledge and Karim's assertion that the consultants' point of view may not always be profit-oriented. The assumption of the existence of a social conflict in the context, for instance, can be the way to transform a profit-oriented vision into an ethically-affected one. Conflictuality can represent an obstacle to the creation of profit via the rehabilitation of the area. This perception, even if not supported by data, can anyway affect the behaviour of entrepreneurs and consultants.

Analysing the process, we can observe that the inclusion of 'relevant others', that is of new groups with new needs and perspectives, enlarges the ethical and moral aspects considered in the reasoning process and creates different points of view among actors at the beginning sharing the same vision. This is the case of planners who share with the real estate consultants the consciousness of the need for social housing but differently look at the subjects to be favoured by a given policy. The inclusion of migrants among the community sectors to be supported through welfare policies creates a conflict between planners and consultants, who respond to different ethical and moral visions and that conflict can induce some consultants not to consider only the market limit as the borderline of his/her feasibility space.

Planning for natural parks: what are the ethical and moral boundaries?

Analyzing the interplay among social, economical and environmental dimensions in planning for natural parks, an immediate and simple question arises: What is the ethically correct relation among these? i.e., how can an ethically correct preferences structure be built?

Ethical and moral dilemmas in planning for natural parks always highlight what is known as an 'intractable conflict' (Burgess and Burgess, 1995): at one end, ethical and moral correctness may suggest careful avoidance of environmental damage (a sort of non-utilitarian ecological utopia) and, at the other end, utilitarian approaches can hide ethical and moral dimensions in terms of economic development perspectives.

Without disapproving of Frolova's (1998) idea of moving the responsibility of facing such dilemmas onto the shoulders of humanity as a whole, it is necessary to consider that changes occurring in environmental awareness lead to the creation of new forms of environmental protection and also of natural parks planning, that encompass whole landscapes and an awareness that traditional parks are integrated in their territorial setting (Bray, 2003). Cognitive Moral Development theory theory suggests that decision makers will allow ethical/moral considerations to constrain their economic and technical behaviour. When dealing with environmental conflicts, an ethical and moral boundary of the action space does not appear operative.

In the case of the *gravina* (a small canyon with a relevant ecological function) of Gravina in Puglia[8], the process for setting up a natural park is still ongoing. The current situation is that the area has been studied by a group of experts and, therefore, provided with an expert view of its future development. This view is based on two possible hypotheses of zoning and management rules, according to two different environmental protection policies and land management frameworks. The expert views to be submitted to and therefore discussed and re-structured within the large community of the municipality of Gravina in Puglia include environmental associations, industrial and agricultural stakeholders, cultural and tourist agencies. Before starting this far-reaching assessment process, several meetings have been held with some regional officers and municipal administration representatives[9].

The meetings with the regional officers revealed behaviours strongly affected by needs for political consensus and by existing legislation frameworks. With regards to the first issue, during the meetings it appeared clearly that regional officers are oriented to stop the setting up of the natural park in the face of persistent opposition by the municipalities involved, because of their need to avoid political conflicts between regional and municipal administrations. Secondly, it appeared that regional officers did not consider any possibility for environmental protection apart from that envisaged within the current normative framework, that is they do not consider the possibility of developing any new idea on natural parks apart from what is already provided by the law. In short, regional officers show a sort of 'waiting' behaviour: they await an opportunity to start the setting-up process of the natural park in the most piecemeal way, avoiding any forcing. In this perspective, of course, good opportunities are generally considered as those situations where the local municipal administrations show their willingness to accept the environmental protection framework as it is structured by law[10].

During the meetings with the municipal administrators of Gravina in Puglia, no evident opposition to the setting up of the natural park was observed, but the need for restructuring the feasibility assessment was strongly declared: 'We need to know, as far as possible, what consequences could be induced on our economic system. We cannot place our emerging and promising productive economies at risk,' was the Mayor's refrain. Because the repeatedly stated willingness of the municipality of Gravina to seriously take into consideration the actual setting-up of the natural park, no *tout court* application of the norms can be considered as possible: setting up the natural park can take place only if the park will be strongly related to the economic development process currently occurring in the local context. But how can this be possible if no substantial change can be introduced in the regulative scheme? In the *gravina* case, a strong integration between environmental protection goals and local economic development strategies can become real (this is the condition posed by the municipality) only if environment and economy collaboratively shape each other. The goal of environmental protection cannot be considered hierarchically greater than the goal of local economic development within the community of Gravina.

Is not environmental protection an ethical commitment *per se* and, therefore, especially an ethical commitment of the public administration? Should the public administration compulsorily proceed in its implementation of the plan for achieving the regional goals in natural park policy and consider the environmental protection as a top level compulsory goal to be pursued without any restriction? What is ethical in environmental evaluation? Short-term vs. long-term benefits and/or costs considerations represent a wide problematic field. Is a planner allowed to consider long term benefits as more relevant than short term costs? How can the dichotomy of the local/global dimension be faced in terms of ethical behavioural rules and principles? A Frolovas' (1998) problem is emerging, that cannot find easy solution within strict rule application. Considering that interactive processes, like those presented in the *gravina* case, create exposure to the ethical beliefs of 'significant others', the problem becomes that of how to use ethical and moral reasoning taking into account that decisions are plurality affecting.

Very similar to this, but more advanced with regards to the process of setting up a natural park, is the case of the Alta Murgia National Park, again in Apulia. In this case, involving a national and not a regional natural park, a preliminary decision on the zoning and the associated transitory land use rules has already been taken by the Italian Ministry for the Environment. The quarrying activity, a large and lucrative economic sector for the communities that are settled in the area of the park, is a crucial and problematic issue for land use regulation. Considering the number of involved workers, the quarrying activity can be considered a relevant local economic asset. The firms, obviously, have already been affected in terms of a reduction of market demand after the intention of creating a new National Park in their area was announced[11].

The Ministry, in collaboration with the regional administration, had to set the boundaries of the National Park, and a dilemma had to be faced in terms of inclusion/exclusion of the quarrying areas in/from those boundaries. Inclusion would mean interruption of quarrying activities. These are, in fact, strictly forbidden in natural park areas by the national law. A recent decision of the Ministry excluded the quarrying areas from the park area. The fundamental trade-off that has been considered deals with the loss of profit for the quarrying entrepreneurs and the need for immediate environmental reclamation of the quarrying areas for local people. Without discussing the political reasons underlying the Ministry decision, it is however clear that no attempt was made to look for alternative economic development based on environmental resources, thus preventing the process of setting up the natural park from taking on the character of an empty mediation in terms of areas of inclusion/exclusion.

Remarks on the case studies

When dealing with ethical and moral dilemmas, the need for explorative decision-making processes is evident. Decision-making can be compared to a series of transactions. Here the term transaction means momentary cognitive composition of unbalanced conditions characterizing the decision-making processes. This transactional character is particularly visible in spatial planning which is an activity carried out in complex action environments which need to be split up and/or composed into other action environments different in terms of level and dimension. So the decision process should be characterized by the alternation of 'evaluation/decision/action' paths and of other paths which are hardly interpretable through traditional sequential models for their particular creativity, productivity, strong linkage to the context and its conditions, and are therefore extremely contingent. What is needed is contextual-adaptive decision models whose restrictions, constraints and local enlargements can be introduced in a continuous way so that decision processes can reduce the number of instances in which the large dimensions of the decision space involve high uncertainty and risk. By making the restrictions and constraints explicit, it is possible to transform the decision process into a sequence of transactions carried out inside decision spaces whose dimensions are small enough to be managed through the limited knowledge bases of the decision makers involved (Borri and Concilio, 1999).

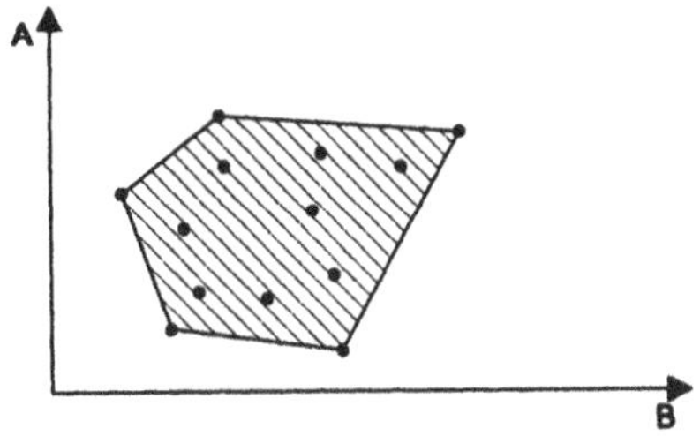

Figure 14.1 Starting feasible space (2D)

14.6 Exploring the action space

In view of the above considerations, ethics can be viewed as an imperative that generates the restructuring of the evaluation environment, by modifying the criteria (which can be reduced or enlarged in numbers, both in the whole evaluation model or simply in a restricted locally explored environment) or by creating new alternatives for action. The role of exploration becomes crucial and with it that of creativity. In this sense, an ethical reasoner should hopefully have the ability to modify the framework of the feasible space, by exploring new action space dimensions and finding new solutions that amplify the value of the subsequent decisions with regards to multiple points of view.

Taking into account the traditional alternatives/criteria model used by decision theory and simplifying the action space in a two-dimensional model (i.e. considering only two criteria, A and B, for the evaluation), the starting feasible space can be represented by the grey area in Figure 14.1.

If the feasibility is not accepted by the existing points of view (i.e. a conflict situation is emerging and trade-offs are not considered acceptable), exploration can be carried out by following the representation in Figure 14.2, that is by maintaining the evaluation dimensions and looking for new, better or modified alternatives. Exploration can also be carried out by introducing new dimensions in the evaluation model, in the evaluation model (Figure 14.3). Referring to the starting feasible space represented in Figure 14.2, the first exploration strategy becomes part of the new one, expanded along with the more valuable axis versus; in the second exploration strategy, instead, the starting feasible space represents a simple section of a multidimensional feasible space.

Therefore, it could be possible to start with an explorative process, looking for new perspectives if the feasibility space is morally unacceptable. Exploration can be stopped when ethical dilemmas seem to be acceptable in terms of the contingent risks.

The interaction between visions (future-oriented evaluation) and solutions and the modification of feasibility domain can be described in terms of evaluation/decision dilemmas in planning practices, with reference to given contexts.

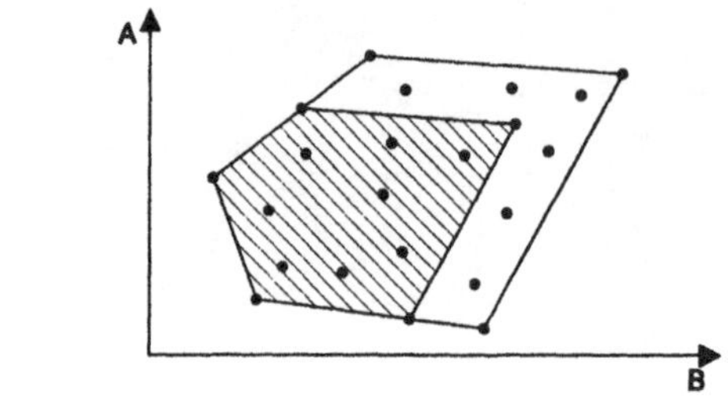

Figure 14.2 Extended feasible space (2D)

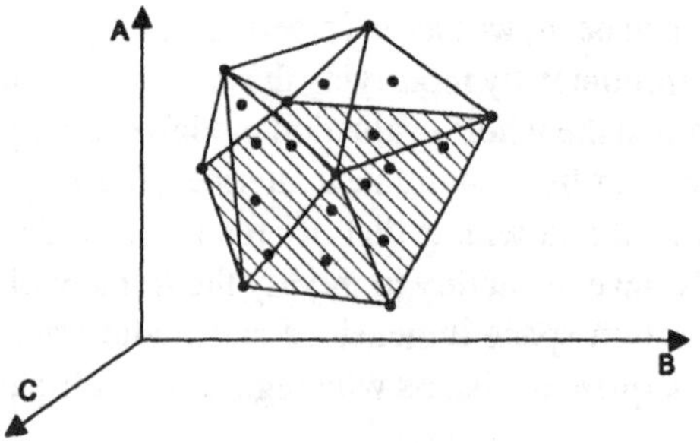

Figure 14.3 Extended feasible space (3D)

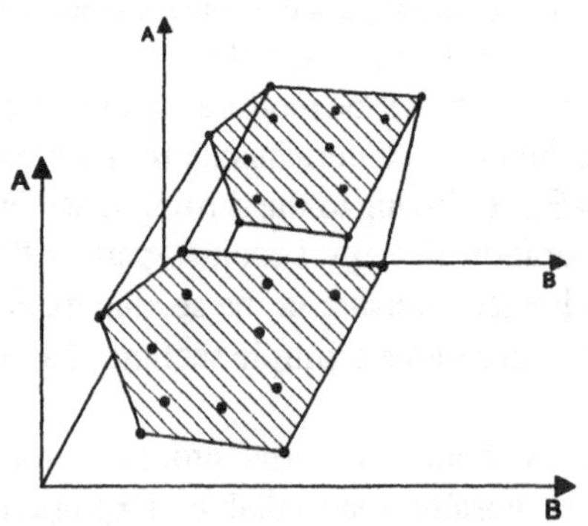

Figure 14.4 Extended feasible space (2D over *t*)

14.7 Perspectives for AI technologies

With regards to the above considerations it is possible to identify two perspectives for AI technologies as regards facing ethical and moral dilemmas in the context of evaluation in spatial planning. The two perspectives are different and at the same time complementary. The first one is based on the opportunity of developing an alerting system, that is a system which is able to recognize the emergence of an ethical and moral dilemma, thus hopefully suggesting possible actions for facing and/or overcoming the dilemma. The second perspective relates to the opportunity of developing a system which is able to support creativity in the planning process, that is exploration of the action space and subsequently evaluation of the new action space.

Ethical alerting systems

An ethical and moral alerting system can have a dual approach to supplying support for the planning process: (i) alerting planners to the ethical and moral dimensions of the actions that are considered so that mistakes can be avoided; (ii) alerting planners to actions which are of a dubious ethical and moral nature. In both cases the system will need computational ability to recognize the ethical and moral dimension of a specific action. Tentatively, and considering that ethical and moral reasoning mainly becomes necessary when conflict situations have to be faced, it is possible to recognize that an ethical and moral dilemma is emerging if — when considering the currently available action space — a decision has to be taken within a conflict environment; that is if a decision is going to be taken although significant others do not agree on it.

A major problem, obviously, is to translate such a definition into a computational model. A possible approach comes from the *trade-off* concept in decision theory. How much can one agent give up with regards to a certain dimension in order to gain a portion of utility with respect to another? This is the basic question posed when using the trade-off model within a decision theory environment. In some cases a mediation solution induces trade-offs which cannot be considered ethically and morally acceptable.

Relating to the above considerations, two possible cases can be considered. Firstly, we can assume that the main interests (economical, environmental, and social) are represented in the model we are considering in an ethically and morally correct manner, such a check is possible for an automatic system if some sort of check lists of relevant stakeholders/interests is created, depending on the problem under discussion. In this case it is necessary to define an unacceptable interval of difference from the utility value considered as the best, in order to make the system able to recognize possible ethical and moral mistakes. Secondly, due to the high complexity of the action under discussion and hence to the uncertainty in terms of the interests affected by the action being decided upon, it is only possible to consider the ethical and moral problem in general terms. Presenting a new economic model that describes the trade-off between profits and ethical principles, Graafland (2002) suggests[12] modelling ethical principles in the same manner as we model profit for a firm, by attaching an intrinsic value to the ethical principle. In our discussion this would mean developing a model for the concept of ethical and moral utility.

A trade-off based model for an ethical and moral alerting system does not cover all the possible ethical and moral dilemmatic situations. When a decision has to be made and an action to be implemented, an evident conflict may even not emerge and a sort of mediation action can appear as the solution to the interests involved in the problem. What about relevant others not involved in the decision making? Such problems, of the (ii) type, represent traditional ethical dilemmas in mediation[13] (Barsky, 1996), and introduce into the possible architecture of an ethical alerting system the need for a sort of 'checking module' which can verify (for example by questioning) whether the main possible ethical and moral implications of the decided action have been considered with regards to relevant others.

It is possible to deduce that in all the cases considered many questions still remain unanswered, and that these questions open a panorama for further explorations on this topic: who are the 'relevant others'? How can 'relevant others' be represented in the system? When are their interests sufficiently protected for it to be considered that ethical and moral issues have been correctly faced?

Exploration support systems

Let us assume that the ethical and moral dimension of the planning evaluation activity is recognized as a dilemmatic one. Then a need arises for identifying promising possible directions for exploring the decision space. Remaining within the trade-off approach it would be possible to consider explorative directions suggested by those evaluation dimensions which show ethical and moral unfeasibility. Obviously this implies an intelligent ability to focus on the actions and opportunities identified by those alternatives presenting a better behaviour precisely with regards to that dimension. This means that the exploration does not necessarily require the creation of a completely new alternative action, and in some cases a solution can be obtained through modifying an already existing one. Analogously, a possible modification of the action alternative can cause the introduction of a temporal dimension (or the modification of the associated weights) into the evaluation. The temporal dimension plays a major role in decision-making processes not only because information integrity fades over time but also because the more deeply into the analysis the process goes the more information and knowledge could need to be produced. Time is, for example, relevant in evaluation when planning under risk (Tsamardinos, Pollack and Horty, 2000). And often a decision postponement enables an improvement of the information level and its sharing[14], especially if what Joslin and Pollack (1996) call active postponement is adopted. On the other hand, supporting explorative behaviour in spatial planning evaluation can also take into consideration some interesting perspectives emerging from AI research related to artificial creativity.

When dealing with exploration and creativity in spatial planning a basic question arises: what does 'creativity' mean? Creativity can be considered as a process of transformation, of re-combination of what already exists in a different form. But, from a social perspective, when can a person or an organization be considered creative? Usually we consider creativity as an innate ability which is manifested 'outside the norms' through original creations which originate or arise out of something which did not exist before. Can a scientist be considered creative in the same sense as an artist? In composition, creativity is an original beginning of a transformation which will then proceed according to an order, a sequence, of an almost musical nature. Are intelligence and creativity related or in opposition? Is creativity related to specialization, to reasoning and acting in a specific domain? Is intelligence related to generalizations, independent of a specific domain? But intelligence and creativity are related to the ability to abstract from contexts and realities. Intelligence appears more comprehensive than creativity; thus creative intelligence should be the highest level of intelligence. How does creativity emerge? Some great creative artists learnt from other creative artists. Does creativity emerge within complex and organized societies? Power can play a role in defining the quality of creativity and affect the judgement of creativity. Museums are extraordinary places of memory and social conventions reflecting mainstream tastes. Creativity is the reduction of complexity, or simplicity emerging from complexity, and allows us to look at complexity from a detached and non conventional point of view.

Do complex systems foster creative behaviour? Biodiverse systems can more easily produce new transformations than a simple system. Creativity, like any other transformation, uses the plurality and the numerousness of the elements from which it arises. Even the openness of each biodiverse system to other systems is a condition for transformation. The higher the number of possible combinations of elements the higher the probability that new, creative transformations will emerge.

Creativity has a probabilistic nature and is associated to great numbers (of people, of resources, etc.). The more people are committed to transformation the more probable it is that creative people will emerge among them. Creating means building and exploring the new: we need new ontologies.

Variety is at the same time alive and the memory of variety: living systems and associated memories are fundamental blocks of life. Deep and shallow memories both exist. They are stratified in some way as in a store, not in a positional, topological framework but as configurations, neuronal schemes.

Memories can be accessed through keys which are 'positional', multi-indexed (temporal, situational, linguistic, associative, etc.). These keys enable different forms of retrieval even when some indexes are lost. Intelligent and creative people have great, durable memory stores and use them to look for schemes for problem solving, for old and new organizations, small blocks serving both for original cognitive transformation and re-combination. Intelligent people produce numerous indexes because of their associative reasoning ability. What is the relationship between memory and creativity? Creativity is about a peculiar attitude towards non conventional transformation of reality which is represented in the form of memory. It depends on contexts, environments, masters, points of reference, and life choices. Memory is a basic component of reasoning and intelligence. Thus, computers are seen as relevant supports for reasoning tasks. Reasoning is at the same time substantive (memory) and procedural (processing for transformation). Procedure is explorative and reactive association which sensorially interacts with reality.

To produce an intelligent plan (that is, search and exploration of action direction within an action space), a machine needs to combine control with reactive adaptation abilities: these are possible only when sensorial skills are given to and agent and experience is consciously acquired by an agent. Such behaviour is hard to reproduce in a machine because it is neither a living system nor able to make autonomous decisions: the machine would need to consider all the possible cases in infinite search space. This introduces the problem of heuristics which are able to guide the search. Moreover, such heuristics should be ethically and morally driven, that is developed or shared in collaborative environment where 'relevant others' have relevant memories and cognitive spaces.

Search activities, as guided exploration of an action space, require wide and structured memories. But the architecture of memory is not well known, even if there is general agreement on the fact that memory has a deep level and an operative one (Anderson, 1982; Damasio, 1994); the latter providing access to the former, probably in terms of two different representations and locations of a unique store (partial, synthetic, and essential for the operative memory, complete for the deep memory).

As noted above, in the memory store, representations, similarly to indexes, are multiple. Memories of events and experiences are stored in both disaggregated (elementary small blocks with relevant links) and aggregated forms (classes of events-experiences). The disaggregated form facilitates implementation, control and revision, while the aggregated one facilitates general comparison, orientation, choice, and decision, and, in general, immediate reactive reasoning. When dealing with ethical and moral dilemmas in AI, in view of the need to include 'relevant others' and to review theories as memory representations of experience and 'reality', a 'theory in action' mechanism, that is a strong continuous link between reasoning and action, is crucial. Explorative planning must be more action-oriented than the traditional deterministic or quasi-deterministic planning approach, because action and evaluation of action and its consequences are fundamental conditions for ample and significant mobilization of the essential mechanism of memory.

14.8 Conclusion

By definition, ethical and moral dilemmas have no easy answer. Further research and discussions on ethical and moral dilemmas in spatial planning evaluation are needed for this field to continue to develop in order to minimize injustice. Therefore, ethical and moral dilemmas call for improvements in evaluation modelling, focusing on values construction and awareness.

Far from being able to define the architecture of an Ethical Artificial Reasoner, the present contribution has attempted to describe some of the main functions and tasks EARs should present: ability, for adopting creative behaviour and seize opportunities to develop/modify spaces of actions which are more feasible with regards to ethics and morality; knowledge base, for recognizing ethical and moral categories; and openness, for accepting the access of 'relevant others' in the decision process. Among others, a relevant characteristic of an EAR appears to be the ability 'to know what it knows'[15] and this appears important for both the envisaged approaches (alerting/exploring systems). In a certain sense, an EAR needs to be able to judge its knowledge in order to operationalize it, by linking it to the real context and — still more relevantly — to the contextual ethics and morality. Such cognitive operationalization needs to be made by working on two different levels: a case-based one, related to the specific problem at hand and to its ethical and moral needs, and a more general one, related to the definition of the 'ethical and moral environment' in which the system acts. Neither of these two levels is subordinate, as the two levels appear reciprocally linked in a process that moves from one level to the other and concurrently defines them.

A relevant role in managing ethical and moral dilemmas is also played by creativity, which is important both to guide exploration of action spaces and/or creation of new portions of them. This is done by defining possible directions or strategies for exploration, deducing new action options from already available options, and creating new action options in view of the characteristics of the dilemmas. Creativity plays a relevant role also when envisaging an EAR, due to the fact that an EAR should have the ability to generate categories; if possible 'ethical and moral categories' of contexts, facts, events, actors. Creativity, when facing ethical and moral dilemmas, calls for a profound understanding of the issues at hand. In a sense, it needs to be context-dependent, in order to develop strategies or actions which are sensitive to the ethical and moral question at hand.

Many further questions emerge: how can creativity be addressed towards specific ethical and moral problems? Can we speak of 'ethical creativity'? Is creativity influenced by the ethics and morality that the creative reasoning is referring to? Can creativity be value-free? How can ethical and moral creativity become transformational, reducing ethical and moral dilemmas in action?

In some cases, ethical and moral issues can be considered as limiting factors to creativity. Therefore, to what extent can we consider ethical constraints to creativity as good and acceptable constraints?[16]

Many questions and problems have been discussed and still others are posed within this contribution, where the role of evaluation processes is considered to be gaining more and more relevance due to their task of managing and operationalizing systems of values. When speaking of ethical and moral dilemmas, the concept of systems of values needs to be discussed within an approach that accepts the challenge to address values towards the action environment, thus requiring that conflicts and differences, similarities and complementarities in practices, behaviour, reasoning styles, social rules, and principles be made explicit.

Notes

1 The contribution is the result of a collective work: section 14.1 'Introduction' (G. Concilio); section 14.2 'The ethical and moral problem in planning' (F. Selicato); section 14.3 'When and how does ethical and moral reasoning emerge in spatial planning evaluation?' (C. M. Torre); section 14.4 'Recent advances in ethical and moral artificial reasoning' (G. Concilio); section 14.5 'Considerations from two case studies' (first subsection C. Torre, second and third subsection G. Concilio); section 14.6 'Exploring the action space' (C. M. Torre); section 14.7 'Perspectives for AI technologies' (first subsection G. Concilio, second subsection D. Borri); section 14.8 'Conclusion' (D. Borri).

2 The term 'computer ethics' was coined in the mid 1970s by Walter Maner (1980) to refer to that field of applied professional ethics dealing with ethical problems aggravated, transformed or created by computer technology. For nearly two decades, the term 'computer ethics' kept this focused meaning.

3 Such distinction pushed some authors to discuss the role of 'Artificial Evil' (Floridi and Sanders, 2001).

4 Tridle, Chen and Zand distinguish in their study the Guinea Pig Treatment Ethics, the Synergistic Ethics, and the Side Effect Ethics (p. 25), each affordable with different behaviours.

5 James Gips (1995), exploring the possibility for the construction of a moral computer, suggests a virtue ethic.

6 Computational agents are intended by Colemann (2001) as computers able to undertake tasks, once assigned, with little assistance or intervention aside from the initial assignment.

7 Editor's note: see Note 3 at p. 200 (Fusco Girard, Cerreta and De Toro, here) for details on Italian case studies.

8 There is a regional law defining a list of several natural relevant sites in Apulia Region, where natural parks should be established. See also Note 7.

9 The regional administration is the formal agent charged of the natural parks establishment and management. Moreover, considering the expert advice, in order to guarantee the environmental protection of the 'gravina' (in the local dialect, a stream flowing through a canyon-like geological formation) within an integrated view of the geological emergency and its territorial context, a large part of Gravina municipal territory should be annexed to the natural park so that role and consensus of the municipal administration are crucial.

10 The reader should consider that the Italian natural park regulative framework is scarcely flexible and that very few modifications can be introduced when instituting a new national park in terms of land use categories and their relative management (possible and forbidden uses) rules.

11 Before the designation of the natural park a large order of stone material had been made by a Japanese construction enterprise: this order was completely cancelled immediately after the news because of the risk of only partial fulfilment for the restrictions related to the new park.

12 Observing that ethical behaviour is not always rewarded by a competitive advantage over agents that are not ethical, Graafland has developed a trade-off model to derive the optimal balance between profits and principles. The model analyzes the impact of consumer concerns, competition on the goods market and the intertemporal trade-off between short term profitability and long term reputation on the ethical standards of the company.

13 Barsky's discussion shows some risks of mediation with regards to ethical dilemmas.

Still mediation appears a possible approach to situations facing ethical dilemmas (Lampe, 2001): 'Mediation, although not a panacea, is an effective and constructive process. It is a non-adversarial method that attempts to resolve conflict through mutual understanding, communication, and collaboration, offering the unique opportunity to preserve and promote relationship under difficult circumstances' (p. 172).

14 Consider for example that the formal process for the setting up of a natural park in Apulia presents a strong temporal-scheduled plan, starting with the first formal action by the responsible regional officers: in fact, following the invitation to several stakeholders to participate in a formal meeting (the *preconferenza*), a strict temporal path to be respected starts; often such scheduling is unacceptable to local communities so that significant parts of the decisions have already been taken before giving rise to the formal process, in order to leave to the decision process the necessary temporal space.

15 In SIROCCO, a case-based System for Intelligent Retrieval of Operationalized Cases and Codes (McLaren, 2003; McLaren and Ashley, 2001), it is explored how the system can know the limitations of its expertise: having found the known source-cases most relevant to a target problem, how can a system assess whether those cases are similar enough to the target to warrant venturing advice?

16 Ethical constraints to creativity are widely investigated in education (Craft, 2003).

References

Anderson, R. (1982), *The Architecture of Cognition*, Wiley, New York, NY (USA).

Barsky, A. (1996), *Ethical dilemmas in community mediation: do the right thing Part 1*, The Conflict Resolution Information, University of Colorado, Boulder, CO (USA).

Borri D. and Concilio G. (1999), 'Sistemi Intelligenti Multiagente di Supporto alle Decisioni' (Intelligent Multi-Agent Decision Support Systems), in IPiGeT – CNR Napoli, *Atti della XX Conferenza Italiana di Scienze Regionali, Piacenza 5-7 ottobre*, (Proceedings of the 20th Italian Regional Science Conference, Piacenza 5-7 October), CD-ROM, ISBN 88-87788-00-6, AISRe, Milano (Italy).

Bray, P. M. (2003), 'New approaches to integrating park and protected area planning with territorial planning in New York State', *Urbanistica*, No. 120, forthcoming.

Burgess G. and Burgess H. (1995), 'Beyond the limits: dispute resolution of intractable environmental conflicts', in J. W. Blackburn and W. M. Bruce (eds.), *Mediating Environmental Conflicts. Theory and Practice*, Greenwood, Quorum Books, Westport, CT (USA), pp. 101-119.

Colemann, K. G. (2001), 'Android arête: toward a virtue ethic for computational agents', *Ethics and Information Technology*, Vol. 3, No. 4, pp. 247-265.

Craft, A. (2003), 'The Limits to Creativity in Education: Dilemmas for the Educator', *British Journal of Educational Studies*, Vol. 51, No. 2, pp. 113-127.

Damasio, A. (1994), *Descartes' Error: Emotion, Reason and the Human Brain*, Grosset/Putnam, New York, NY (USA).

Daviss, B. (1999), 'Profits from principle: Five forces redefining business', *The Futurist*, Vol. 33, No. 3, pp. 28-33.

Floridi L. and Sanders J. W. (2001), 'Artificial evil and the foundation of computer ethics', *Ethics and Information Technology*, Vol. 3, No. 1, pp. 55-66.

Forester, J. (1989), *Planning in the Face of Power*, California University Press, Berkeley, CA (USA).

Forester T. and Morrison P. (1993), *Computer Ethics: Cautionary Tales and Ethical Dilemmas in Computing* (2nd ed.), The MIT Press, Cambridge, MA (USA).

Fritz, W. (1996), *Intelligent Systems and their Societies*, free e-book New Horizon Press, http://www.intelligentsystems.com.ar/intsyst/.

Frolova, A. (1998), 'Ecological reasoning: Ethical alternatives', *Ecological Economics*, Vol. 24, No. 2-3, pp. 169-182.

Funtowicz, S. and Ravetz, J. L. (1992), 'Three Types of Risk Assessment and the Emergence of Post-Normal Science', in S. Krimsky and D. Golding (eds.), *Social Theories of Risk*, Greenwood, Westport, CT (USA), pp. 251-273.

Fusco Girard, L. and Forte, B. (2000), *Città sostenibile e sviluppo umano* (Sustainable cities and human development), Franco Angeli, Milano (Italy).

Gambino, R. (2001), 'Per ricostruire il rapporto uomo-natura' (In order to rebuild the relationship between man and nature), *Parchi*, No. 32.

Giddens, A. (1984), *The Constitution of Society*, Polity Press, Cambridge (UK).

Gips, J. (1995), 'Towards the Ethical Robot', in K. Ford, C. Glymour and P. Hayes (eds.), *Android Epistemology*, AAAI Press/The MIT Press, Menlo Park, CA (USA), pp. 243-252.

Gottman, J. (1987), *Megalopolis Revisited: 25 Years Later*, The University of Maryland Institute for Urban Studies, College Park, MD (USA).

Graafland, J. J. (2002), 'Modelling the trade-off between profits and principles', *De Economist*, Vol. 150, No. 2, pp. 129-154.

Granitz, N. A. and Ward, J. C. (2001), 'Actual and Perceived Sharing of Ethical Reasoning and Moral Intent Among In-group and Out-group Members', *Journal of Business Ethics*, Vol. 33, No. 4, pp. 299-322.

Hamilton, B. and Rao, S. (1996), 'The Effect of Published Reports of Unethical Conduct on Stock Prices', *Journal of Business Ethics*, Vol. 15, No. 12, pp. 1321-1330.

Joslin, D. and Pollack, M. E. (1996), 'Passive and Active Decision Postponement in Plan Generation', in M. Ghallab and A. Milani (eds.), *New Directions in AI Planning*, Proceedings of the Third European Conference on Planning, Assisi, Italy, September 1995, IOS Press, Amsterdam (The Netherlands), pp. 37-48.

Karlsson, J. (1997), *Learning to Solve Multiple Goals*, PhD Thesis, Department of Computer Science, University of Rochester, NY, USA.

Khakee, A. (1998), 'Evaluation and planning, inseparable concepts', *Town Planning Review*, No. 64, pp. 359-374.

Lampe, M. (2001), 'Mediation as an Ethical Adjunct of Stakeholder Theory', *Journal of Business Ethics*, Vol. 31, No. 2, pp. 165-173.

Maciocco, G. (2000), 'Etica e Pianificazione Ambientale' (Ethics and Environmental Planning), in G. Maciocco, G. Deplano and G. Marchi (eds.), *Etica e Pianificazione Spaziale*, (Ethics and Spatial Planning), Franco Angeli, Milano (Italy), pp. 7-24.

Maner, W. (1980), *Starter Kit in Computer Ethics*, Helvetia Press (published in cooperation with the National Information and Resource Center for Teaching Philosophy), Hyde Park, NY (USA), originally self-published by the author in 1978.

Maner, W. (1999), 'Is Computer Ethics Unique?', *Etica&Politica-Ethics&Politics*, Vol. 1, No. 2, special issue ('Monographica') on Computer Ethics, edited by L. Floridi, http://www.units.it/ etica/1999_2.

McHarg, I. L. (1969), *Design with Nature*, Natural History Press, New York, NY (USA).

McHarg, I. L. (1996), *A Quest for Life*, Wiley, New York, NY (USA).

McLaren, B. M. (2003), 'Extensionally Defining Principles and Cases in Ethics: An

AI Model', *Artificial Intelligence Journal*, Vol. 150, pp. 145-181, November, http://www.pitt.edu/ bmclaren/publications.html.

McLaren, B. M. and Ashley, K. D. (2001), paper presented at the International Conference on Case-Based Reasoning, Vancouver, BC (Canada), August.

Menzel, P. T. (1999), 'How Should What Economists Call "Social Values" Be Measured?', *The Journal of Ethics*, Vol. 3, No. 3, pp. 249-273.

Munda, G. (1995), *Multicriteria Evaluation in a Fuzzy Environment. Theory and applications in ecological economics, Contributions to Economics Series*, Physica-Verlag, Heidelberg (Germany).

Nijhof, A. and Fisscher, O. (1997), 'Dealing with Ethical Dilemmas in Organizational Change Processes', *International Journal of Value-Based Management*, Vol. 10, No. 2, pp. 173-192.

Palermo, P. C. (2000), 'Autori e paradigmi. Temi e figure emergenti nel corso evolutivo dell'urbanistica italiana' (Authors and paradigms. Emerging themes and personalities during the evolution of Italian urbanistics), in G. Maciocco, G. Deplano and G. Marchi (eds.), *Etica e Pianificazione Spaziale*, (Ethics and Spatial Planning), Franco Angeli, Milano (Italy), pp. 25-44.

Rutledge, R. W. and Karim, K. E. (1999), 'The influence of self-interest and ethical considerations on managers' evaluation judgments', *Accounting, Organizations and Society*, Vol. 24, No. 2, pp. 173-184.

Scandurra, E. (1997), *Città di Terzo Millennio* (Cities of the Third Millennium), La Meridiana, Molfetta (Italy).

Schön, D. A. (1983), *The Reflective Practitioner*, Basic Books, New York, NY (USA).

Tagliagambe, S. (2000), 'Che cosa significa etica della pianificazione nelle organizzazioni complesse?' (What does planning ethics mean within complex organizations?), in G. Maciocco, G. Deplano and G. Marchi (eds.), *Etica e Pianificazione Spaziale*, (Ethics and Spatial Planning), Franco Angeli, Milano (Italy), pp. 98-133.

Tridle, J. J., Chen, Z. and Zand, M. K. (1995), 'Building Expert Critics for Ethical Testing', *Expert Systems with Applications*, Vol. 8, No. 1, pp. 23-32.

Tsamardinos, I., Pollack, M. E. and Horty, J. F. (2000), 'Merging Plans with Quantitative Temporal Constraints, Temporally Extended Actions and Conditional Branches', in S. Chien, S. Kambhampati and C. Knoblock (eds.), *Proceedings of the 5th International Conference on AI Planning Systems, Breckenridge, CO, April*, AAAI, Menlo Park, CA (USA), pp. 264-272, http://www.eecs.umich.edu/ pollackm/Pollackweb_files/distrib/aips00merg.pdf.

Zeleny, M. (1983), *Multiple Criteria Decision Making*, McGraw-Hill, New York, NY (USA).

PART IV
ORGANIZATIONAL AND INSTITUTIONAL CONTEXT OF EVALUATION AND DECISION

Chapter 15

Towards a Conceptual Framework for Evaluating Governance Capacities in European Polycentric Urban Regions

Simin Davoudi

15.1 Introduction

Changes in social, economic and spatial structure of urban areas are reflected in and reinforced by considerable changes in the way cities and regions are governed and organized. The debate on the dynamics of these changes is currently focused on the transformation of the traditional forms of *government*, understood as the formal organizations and procedures of public sector, into *governance*, understood as the multiplicity of governmental and non-governmental organizations.

There is an increasing recognition among the research community and the policy makers that the existence of effective governance relations is an important prerequisite for developing and sustaining economically, socially and environmentally balanced regions across Europe. The capacity of urban governance and the quality of institutional relationships can significantly influence the direction of economic potential and the successful implementation of policy.

Creating horizontal and vertical co-operation between various levels of government as well as integration between disparate responsibilities have now become the central focus of effective governance. This is particularly the case with regard to the promotion of the polycentric development of the European territory which forms a key spatial policy theme in the European Spatial Development Perspective (ESDP, 1999).

This contribution is part of an attempt towards the development of a conceptual framework for describing and evaluating governance relations and power dynamics with specific reference to polycentric urban regions in Europe. Emphasis is placed on evaluating the governance capacities for capturing the opportunities and alleviating the threats that are embedded in and arise from a polycentric urban structure. The contribution is structured around the following themes: firstly, a brief review of the significance of place and territory in economic development and its recent uptake within the European Union policy agenda and in particular the ESDP; secondly, an outline of the way in which the concept of polycentricity is used in the ESDP and the debate around the definition of polycentric urban regions (PUR); thirdly, a review of literature on the transition from government to governance and the key challenge of governance particularly in the context of PURs; and finally, an outline of a conceptual framework for evaluating governance capacities with references to some of the methodological challenges facing the design of appropriate indicators for measuring these capacities and the role of policy intervention in steering new forms of governance.

15.2 Territory — a new dimension in European policy

There has been a rediscovery of the significance of place and territory in the discussion around local economic development, environmental sustainability and quality of life. This renewed interest in place is taking place in the context of globalization of the economy, technological advances in transport and telecommunication, the growing influence of multi-national corporations and a concern for global environmental problems. It is argued that as capital is becoming ever more stretched out and mobile, it is the place-specific qualities that are becoming the defining factors in its search for profitable production sites (Hudson, 1997). These developments clearly raise a number of challenges for the relationship between the state and society and for spatial planning systems in particular. This is not only because planning is a major component of that relationship, but also because of its central concern with place-making and territorial development.

Cities and regions are faced with the challenge of becoming economically more competitive, socially more cohesive and environmentally more sustainable. As theories of social ecology have shown, these developmental, environmental and distributive domains constitute the critical objectives of policy making (Liepietz, 1995). In most western societies, the planning system has traditionally provided a key arena within which economic, social and environmental concerns are played out in the context of the decisions made over the use of land (Campbell, 1999; Davoudi, Hull and Healey, 1996).

The widespread recognition of the significance of place in integrating these key policy domains and the potential role played by spatial planning have gradually opened their way on the EU policy agenda. They finally made their mark through the publication of the ESDP in 1999. The ESDP promotes spatial 'territory' as a new dimension of European policy and argues that by focusing on territory, a better integration of EU sectoral policies can be achieved. A major concern of the ESDP is 'to reconcile the social and economic claims for spatial development with the area's ecological and cultural functions and hence contribute to a sustainable, and balanced territorial development' (ESDP, 1999; p. 10). One of the cornerstones of its 'policy options' for achieving this three-fold objective is the promotion of polycentric development through spatial planning strategies.

15.3 The concept of polycentricity

The notion of polycentricity, however, has remained an elusive one. It means different things to different people. It also means different things when applied at different spatial scales. ESDP uses the concept at two levels: the level of Europe as whole and the inter-urban or regional scale. At the European level, polycentric development is promoted by the ESDP as a way of enhancing its economic competitiveness in the world market by developing multiple centres of globally significant economic growth zones across Europe. These zones complement the only 'zone of global economic integration' in Europe, called the 'pentagon' and defined by the metropolises of London, Paris, Milan, Munich and Hamburg. Although this area accounts for only 20 per cent of the EU territory, it produces 50 per cent of its Gross Domestic Product (GDP) and accommodates 40 per cent of its population. The lack of any other such zones is seen as a disadvantage for the future economic competitiveness of Europe when compared with other major trading blocks such as the USA (ESDP, 1999; paragraph 68). Moreover, promotion of polycentric development is seen as a way of alleviating the persisting regional disparities in Europe, which are set to widen following the EU's eastward enlargement, and achieving social cohesion. In short, the concept of polycentricity is used to challenge the dominant core-periphery image of Europe, where a prosperous core stands against an under-developed periphery, and promote a more balanced and sustainable territorial development.

Whilst this seems an attractive policy response to regional disparities, as Copus (2001; p. 548) points out, it is not without its 'weaknesses and pitfalls'. Key to this debate is the existence of a fundamental incompatibility between the EU's two policy objectives of economic growth and social cohesion in the way that progress towards economic competitiveness through market integration may lead to a slow down of progress towards or even divergence from social cohesion (Mayes, 1995; Perrons, 1999). Nevertheless, making Europe economically more competitive and socially and spatially more equitable has remained at the heart of the Community's policy agenda.

At the regional level, the ESDP promotes polycentricity as a specific spatial structure, which if promoted through spatial planning strategies can enhance economic development. It suggests that, 'the economic potential of all regions of the EU can only be utilized through the further development of a more polycentric European settlement structure ... A network of internationally accessible metropolitan regions and their linked hinterland', rather than a single dominant urban centre, is seen as 'an essential prerequisite for the balanced and sustainable development of the local entities and regions' (ESDP, 1999; paragraphs 67, 70, and 71). What is a polycentric urban region and how can it be identified?

15.4 Defining polycentric urban regions

A polycentric urban region is defined as a region with two or more historically and politically separate cities, without a clear hierarchical ranking, in a reasonable proximity and with functional interconnection (EC, 1999). European examples of PUR can be found in the Flemish Diamond in Belgium bounded by cities of Brussels, Leuven, Antwerp and Ghent (Albrechts, 1998); Rhine-Ruhr in Germany consisting of cities of Dortmund, Essen, Düsseldorf, Cologne and Bonn (Blotevogel, 1998; Knapp, 1998); and the Padua-Treviso-Venice area in Northern Italy (Camagni and Salone, 1993). Outside Europe, southern California in the USA and Kansai area (including Osaka, Kyoto and Kobe cities) in Japan are mentioned (Batten, 1995). But, a polycentric urban region *par excellence* remains to be the Randstad in Holland (Priemus, 1998). This is an area bounded roughly by four large cities each thriving on a different, yet complementary, economic basis: Amsterdam benefits from proximity to Schiphol airport, tourism and finance; Utrecht has the service sector and nice surroundings; The Hague is the seat of government, and Rotterdam lives off its port. In the middle is the Green Heart, an area of farmland and water with high environmental values. The Randstad is not an administrative or political unit, but given the proximity and interactions amongst its constituent cities, it has been increasingly promoted and treated by the Dutch planning community as a single coherent region and as the next European metropolis capable of competing with London and Paris.

The conceptualization of polycentricity at the regional level is still at an early stage of development. Elsewhere, I have argued that the concept is characterized by a lack of clear definition and little agreement on criteria and thresholds for analysis (Davoudi, 2002; Davoudi, 2003). For example, it is not clear what is a *reasonable proximity* between the constituent cities and how *functional interconnection* between the centres can be measured. I have also discussed in detail the potential problems associated with adopting this strategy as a one-size-fits-all model. I have emphasized the need for further theoretical underpinning and robust empirical evidence which clearly show the advantages of the PUR compared with other models of spatial structure in achieving economic competitiveness and social cohesion. However, despite a lack of theoretical vigour and limited empirical research, the concept of the PUR is gathering momentum particularly in the context of the European spatial planning. In fact, it can be argued that it owes its widespread usage to the fact that it is ambiguous and can be interpreted and/or operationalized in different ways. It could also be that the PUR provokes a positive image, almost analogous to pluralism, multi-culturalism and inclusiveness, which is 'politically' appealing and difficult to challenge. Indeed, it is this political dimension of polycentricity that is the focus of this contribution, rather than the argument for or against the PUR as a 'good thing'. My proposition is that the quality of governance matters if a PUR is to be developed and sustained. In other words, a polycentric urban region needs polycentric governance.

This has already been recognized by the ESDP along with several other European, national and regional policy documents. Using the discourse of business competition and the role of clustering and networking in the economic competitiveness of firms, they argue that cities and regions can become equally successful if they develop associational structures in their social relationships. The ESDP states that, 'in smaller towns in less densely settled and economically weaker regions, co-operation between urban centres to develop functional complementarity may be the only possibility for achieving viable markets and maintaining economic institutions and services' (ESDP, 1999; paragraph 76). It also emphasizes that, 'a pre-requisite [therefore] is the voluntary nature of the co-operation and the equal rights of the partners' (ESDP, 1999; paragraph 74). Other proponents of PURs argue that by encouraging interaction between neighbouring cities and towns and by pooling together and sharing labour market and infrastructure facilities amongst them, economic innovation will be enhanced and functional synergies will be created (Priemus, 1994; Albrechts, 1998; Batten, 1995).

My argument is that if such synergies are to be developed in European polycentric urban regions, there is a clear need for not only the 'hard infrastructure' such as an efficient transport and telecommunication network between and within the regions, but also the 'soft infrastructure' including in particular the appropriate forms of institutional arrangements. Existence of effective governance relations is an important prerequisite for developing and sustaining the economically, socially and environmentally balanced regions across Europe. The institutional structure and the nature of mechanisms for decision-making, co-operation and power partitioning can significantly influence the direction taken by European cities and regions and the successful implementation of ESDP's spatial policy options. The reason is that, whilst industry, businesses and households operate on the basis of functionally defined areas particularly in polycentric urban regions, governance institutions are often organized and operate on the basis of administratively defined areas such as communes, municipalities, boroughs or Kreise. It is in this context that the ESDP emphasizes the need for building up co-operations and partnerships between towns and cities and their surrounding rural areas to enable the development of sustainable polycentric territories. As Sellers (2002; p. 93) argues, 'within an urban region that faces common problems, the multiple local jurisdictions that typically divide up the urban space often must coordinate with one another or come together in collective action. Throughout the advanced industrial world urban and regional planning has emerged as one of the most important local means to this end'.

The questions that follow are: what are the key characteristics of effective partnership working and governance relations, and how can we identify and evaluate them. There is a growing body of the literature on governance and 'institutional capital'. These provide a useful starting point for developing a conceptual framework to underpin such evaluation, but they rarely tackle the methodological challenges of designing appropriate indicators for measuring these qualities. However, developing a conceptual framework for studying and evaluating the performance of governance requires an understanding of what 'governance' means, how it differs from 'government', and what constitute the key challenges of governance.

15.5 From government to governance

The concept of governance has found a central place in social science debate. As an analytical concept, it has emerged in a range of research fields including urban politics (Stoker, 1997), political economy (Campbell, Hollingsworth and Lindberg, 1991; Hall, 1986), and international and comparative politics (Hyden, 1992). The main focus of the debate has been on the transformation of the prevalent modes of governing advanced economies from *government* into what has come to be called *governance*. Various theoretical perspectives have tried to conceptualize this transformation and its outcome (Pierre, 1999; Pierre, 2000; Peters, 2000). For example, regulation theorists argue that the shift from government to governance is part of and a response to the wider process of socio-economic changes manifested in a move away from a Fordist mass production system and an established Keynesian welfare state towards a 'post-Fordist' flexible specialization (Jessop, 1995a; Jessop, 1995b; Piore and Sabel, 1984) and a relentless search for a new 'institutional fix' (Peck and Tickell, 1994). Jessop (1997) argues that, central to these developments is the profound restructuring of state and its changing role in governing the relationships between society and economy. It is suggested that the 'denationalization of the state', or the 'hollowing out' process, has led to a continuing loss of state functions and shift of power upwards to supranational bodies such as the EU, downwards to special purpose bodies at the sub-national levels and sideways to a range of semi-public and semi-autonomous agencies (Jessop, 1995a; Jessop, 1995b; Rhodes, 1997; Rhodes, 2000). These restructuring processes have marked a number of changes including:

- A relative decline in the role of state in management of social and economic relationships;
- The involvement of non-governmental actors in a range of state functions at a variety of spatial scales;
- A change from hierarchical forms of government structures to more flexible forms of partnership and networking;
- A shift from provisions by formal government structures to the contemporary sharing of responsibilities and service provision between the state and civil society;
- The emergence of local and regional forms of governance as a result of mobilization and construction of scale-specific state policies and institutions (Brenner, 2000).

In summary, the outcome of these restructuring processes is now widely understood as a shift from 'government' to 'governance'. Here, *government* refers to the dominance of state power organized through the formal public sector agencies and bureaucratic procedures, and is characterized by Healey et al. (2002) as:

- Hierarchical organization of responsibilities between different territorial (national and local) scales in Europe;
- Sectoral separation of competencies between various functions of the public sector;

- Perceptual distinction between politics (managed through representative democracy), professionals and experts (based on technical and instrumental rationality) and lay people;
- Functional division between the roles and interests of public (state), private (market) and community (civil society);
- Universalist welfare state structure of service delivery.

These neat and simple dividing lines, however, have been increasingly fading away and replaced with overlapping and complex relationships which have come to be known as *governance*. Healey et al. (2002), argue that governance, in its *descriptive* sense, directs attention to the proliferation of agencies, interests, service delivery and regulatory systems which are involved in making policies and taking actions. In its *normative* sense, governance is defined as an alternative model for managing collective affairs. It is seen as 'horizontal self-organization among mutually interdependent actors' (Jessop, 2000; p. 15), of whom government is only one and with only 'imperfect control' (Rhodes, 1997; p. 8).

Today, the modern urban systems are characterized by complex patterns of interdependencies between actors, institutions, functional activities and spatial organizations. Controlling, managing or even steering the complex, fragmented and often competing societal interests is beyond the capacity of state as an agent of authority. City governments are no longer the key locus for integration of urban relationships but merely one of many actors competing for access to resources and control of policy agenda (Davoudi, 1995). In this context, urban governance is defined as 'the actions and institutions within an urban region that regulate or impose conditions for its political economy' (Sellers, 2002; p. 9).

15.6 The challenge of governance

The move to governance has not only led to fragmentation of local government, it has also led to disruption of established channels, networks and alliances through which local government linked to the citizens and businesses. It has resulted in decay of established forms of political representation. Old networks are disintegrating, new ones forming, focusing on new arenas and different forms of representation (Stoker and Young, 1993). Hence, the challenge of governance is how to create new forms of integration out of fragmentation, and new forms of coherence out of inconsistency. As Stoker points out, governance is 'a concern with governing, achieving collective action in the realm of public affairs, in conditions where it is not possible to rest on recourse to the authority of the state' (Stoker, 2000; p. 93). It is about how collective actors emerge from a diverse group of interests (Le Gales, 1998). A key concern is the availability of strategies of co-ordination to actors involved in the governing of places in the context of a globalized market economy. The capacity to govern depends on 'effective co-ordination of interdependent forces within and beyond the state' (Jessop, 1997; p. 96).

In the context of a polycentric urban region, which is made of a number of cities that are historically and politically independent, actors are not only drawn from beyond the boundaries of formal institutions of government, and spread among public, private and voluntary sectors. They also spread across the boundaries of different political and administrative jurisdictions which traditionally do not share a place-based identity. Moreover, the policy objective with which they are preoccupied, i.e. the development of a spatial planning strategy which enables and enhances the development of a PUR, is highly complex, demanding and dependent on the actions of a wide range of actors outside the public sector. All this leads to a higher degree of fragmentation and poses an even greater challenge for effective governance. In other words, in the context of a PUR, creating a favourable condition to meet the challenge of collective action is even more problematic.

Previously, following the work of Logan and Molotch (1987), the literature, largely from the United States, provided a powerful argument about the role of growth coalition in creating the condition for collective action. However, the narrow focus of this literature on economic growth is of little use to the complex and highly conflicting task of developing spatial planning strategies which aim to strike a balance between economic, social and environmental goals. As Sellers Sellers (2002) argues, to assess how much of a difference urban governance can make requires an analysis of its role in all three areas of promoting growth, protecting environmental quality and remedying inequities.

For that, regime theory has provided a wider perspective. Following Clarence Stones' (1989) study of urban regime formation in Atlanta, regime theorists have moved beyond growth coalition and focused on the formation of regimes whose remit is wider than economic growth and can include other shared purposes and common goals. From the regime theory perspective, the problem of governance, i.e. the challenge of collective action, can be resolved by forming governing coalitions or regimes that are informal, stable, have access to institutional resources, have sustained roles in decision-making and draw on actions from public and non-public sectors (Stoker, 2000). It is argued that substantive policy outcome can be achieved if organizations from various sectors come to co-operate as a result of recognizing mutual dependency in objectives, resources, power or knowledge (Bryson and Crosby, 1992).

15.7 Towards a conceptual framework for evaluating governance capacities

The discussion above has established that the key challenge of governance is to create the condition which allows collective action to take place. Hence, the critical question for evaluation is: what are the key factors for creating such a condition? What are the key ingredients of a favourable climate in which collective action can emerge? What relational qualities are required for creating a capacity to govern (i.e. to get things done) in the midst of diversity?

Many commentators have tried to identify specific sets of relationships for assessing the performance of governance and its capacity to act collectively. For example, Amin and Thrift (1995) coined the concept of 'institutional thickness' and argued that the nature of institutional relations is a significant factor in the economic and social health of localities. Institutional thickness refers to five main factors:

- A plethora of civic associations;
- A high level of inter-institutional interaction;
- A culture of collective representation which cross individual interests;
- A strong sense of common purpose; and
- A shared set of cultural norms and values.

Coffey and Bailly (1996) used the concept of 'innovative milieu', which was first developed in the French speaking world in the 1980s. This defines a broadly based local milieu, which encompasses economic, social, cultural and institutional factors that affect the competitive advantage of cities. An innovative milieu includes:

- A group of actors (firms and institutions) that are relatively autonomous in terms of decision making and strategy formulation;
- A specific set of material (infrastructure), immaterial (knowledge, know-how) and institutional elements (authorities, legal framework);
- Interaction between local actors based on co-operation;
- Self-regulating dynamics that lead to learning, and ability to adapt to changing environment.

This approach emphasizes the significance of the complex web of relations that tie different actors and agencies together. Here, the territory is not seen as a 'container' but rather as a 'created space' that is both a result of and a precondition for learning (Malmberg and Maskell, 1997). It is an active resource rather than a passive surface (Coffey and Bailly, 1996).

More recently, Innes et al. (1994), in a study of growth management through consensus building in California, have argued that 'consensus building achieves its coordination effects in great part by creating or amplifying three types of capital: social, intellectual, and political capital' (p. 46). They use the term capital as it represents 'shared value that can grow as it is used. Once created, this capital lives on among participants even after the group [coalition] disbands, and it facilitates future coordination' (pp. 46-47).

Similarly, de Magalhães, Healy and Madanipour (2002) in their study of an urban regeneration project in Newcastle draw on the work of Innes and Booher (1999) on consensus-building processes and use the notion of 'institutional capital' as a conceptual device for linking these three forms of capital.

Regime theory confirms the significance of these factors and makes more explicit a number of other factors which are seen as essential for a regime to achieve a sustained capacity to act and influence developments in key policy areas (Stoker, 1995; Stone, 1993). These include: composition of the governing coalition, nature of relations among members of the governing coalition, and the resources that members bring to the coalition.

Drawing on these perspectives and adding a fourth form of capital, i.e. material capital, it can be concluded that the following set of capitals are key to the success of a self-organized voluntary coalition in terms of its ability to act collectively and to develop the capacity to achieve its goals and objectives:

- Intellectual capital: knowledge resources that are socially constructed and flow among the actors;
- Social capital: relational resources and the nature of relations between the actors;
- Political capital: power relations and the capacity to mobilize resources and to take action;
- Material capital: financial and other tangible resources that are made available to the actors and the coalition/group.

Creating, sustaining and making use of these capitals, however, depends on a number of factors, as outlined below. These factors can also be drawn upon as criteria for examining/evaluating the quality of governance relations in polycentric urban regions. The remaining part of this contribution aims to provide a clearer understanding of these capitals and what they entail as well as an outline of the key factors affecting their development.

15.8 Social capital

Building social capital is the first step towards the formation of effective coordination and collective action, particularly given the voluntary and independent nature of governance coalitions. It is a crucial part of a shared sense of community which allows the participants to respond flexibly to complex issues involved in the formulation of a spatial strategy for an area which cut across formal administrative and political boundaries and is faced with multiple claims.

The concept of social capital links to other concepts, notably the concept of 'civic society' or 'civic virtues' which were coined by Putnam and his colleagues following their work based on a longitudinal study of Italian regional institutions (Putnam, 1993). This study showed that the presence of 'civil society' is a causal factor in explaining institutional performance and ultimately economic development. Putnam argued that civic context matters for the institutions' work, and defined civic virtues as encompassing 'an active, public-spirited citizenry, by egalitarian political relations, by a social fabric of trust and co-operation' (Putnam, 1993; p. 15).

Using these ideas in the context of coalitions and partnerships, it is argued that creating and maintaining co-operation depends on setting up relations based on:

- *Solidarity* among the actors and learning to talk and listen to one another despite previous rivalries;
- *Relationships* which are based on loyalty and trust rather than hierarchy and bargaining;

- *Mutual support* for the actions that have been agreed;
- *Shared sense of purpose*, given that the most common form of achieving co-operation is by mutual self-interest. Selective incentives create the conditions for collective action. However, another form of achieving co-operation is through a deeply held commitment to a shared social purpose (Stoker and Mossberges, 1995).

15.9 Intellectual capital

This refers to knowledge resources. Knowledge in this context is seen as a non-linear, interactive and socially constructed resource. It encompasses all forms of knowledge ranging from technical and scientific knowledge, often presented by the experts and professionals, to tacit and experiential knowledge, often held by non-expert and lay people. Such knowledge is not considered as given and fixed, but rather as created over time and through a dynamic process of interaction between the actors. As argued by de Magalhães, Healy and Madanipour (2002), the building up of intellectual capital depends on:

- The *range* of knowledge available to the actors. In the case of coalitions which aim to develop a coordinated spatial strategy, the range includes, for example, knowledge of spatial structure of cities and regions and the ways in which they evolve, knowledge of complex socio-economic processes and their impact on spatial development, knowledge of the ways in which institutions operate and so on.
- *Frames of reference* to turn the information into meaningful and integrated knowledge and to make sense of it. Knowledge can be used and interpreted in different ways by different people. To develop a shared understanding of the available knowledge, a common frame of reference between the actors needs to be developed in the process of co-operation.
- *Transparency* in the flow of knowledge to allow the sharing of information between the actors.
- *Learning capacity* of actors, which includes both willingness to learn and openness to new ideas.

The key areas for which the development of shared knowledge is crucial are the problem definition and the realization of the mutual interdependency between the actors.

15.10 Political capital

Political capital is about the capacity to mobilize and depends on power relations. Power in this context refers to power *to* act rather than power *over* the action others. Dyeberg (1997) argues, power can be seen as both the power to control the actions of others and the power to act, to get things done. It is seen as a matter of social production rather than social control. 'The power struggle concerns not control and resistance but gaining and fusing a capacity to act — power to, not power over' (Stone, 1989; p. 229). However, it is clear that in the social relations of governance processes, both forms of power exist and remain in tension.

Stoker (2000) argues that the move away from a traditional model of hierarchical and mainly political power to a system where the power is shared and split between a variety of political and non-political stakeholders has led to further diffusion of power with multiple characteristics. Although those with systemic power (i.e. power emerging from the position of actors in society and socio-economic structure) and those with command power (i.e. power emerging from the ability of actors to mobilize resources including information, finance, rules and popularity) have advantage in governance relations, they can only make use of their position if they turn that power into pre-emptive power, which is the power to act as 'a collective actor to guide the community's policy response to social change and alter the terms on which social cooperation takes place' (Stone, 1988; p. 102). In other word, it is the power of social production that requires leadership, not of individual but a group of interests, for solving collective action problems and building capacity to govern.

15.11 Material capital

Assembling and blending resources is a daunting task. Even if a form of co-operation is developed, for a governing coalition to be viable in the long term, it 'must be able to mobilize resources commensurate with its main policy agenda' (Stone, 1993; p. 21). This is the 'iron law' of governing.

In addition to *intangible resources* that members bring to the coalition such as political popularity and possession of strategic knowledge of social transactions and a capacity to act on the basis of that knowledge (Stone, 1986), there are also tangible resources, such as financial and asset based resources that are important for the continuity of the governance relations.

The task of governance formation is about recognizing mutual interdependence and gaining a shared sense of purpose and direction. The latter, in turn, is influenced by an understanding of what is feasible. However, feasibility favours linking with resource-rich actors and marginalizes the resource-poor players. This often gives a stronger voice to businesses, politicians and professionals as compared with community groups and voluntary organizations. It also favours some goals over others.

However, as mentioned above, although such stronger voices may lead to greater systemic or command power, it does not necessarily lead to a pre-emptive power of leadership which is key to collective action in the condition of diffused and multifaceted forms of power where no one agency had the sole power to control the outcome. Furthermore, as suggested by Stone (1986), politics in regime theory is about *production* rather than *distribution* of benefits. In this context, power is created by bringing together cooperative actors, not as equal claimants but as unequal contributors to a shared set of purposes.

15.12 The significance of institutional capacity

Creating and enhancing new forms of governance and creating strategic capacity to capture emerging opportunities require progress towards all four forms of capital. This is particularly important in relation to spatial planning aimed at promoting a polycentric Europe. The processes through which these capitals are developed reinforces one another, as Innes et al. (1994) put it:

> As participants learn to communicate and trust each other — i.e. as they amass social capital — they are more likely to agree on a common indicator of problem. As participants come to understand one another's policy needs, they are more likely to overcome previous mutual distrust, even if they still don't agree. And, as social and intellectual capitals are amassed, a group is in a better position to deal with the outside world and create the political capital necessary to turn agreements into action (Innes et al., 1994; p. 47).

Given the new condition of governance, the capacity of institutions to create new relationships for engaging in purposeful, collective action is key in success or failure of cities and regions in taking advantage of the globalized economy. However, the conditions affecting institutional capacity varies between different localities. As Healey (1998; p. 1531) argues, 'a key element of such capacity lies in the quality of local political culture. Some are well-integrated, well-connected, well-informed and can mobilize readily to capture opportunities and enhance local conditions. Others are fragmented, lack the connections to sources of power and knowledge and the mobilization capacity to organize to make a difference'. In short, in some governance relations and institutional arrangements the four forms of capitals are well developed, whilst in others they are either non-existent or premature. Two questions arise from this observation, one is a research question and in particular the issue of evaluation; the other is a policy question and the role policy intervention in the development of institutional capacities and effective governance relations.

15.13 Measuring governance relations

The conceptual framework outlined above provides a better understanding of governance relations in a locality and identifies key criteria for examining the effectiveness of such relations in achieving collective action. The next step in any evaluation exercise is to develop indicators with which these criteria and the quality of governance relations can be measured and evaluated. This poses major methodological challenges such as: how do we measure the degree of trust among the actors, the learning capacity of the partners, or the level of pre-emptive power of the leadership. Whilst this contribution acknowledges the methodological difficulties of undertaking an objective evaluation of governance relations based on the proposed conceptual framework, further research is needed to identify appropriate indicators and to design new methodologies.

Given the growing interest in the research community in gaining a better understanding of the complex nature of governance formation and institutional capacity building, it will not be long before further innovative methodologies will be developed. Until such time, the most useful way forward seems to be the case study approach involving a triangulation of evidence collected through both survey materials and more importantly in-depth semi-structured interviews with the actors involved in governance formation. The two research projects mentioned in the acknowledgment above, have utilized both of these techniques and, although they faced methodological difficulties, enabled an insight into the way in which partnerships are working and governance relationships are developed. By using this conceptual framework, the researchers have been able to identify key barriers and opportunities for developing the institutional conditions which enable collective action.

15.14 The role of policy intervention

Whilst it might be argued that in the United States (where discussions on governance and urban regime were pioneered), coalitions are 'natural', in the EU countries governments have attempted to actively steer processes of coordination and collective action across public, private and voluntary sector boundaries. The notion of 'steer' in the context of governance is used to acknowledge that 'government cannot impose its policy but must rather negotiate both policy and implementation with partners in public, private and voluntary sectors' (Stoker, 2000; p. 98). A new 'operating code' is based less on government's authority to make decisions and more on creating the condition for positive-sum partnership.

It is therefore argued that governments can establish a framework for effective collective action. In the UK for example, the election of the Labour Government accelerated the search for a 'modernized' form of government. As Harding (1998) argues, the UK's interest in regime comes out of a growing awareness of the limits to direct action by the state, and the need for partnership with other actors including the private sector and the civil society. Similar attempts have been made in France and Spain to promote local coalition building (Le Gales, 1998).

At the local level, local government has an important role to play in promoting new forms of governance and enhancing local institutional capacities given that it is situated at the crossing point between the traditional vertical axis of power and public administration and the new horizontal axis of partnership between government, private and civil sector.

At the EU level, research undertaken on the impact of governance structure and institutional performance on delivery of the Structural Funds in southern Europe concluded that an important factor influencing the degree to which EU policies can be implemented is based on the institutional capacity of the localities (Batterbury, 2002). Such capacity can be enhanced by the action of the European Union aimed at enabling local institutions to operate effectively.

Most of the EU policies are embedded in a system of multi-level governance where European, national and regional government play a role. These mediate policy implementation through local governance structures. In many EU countries, Structural Funds, for example, have effectively become a mechanism for regional capacity building, a role as important as the delivery of regional assistance itself (Grote, 1996). However, some regions have been more successful in adapting themselves to the requirement of policy, while others have faced a difficult challenge, due to a lack of institutional capacity. These problems are exacerbated when institutions are faced with achieving new policy goals. The concept of polycentric development, simple as it may look, is a complex one with potential for being interpreted in different ways. Key to successful application of this policy framework is effective governance relations and a capacity to capture opportunities offered by polycentrism.

Hence, it is important that part of the EU and national resources is explicitly allocated to enhancing governance relations at a variety of scales and on building up of institutional capacity by, for example, focusing on the four capitals mentioned above.

References

Albrechts, L. (1998), 'The Flemish Diamond: precious gem and virgin area', *European Planning Studies*, Vol. 6, No. 4, pp. 411-424.

Amin, A. and Thrift, N. (1995), 'Globalisation, "institutional thickness" and the local economy', in P. Healey et al. (eds.), *Managing Cities*, Wiley, Chichester (UK), pp. 91-108.

Batten, D. F. (1995), 'Network cities; creative urban agglomerations for the 21st Century', *Urban Studies*, Vol. 32, No. 2, pp. 313-327.

Batterbury, S. C. E. (2002), 'Evaluating policy implementation: The European Union's Small and Medium Sized Enterprises in Galicia and Sardinia', *Regional Studies*, Vol. 36, No. 8, pp. 861-877.

Blotevogel, H. H. (1998), 'The Rhine-Ruhr metropolitan region: reality and discourse', *European Planning Studies*, Vol. 6, No. 4, pp. 395-410.

Brenner, N. (2000), 'Building Euro-regions: locational politics and the political geography of neoliberalism in post-unification Germany', *European Urban and Regional Studies*, Vol. 7, No. 4, pp. 319-345.

Bryson, J. M. and Crosby, B. C. (1992), *Leadership for the common good. Tackling public problems in a shared power world*, Jossey-Bass Publisher, San Francisco, CA (USA).

Camagni, R. and Salone, C. (1993), 'Network Urban Structures in Northern Italy: Elements for a Theoretical Framework', *Urban Studies*, Vol. 30, No. 6, pp. 1053-1064.

Campbell, J. L., Hollingsworth, J. R. and Lindberg, L. N. (eds., 1991), *Governance of the American Economy*, Cambridge University Press, Cambridge, MA (USA).

Campbell, S. (1999), 'Planning, Green Cities, Growing Cities, Just Cities? Urban Planning and the contradictions of sustainable development', in D. Satterthwaite (ed.), *Sustainable Cities*, Earthscan Publications, London (UK).

Coffey, W. and Bailly, A. (1996), 'Economic restructuring: A conceptual framework', in A. Bailly and W. Lever (eds.), *The Spatial Impact of Economic Changes in Europe*, Averbury, London (UK).

Copus, A. K. (2001), 'From core-periphery to polycentric development: concepts of spatial and aspatial peripherality', *European Planning Studies*, Vol. 9, No. 4, pp. 539-552.

Davoudi, S. (1995), 'Dilemmas of Urban Governance', in P. Healey et al. (eds.), *Managing Cities - The new urban context*, John Wiley, Chichester (UK).

Davoudi, S., Hull, A. and Healey, P. (1996), 'Environmental Concerns and Economic Imperatives in Strategic Plan-making', *Town Planning Review*, Vol. 67, No. 4, pp. 421-436.

Davoudi, S. (2000), 'Making sense of the ESDP', *Town and Country Planning*, Vol. 68, No. 12, pp. 367-369.

Davoudi, S. (2002), 'Polycentricity - modelling or determining reality?', *Town and Country Planning*, Vol. 71, No. 4, pp. 114-117.

Davoudi, S. (2003), 'Polycentricity in European spatial planning: from an analytical tool to a normative agenda', *European Planning Studies*, Vol. 11, No. 8, pp. 979-999.

Dyeberg, T. (1997), *The Circular Structure of Power*, Verso, London (UK).

European Commission (1999), *6th Periodic Report on Social and Economic Situation and Development of Regions in the EU*, EC, Brussels (Belgium).

European Spatial Development Perspective (1999), *Towards balanced and sustainable development of the territory of the European Union. Agreed at the Informal Council of Ministers responsible for Spatial planning in Potsdam, May 1999*, EC, Luxembourg.

Grote, J. R. (1996), 'Cohesion in Italy: a view on non-economic disparities', in L. Hooghe (ed.), *Cohesion policy and European integration: building multi-level governance*, Oxford University Press, Oxford (UK).

Hall, P. (1986), *Governing the Economy*, Oxford University Press, Oxford and New York (UK and USA).

Harding, A. (1998), 'Regime formation in Manchester and Edinburgh', in G. Stoker (ed.), *The New Politics of British Local Governance*, Macmillan, London (UK), pp. 54-71.

Healey, P. (1998), 'Building institutional capacity through collaborative approaches to urban planning', *Environment and Planning A*, Vol. 30, No. 9, pp. 1531-1546.

Healey, P., Cars, G., Madanipour, A. and de Magalhaes, C. (2002), 'Transforming governance, institutional analysis and institutional capacity', in G. Cars et al. (eds.), *Urban Governance, Institutional Capacity and Social Milieux*, Ashgate, Aldershot (UK), pp. 6-28.

Hudson, R. (1997), 'Regional Futures: industrial restructuring, new high volume production concepts and spatial development strategies in the new Europe', *Regional Studies*, Vol. 31, No. 5, pp. 467-479.

Hyden, G. (1992), 'Governance and the Study of Politics', in G. Hyden and M. Bratton (eds.), *Governance and Politics in Africa*, Lynne Reinner, London (UK).

Innes, J. and Booher, D. (1999), 'Consensus-building and complex adaptive systems: a framework for evaluating collaborative planning', *Journal of the American Planning Association*, Vol. 65, No. 4, pp. 412-423.

Innes, J., Gruber, J. Thompson, R. and Neuman, M. (1994), *Co-ordinating growth and environmental management through consensus-building. Report to the California Policy Seminar*, University of California, Berkeley, CA (USA).

Jessop, B. (1995a), 'The regulation approach, governance and post-fordism: alternative perspectives on economic and political change', *Economy and Society*, Vol. 24, pp. 307-333.

Jessop, B. (1995b), 'Towards a Schumpeterian workfare regime in Britain? Reflections on regulation, governance and the welfare state', *Environment and Planning A*, Vol. 27, No. 10, pp. 1613-1626.

Jessop, B. (1997), 'Governance of complexity and the complexity of governance: preliminary remarks on some problems and limits of economic guidance', in A. Amin and J. Hausner (eds.), *Beyond market and hierarchy: interactive governance and social complexity*, Edward Elgar, Cheltenham (UK), pp. 95-108.

Jessop, B. (2000), 'Governance Failure', in G. Stoker (ed.), *The New Politics of British Local Governance*, Macmillan, London (UK), pp. 11-32.

Knapp, W. (1998), 'The Rhine-Ruhr area in transformation: towards a European metropolitan region?', *European Planning Studies*, Vol. 6, No. 4, pp. 379-393.

Le Gales, P. (1998), 'Regulation and governance in European Cities', *International Journal of Urban and Regional Research*, Vol. 22, No. 3, pp. 482-506.

Liepietz, A. (1995), *Green Hopes: The Future of Political Ecology*, Translated by Malcolm Slater, Polity Press, Cambridge (UK).

Logan, J. and Molotch, H. (1987), *Urban Fortunes: the political economy of place*, University of California, Berkeley and Los Angeles, CA (USA).

de Magalhães, C., Healy, P. and Madanipour, A. (2002), 'Assessing institutional capacity for city centre regeneration: Newcastle's Grainger Town', in G. Cars et al. (eds.), *Urban Governance, Institutional Capacity and Social Milieux*, Ashgate, Aldershot (UK), pp. 45-62.

Malmberg, A. and Maskell, P. (1997), 'Towards an explanation of regional specialisation and industry agglomeration', *European Planning Studies*, Vol. 5, No. 1, pp. 24-41.

Mayes, D. (1995), 'Conflict and cohesion in the Single European Market: a reflection', in A. Amin and J. Tomaney (eds.), *Behind the myth of the European Union: prospects for cohesion*, Routledge, London and New York (UK and USA).

Painter, J. and Goodwin, M. (2000), 'Local governance after Fordism: A regulationist perspective', in G. Stoker, *The new politics of British governance*, Macmillan Press, London (UK), pp. 33-53.

Peck, J. and Tickell, A. (1994), 'Too many partners...the future of regeneration partnerships', *Local Economy*, Vol. 9, pp. 251-265.

Perrons, D. (1999), 'Deconstructing the Maastricht myth? Economic and social cohesion in Europe: regional and gender dimension of inequality', in R. Hudson and A. M. Williams (eds.), *Divided Europe: society and territory*, Sage, London (UK).

Peters, G. B. (2000), 'Governance and comparative politics', in J. Pierre (ed.), *Debating Governance*, Oxford University Press, Oxford (UK).

Pierre, J. (ed., 2000), *Debating Governance*, Oxford University Press, Oxford (UK).

Pierre, J. (ed., 1999), *Governance*, Oxford University Press, Oxford (UK).

Piore, M.J. and Sabel, C.F. (1984), *The Second Industrial Divide: possibilities for prosperity*, Basic Books, New York, NY (USA).

Priemus, H. (1994), 'Planning the Randstad: between economic growth and sustainability', *Urban Studies*, Vol. 31, No. 3, pp. 509-534.

Priemus, H. (1998), 'The Randstad and the Central Netherlands Urban Ring: Planners waver between two concepts', *European Planning Studies*, Vol. 6, No. 4, pp. 443-466.

Putnam, R. (1993), *Making democracy work: civil tradition in modern Italy*, University of Princeton Press, Princeton, NJ (USA).

Rhodes, R. (1997), *Understanding Governance — Policy networks, governance reflexivity and accountability*, Open University Press, Buckingham and Philadelphia, PA (UK and USA).

Rhodes, R. (2000), 'Governance and Public Administration', in J. Pierre (ed.), *Debating Governance*, Oxford University Press, Oxford (UK).

Sellers, J. M. (2002), *Governance from Below, Urban regions and the global economy*, Cambridge University Press, Cambridge (UK).

Stoker, G. (1995), 'Regime Theory and Urban Politics', in D. Judge, G. Stoker and H. Wolman (eds.), *Theories of Urban Politics*, Sage, London (UK).

Stoker, G. (1997), 'Public-private partnerships in urban governance', in J. Pierre (ed.), *Partnerships in Urban Governance, European and American experience*, Macmillan, London (UK).

Stoker, G. (2000), 'Urban Political Science and the challenge of urban governance', in J. Pierre (ed.), *Debating Governance*, Oxford University Press, Oxford (UK).

Stoker, G. and Mossberges, K. (1995), 'The post-Fordist local state: the dynamic of its development', in J. Stewart and G. Stoker (eds.), *Local government in the 1990s*, Macmillan, Basingstoke (UK), pp. 210-227.

Stoker, J. and Young, S. (1993), *Cities in the 1990s*, Longman, London (UK).

Stone, C. (1986), 'Power and Social Complexity', in R. Waste (ed.), *Community power: Directions for future research*, Sage, Newbury Park, CA (USA).

Stone, C. (1988), 'Pre-emptive power: Floyd Hunter's 'Community power structure reconsidered', *American Journal of Political Science*, Vol. 32, pp. 82-104.

Stone, C. (1989), *Regime Politics: Governing Atlanta, 1946-1988*, University Press of Kansas, Lawrence, KS (USA).

Stone, C. (1993), 'Urban regimes and the capacity to govern: a political economy approach', *Journal of Urban Affairs*, Vol. 15, No. 1, pp. 1-28.

Acknowledgement The contribution draws on the literature review which was carried out by the author as part of two research projects during 2002-2003, one funded by the UK Economic and Social Research Council on 'Regionalisation and the New Politics of Waste' and the other funded by the European Commission under the ESPON (European Spatial Planning Observation Network) Programme on 'The Role, Specific Situation and Potentials of Urban Areas as Nodes in a Polycentric Development'.

Chapter 16

Implementing Norms in Practice — The Institutional Design of Evaluation

Ernest Alexander

16.1 Introduction

This book addresses some common problems in current evaluation practice. One is the neglect of non-economic aspects: the tendency to focus evaluation on market-related factors in evaluating development strategies and plans, underplaying the assessment of environmental, social and cultural impacts. Another is the reluctance to confront constraints of ignorance, uncertainty, and contested values.

Many responses (including some chapters in this book) suggest that these are actually problems either of wrong values, or methodological limitations. In the first view, these problems are the result of mistaken norms that guide the development and application of policy-, plan- and project-evaluation methods. In the second, the problem is the limits of the evaluation approaches that have been developed and applied. Each of these views also implies its solution.

The first is ultimately to change accepted values and practice norms by consciousness-raising. This means educating practitioners to adopt different and better norms, such as a human values-based ethics (Borri et al., here) or 'sustainability' as a meta-criterion for evaluation (Fusco Girard, Cerreta and De Toro, here) and institutionalizing their practice. The second proposes new evaluation approaches that transcend the limits of prevailing methods, e.g. Strategic Impact Assessment (Partidário, here) or scenarios (Barbanente and Khakee, here).

Both these views, I believe, are mistaken. Though each approach may effect some improvements in how we evaluate projects and plans, I suspect that they offer only a poor prospect of solving the basic problems or making significant contributions to evaluation practice. I will argue that the observed problems are less the result of wrong values and norms, or the limits of existing methods, than the results of structural flaws in the evaluation process' institutional context. In other words, the main problems with plan and project evaluation today cannot be solved with consciousness-raising or better methods: they demand deliberate and effective institutional design.

Current planning paradigms give planners, evaluators and analysts a 'scientifically' objective position or a socially benign role in a 'neutral' evaluation process. These norms are demonstrably incompatible with our actual life-world, as I will show through some historical cases of plan evaluation. Reality is different: evaluation methods and frameworks are weapons in a planning process that is (when significant values or resources are at stake) a partisan debate between conflicting interests, and evaluation is usually a contested, not a consensual process.

The case analyses that follow will show how the institutional design (either intentionally proactive or reactive, or the inertial product of preceding institutionalization) of planning and evaluation processes generates particular methods and practices to produce the observed outcomes. The conclusion is inescapable: 'good' evaluation demands a prior investment of institutional design of the planning and evaluation process. Such institutional design recognizes that often policy, project and plan evaluations are the arenas for resolving conflicting claims.

The contribution closes with a brief review of institutional design in general, and its application to evaluation processes in particular. Some norms are proposed for 'designing' effective evaluation processes. These norms prescribe supportive institutional contexts for the development of evaluation frameworks that empower affected parties, facilitate the adoption of appropriate evaluation methods, and enable the enaction of 'right' evaluation practices.

16.2 Planning paradigms and evaluation — myth and reality

Most discussions of evaluation methods and practice are premised on one or another of two prevailing planning paradigms: rational planning and communicative practice[1]. In rational planning the adopted framework for assessing the relative merit of alternative courses of action is supposed to facilitate the processing of objective information, to arrive at conclusions that warrant a collective decision.

Evaluation methods that reflect instrumental rationality *par excellence* are the various forms of investment analysis, which apply simple criteria of economic efficiency: benefit-cost ratio, net present value (NPV), internal rate of return (IRR) etc. When the parties involved in a planning process agree on these methods, they are presumed to agree on the criteria and methodology. These are applied to 'objective' data or scientific information to produce an 'automatic' consensus on the collective decision: to 'go' or not in implementing the proposed project or plan, or which option to choose as the optimal alternative.

Substantive rationality is associated with more sophisticated evaluation methods: various models of multi-criterion decision analysis (MCDA), which incorporate discussion and prioritization of values in the form of specified and weighted objectives and criteria. Here the application can range from more rational-'scientific' approaches, eliciting weights through paired comparisons or trade-off functions, to more interactive ones (e.g. Delphi surveys), but the evaluation process is still viewed as an objective way of identifying, expressing and aggregating the diverse subjective values, preferences, and priorities of the interested parties and decision makers.

In communicative practice (more preached than practiced) the evaluation is expected to promote an interactive discourse on values, which yields a consensus on the preferred plan or strategy. This may involve the development and presentation of some form of impact analysis[2] as a framework for an essentially political debate on the respective merits of the alternatives. Or it may be through more interactive applications of MCDA methods, which can include active discourse on determining and prioritizing criteria and goals, and focused debate about planning-related values if sensitivity analysis reveals that these are critical in choosing between two superior alternatives (Alexander, 2000). The evaluators are benign advisors to decision makers: professional information generators, processors and analysts, or facilitators of the planning-dialogue.

But does evaluation conform to these images in reality? Is the planning process in which plan- or project-evaluation is embedded really the neutral kind of process these paradigms imply? Is evaluation really a matter of objective fact-finding regarding the expected impacts of alternative courses of action, and rational choice between them on the basis of criteria reflecting an agreed-on goal, according to instrumental rationality? Does it also include reasonable discussion and agreement on the priorities of relevant objectives, as substantive rationality demands? Or does a consensus emerge from an open discourse among parties and decision makers on their respective values and preferences, in the framework of an interactive evaluation process as communicative practice prescribes?

Perhaps reality is not like this at all. There is ample literature and experience to suggest that planning is not the scientifically objective or benign process these paradigms imply, but that planning decisions are the outcomes of a political process[3]. If this is so, then real-life plan- and project-evaluation is not the neutral and consensual practice that prevailing and proposed approaches and methods imply, but essentially an institutionalized framework for debating and resolving conflicting claims.

16.3 Evaluation cases — the lessons of experience

section 16.6 presents and analyses four case histories of plan and project evaluation to explore which of these models gives a truer picture of reality. In the two other cases the author was a participant-observer.[4] These cases show that generally the conflict-resolution model of evaluation is more accurate than the normative image of neutral evaluation. Looking at the evaluation process as an arena for resolving the conflicting claims of opposing values and competing interests provides a better way to understand what happened, why, and explain the evaluations' outcomes.

In the *Third London Airport* case the Roskill Commission's evaluation should have produced a consensual recommendation, but suffered from basic institutional design flaws in the Commission's charge and execution. Here two kinds of conflict remained unresolved. In one, local populations and community interests confronted central government's essentially economic view of the public interest (later modified under public and political pressure). The other expressed conflicting values of economic and operational effectiveness vs. less tangible 'planning considerations' involving land preservation and environmental impacts. Here a technically superior evaluation failed because the process and methods adopted were inappropriate for mediating these conflicts.

The *EU T-TEN*[5] *project evaluation* case illustrates a process of institutional design that was itself the arena for struggle between conflicting interests and values. The opposing parties here were, on the one side, economic and transportation-related interests that were the original initiators and supporters of the program, and on the other side were groups advocating environmental values. Both recognized that the institutional design of the evaluation process would determine the adoption of particular methods and thus critically affect the evaluation results and consequent project-related decisions. A decade of interaction between EU institutions, governments, and lobbyists for the opposing interests produced the staged evaluation process that was adopted.

Israel's Highway #6 (the 'Trans-Israel Highway') involved much the same kinds of conflict as the EU case did. But here one side — transportation interests making government policy — determined the institutional design of the evaluation process. Only limited evaluations were done: a benefits cost analysis (BCA) -based feasibility analysis, and later the legally required environmental impact statement (EIS) for segments of the project. Evaluations were internal to established planning processes and agencies: their arguments were not rationales but rationalizations of decisions. Opposing interests were reduced to ineffective legal objections and political protest. The institutional design of evaluation succeeded in its aim: to ensure project implementation. The question is still open, however, about the quality of the evaluations and of the project approval decision.

In reviewing the strategic plan for *Ben Gurion International Airport*, the national planning authority recognized the conflict-mediating potential of the evaluation process. It formed a professional advisory committee, which included some of the affected interests and sought the participation of others. This involved El-Al (the national airline), the Israel Defense Forces (IDF), and some adjacent municipalities in an interactive process of incremental and informal evaluation of alternative plans. Conflicts between opposing interests and values included cost, safety and operating efficiency vs. environmental (mainly noise) impacts, and the competing interests of communities in different locations. These conflicts were partially resolved in an agreed development plan and 'flexible' operations model. Success was only partial, however, because limited investment in the evaluation process and under-representation of some interests left room for serious objections.

Producing the *Tel-Aviv Metropolitan Development Policy* included evaluating three schematic spatial development options, which the planning team had designed: CU (concentrated urbanization), MU (multipolar urbanization), and CD (controlled dispersion). Conflicting interests and values that were involved included Tel-Aviv (the core city), other municipalities, suburban and exurban communities, development and real-estate interests, and environmental values. One evaluation failed, because one party (Tel-Aviv, which favored CU) successfully attacked its conclusions. A new evaluation used MCDA as a framework for expressing conflicting values and preferences. This evaluation identified one alternative (MU) as intrinsically superior. Here, explicit consideration of subjective preferences succeeded in producing agreement and a consensual plan (Alexander, 2000; pp. 322-329).

The Haifa Marina has been a controversial project for over a decade. The national planning authority rejected a proposed development plan for the marina, which included substantial residential development on reclaimed land, as incompatible with the national shoreline development plan. At the same time, it commissioned a detailed amendment plan for the Haifa shoreline, which included the development and evaluation of alternative locations and configurations for the Haifa marina.

This plan has pitted opposing interests — real-estate and development interests including Haifa municipality on one side, and environmental interests (the Ministry for Environmental Quality and 'Green' NGOs) on the other — against each other in structuring and implementing the evaluation of a set of planner-designed alternatives.

One participating NGO objected to the upcoming evaluation, claiming that the planners had offered an incomplete set of options, and proving that the proposed evaluation method was flawed. With some additional alternatives to meet these objections, and modification of the evaluation method, the evaluation is now in progress. However, its results and the subsequent decisions will not only be affected by the evaluation method and its application, but by the structure of the planning process itself: who are the active participants and how they make their decisions.

All these cases have two things in common. One is the involvement of conflicting interests and values in the planning and evaluation process. The other is the importance of institutional design — determining how these processes are structured and managed — in affecting the quality of the evaluation and its success or failure. The conclusion is inescapable that good evaluation demands anticipatory institutional design of the evaluation structure and process, so as to make project or plan evaluation an effective framework for debating conflicting claims and resolving them in a consensual policy or plan.

16.4 Designing evaluation frameworks and processes

If we understand evaluation as an arena for debating and resolving conflicting claims, the institutional design of the evaluation process must address the factors affecting the decisions on how these claims are resolved. Some of these factors are easy to identify, using sound intuition and simple common sense.

Who are the actors in the evaluation process, what are their assigned roles and prescribed interactions? For example, in the last case described above, the evaluation was to be carried out by the principal members of the planning team together with the members of the statutory Steering Committee appointed to supervise the planning and to make planning policy decisions. Anticipatory institutional design would address the representation of relevant interests on the Steering Committee, and specify their voting power to influence critical decisions.

How is the evaluation process structured, in terms of the content and sequence of critical decisions? This question is and should be of legitimate concern to the interested participants in the planning process. Many complex project evaluations, for instance, are actually a series of decisions at increasing levels of detail, where choices made at an early stage of the process preclude options for later assessment. The awareness of this structured the debate between opposing economic and environmental interests in the EU T-TEN case, with each group arguing for consideration of its criteria at the earliest possible stage of the process.

What will be the object of the proposed evaluation, and how is it to be formed? This question addresses the process of designing and presenting alternatives, which is an integral (though often neglected or ignored) part of evaluation. Who will design and present the prospective alternatives? What is or will be the alternative designer's program brief, and who or what is its source? The range and content of alternatives can critically affect any evaluation and its results. After all, if the 'best' option (from any particular interest's point of view) is not included, it will not be chosen!

In the last case presented above, institutional design of the planning process neglected this issue. It was confronted just before it was too late, when a patently manipulative evaluation exercise offered alternatives that included the project the planners (and the interests to whom they are apparently responsive) favored. This case also illustrates the importance of the program brief, here the formal instructions commissioning the plan. These were ambiguous (and may still become the subject of legal interpretation) as to whether the plan should include a marina project or not.

The question of the program behind the design and evaluation of alternatives raises another critical issue: the institutional context of the subject planning process in general, and the institutional structure of the planning and evaluation process in particular. Each of the cases illustrates different contexts and planning processes and structures, and they are quite suggestive of the impact these may have. Statutory planning processes, for example, set their own constraints, which limit institutional design but also indicate useful possibilities. The cases show how locating an evaluation process deep in an established agency may contribute towards one outcome, while setting up an institutionally independent evaluation might produce another.

In spite of its importance, as we have seen, practitioners of planning and evaluation have little awareness and even less knowledge of institutional design. I want to close this chapter, therefore, by describing (necessarily too briefly) institutional design: what it is, who does it, and what we know about how to do it.

16.5 Institutional design[6]

Before answering the question: What is institutional design? I have to explain what institutions are. 'Institutions are the rules of the game in society … the humanly devised constraints that shape human interaction' (North, 1990; p. 3). Institutions may take the form of organizations, or of norms or rules enabling or constraining action. Institutions are created (e.g. the French 4th Republic, the University of Venice) or evolve over time (e.g. the UK statutory planning system, the Catholic

Table 16.1 Institutional-agent interactions — Elements of institutional design

Type	Public/formal	Tacit/informal
Performative	Transactions*[7]	Episodes
		Events*
		Customary behaviors*
Structural	'Cultural' Institutions	'Ontological' Institutions
[Agency, Process]	*Laws*	Norms*
	Rules/regulations	Habits*
	Standards	Practices*
[Structure]	*Governments*	Knowledge/world-views*
	Markets:	Languages
	• *'hybrid' markets*[8]	'Games'
	• *artificial/quasi-markets*[9]	Informal social networks
	Interorganizational networks[10]	Associational/kinship networks
	Organizations	

Source: Adapted from Table 2: A map of institutional/agent interaction, in Bolan (2000), 'Social interaction and institutional design: The case of housing in the U.S.', p. 29. Elements of institutional design in the table (e.g. *Laws, Governments*) are shown in italics. Impacts, or interactions intended to be affected by institutional design (e.g. Transactions, Practices) are marked by an asterisk (*)

Church); they range from the U.S. Constitution to the Thursday night card game at O'Brady's bar.

Institutional design, then, means devising and realization of rules, procedures, and organizational structures that will enable and constrain behavior and action so as to accord with held values, achieve desired objectives, or execute given tasks. By this definition institutional design is pervasive at all levels of social deliberation and action, including legislation, policymaking, planning and program design and implementation. The 'media' and objects of institutional design are shown in Table 16.1. It is a simple task to convert these relatively abstract categories into specific and concrete elements of plan evaluation and evaluation processes.

We can think of three different 'levels' of institutional design: 1) The macro-level, affecting whole societies or polities; this has sometimes been (wrongly) identified with 'constitution writing'. 2) The meso-level involves planning and implementation structures and processes, the creation of new organizations and interorganizational networks or transforming existing ones, and devising incentives and constraints (laws, regulations and resources) to form and implement policies, programs and plans. 3) The 'micro' level involves intraorganizational or informal units, processes and interactions: committees, teams, work groups, task forces etc. The micro level is mainly oriented to ensure effective and timely task performance, and is a universal if generally unacknowledged aspect of most administration and management. Institutional design for planning and evaluation may involve either or both of the meso- and micro-levels.

The burdens of complexity and the constraints of ignorance mean that the 'Handbook of Institutional Design' will never be written. But there are some areas of knowledge that may help the practitioner to understand the context and define the institutional design problem, or that may even be practically applicable for institutional design. These cover three issues which are central to institutional design, and which roughly match the 'levels' of institutional design described above.

The first is *governance*, which is highly relevant at the 'constitution writing' level of institutional design, but also at the meso-level involving organizational and interorganizational design and the delivery of policies, programs and plans. The second is *coordination*, applicable mainly at the meso-level as organizational and interorganizational coordination, but in its macro- and micro-forms reaching 'up' and 'down' to the other 'levels' as well. The third is *agency*, which is most salient at the 'lowest' level of task performance, though agency issues arise at other levels too.

Conscious and deliberate institutional design must begin with institutional analysis of the design setting. For this purpose, several tools are available: transaction cost analysis is one; organizational network analysis is another. Transaction cost theory also offers the would-be institutional designer a repertoire of alternative forms of governance as possible design options at the meso-level, while other research suggests an array of organizational and interorganizational coordination structures at the meso- and micro-levels. Some organization-related studies and a good deal of agency theory give some insight into the relative fit and effectiveness of these design 'solutions' for various purposes and contexts.

16.6 Four case histories

This section presents four brief evaluation cases, which are compiled from secondary sources. One is by now a classic story: the Roskill Commission report on a Third London Airport and what followed it (Lichfield, Kettle and Whitbread, 1973; pp. 271-289, 294-309) (Hall, 1980; pp. 15-55). The second is a well-observed case of emerging practice in evaluating EU-funded T-TEN projects (Richardson, 1997). The third is the evaluation and EIA of the Trans-Israel Highway (Alexander, 1998b; Alexander, 1998c; Levine and Garb, 1997). The fourth is the evaluation of alternative development and operational options for Ben Gurion International Airport (Alexander, 1998d; pp. 306-310).[11]

A third London airport

After about five years (1963-1968) of public debate and formal enquiry into the need for and location of a third international airport for London (to supplement the existing airports at Heathrow and Gatwick), the government appointed a special commission (chaired by Lord Roskill) to decide when and where a third airport should be constructed. The Roskill Commission applied a model process of staged alternatives development (from 78 possible sites to a short list of four) and evaluation — from basic feasibility analysis to fully detailed benefit-cost analysis (BCA) of the final options — to issue a report in January 1971 that identified Cublington as the optimal location for the proposed airport.

However, this recommendation was already controversial when it appeared. A minority report (by Prof. Buchanan) preferred another site, Foulness (or Maplin Sands), for its better environmental quality, though it had been eliminated earlier (primarily on access cost considerations) by the Commission's analysts: it was simply too distant to be feasible. Intensive public debate followed, which the opponents of the Cublington option (who included residents of the selected area and broader environmental interest groups) won: in April 1971 the government adopted Maplin as the location for the new airport.

But the Maplin site, too, was problematic. Though it avoided the adverse environmental impacts of the other locations closer to London, that included noise impacts on populated areas and occupying large areas of greenbelt, it had other drawbacks. The Maplin site had high costs and interference in sensitive coastal areas. A series of formal reviews (through 1974 to 1978) led to ultimate abandonment of the Maplin project. The main reason was revision of the demand projections, which had been the incentive for setting up the Roskill Commission in the first place. The final outcome was incremental development of alternative and expanded airports at Heathrow, Stanstead and Luton, demonstrating the impotence of 'classic' comprehensive planning and its best attempts at rational evaluation.

In retrospect this failure can be attributed largely to flaws in institutional design, though this is not how later intelligent analysts (e.g. Nat Lichfield, Peter Self and Peter Hall) described it. They all agree, however, that the primary reason for the consequences of the Roskill Commission report was the Commission's erroneous remit and its persistence in following its charge to the letter. Rather than reexamining the question of whether and to what degree a new third airport was needed at all, the Commission's analysts took the travel demand projections (which are intrinsically speculative) for granted, and focused their attention on finding the best location.

These, of course, are the results of institutional design flaws. The Commission's limited charge was an institutional design error in itself, and its enthusiastic acceptance was the product of the Commission's professional staffing and culture, oriented to rational planning, economic evaluation and quantitative analysis. This also led to the adoption of formal BCA as the primary evaluation method, a decision that, in hindsight, made the debate over the Commission's recommendations almost inevitable.

BCA gave natural primacy to quantifiable factors and economic considerations, depriving advocates (like Prof. Buchanan) of other 'planning considerations' (primarily environmental impacts) of an institutionalized arena for raising their concerns. The institutional design of the Roskill Commission's evaluation process made it incapable of mediating disputes over the relative importance of different, here even conflicting, values (economic efficiency vs. environmental quality) internally, so that these principled disagreements were postponed and revealed on publication of the Commission's report. This case, then, well illustrates the interdependence between institutional design, choice and use of evaluation methods, and ultimate success or failure.

Evaluating EU T-TEN projects

The development of evaluation frameworks to assess EU-funded T-TEN projects is an excellent example of influence of institutional design on the choice and application of evaluation methods. It also shows how evaluation is really an arena for resolving conflicting values and claims, and how, recognizing that fact, interested parties invoke deliberate institutional design to determine evaluation outcomes.

On one side of the conflicting interests were national transportation planning agencies and the program's 'spiritual progenitors', the European Round Table of Industrialists, who lobbied for its adoption. On the other side was the 'environmental lobby' — Green parties, national environmental agencies, and environmental NGOs partly associated in the European Federation for Transportation and the Environment who were latecomers to the debate.

The basic justification for the T-TEN program was economic rationality: the claim that its projects were needed to realize the economic benefits of the Single European Market. For project appraisal, this paradigm uses BCA, already well tried in evaluating national strategic infrastructure projects. But in the 1990s the European Parliament demanded justification of the programs' investments in European terms, not only the strictly national benefits of its projects. The response was the development of an improved BCA focused on 'Community Benefits', with macroeconomic research confirming the positive expectations of the program as a whole.

However, just then an environmental movement had begun to campaign against the TENs. Many of its objections were to specific projects (e.g. the Somport Tunnel through the Pyrenees) that had begun without consideration of alternatives or environmental impacts. But these also generated the demand for a more comprehensive assessment to integrate economic and environmental considerations into a strategic evaluation framework. The advocated evaluation method was called Strategic Environmental Assessment (SEA).

The debate in EU institutions continued from 1992 to 1995. It involved DG XI (Environment, Nuclear Safety and Civil Protection), DG XVII (Transport), the EU Commission[12], the European Parliament[13] (whose review of the T-TEN program concluded in a demand for SEA and stronger environmental conditions) and the European Council[14], whose opposition to SEA reflected the resistance of national governments to EU involvement in evaluating their pet projects.

After a formal conciliation process to resolve the stand-off between the Council and Parliament, a weak form of SEA was incorporated into the T-TEN evaluation process. This is now structured in a hierarchy that reflects the uneasy combination of conflicting paradigms: the economic paradigm based on utilitarian rationality, and the environmental paradigm based on ecological principles. Non-mandatory SEA, at the highest level of this hierarchy, is designed to evaluate TEN networks as a whole, while at lower levels project proposals are evaluated using BCA to identify 'Community benefits', and 'Corridor Analysis' incorporating environmental considerations (Richardson, 1997; pp. 3-11).

The Trans-Israel Highway: project and implementation evaluation

A 'Trans-Israel Highway', linking the country's northern and southern peripheries with its center along its eastern border, was already included in the national statutory highway plan that was approved in 1970. But the project remained dormant until the late 1980s, when growing congestion stimulated its revival as a critical addition to Israel's infrastructure.

When the government (the DPW) undertook detailed project planning there was no consideration or evaluation of strategic or policy alternatives: Highway #6 and its designated corridor were foregone conclusions. The only assessment that was done was a detailed feasibility analysis, which was clearly intended to establish the project's economic rationale. The centerpiece of this is a conventional BCA, which confirmed the project's benefits in terms of its high benefit-cost ratio[15].

As soon as it was revived as a strategic national infrastructure project, HW#6 was controversial, and vehemently opposed by two groups: environmental groups and communities on its right of way (ROW) that would be negatively impacted. At the same time, powerful interests mobilized in its support, and succeeded in short-circuiting some avenues of opposition. An Act that gave the newly created special agency authority for preemptive land expropriation neutralized potential legal action by affected communities and landowners[16].

The BCA that justified the project was the subject of considerable criticism (Levine and Garb, 1997), but to no avail in terms of changing the decision to proceed. Objections included its failure to take account of second-order effects (including foreseeable urbanization impacts and their traffic-related consequences) and its understatement of some costs, e.g. compensation for compulsory land acquisition, which could reverse the final assessment of economic benefits.

Another major critique was the neglect of environmental impacts informing the decision on project implementation. This became the central issue in an appeal of the final project approval decision (taken by the country's highest planning authority), demanding compliance with contemporary EIA requirements[17] in the form of a comprehensive EIS. But the HW#6 agency found a way for achieving technical conformity with rational planning norms of evaluating alternatives, and with statutory EIS requirements.

The division of the whole 300 km long highway project into segments (obviously needed for detailed engineering and planning/monitoring construction) became the rationale for segmented evaluation too. Thus the only alternatives evaluation for this project was the assessment of alternative routes of segments, within the broad corridor that had already been approved for the project as a whole. These evaluations combined engineering-cost assessments with the EIS required by law. Naturally, they had no bearing on the disputed strategic decisions, or any substantive effect on their outcomes.

Evaluation had a similar role in another project-related decision: by whom and how was the project to be funded and implemented. Here a poorly executed MCDA provided an ostensibly 'scientific' justification for the choice of a private corporation to plan, construct and operate the highway, which would be funded by its expected toll revenue[18]. In the final event, the franchisee's lack of faith in the government's revenue estimates was demonstrated by his demand for minimum revenue guarantees[19].

This case is another striking illustration of the political use of evaluation. But here the evaluation is not intended to bias open decisions in favor of a particular interest's preferred alternative. Rather, evaluation is used to rationalize a choice that has already been made. Again, it is the institutional design of the evaluation process, performed here as essentially a rational-technical exercise carried out internally by the planning-implementing agency, which enables this transformation of planning rationality into specious rationalization.

Ben Gurion International Airport

Ben Gurion Airport (BGA) has grown incrementally from its modest origins as an air force base to become Israel's main international airport, now serving 5 million travellers a year. Up to the mid-1970s planning BGA was a mainly technical process, involving the Airports Authority and its consultants, and the airport's main users: El-Al and the IDF. Nearby communities could only try political influence on the Ministry of Transportation, the Airports Authority's overlord.

But airport development planning was not confined to the transportation sector. The statutory land use planning process provided another arena for affected interests. As a result, the BGA development plan proved contentious when it was presented to the National Council for Planning and Building (NCPB), the supervising body of the statutory land use planning system. To review this plan the NCPB set up a Professional Advisory Committee in 1984, called the Brovender Committee after its chairman.

The Committee was charged to assess environmental effects (primarily noise impacts) and present mitigation proposals, but later its terms of reference were broadened to consider other alternatives. Dr. Brovender's October 1986 report recommended a 'Flexible Plan' for BGA's development and operations. Less a development plan than an organizational and operational model, the 'Flexible Plan' proposed adapting airport operations so as to minimize cumulative noise impacts, and included an environmental impact monitoring and control system.

In its Report the Committee describes the development and evaluation of two options: the Airports Authority's previous plan, and an alternative system of parallel runways with horizontal separation. The evaluation (exclusively on economic and operational criteria) shows the clear superiority of the first option, but noise impacts are only superficially discussed. It is silent on how it developed its own plan, and totally unclear on how it arrived at its conclusions.

How the Brovender Committee actually created its 'Flexible Plan' is much more interesting than the (barely competent) method it describes, involving the interaction of various interests in the course of developing, evaluating and discussing a succession of alternatives. Taking the Airports Authority's plan as its point of departure, the committee reviewed and evaluated two other plans which interested parties (El-Al, and communities to the north of the airport) had offered as alternatives. These were informal evaluations, based on cost, operational, and noise impact considerations.

Upon agreeing on a modified runway configuration, the Committee focused on the airport's operational pattern. Protracted debate on approach configurations and the allocation of landings between two runways, which had different impacts on the surrounding communities, was inconclusive. Failure to reach agreement generated the 'Flexible Plan'. After deliberating on numerous objections, the NCPB adopted the Brovender Report at the end of 1986, charging the Advisory Committee with submitting a draft statutory plan. This was the base for the Airport Authority's 'BGA 2000' strategic development plan, which was submitted to the NCPB in 1994.

Relying on the NCPB's previous approval, the plan did not encounter any opposition there, but several formal objections were lodged. Opponents included 'green' interests, who objected to the airport's expansion, disputed the plan's need and capacity projections, and claimed that its environmental impacts were understated. Noise-impacted neighboring communities also objected, arguing that the 'Flexible Plan' was a surrender to political interests, and pleading for an alternative rigid plan avoiding the use of one runway.

A statutory Inspector took nearly two years to hear the objections and make recommendations. In April 1997 the new statutory land use plan for BGA was approved, with some minor modifications of the original proposals to address some objections and mitigate negative environmental impacts. The 'Flexible Plan' has governed BGA operations since its adoption, and implementation of the BG-2000 plan is in progress.

This case is of interest in the institutional design and application of the plan evaluation process. Its (limited) success is due to two factors. First, the recognition of evaluation as a political process, resulting in the creation of a professional advisory committee as an arena for debating and resolving conflicting interests. Second, the committee's own (implicit) recognition of this fact, leading it to structure its proceedings as an interactive and iterative evaluation process with active participation by many interested parties, including El-Al, the Air Force, and some adjacent municipalities.

The failure of this effort is reflected in the number and intensity of the objections to the BG-2000 plan[20]. Insufficient attention and resources were devoted to structuring and managing the committee's interactive evaluation process (which was in large measure informal) and, more important, several important interests (environmental groups, some neighboring towns) were underrepresented. The objections to the final plan were the result of the failure to bring all parties aboard and to really exploit the evaluation process to develop a consensual plan.

Notes

1 For a more detailed discussion of the relation between planning paradigms and evaluation methods see Alexander (1998a).

2 Such as Environmental Impact Assessment, social impact assessment and Community Impact Evaluation (Lichfield, 1996).

3 Today this is so axiomatic and widely recognized that supporting citations are unnecessary.

4 In the first I was a member of the planning team for this project (which was a metropolitan policy plan to provide the foundation for the statutory District plan for the Tel-Aviv District), and responsible for the evaluation. In the second I was an expert consultant to one of the 'Green' NGOs participating in the evaluation as a member of the plan's Steering Committee.

5 A European Union-funded program to subsidise the planning and construction of *Trans-European Networks*: major international transportation (highway and rail) arteries.

6 Alexander (2002) gives a more extended exposition of this section.

7 As defined in Alexander (2001; pp. 50-51).

8 See Alexander (2001; p. 55) and Williamson (1985).

9 See Alexander (1995; pp. 227-235).

10 See Alexander (1995; pp. 199-266).

11 Although the source citations may suggest that I was a participant in the third and fourth cases, I was not. I wrote the referenced articles as an outside observer, although peripherally involved in each of the cases as an expert witness in court appeals of planning decisions on the projects' approval.

12 Editor's note: the European Commission (EC) 'is a body with powers of initiative, implementation, management and control. It is the guardian of the Treaties and the embodiment of the interests of the Community. It is composed of twenty independent members (two each from France, Germany, Italy, Spain and the United Kingdom and one each from all the other countries), including a President and two Vice-Presidents. It is appointed for a five-year term by the Council, acting by qualified majority in agreement with the Member States. It is subject to a vote of appointment by the European Parliament, to which it is answerable. The Commissioners are assisted by an administration made up of directorates-general and specialised departments whose staff are divided mainly between Brussels and Luxembourg' (EU on-line glossary at http://www.europa.eu.int/scadplus/leg/en/cig/g4000.htm).

13 Editor's note: the parliament of the EU (European Parliament, EP) is elected each five years directly by all eligible voters of the EU member states and represents, in the words of the 1957 Treaty of Rome, 'the peoples of the States brought together in the European Community'. See also the EP's web site at http://www.europarl.eu.int/presentation/default_en.htm.

14 Editor's note: the Council of the European Union (Council, sometimes referred to as the Council of Ministers) is the Union's main decision-making institution. The ministers of the member states meet within the Council of the European Union. Depending on the issue on the agenda, each country will be represented by the minister responsible for that subject (foreign affairs, finance, social affairs, transport, agriculture, etc.). Despite the existence of these different configurations depending on the area of activity, the Council is nonetheless a single institution. The Presidency of the Council is held for six months by each member state on a rotational basis (definitions taken from the official website of

the Council at http://ue.eu.int/showPage.asp?lang=en and from the EU on-line glossary at http://www.europa.eu.int/scadplus/leg/en/cig/g4000.htm).

15 A potential point of weakness in this analysis was anticipated: since the primary positive project impact was travel time saving, the estimated benefits might be critically dependent on the imputed value of travel time. Sensitivity analysis over a wide range of possible values eliminated this possibility.

16 Though this has no direct bearing on the evaluations that are the topic of this case history, it sets the stage of the context in which these evaluations were carried out.

17 Which, however, did not exist in 1973 when the project was first approved as part of the national transportation master plan, an approval that gave the court the technical grounds for dismissing the appellants' petition.

18 A detailed account and critique of this evaluation and its subject options is provided in Alexander (1998b).

19 The government had no choice but to meet this demand (by the Israeli syndicate negotiating for the franchise) because potential foreign sources of financing had even less confidence in this project's economic projections and showed no interest whatsoever.

20 Though they were finally overruled and the plan is now some years into implementation, environmental interests and some communities are still dissatisfied, and are still actively promoting the transfer of the country's major international airport to the remote Negev.

References

Alexander, E. R. (2000), 'Devaluing evaluation', in H. Voogd (ed.), *Evaluation in Spatial Planning*, GeoPress, Groningen (The Netherlands), pp. 319-340.

Alexander, E. R. (1995), *How Organizations Act Together: Interorganizational coordination in theory and practice*, Gordon and Breach, Amsterdam (The Netherlands).

Alexander, E. R. (1998a), 'Conclusions: Where do we go from here', in N. Lichfield et al. (eds.), *Evaluation in Planning*, Kluwer, Dordrecht (The Netherlands), pp. 355-374.

Alexander, E. R. (1998b), 'Evaluation in Israeli spatial planning', in N. Lichfield et al. (eds.), *Evaluation in Planning*, Kluwer, Dordrecht (The Netherlands), pp. 299-310.

Alexander, E. R. (1998c), 'Planning theory in practice: The case of planning Highway 6 in Israel', *Environment and Planning B: Planning and Design*, Vol. 25, No. 3, pp. 435-446.

Alexander, E. R. (1998d), 'Planning and implementation: Coordinative planning in practice', *International Planning Studies*, Vol. 3, No. 3, pp. 303-320.

Alexander, E. R. (2001), 'A transaction-cost theory of land use planning and development control', *Town Planning Review*, Vol. 72, No. 1, pp. 45-76.

Alexander, E. R. (2002), 'Acting Together: From Planning to Institutional Design', in AESOP, *XVI Association of European Schools of Planning Conference, 10-14 July 2002, Vólos*, (Planning and Regional Development Issues in Border Regions), AESOP, Newcastle upon Tyne (UK), available from author.

Bolan, R. J. (2000), 'Social interaction and institutional design: The case of housing in the U.S.', in W. Salet and A. Faludi (eds.), *The Revival of Strategic Spatial Planning*, Royal Netherlands Academy of Arts & Sciences, Amsterdam (The Netherlands), pp. 25-38.

Hall, P. (1980), *Great Planning Disasters*, University of California Press, Berkeley, CA (USA).

Levine, J. and Garb, Y. (1997), *The Trans-Israel Highway: Do We Know Enough to Proceed?*, The Floersheimer Institute for Policy Studies, Jerusalem (Israel).

Lichfield, N. (1996), *Community Impact Evaluation*, UCL Press, London (UK).

Lichfield, Kettle and Whitbread, Lichfield, N., Kettle, P. and Whitbread, M. (1973), *Evaluation in the Planning Process*, Pergamon, Oxford (UK).

North, D. (1990), *Institutions, Institutional Change and Economic Performance*, Cambridge University Press, New York, NY (USA).

Richardson, T. (1997), 'The Trans-European Transport Network: Environmental policy integration in the European Union', *European Urban and Regional Studies*, Vol. 4, No. 4, pp. 333-346.

Williamson, O. E. (1985), *The Economic Institutions of Capitalism*, Free Press, New York, NY (USA).

Index